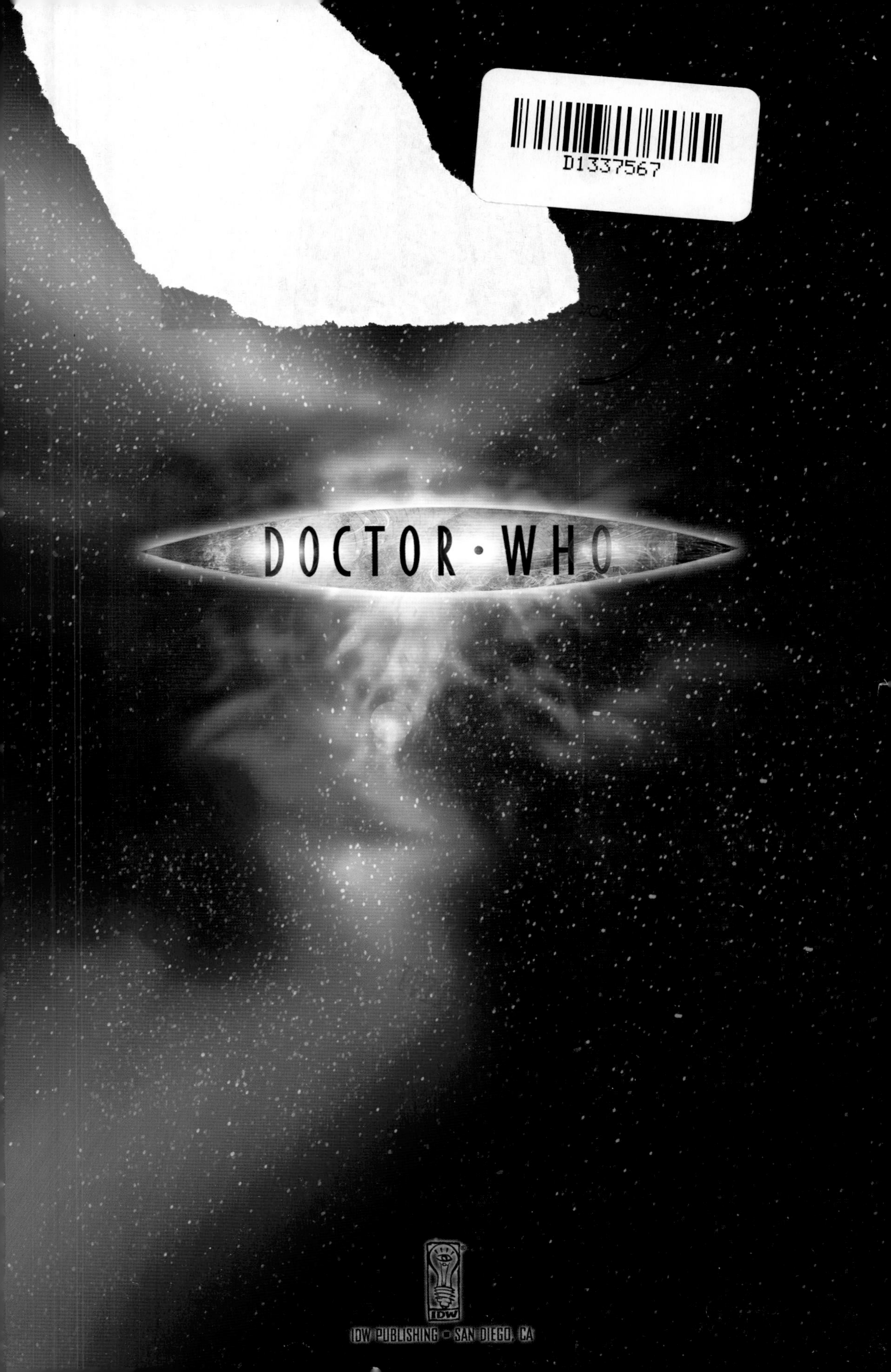

DOCTOR · WHO
IDW PUBLISHING • SAN DIEGO, CA

DOCTOR WHO: AGENT PROVOCATEUR

WRITTEN BY GARY RUSSELL

ART BY NICK ROCHE [CH. 1], JOSE MARIA BEROY [CH. 2], STEFANO MARTINO [CH. 3 & 6], AND MIRCO PIERFEDERICI [CH. 4-5],

ART ASSIST BY JOE PHILLIPS [CH. 1]

INKING ASSIST BY GERMAN TORRES [CH. 1]

COLORS BY CHARLIE KIRKOFF [CH. 1-3] AND TOM SMITH [CH. 4-6]

LETTERS BY CHRIS MOWRY, AMAURI OSORIO, AND NEIL UYETAKE

SERIES EDITS BY SCOTT DUNBIER, CHRIS RYALL, AND DENTON J. TIPTON

COLLECTION EDITS BY JUSTIN EISINGER

COLLECTION DESIGN BY NEIL UYETAKE

ISBN: 978-1-60010-196-0
11 10 09 08   1 2 3 4
WWW.IDWPUBLISHING.COM

Special thanks to Jordana Chapman and Anna Hewitt at BBC Worldwide, Russell T. Davies, and Marc Mostman for their invaluable assistance.

IDW Publishing

Operations:
Moshe Berger, Chairman
Ted Adams, President
Clifford Meth, EVP of Strategies
Matthew Ruzicka, CPA, Controller
Alan Payne, VP of Sales
Lorelei Bunjes, Dir. of Digital Services
Marci Hubbard, Executive Assistant
Alonzo Simon, Shipping Manager

Editorial:
Chris Ryall, Publisher/Editor-in-Chief
Scott Dunbier, Editor, Special Projects
Justin Eisinger, Editor
Kris Oprisko, Editor/Foreign Lic.
Denton J. Tipton, Editor
Tom Waltz, Editor

Design:
Robbie Robbins, EVP/Sr. Graphic Artist
Ben Templesmith, Artist/Designer
Neil Uyetake, Art Director
Chris Mowry, Graphic Artist
Amauri Osorio, Graphic Artist

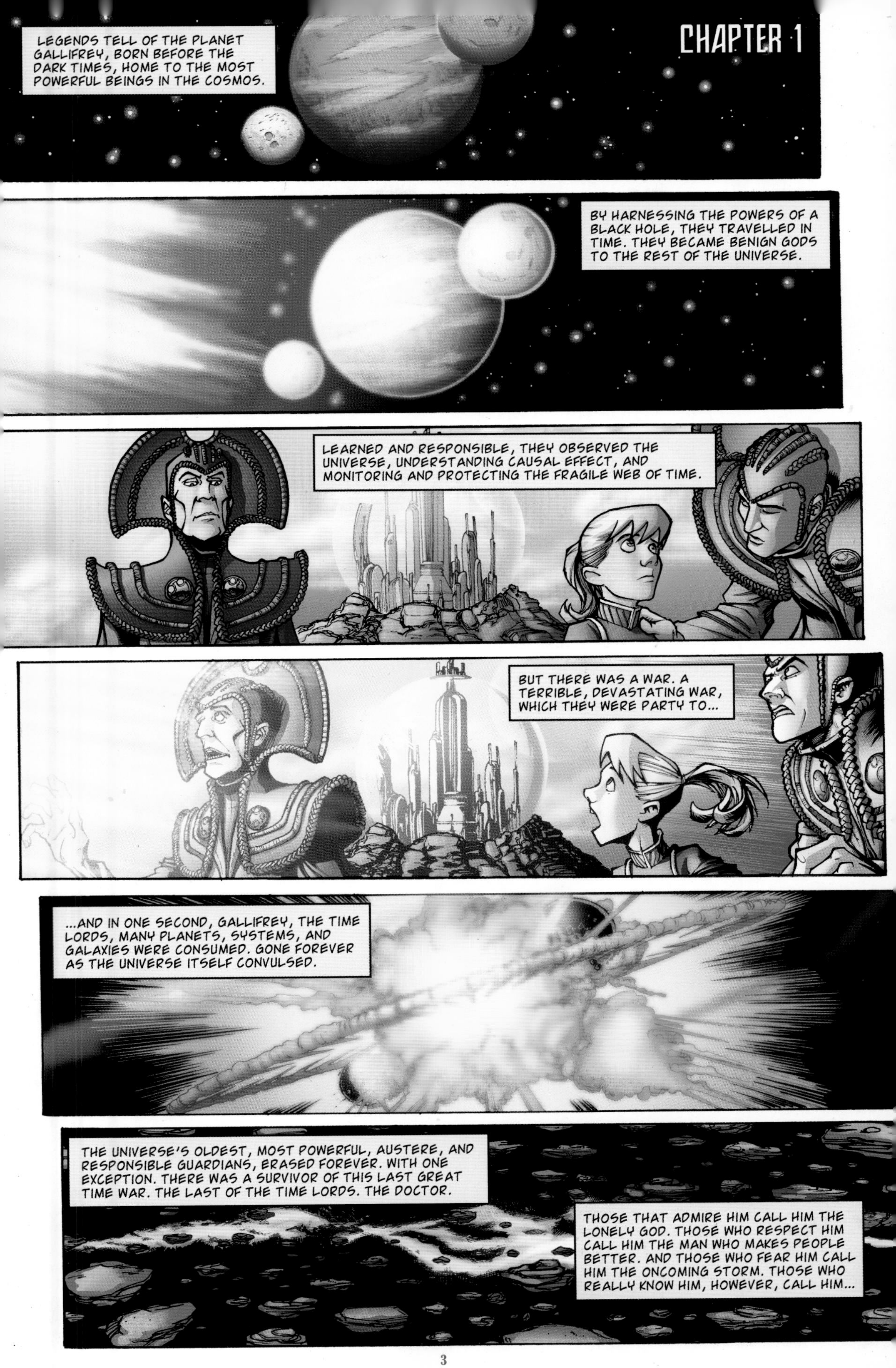
CHAPTER 1
LEGENDS TELL OF THE PLANET GALLIFREY, BORN BEFORE THE DARK TIMES, HOME TO THE MOST POWERFUL BEINGS IN THE COSMOS.
BY HARNESSING THE POWERS OF A BLACK HOLE, THEY TRAVELLED IN TIME. THEY BECAME BENIGN GODS TO THE REST OF THE UNIVERSE.
LEARNED AND RESPONSIBLE, THEY OBSERVED THE UNIVERSE, UNDERSTANDING CAUSAL EFFECT, AND MONITORING AND PROTECTING THE FRAGILE WEB OF TIME.
BUT THERE WAS A WAR. A TERRIBLE, DEVASTATING WAR, WHICH THEY WERE PARTY TO...
...AND IN ONE SECOND, GALLIFREY, THE TIME LORDS, MANY PLANETS, SYSTEMS, AND GALAXIES WERE CONSUMED. GONE FOREVER AS THE UNIVERSE ITSELF CONVULSED.
THE UNIVERSE'S OLDEST, MOST POWERFUL, AUSTERE, AND RESPONSIBLE GUARDIANS, ERASED FOREVER. WITH ONE EXCEPTION. THERE WAS A SURVIVOR OF THIS LAST GREAT TIME WAR. THE LAST OF THE TIME LORDS. THE DOCTOR.
THOSE THAT ADMIRE HIM CALL HIM THE LONELY GOD. THOSE WHO RESPECT HIM CALL HIM THE MAN WHO MAKES PEOPLE BETTER. AND THOSE WHO FEAR HIM CALL HIM THE ONCOMING STORM. THOSE WHO REALLY KNOW HIM, HOWEVER, CALL HIM...

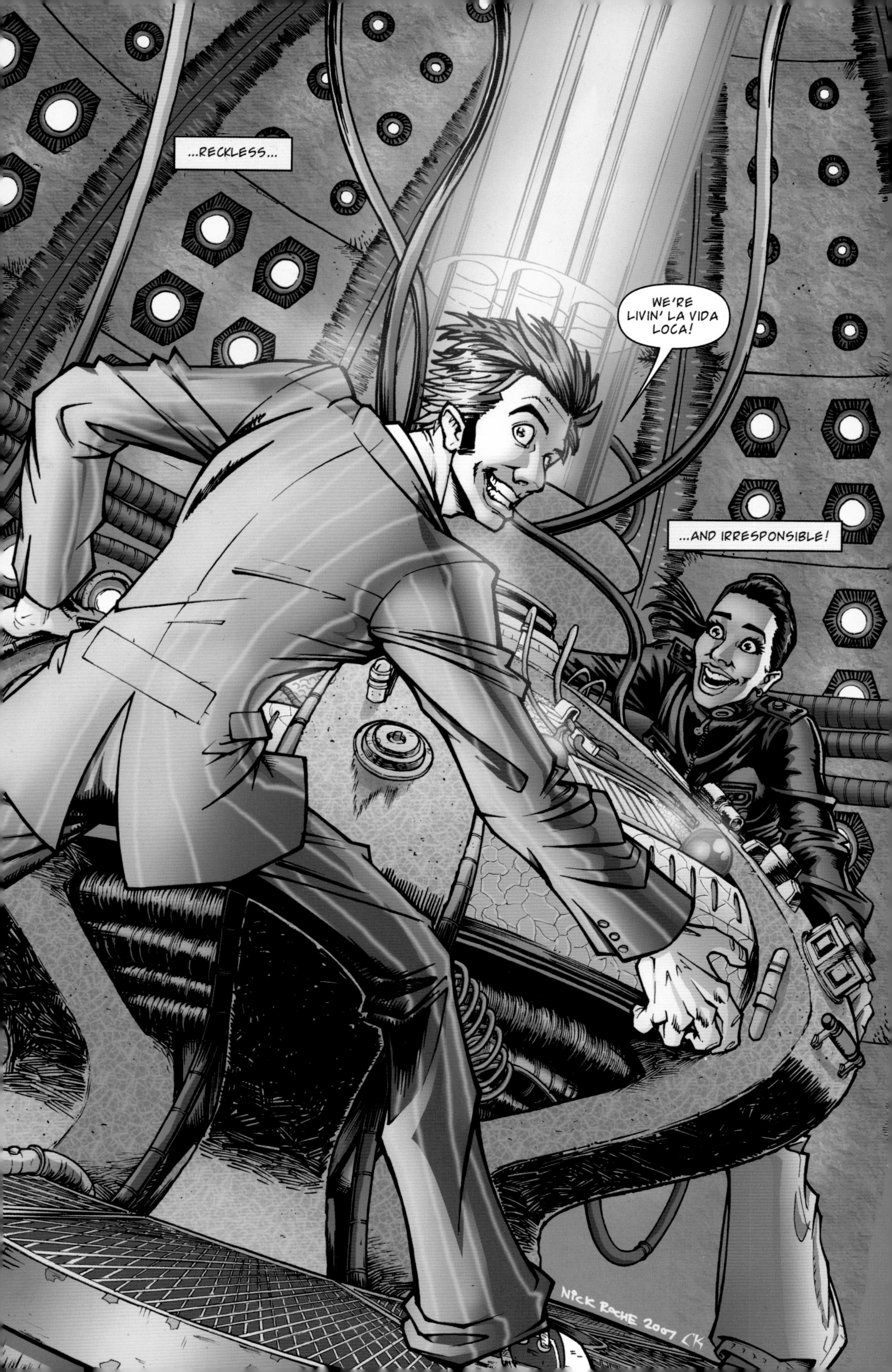
...RECKLESS...
WE'RE LIVIN' LA VIDA LOCA!
...AND IRRESPONSIBLE!
NICK ROCHE 2007 CK

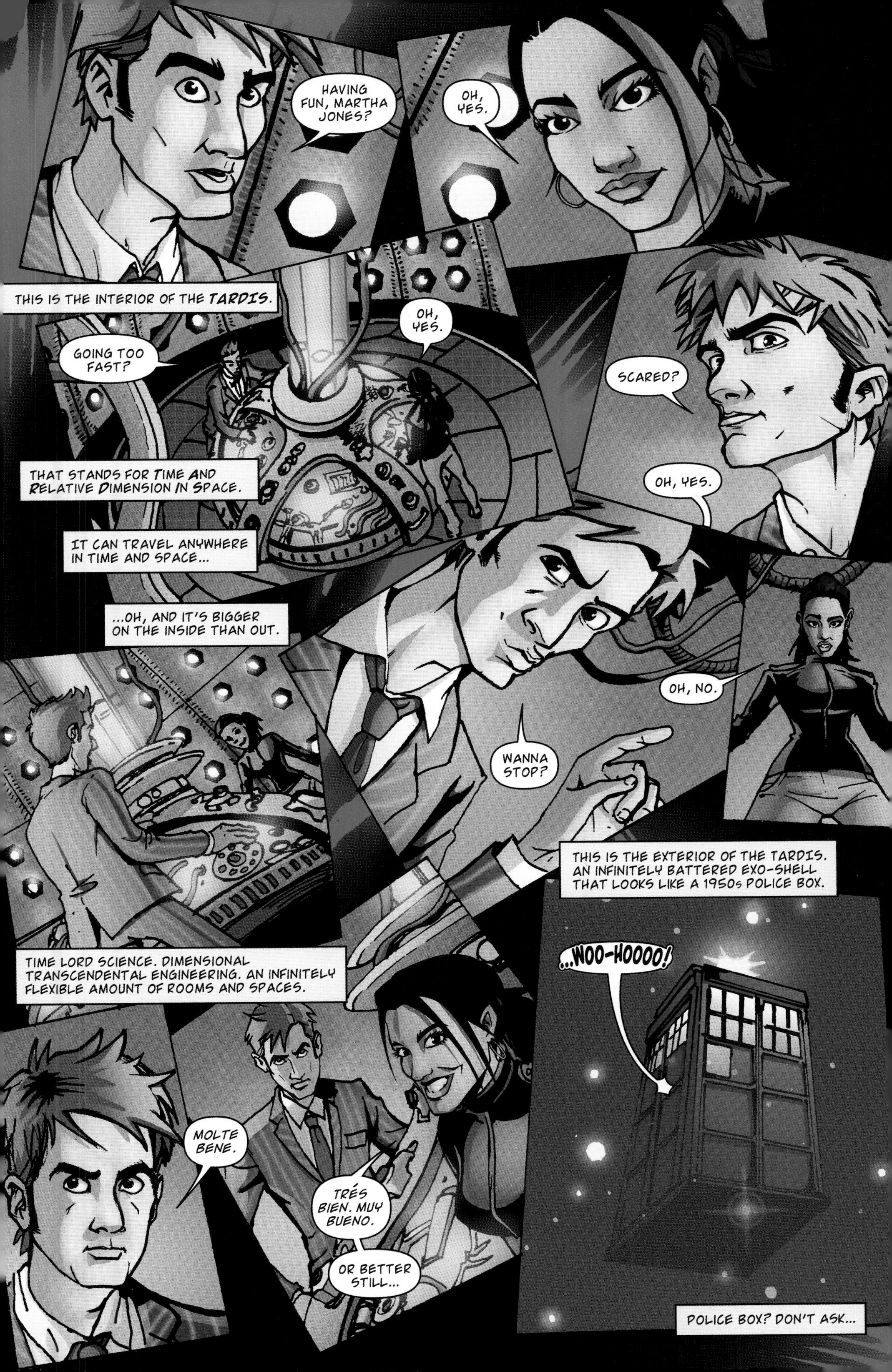
HAVING FUN, MARTHA JONES?
OH, YES.
THIS IS THE INTERIOR OF THE TARDIS.
GOING TOO FAST?
OH, YES.
SCARED?
OH, YES.
THAT STANDS FOR TIME AND RELATIVE DIMENSION IN SPACE.
IT CAN TRAVEL ANYWHERE IN TIME AND SPACE...
...OH, AND IT'S BIGGER ON THE INSIDE THAN OUT.
WANNA STOP?
OH, NO.
THIS IS THE EXTERIOR OF THE TARDIS. AN INFINITELY BATTERED EXO-SHELL THAT LOOKS LIKE A 1950s POLICE BOX.
TIME LORD SCIENCE. DIMENSIONAL TRANSCENDENTAL ENGINEERING. AN INFINITELY FLEXIBLE AMOUNT OF ROOMS AND SPACES.
MOLTE BENE.
TRÉS BIEN. MUY BUENO.
OR BETTER STILL...
...WOO-HOOOO!
POLICE BOX? DON'T ASK...

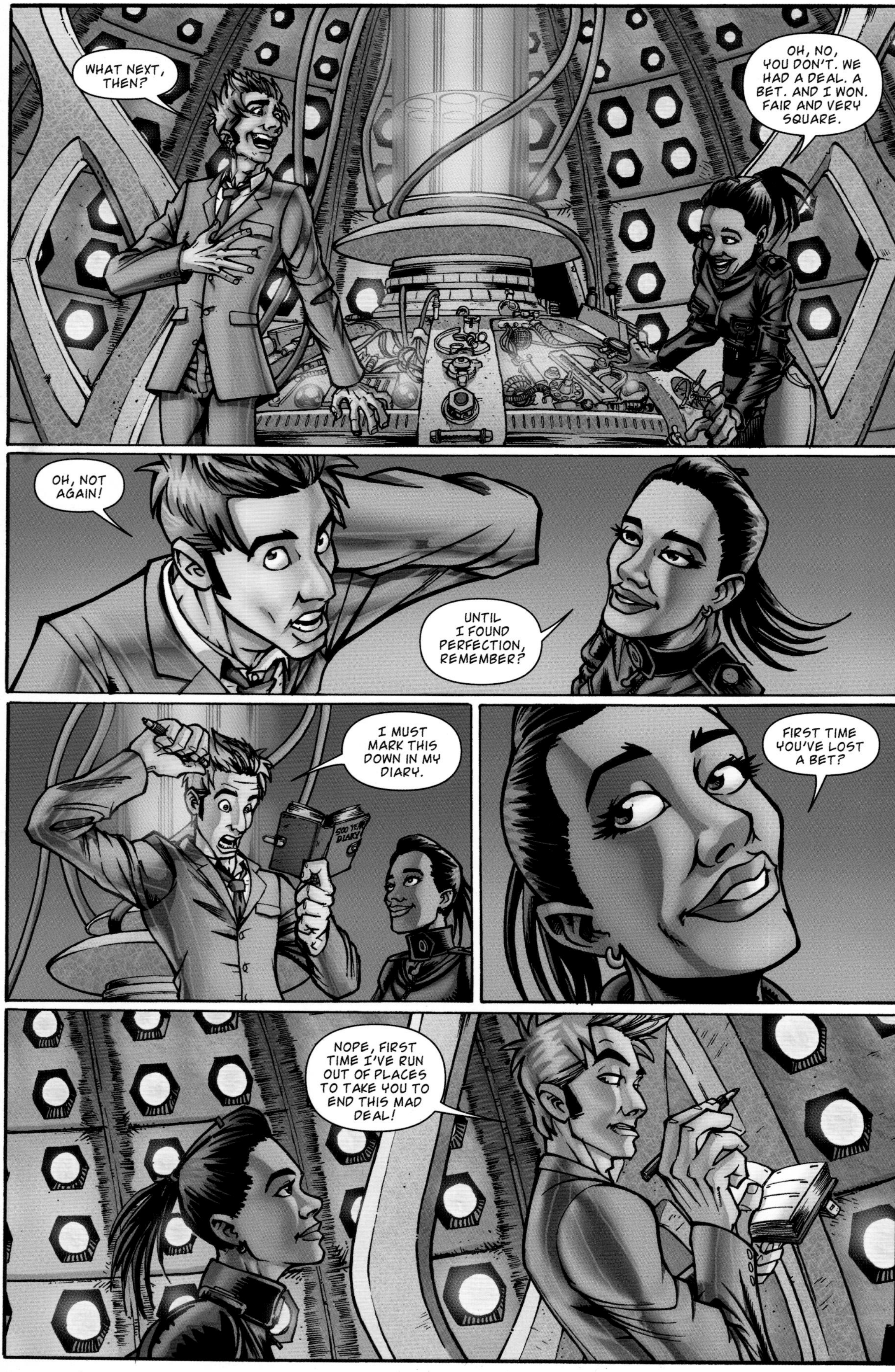
WHAT NEXT, THEN?
OH, NO, YOU DON'T. WE HAD A DEAL. A BET. AND I WON. FAIR AND VERY SQUARE.
OH, NOT AGAIN!
UNTIL I FOUND PERFECTION, REMEMBER?
I MUST MARK THIS DOWN IN MY DIARY.
FIRST TIME YOU'VE LOST A BET?
NOPE, FIRST TIME I'VE RUN OUT OF PLACES TO TAKE YOU TO END THIS MAD DEAL!

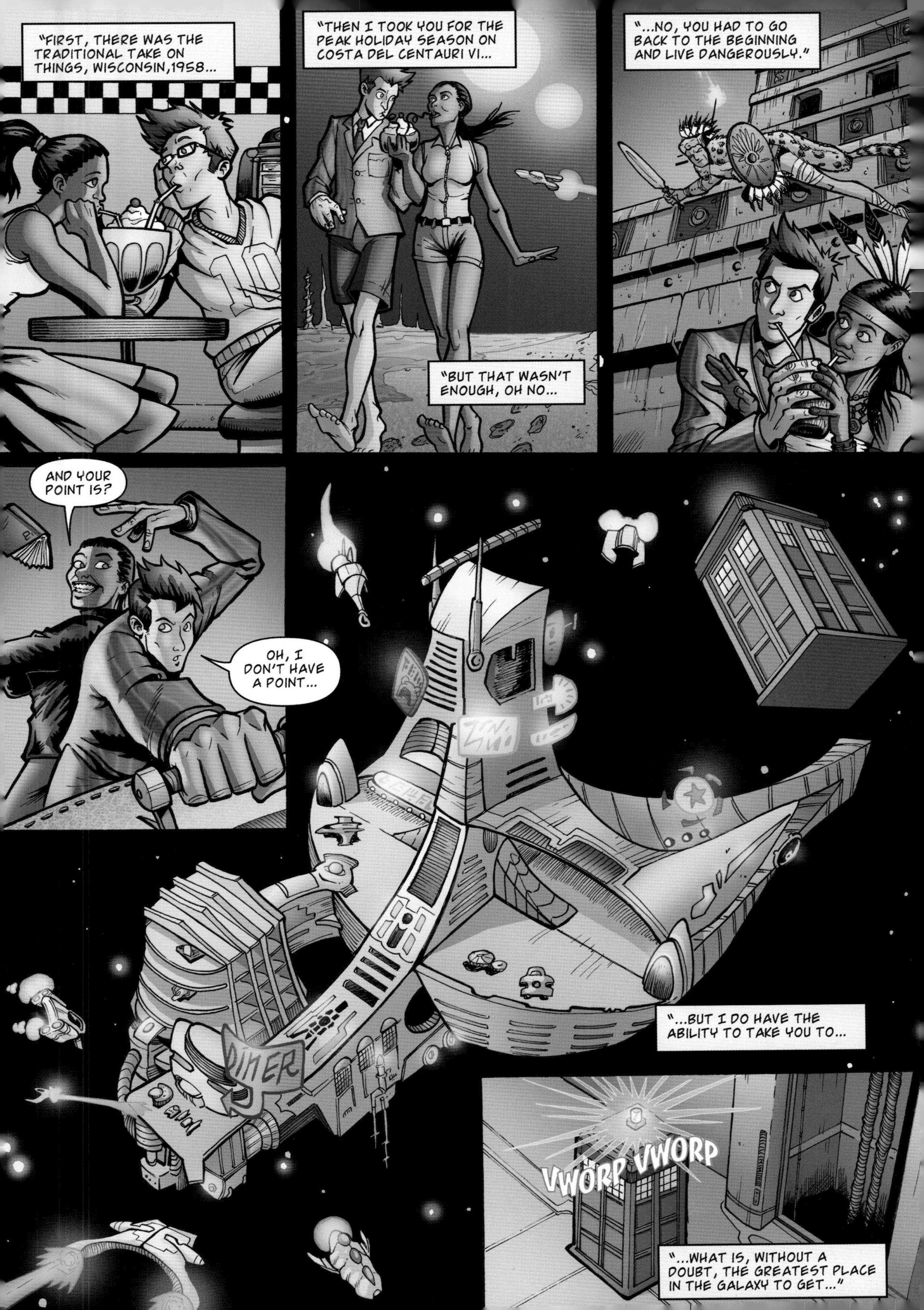
"FIRST, THERE WAS THE TRADITIONAL TAKE ON THINGS, WISCONSIN,1958...
"THEN I TOOK YOU FOR THE PEAK HOLIDAY SEASON ON COSTA DEL CENTAURI VI...
"BUT THAT WASN'T ENOUGH, OH NO...
"...NO, YOU HAD TO GO BACK TO THE BEGINNING AND LIVE DANGEROUSLY."
AND YOUR POINT IS?
OH, I DON'T HAVE A POINT...
DINER
"...BUT I DO HAVE THE ABILITY TO TAKE YOU TO...
VWORP VWORP
"...WHAT IS, WITHOUT A DOUBT, THE GREATEST PLACE IN THE GALAXY TO GET..."

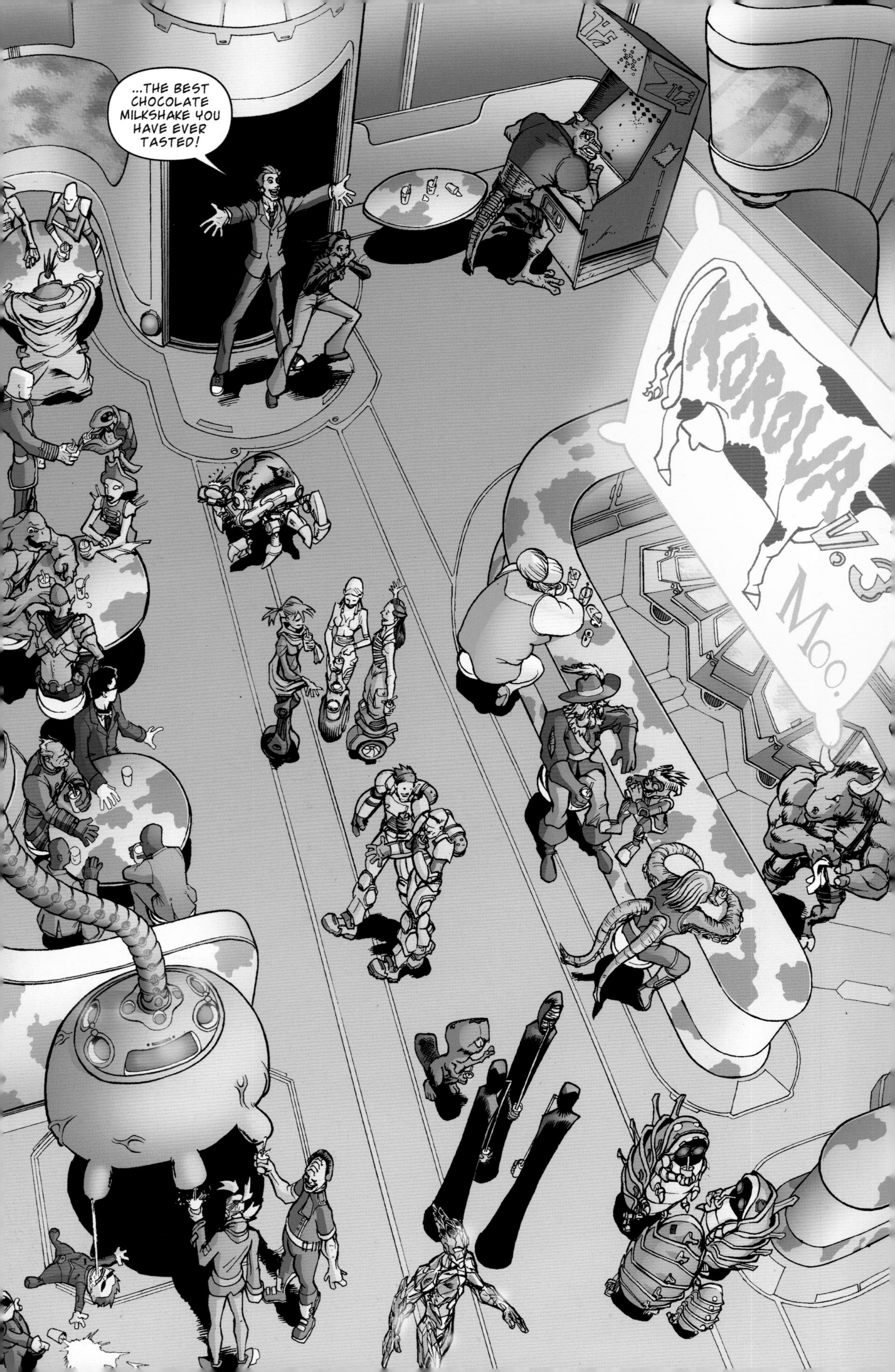
...THE BEST CHOCOLATE MILKSHAKE YOU HAVE EVER TASTED!
KOROVA V.3
Moo.

SO, MARTHA JONES, READY TO TASTE THE NECTAR OF THE GODS?

THE GODS OF CHOCOLATE, THAT IS.

AM I EVER!

YOU SPOIL ME, DOCTOR. AND I LOVE IT!

"SO? DARK OR MILK?

"BELGIAN OR SWISS?"

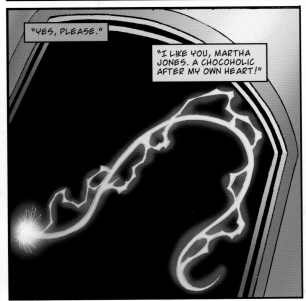

"YES, PLEASE."

"I LIKE YOU, MARTHA JONES. A CHOCOHOLIC AFTER MY OWN HEART!"

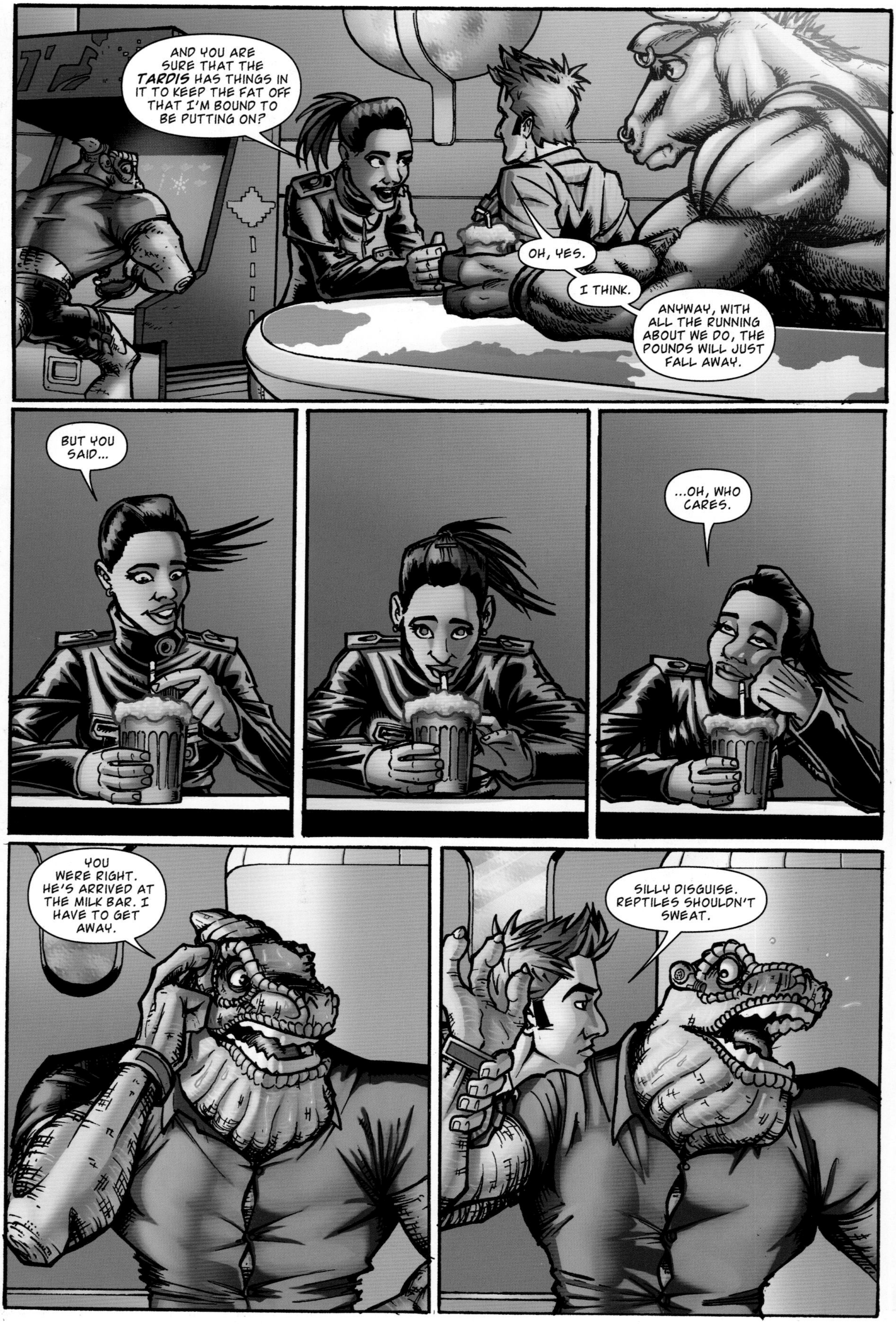
AND YOU ARE SURE THAT THE TARDIS HAS THINGS IN IT TO KEEP THE FAT OFF THAT I'M BOUND TO BE PUTTING ON?
OH, YES.
I THINK.
ANYWAY, WITH ALL THE RUNNING ABOUT WE DO, THE POUNDS WILL JUST FALL AWAY.
BUT YOU SAID...
...OH, WHO CARES.
YOU WERE RIGHT. HE'S ARRIVED AT THE MILK BAR. I HAVE TO GET AWAY.
SILLY DISGUISE. REPTILES SHOULDN'T SWEAT.

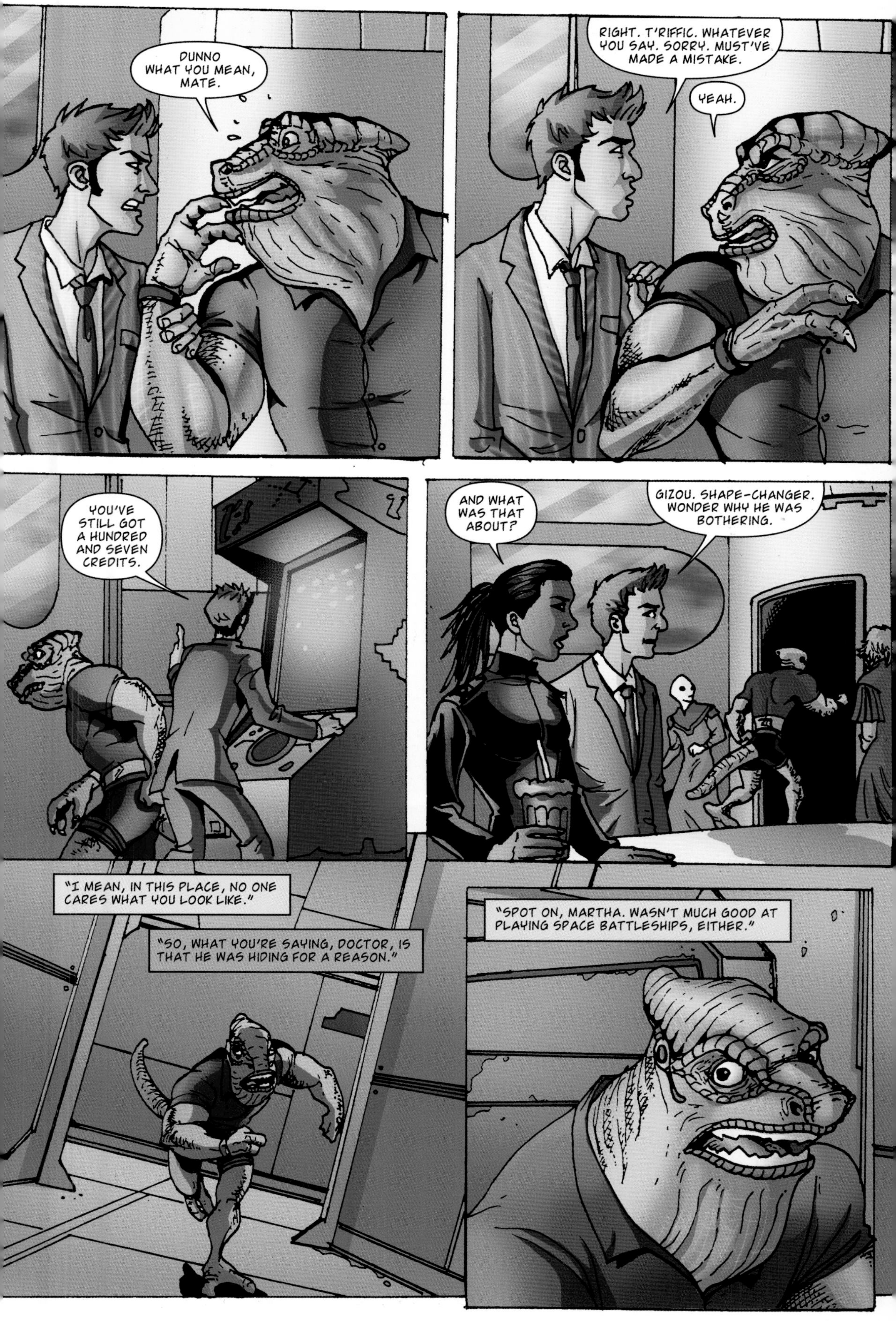
DUNNO WHAT YOU MEAN, MATE.
RIGHT. T'RIFFIC. WHATEVER YOU SAY. SORRY. MUST'VE MADE A MISTAKE.
YEAH.
YOU'VE STILL GOT A HUNDRED AND SEVEN CREDITS.
AND WHAT WAS THAT ABOUT?
GIZOU. SHAPE-CHANGER. WONDER WHY HE WAS BOTHERING.
"I MEAN, IN THIS PLACE, NO ONE CARES WHAT YOU LOOK LIKE."
"SO, WHAT YOU'RE SAYING, DOCTOR, IS THAT HE WAS HIDING FOR A REASON."
"SPOT ON, MARTHA. WASN'T MUCH GOOD AT PLAYING SPACE BATTLESHIPS, EITHER."

YEAH, I DON'T KNOW WHERE HE IS NOW. BUT HE MUST BE HERE SOMEWHERE, I SAW HIM FOLLOW SOME HUMANS IN.

THEN HE VANISHED.

YEEARRGHHHH!!

ZZZZZTT

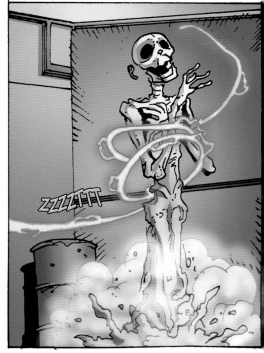

ZZZZZTT

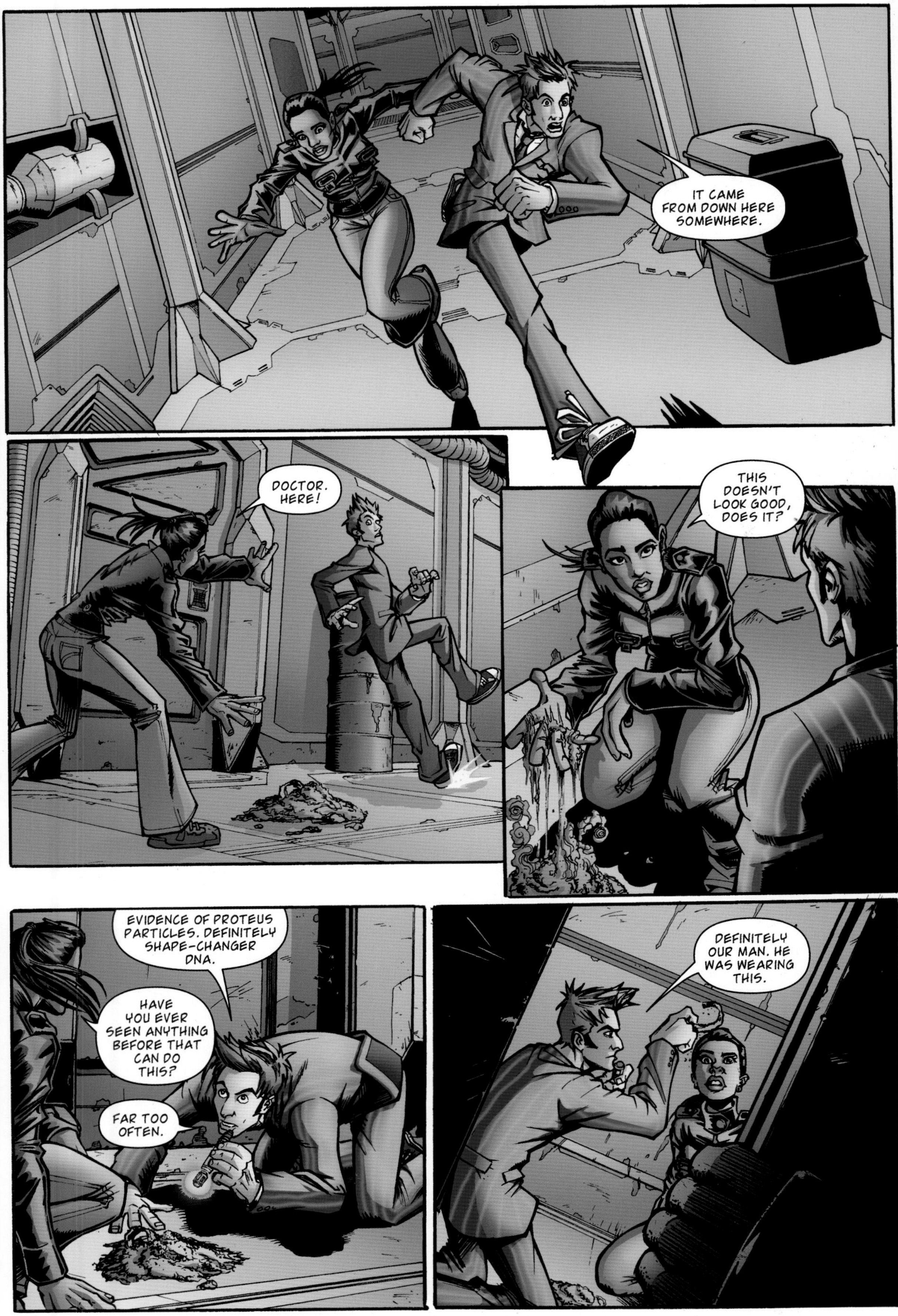
IT CAME FROM DOWN HERE SOMEWHERE.
DOCTOR. HERE!
THIS DOESN'T LOOK GOOD, DOES IT?
EVIDENCE OF PROTEUS PARTICLES. DEFINITELY SHAPE-CHANGER DNA.
HAVE YOU EVER SEEN ANYTHING BEFORE THAT CAN DO THIS?
FAR TOO OFTEN.
DEFINITELY OUR MAN. HE WAS WEARING THIS.

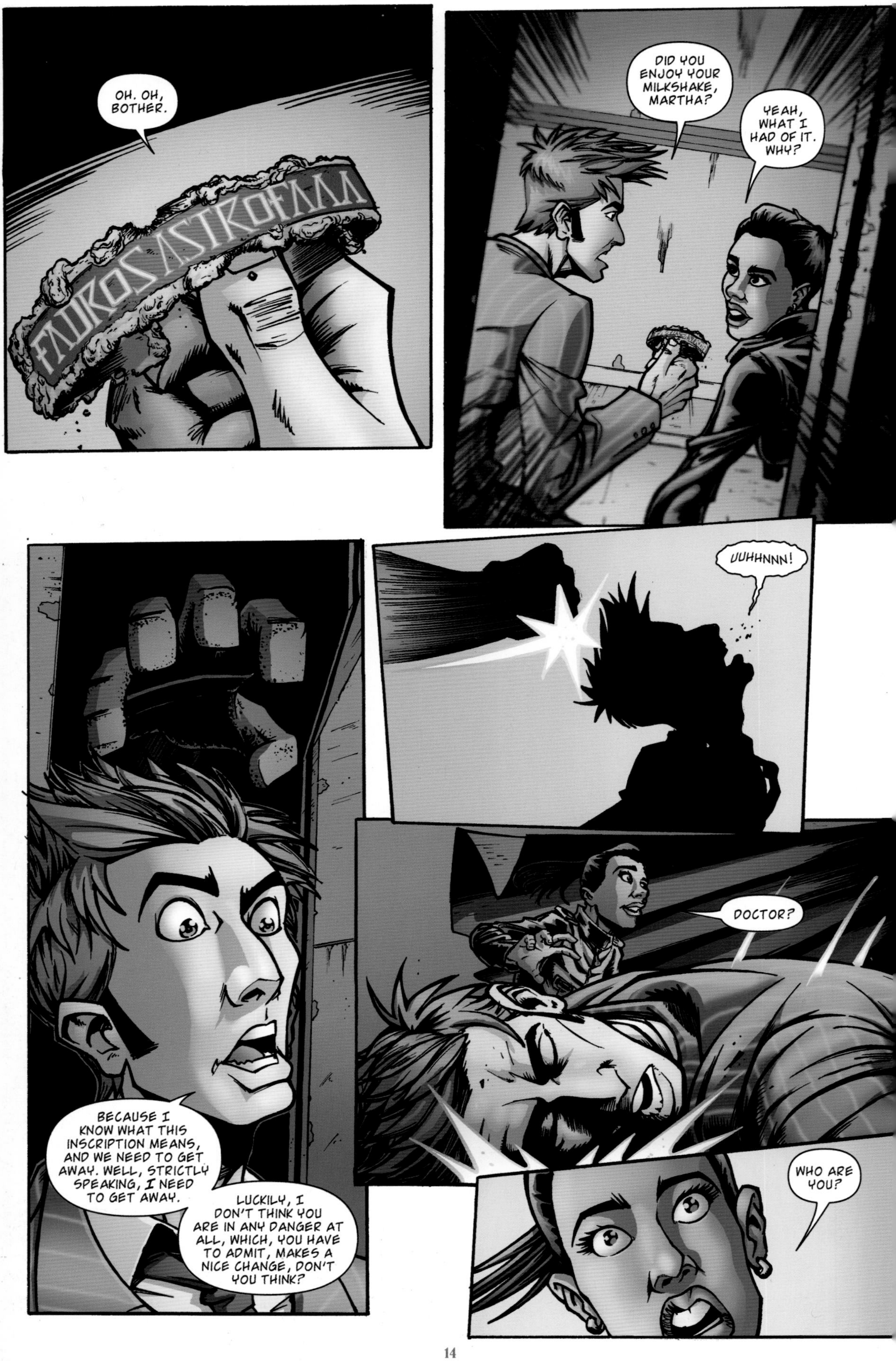
OH. OH, BOTHER.
FAUROS ASTROFAAA
DID YOU ENJOY YOUR MILKSHAKE, MARTHA?
YEAH, WHAT I HAD OF IT. WHY?
BECAUSE I KNOW WHAT THIS INSCRIPTION MEANS, AND WE NEED TO GET AWAY. WELL, STRICTLY SPEAKING, I NEED TO GET AWAY.
LUCKILY, I DON'T THINK YOU ARE IN ANY DANGER AT ALL, WHICH, YOU HAVE TO ADMIT, MAKES A NICE CHANGE, DON'T YOU THINK?
UUHHNNN!
DOCTOR?
WHO ARE YOU?

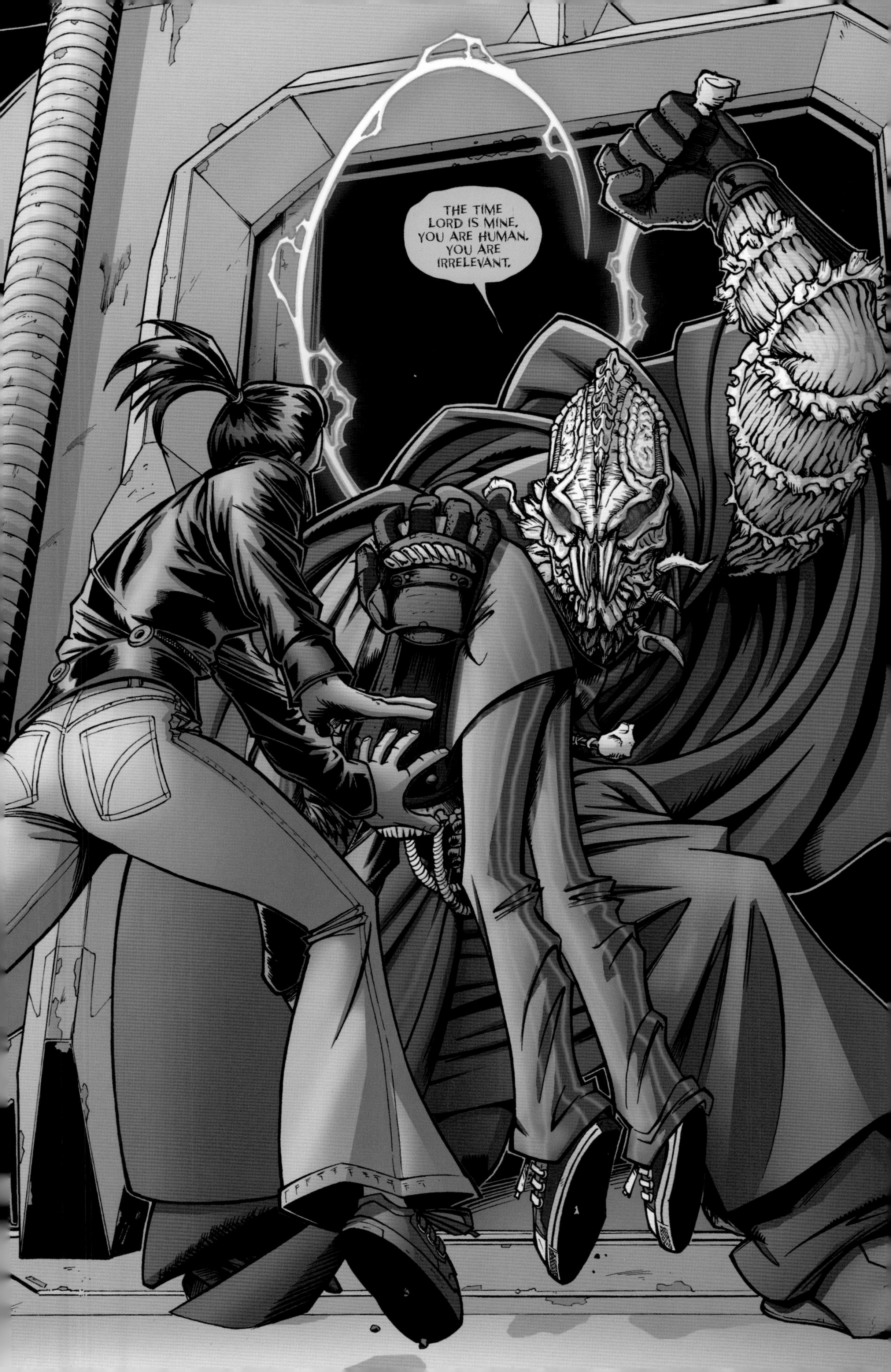
THE TIME LORD IS MINE. YOU ARE HUMAN. YOU ARE IRRELEVANT.

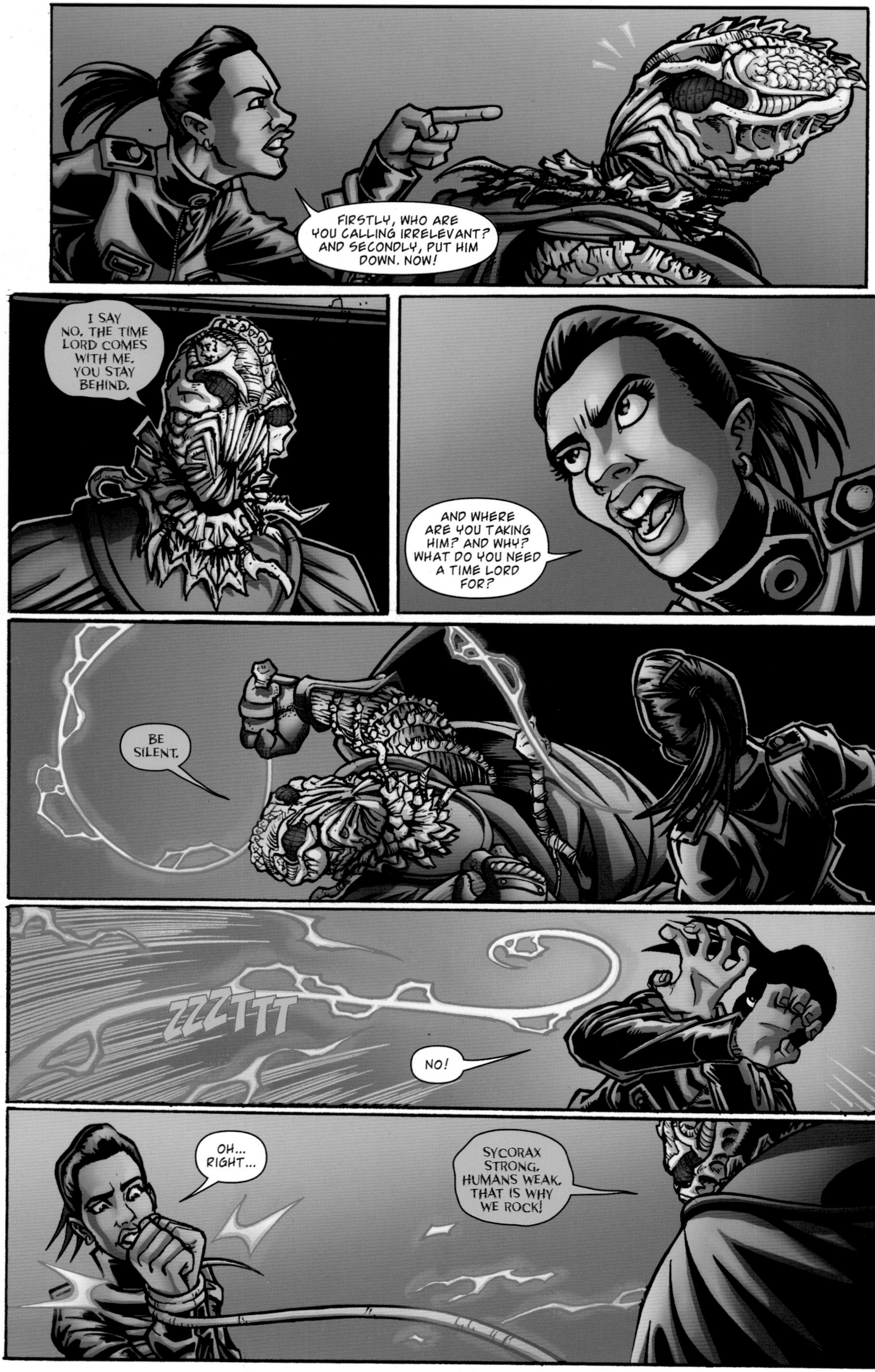
FIRSTLY, WHO ARE YOU CALLING IRRELEVANT? AND SECONDLY, PUT HIM DOWN. NOW!
I SAY NO. THE TIME LORD COMES WITH ME. YOU STAY BEHIND.
AND WHERE ARE YOU TAKING HIM? AND WHY? WHAT DO YOU NEED A TIME LORD FOR?
BE SILENT.
ZZZTTT
NO!
OH... RIGHT...
SYCORAX STRONG. HUMANS WEAK. THAT IS WHY WE ROCK!

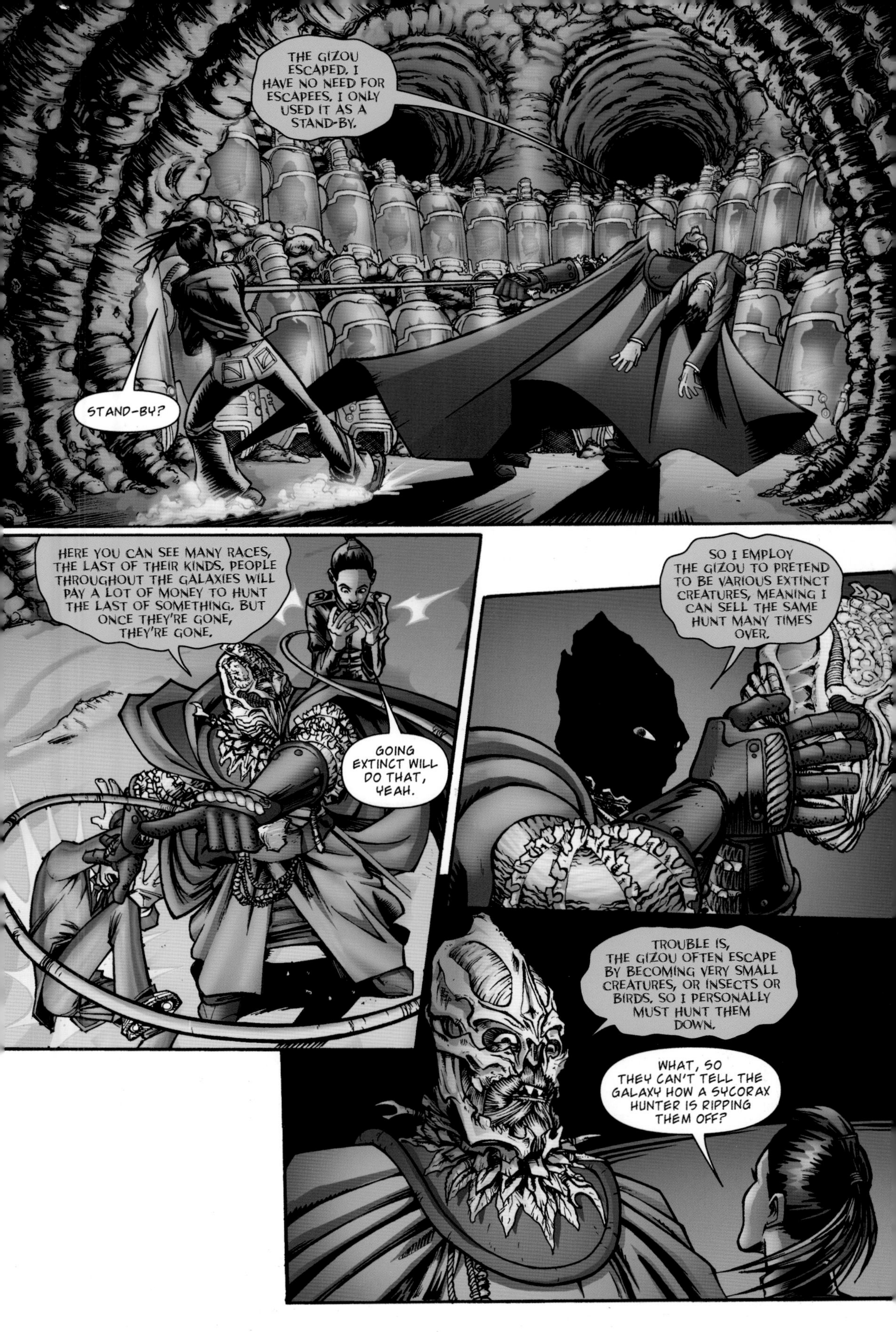
THE GIZOU ESCAPED. I HAVE NO NEED FOR ESCAPEES. I ONLY USED IT AS A STAND-BY.
STAND-BY?
HERE YOU CAN SEE MANY RACES, THE LAST OF THEIR KINDS. PEOPLE THROUGHOUT THE GALAXIES WILL PAY A LOT OF MONEY TO HUNT THE LAST OF SOMETHING. BUT ONCE THEY'RE GONE, THEY'RE GONE.
GOING EXTINCT WILL DO THAT, YEAH.
SO I EMPLOY THE GIZOU TO PRETEND TO BE VARIOUS EXTINCT CREATURES, MEANING I CAN SELL THE SAME HUNT MANY TIMES OVER.
TROUBLE IS, THE GIZOU OFTEN ESCAPE BY BECOMING VERY SMALL CREATURES, OR INSECTS OR BIRDS. SO I PERSONALLY MUST HUNT THEM DOWN.
WHAT, SO THEY CAN'T TELL THE GALAXY HOW A SYCORAX HUNTER IS RIPPING THEM OFF?

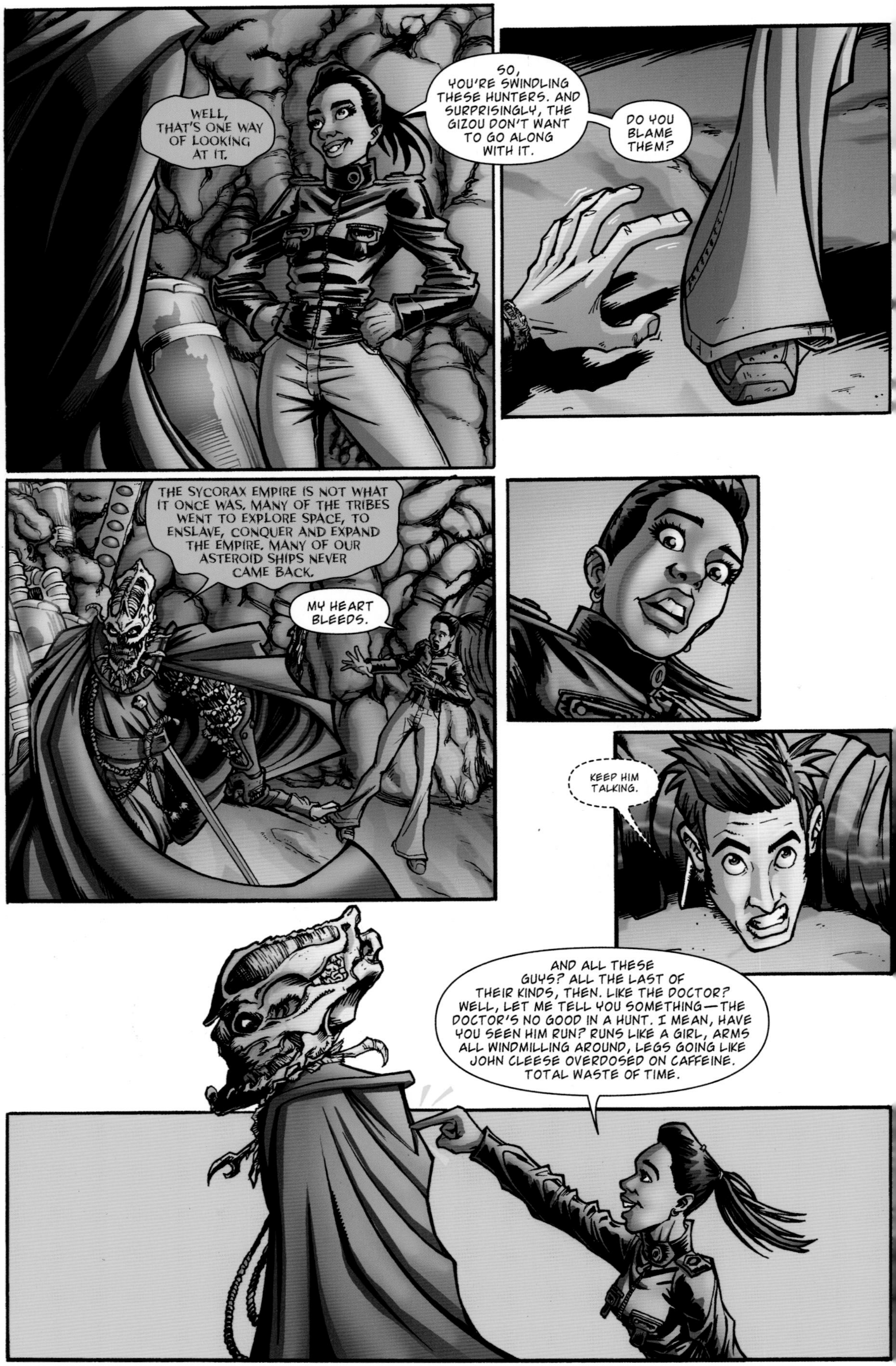
WELL, THAT'S ONE WAY OF LOOKING AT IT.
SO, YOU'RE SWINDLING THESE HUNTERS. AND SURPRISINGLY, THE GIZOU DON'T WANT TO GO ALONG WITH IT.
DO YOU BLAME THEM?
THE SYCORAX EMPIRE IS NOT WHAT IT ONCE WAS. MANY OF THE TRIBES WENT TO EXPLORE SPACE, TO ENSLAVE, CONQUER AND EXPAND THE EMPIRE. MANY OF OUR ASTEROID SHIPS NEVER CAME BACK.
MY HEART BLEEDS.
KEEP HIM TALKING.
AND ALL THESE GUYS? ALL THE LAST OF THEIR KINDS, THEN. LIKE THE DOCTOR? WELL, LET ME TELL YOU SOMETHING—THE DOCTOR'S NO GOOD IN A HUNT. I MEAN, HAVE YOU SEEN HIM RUN? RUNS LIKE A GIRL, ARMS ALL WINDMILLING AROUND, LEGS GOING LIKE JOHN CLEESE OVERDOSED ON CAFFEINE. TOTAL WASTE OF TIME.

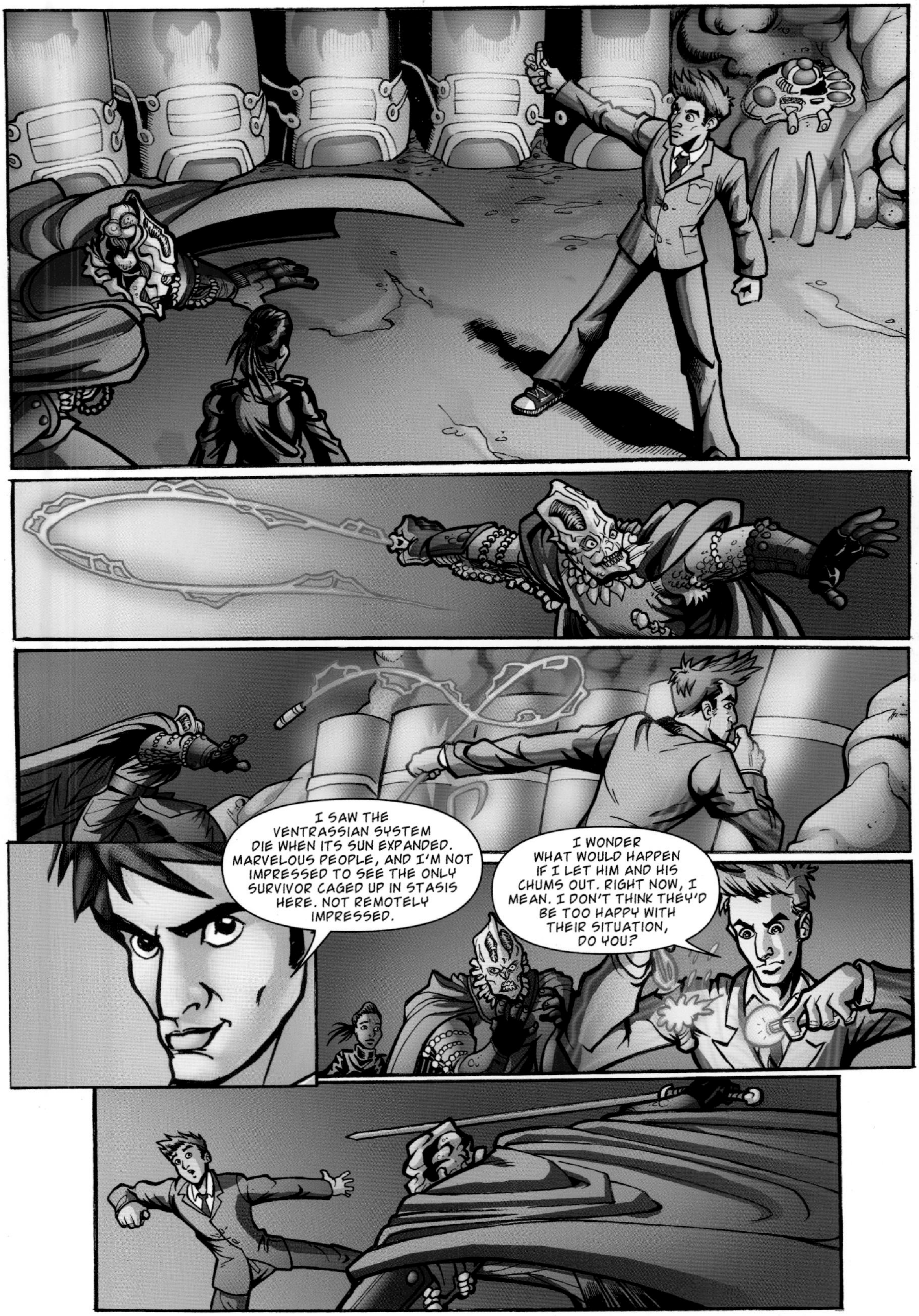
I SAW THE VENTRASSIAN SYSTEM DIE WHEN ITS SUN EXPANDED. MARVELOUS PEOPLE, AND I'M NOT IMPRESSED TO SEE THE ONLY SURVIVOR CAGED UP IN STASIS HERE. NOT REMOTELY IMPRESSED.
I WONDER WHAT WOULD HAPPEN IF I LET HIM AND HIS CHUMS OUT. RIGHT NOW, I MEAN. I DON'T THINK THEY'D BE TOO HAPPY WITH THEIR SITUATION, DO YOU?

THWEEEP

WHO NEEDS WHIPS AND SWORDS WHEN A LITTLE SONIC SCREWDRIVER CAN DO ALL THIS?

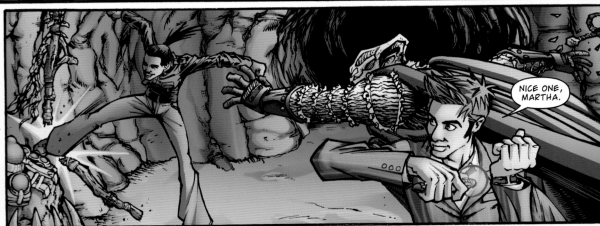

NICE ONE, MARTHA.

WHIPS, NEUTRALISED. BROADSWORD, SHATTERED. STAFF, SNAPPED. YOU'VE NO WEAPON, NO TROPHIES, AND NOT MUCH IN THE WAY OF HONOR NOW. I'D GO HOME IF I WERE YOU.

THE TRIBE OF ASTROPHIA, YEAH?

BUT YOU, YOU'RE THE LAST OF THIS TRIBE. DIED OUT DURING THE VALHALLA WARS OF THE 41ST CENTURY. MAYBE YOU SHOULD BE UP IN ONE OF THOSE CAPSULES, YEAH?

SOMEONE SHOULD SELL YOU OFF TO THE HUNT!

LEGENDS SAY, MARTHA JONES, THAT THE SYCORAX WILL BE ONE OF THE LAST THREE RACES LEFT WHEN THE UNIVERSE FINALLY DIES. YOUR LOT, HUMANS, BY THE WAY, ARE ONE OF THE OTHER TWO.

SYCORAX STRONG. SYCORAX MIGHTY. SYCORAX—

ROCK—YEAH, GOT THAT, THANKS.

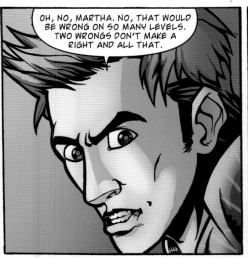

OH, NO, MARTHA. NO, THAT WOULD BE WRONG ON SO MANY LEVELS. TWO WRONGS DON'T MAKE A RIGHT AND ALL THAT.

BUT SHE DOES HAVE A POINT—BECAUSE ALTHOUGH I MIGHT NOT BE ONE TO SELL THE LAST SURVIVORS OF VARIOUS RACES TO SLAUGHTER, MATEYKINS UP THERE IN HIS CYLINDER AND HIS CHUMS MAY NOT AGREE WITH ME.

SHALL WE LET THEM OUT AND ASK THEM?

NO, NO... PLEASE, I'LL TAKE THEM SOMEWHERE—ANYWHERE—AND LET THEM GO FREE.

AND WHY WOULD YOU DO THAT?

INDEED. AND WHAT GUARANTEE HAVE WE GOT?

I'LL TELL YOU WHAT I'LL DO...

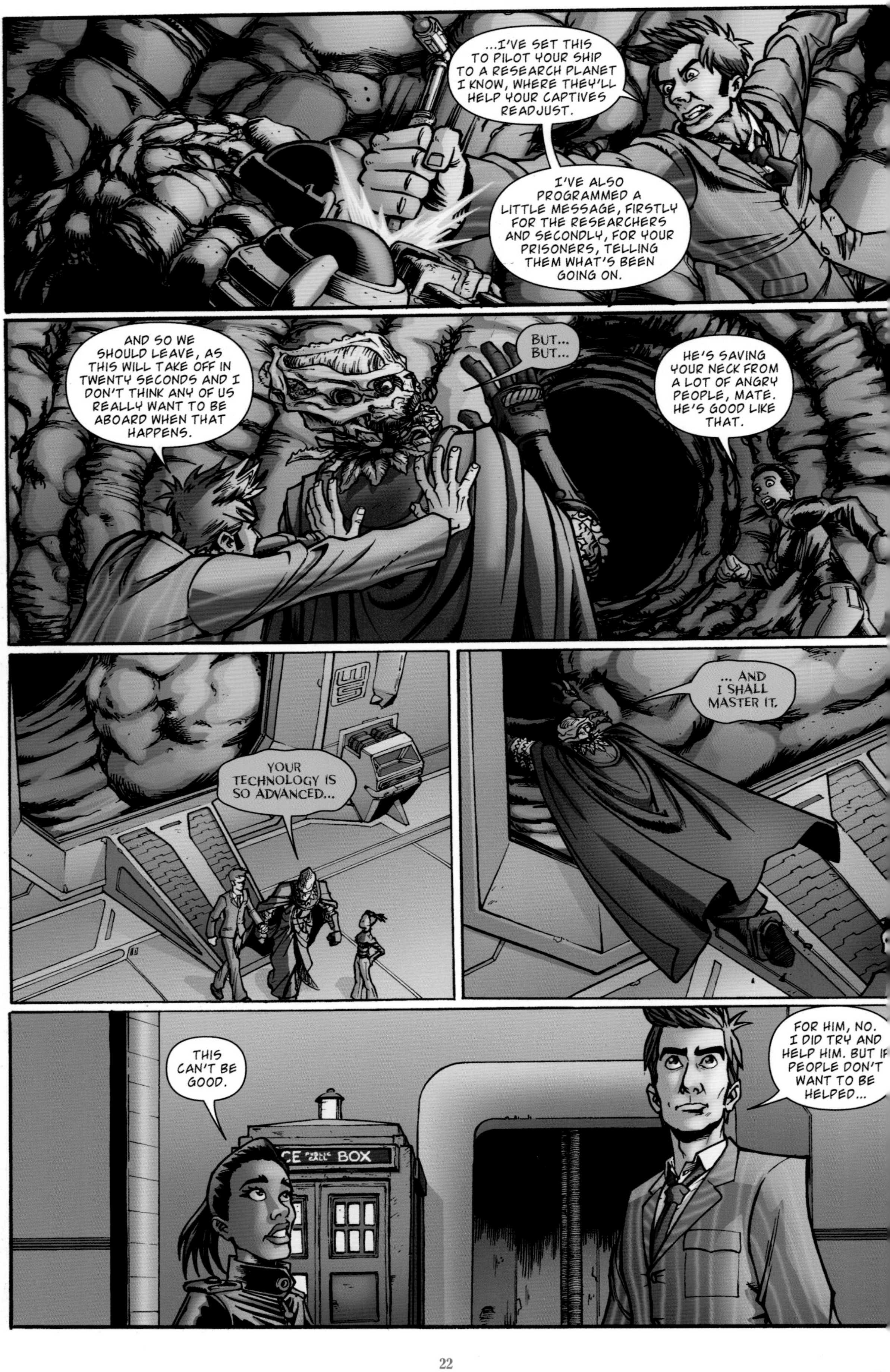
...I'VE SET THIS TO PILOT YOUR SHIP TO A RESEARCH PLANET I KNOW, WHERE THEY'LL HELP YOUR CAPTIVES READJUST.
I'VE ALSO PROGRAMMED A LITTLE MESSAGE, FIRSTLY FOR THE RESEARCHERS AND SECONDLY, FOR YOUR PRISONERS, TELLING THEM WHAT'S BEEN GOING ON.
AND SO WE SHOULD LEAVE, AS THIS WILL TAKE OFF IN TWENTY SECONDS AND I DON'T THINK ANY OF US REALLY WANT TO BE ABOARD WHEN THAT HAPPENS.
BUT... BUT...
HE'S SAVING YOUR NECK FROM A LOT OF ANGRY PEOPLE, MATE. HE'S GOOD LIKE THAT.
YOUR TECHNOLOGY IS SO ADVANCED...
... AND I SHALL MASTER IT.
THIS CAN'T BE GOOD.
FOR HIM, NO. I DID TRY AND HELP HIM. BUT IF PEOPLE DON'T WANT TO BE HELPED...
BOX

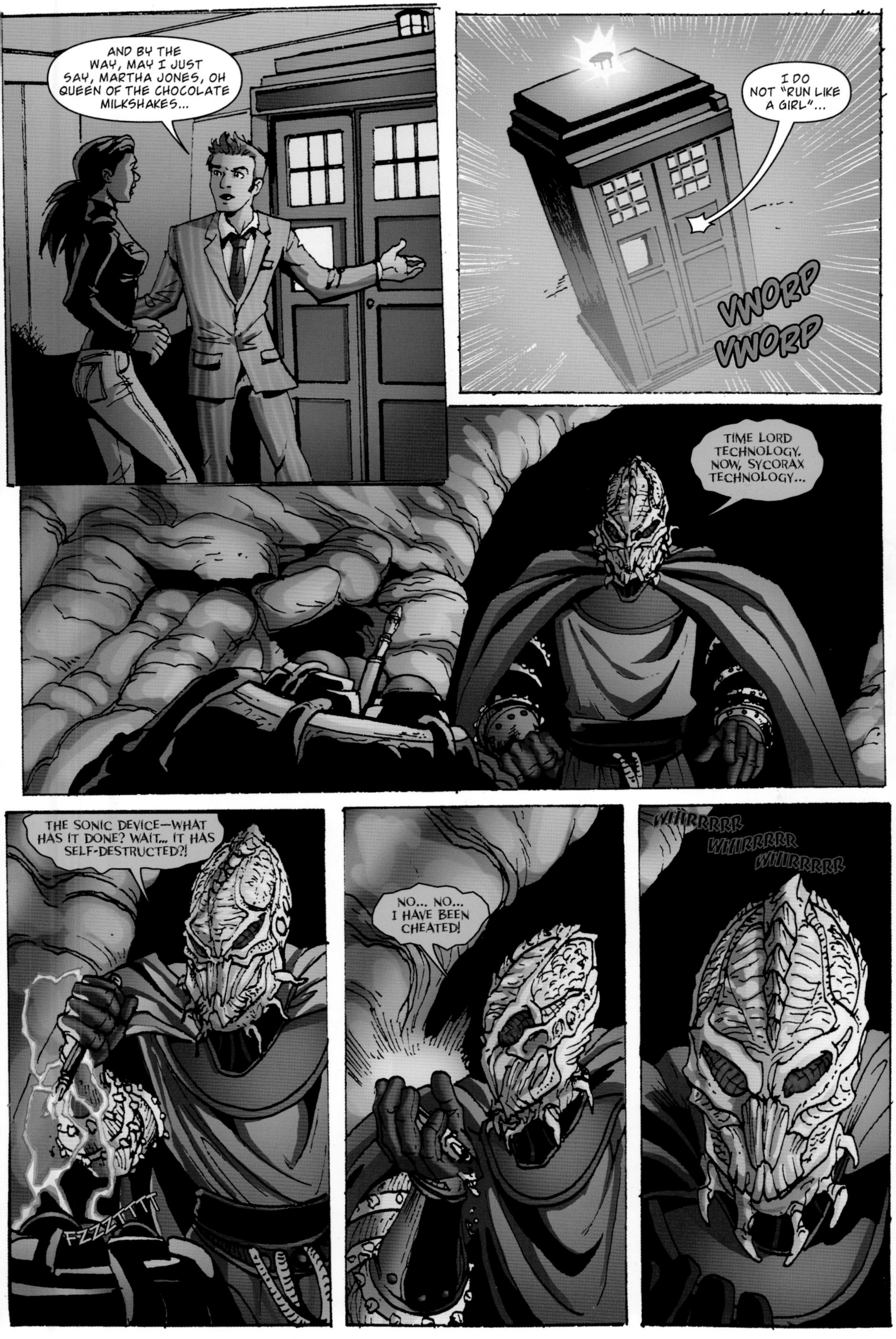
AND BY THE WAY, MAY I JUST SAY, MARTHA JONES, OH QUEEN OF THE CHOCOLATE MILKSHAKES...
I DO NOT "RUN LIKE A GIRL"...
VWORP VWORP
TIME LORD TECHNOLOGY. NOW, SYCORAX TECHNOLOGY...
THE SONIC DEVICE—WHAT HAS IT DONE? WAIT... IT HAS SELF-DESTRUCTED?!
FZZZTTTT
NO... NO... I HAVE BEEN CHEATED!
WHIRRRRR
WHIRRRRR
WHIRRRRR

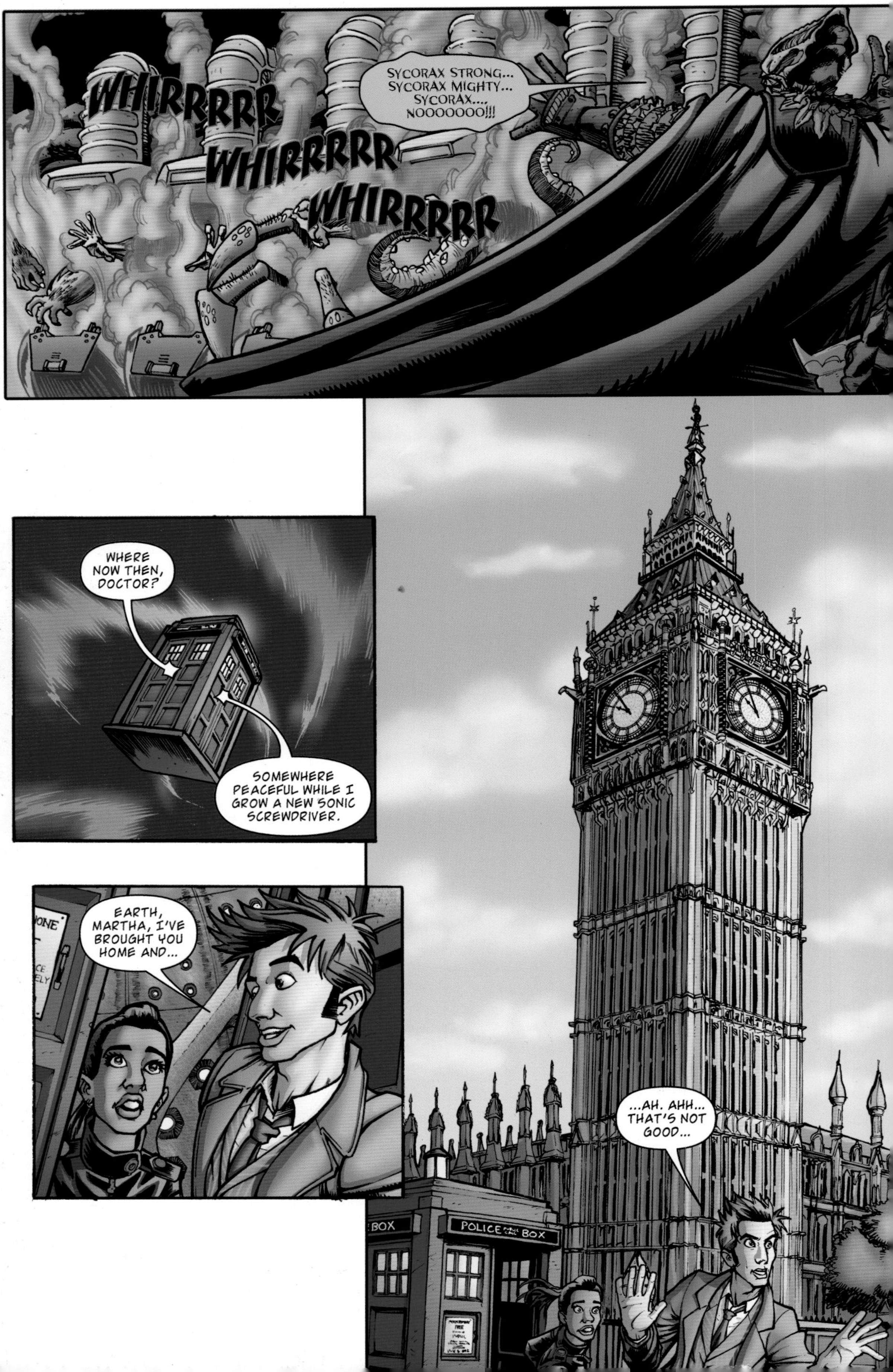

WHIRRRRR
SYCORAX STRONG... SYCORAX MIGHTY... SYCORAX.... NOOOOOOO!!!
WHIRRRRR
WHIRRRRR
WHERE NOW THEN, DOCTOR?
SOMEWHERE PEACEFUL WHILE I GROW A NEW SONIC SCREWDRIVER.
EARTH, MARTHA, I'VE BROUGHT YOU HOME AND...
...AH. AHH... THAT'S NOT GOOD...
POLICE BOX

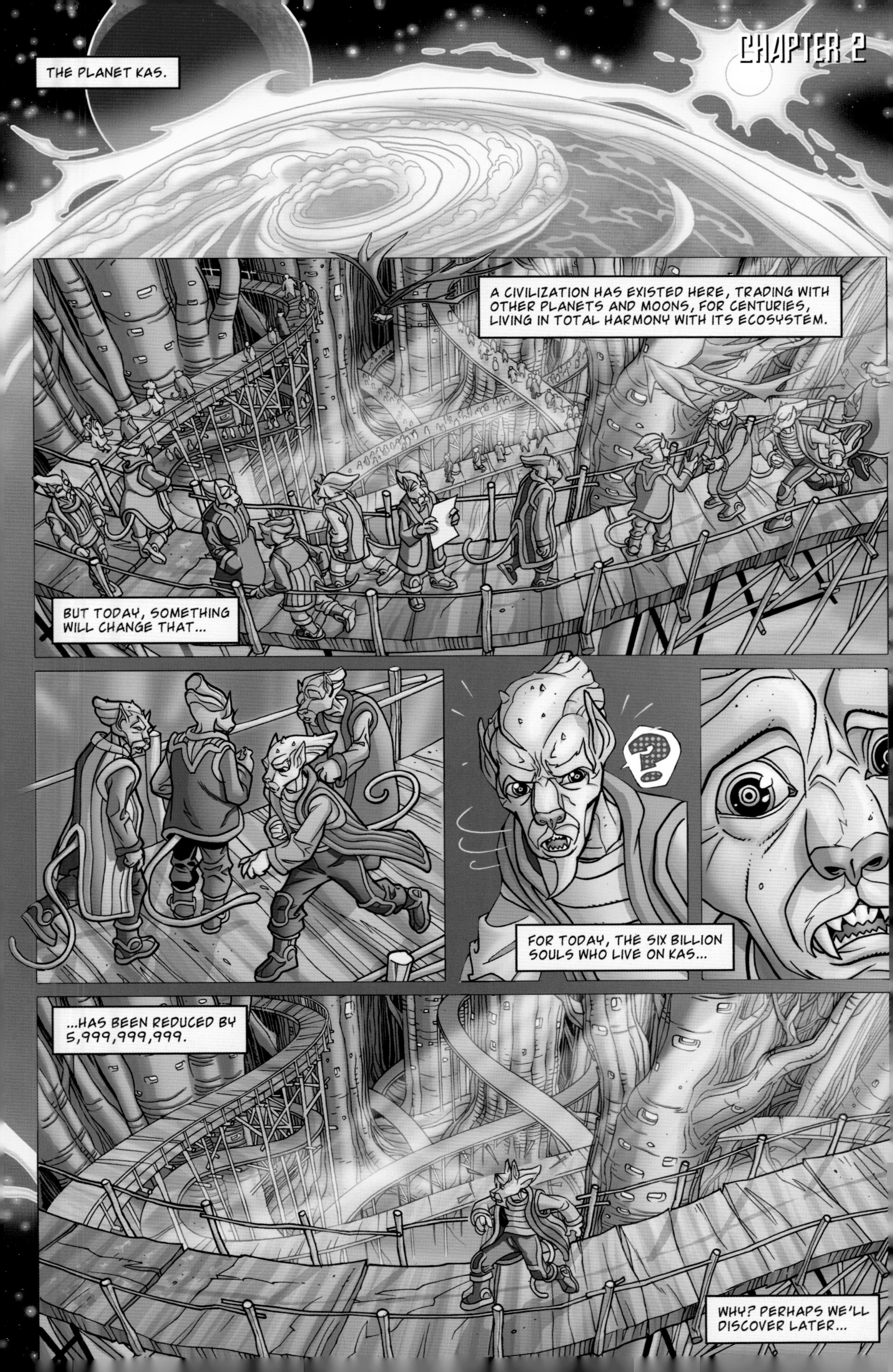
CHAPTER 2
THE PLANET KAS.
A CIVILIZATION HAS EXISTED HERE, TRADING WITH OTHER PLANETS AND MOONS, FOR CENTURIES, LIVING IN TOTAL HARMONY WITH ITS ECOSYSTEM.
BUT TODAY, SOMETHING WILL CHANGE THAT...
?
FOR TODAY, THE SIX BILLION SOULS WHO LIVE ON KAS...
...HAS BEEN REDUCED BY 5,999,999,999.
WHY? PERHAPS WE'LL DISCOVER LATER...

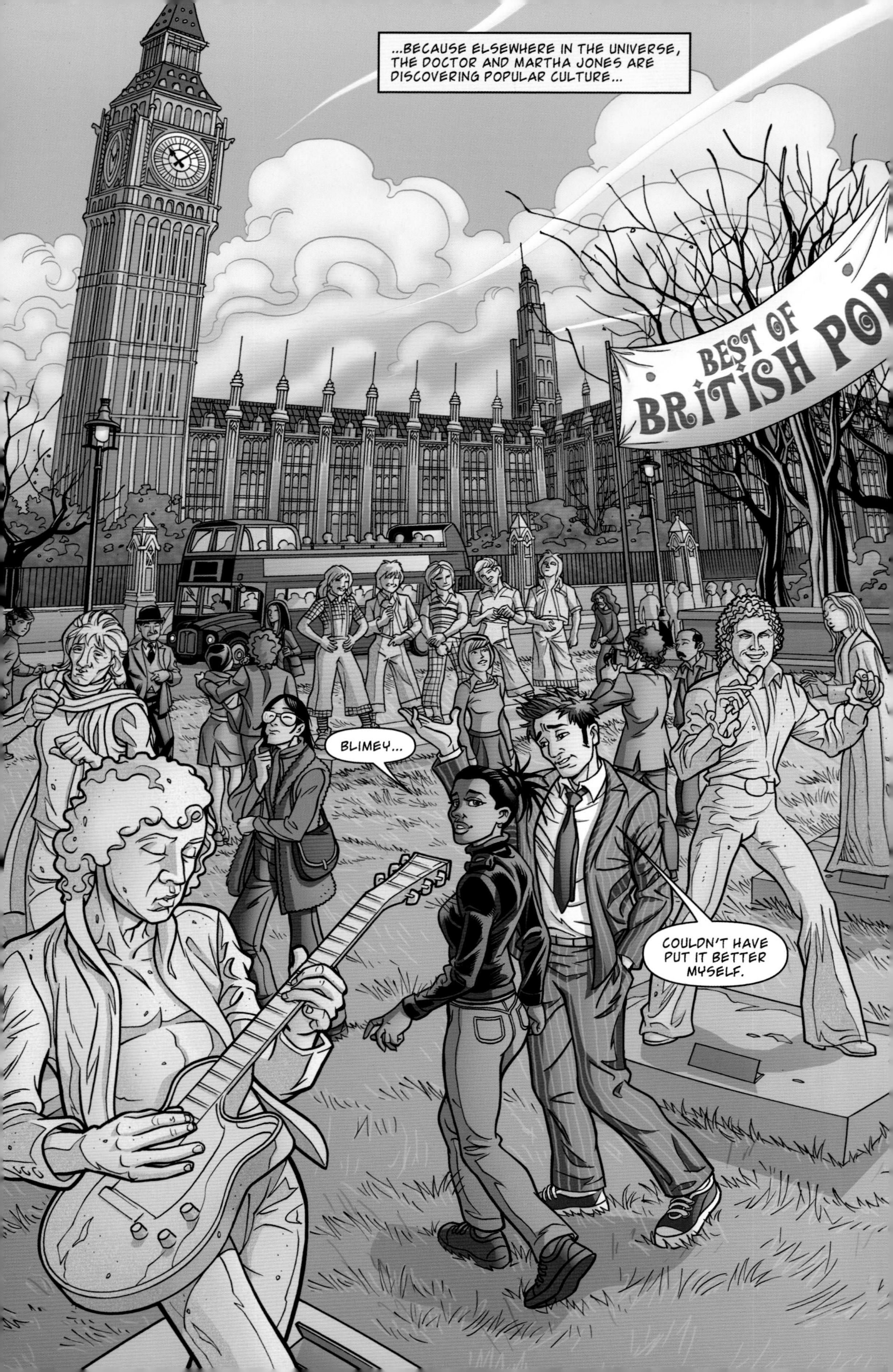
...BECAUSE ELSEWHERE IN THE UNIVERSE, THE DOCTOR AND MARTHA JONES ARE DISCOVERING POPULAR CULTURE...
BEST OF BRITISH POP
BLIMEY...
COULDN'T HAVE PUT IT BETTER MYSELF.

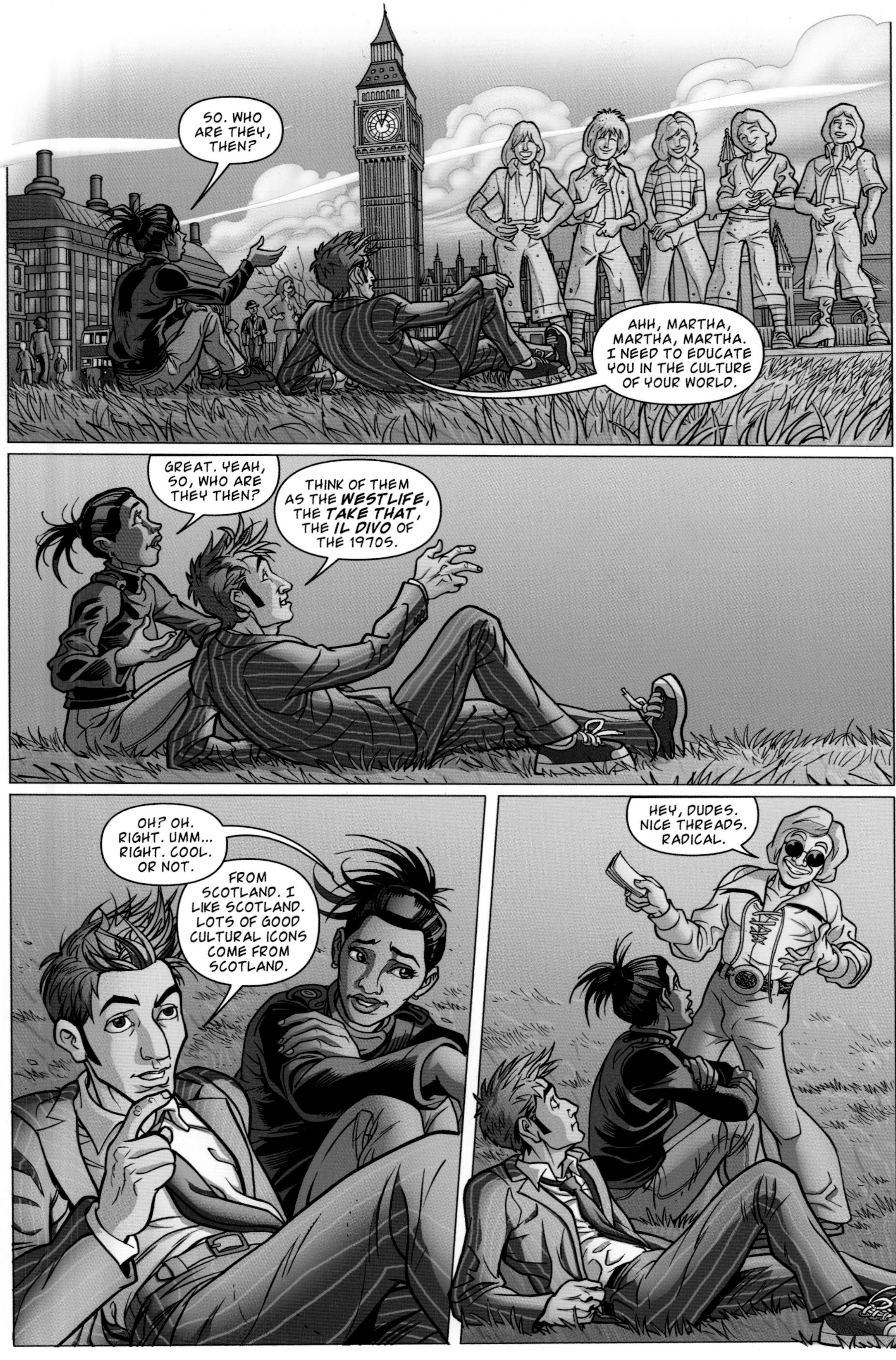

SO. WHO ARE THEY, THEN?
AHH, MARTHA, MARTHA, MARTHA. I NEED TO EDUCATE YOU IN THE CULTURE OF YOUR WORLD.
GREAT. YEAH, SO, WHO ARE THEY THEN?
THINK OF THEM AS THE WESTLIFE, THE TAKE THAT, THE IL DIVO OF THE 1970S.
OH? OH. RIGHT. UMM... RIGHT. COOL. OR NOT.
FROM SCOTLAND. I LIKE SCOTLAND. LOTS OF GOOD CULTURAL ICONS COME FROM SCOTLAND.
HEY, DUDES. NICE THREADS. RADICAL.

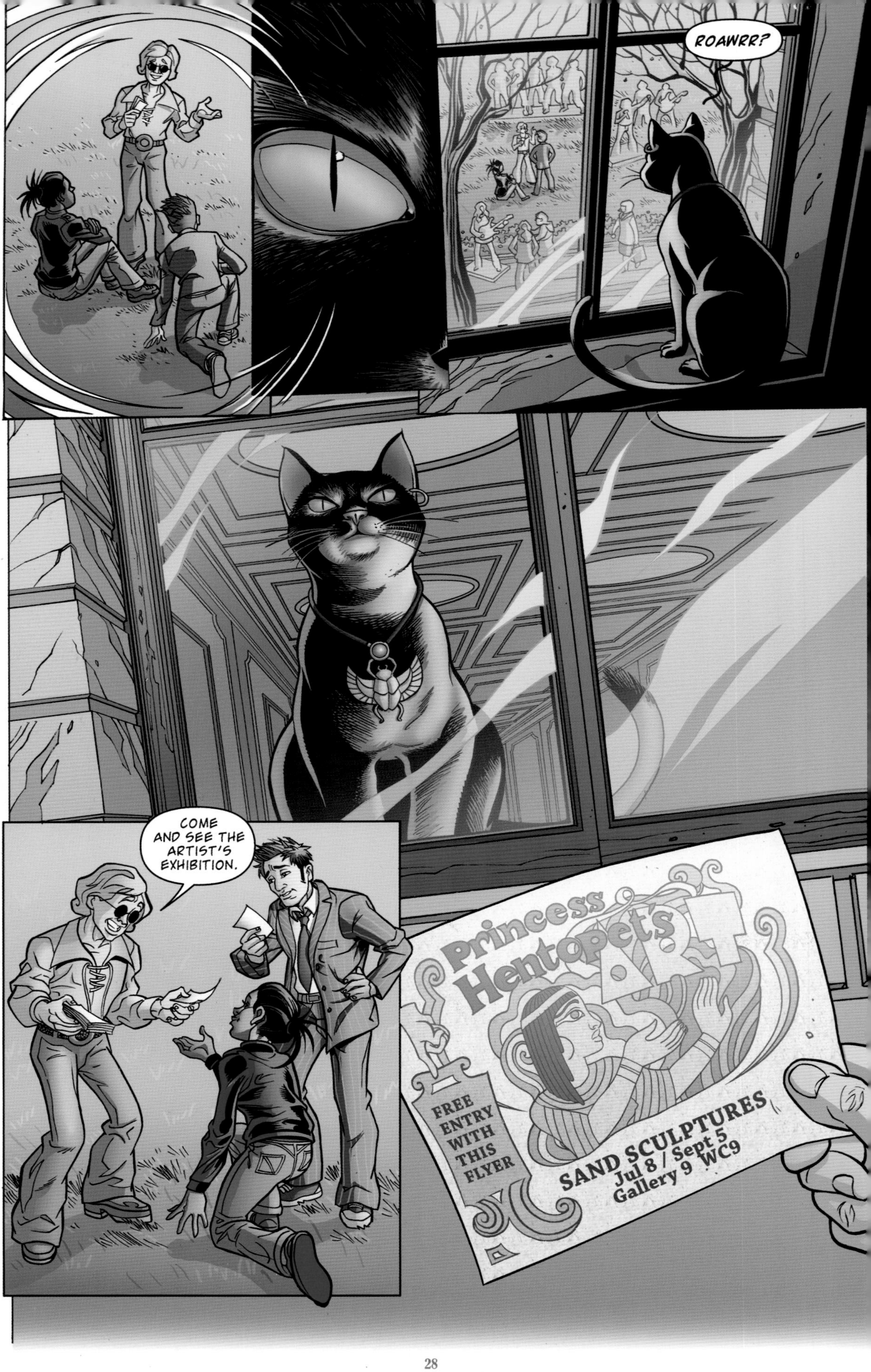
ROAWRR?
COME AND SEE THE ARTIST'S EXHIBITION.
Princess Hentopet's ART
FREE ENTRY WITH THIS FLYER
SAND SCULPTURES
Jul 8 / Sept 5
Gallery 9 WC9

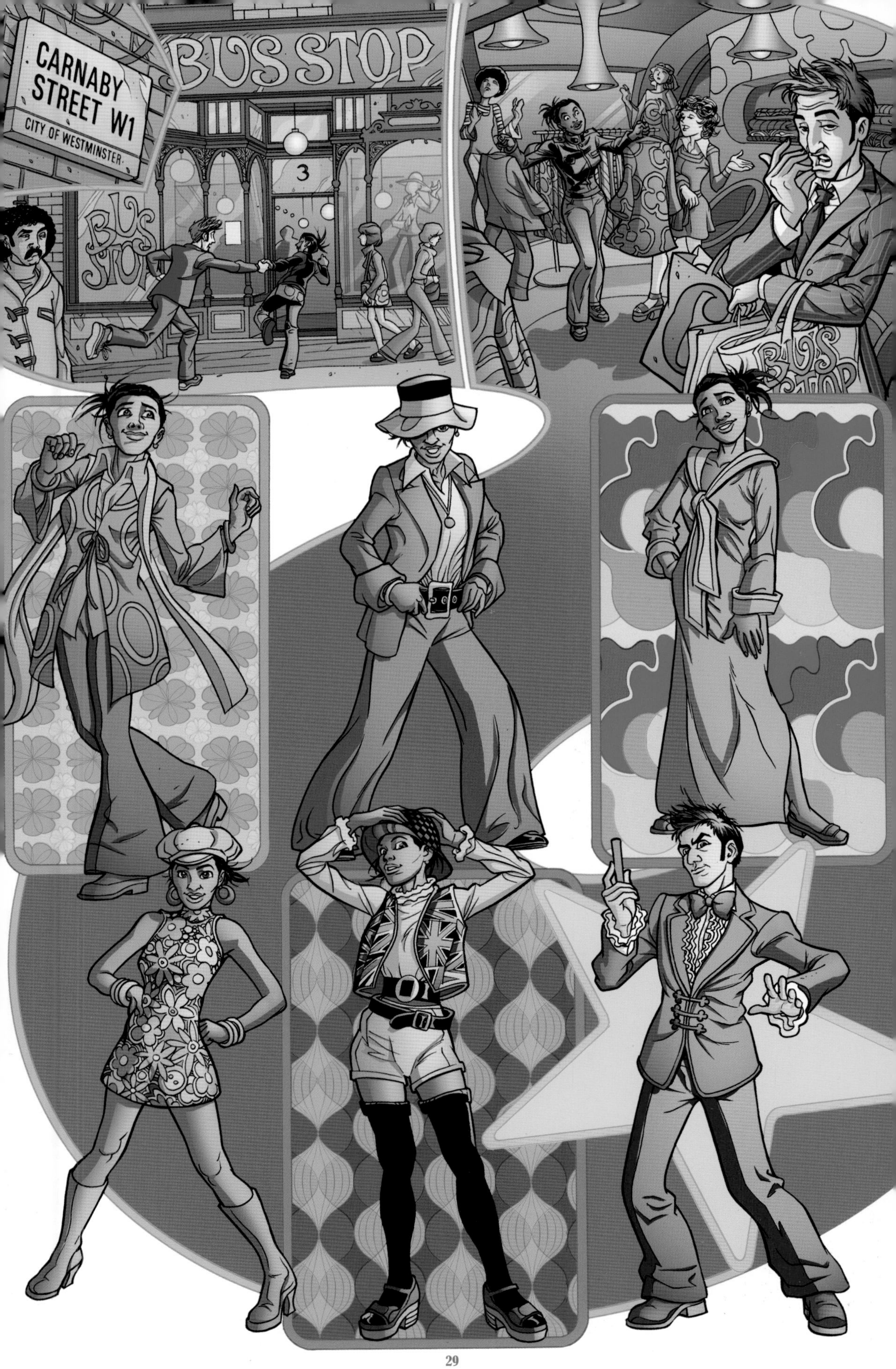
CARNABY
STREET W1
CITY OF WESTMINSTER
BUS STOP
3
BUS STOP
BUS STOP

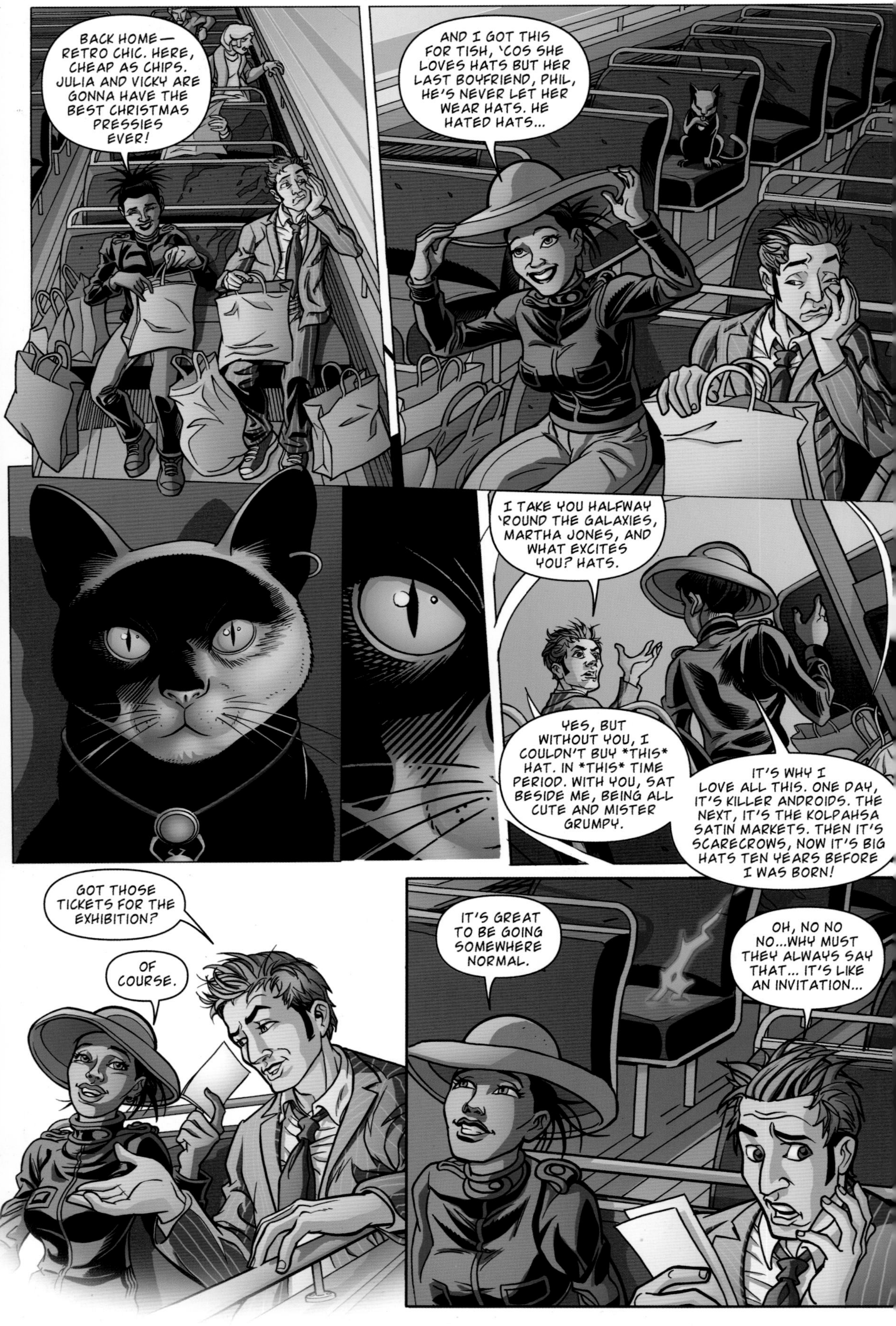
BACK HOME— RETRO CHIC. HERE, CHEAP AS CHIPS. JULIA AND VICKY ARE GONNA HAVE THE BEST CHRISTMAS PRESSIES EVER!
AND I GOT THIS FOR TISH, 'COS SHE LOVES HATS BUT HER LAST BOYFRIEND, PHIL, HE'S NEVER LET HER WEAR HATS. HE HATED HATS...
I TAKE YOU HALFWAY 'ROUND THE GALAXIES, MARTHA JONES, AND WHAT EXCITES YOU? HATS.
YES, BUT WITHOUT YOU, I COULDN'T BUY *THIS* HAT. IN *THIS* TIME PERIOD. WITH YOU, SAT BESIDE ME, BEING ALL CUTE AND MISTER GRUMPY.
IT'S WHY I LOVE ALL THIS. ONE DAY, IT'S KILLER ANDROIDS. THE NEXT, IT'S THE KOLPAHSA SATIN MARKETS. THEN IT'S SCARECROWS, NOW IT'S BIG HATS TEN YEARS BEFORE I WAS BORN!
GOT THOSE TICKETS FOR THE EXHIBITION?
OF COURSE.
IT'S GREAT TO BE GOING SOMEWHERE NORMAL.
OH, NO NO NO...WHY MUST THEY ALWAYS SAY THAT... IT'S LIKE AN INVITATION...

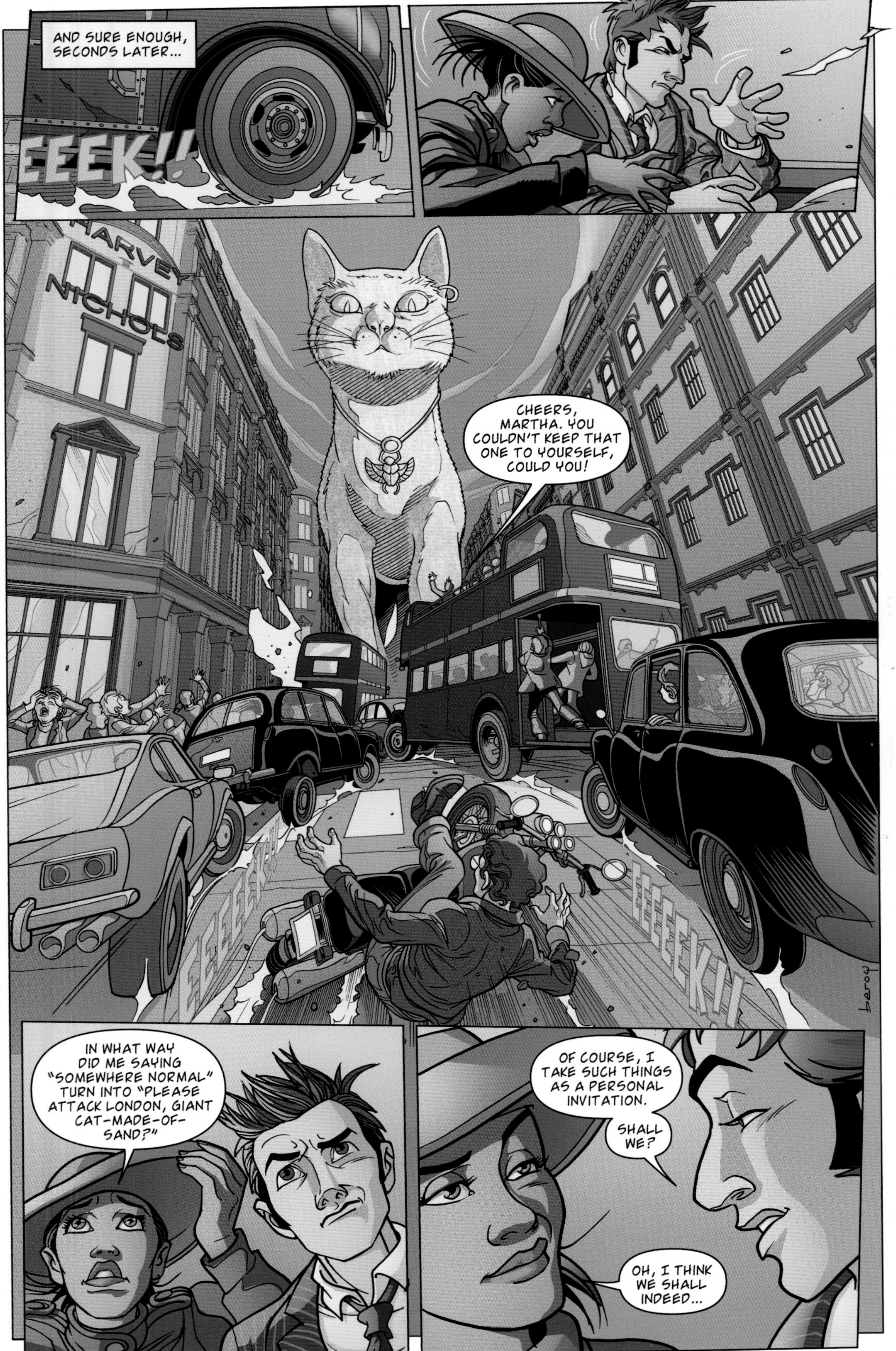
AND SURE ENOUGH, SECONDS LATER...
EEEK!!
HARVEY NICHOLS
CHEERS, MARTHA. YOU COULDN'T KEEP THAT ONE TO YOURSELF, COULD YOU!
EEEEEK!!
EEEEK!!
IN WHAT WAY DID ME SAYING "SOMEWHERE NORMAL" TURN INTO "PLEASE ATTACK LONDON, GIANT CAT-MADE-OF-SAND?"
OF COURSE, I TAKE SUCH THINGS AS A PERSONAL INVITATION.
SHALL WE?
OH, I THINK WE SHALL INDEED...

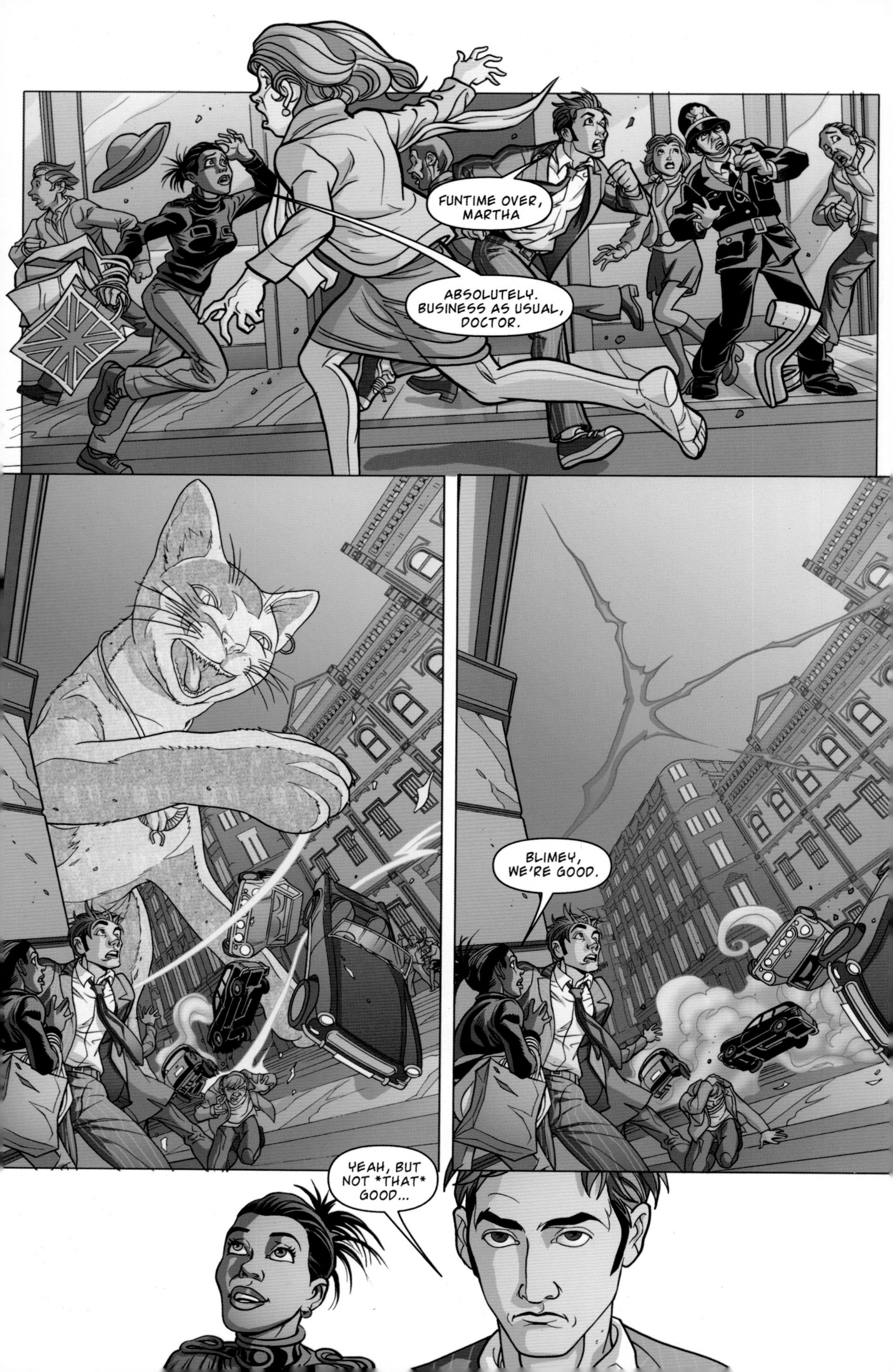
FUNTIME OVER, MARTHA
ABSOLUTELY. BUSINESS AS USUAL, DOCTOR.
BLIMEY, WE'RE GOOD.
YEAH, BUT NOT *THAT* GOOD...

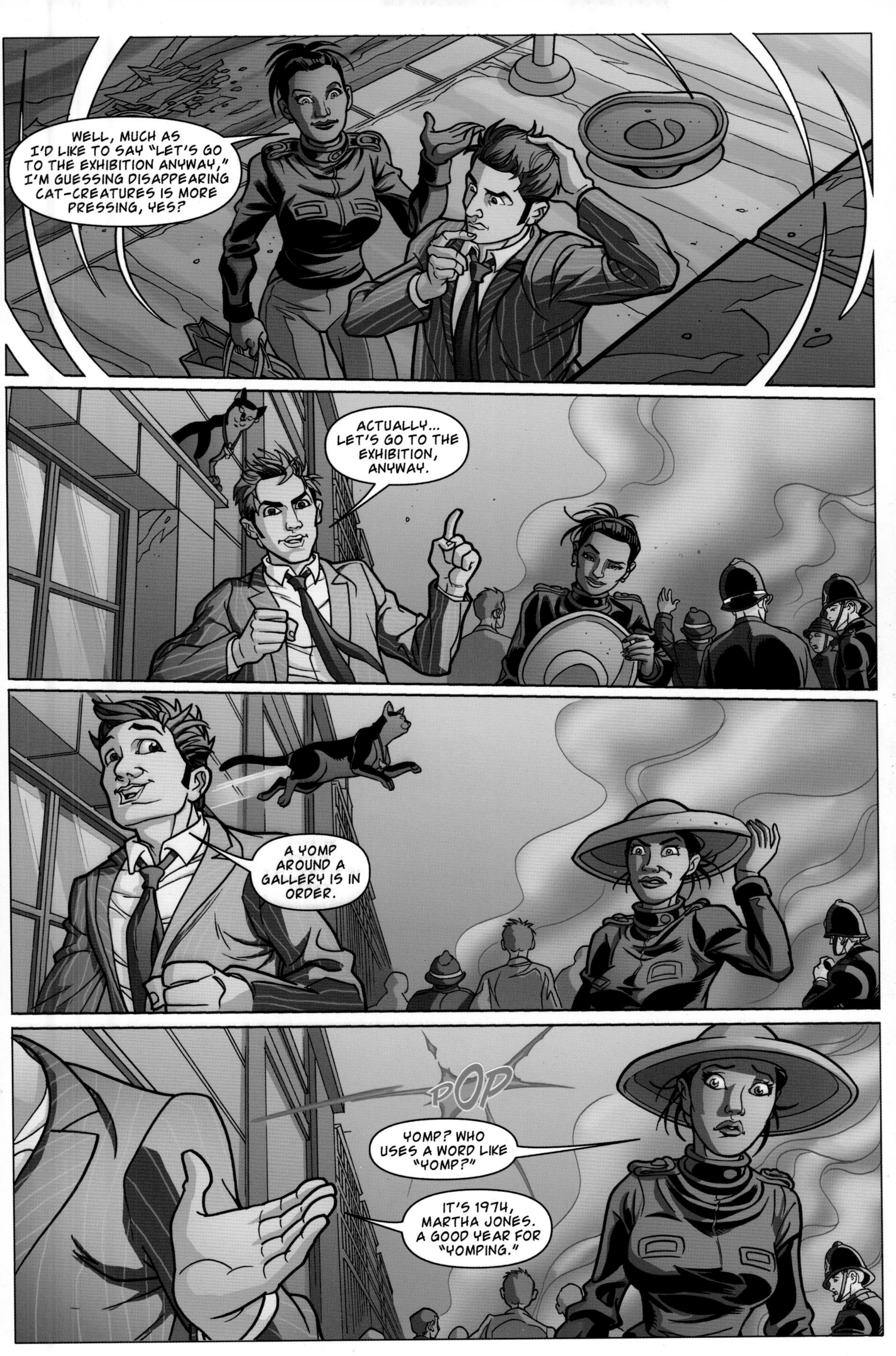
WELL, MUCH AS I'D LIKE TO SAY "LET'S GO TO THE EXHIBITION ANYWAY," I'M GUESSING DISAPPEARING CAT-CREATURES IS MORE PRESSING, YES?
ACTUALLY... LET'S GO TO THE EXHIBITION, ANYWAY.
A YOMP AROUND A GALLERY IS IN ORDER.
POP
YOMP? WHO USES A WORD LIKE "YOMP?"
IT'S 1974, MARTHA JONES. A GOOD YEAR FOR "YOMPING."

ELSEWHERE...

THE PLANET *NYRRUH 4.*

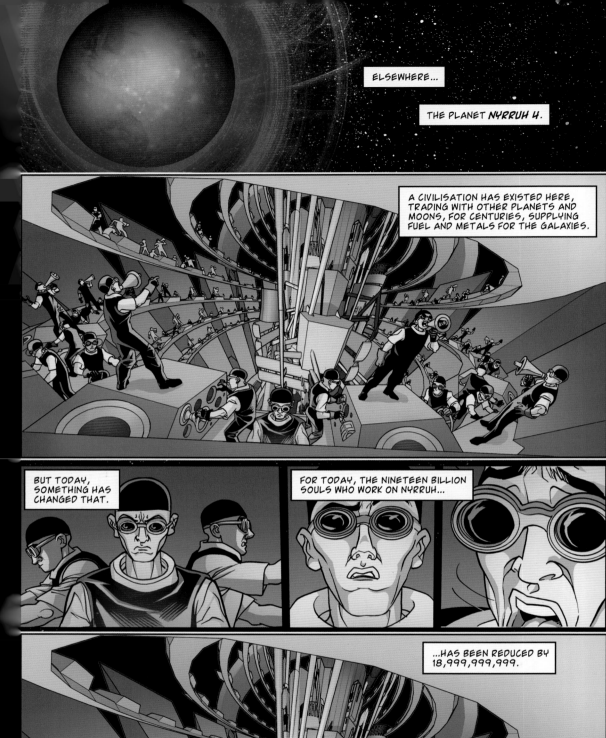

A CIVILISATION HAS EXISTED HERE, TRADING WITH OTHER PLANETS AND MOONS, FOR CENTURIES, SUPPLYING FUEL AND METALS FOR THE GALAXIES.

BUT TODAY, SOMETHING HAS CHANGED THAT.

FOR TODAY, THE NINETEEN BILLION SOULS WHO WORK ON NYRRUH...

...HAS BEEN REDUCED BY 18,999,999,999.

SOMETHING IS GOING ON...

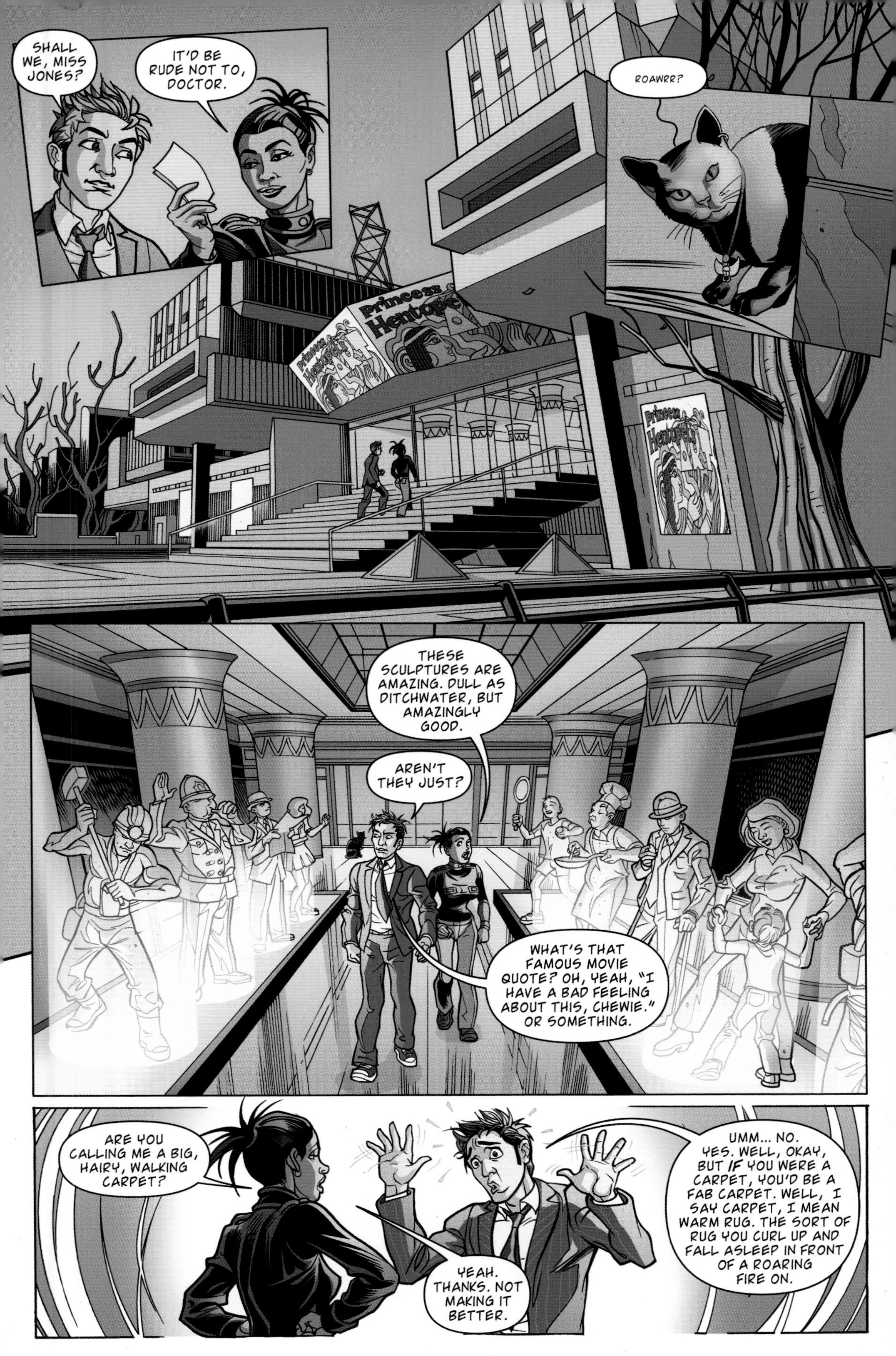
SHALL WE, MISS JONES?
IT'D BE RUDE NOT TO, DOCTOR.
ROAWRR?
Princess Hentopet
THESE SCULPTURES ARE AMAZING. DULL AS DITCHWATER, BUT AMAZINGLY GOOD.
AREN'T THEY JUST?
WHAT'S THAT FAMOUS MOVIE QUOTE? OH, YEAH, "I HAVE A BAD FEELING ABOUT THIS, CHEWIE." OR SOMETHING.
ARE YOU CALLING ME A BIG, HAIRY, WALKING CARPET?
UMM... NO. YES. WELL, OKAY, BUT *IF* YOU WERE A CARPET, YOU'D BE A FAB CARPET. WELL, I SAY CARPET, I MEAN WARM RUG. THE SORT OF RUG YOU CURL UP AND FALL ASLEEP IN FRONT OF A ROARING FIRE ON.
YEAH. THANKS. NOT MAKING IT BETTER.

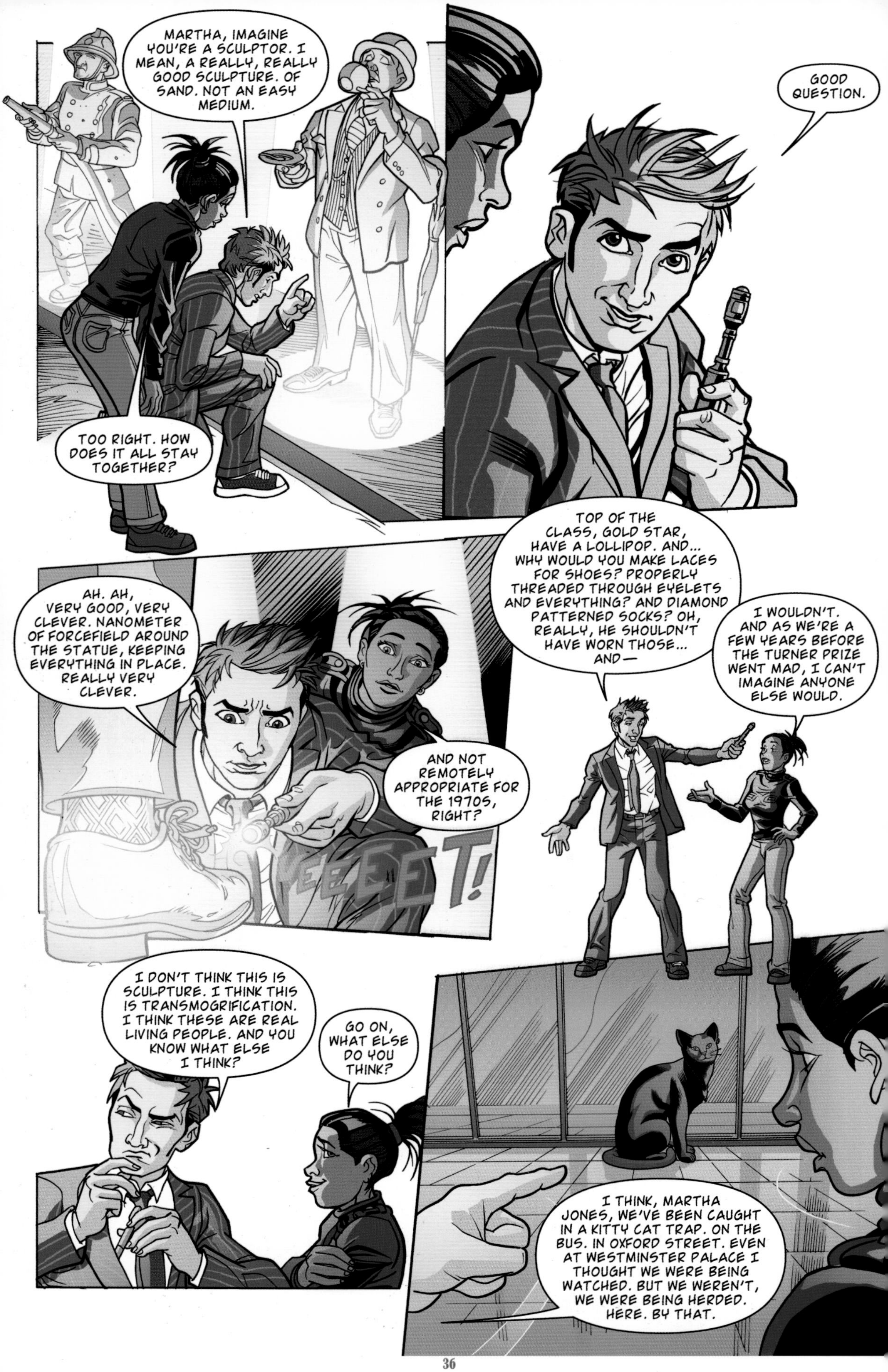
MARTHA, IMAGINE YOU'RE A SCULPTOR. I MEAN, A REALLY, REALLY GOOD SCULPTURE. OF SAND. NOT AN EASY MEDIUM.
TOO RIGHT. HOW DOES IT ALL STAY TOGETHER?
GOOD QUESTION.
AH. AH, VERY GOOD, VERY CLEVER. NANOMETER OF FORCEFIELD AROUND THE STATUE, KEEPING EVERYTHING IN PLACE. REALLY VERY CLEVER.
AND NOT REMOTELY APPROPRIATE FOR THE 1970S, RIGHT?
VEEEET!
TOP OF THE CLASS, GOLD STAR, HAVE A LOLLIPOP. AND... WHY WOULD YOU MAKE LACES FOR SHOES? PROPERLY THREADED THROUGH EYELETS AND EVERYTHING? AND DIAMOND PATTERNED SOCKS? OH, REALLY, HE SHOULDN'T HAVE WORN THOSE... AND—
I WOULDN'T. AND AS WE'RE A FEW YEARS BEFORE THE TURNER PRIZE WENT MAD, I CAN'T IMAGINE ANYONE ELSE WOULD.
I DON'T THINK THIS IS SCULPTURE. I THINK THIS IS TRANSMOGRIFICATION. I THINK THESE ARE REAL LIVING PEOPLE. AND YOU KNOW WHAT ELSE I THINK?
GO ON, WHAT ELSE DO YOU THINK?
I THINK, MARTHA JONES, WE'VE BEEN CAUGHT IN A KITTY CAT TRAP. ON THE BUS. IN OXFORD STREET. EVEN AT WESTMINSTER PALACE I THOUGHT WE WERE BEING WATCHED. BUT WE WEREN'T, WE WERE BEING HERDED. HERE. BY THAT.

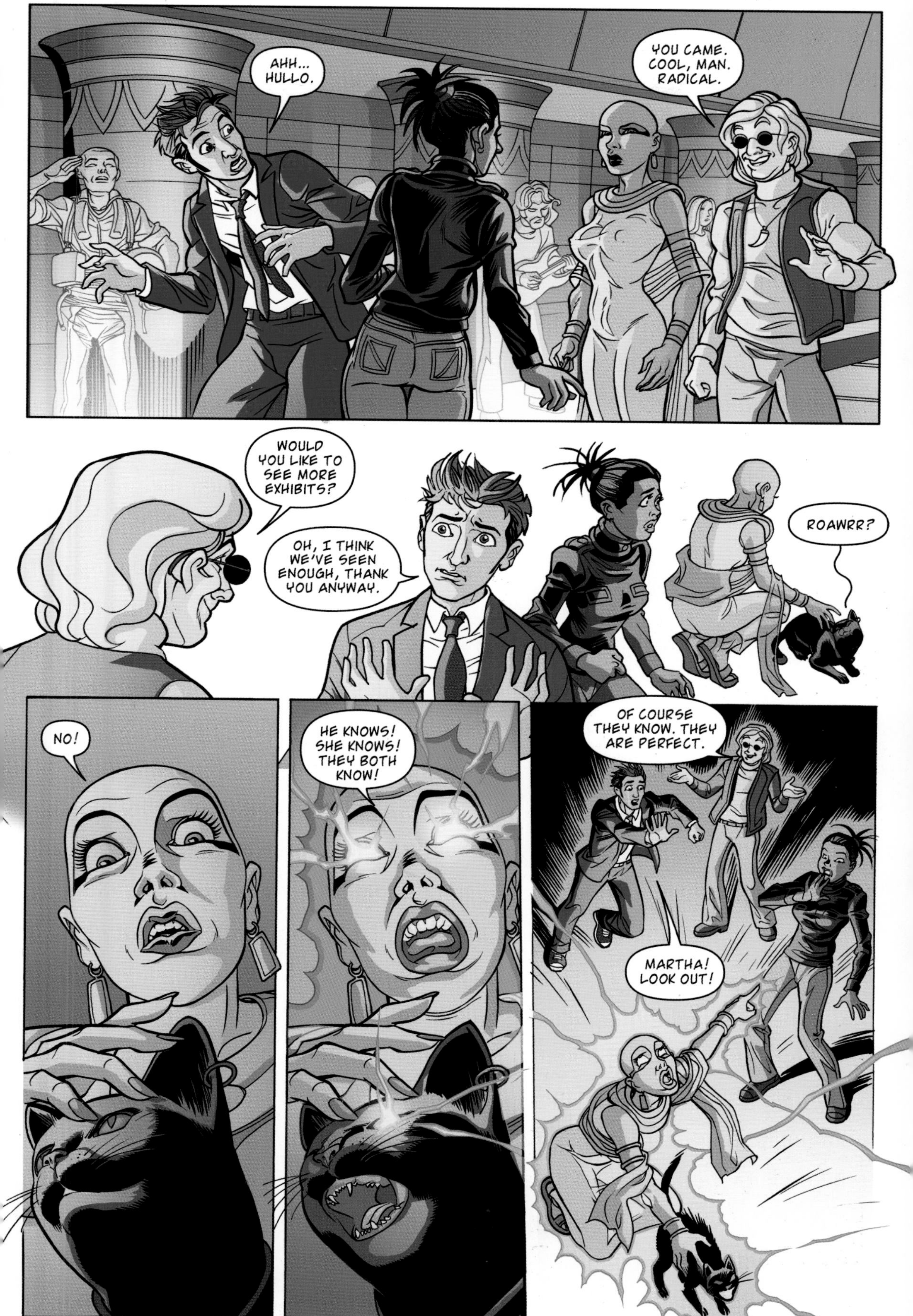
AHH... HULLO.
YOU CAME. COOL, MAN. RADICAL.
WOULD YOU LIKE TO SEE MORE EXHIBITS?
OH, I THINK WE'VE SEEN ENOUGH, THANK YOU ANYWAY.
ROAWRR?
NO!
HE KNOWS! SHE KNOWS! THEY BOTH KNOW!
OF COURSE THEY KNOW. THEY ARE PERFECT.
MARTHA! LOOK OUT!

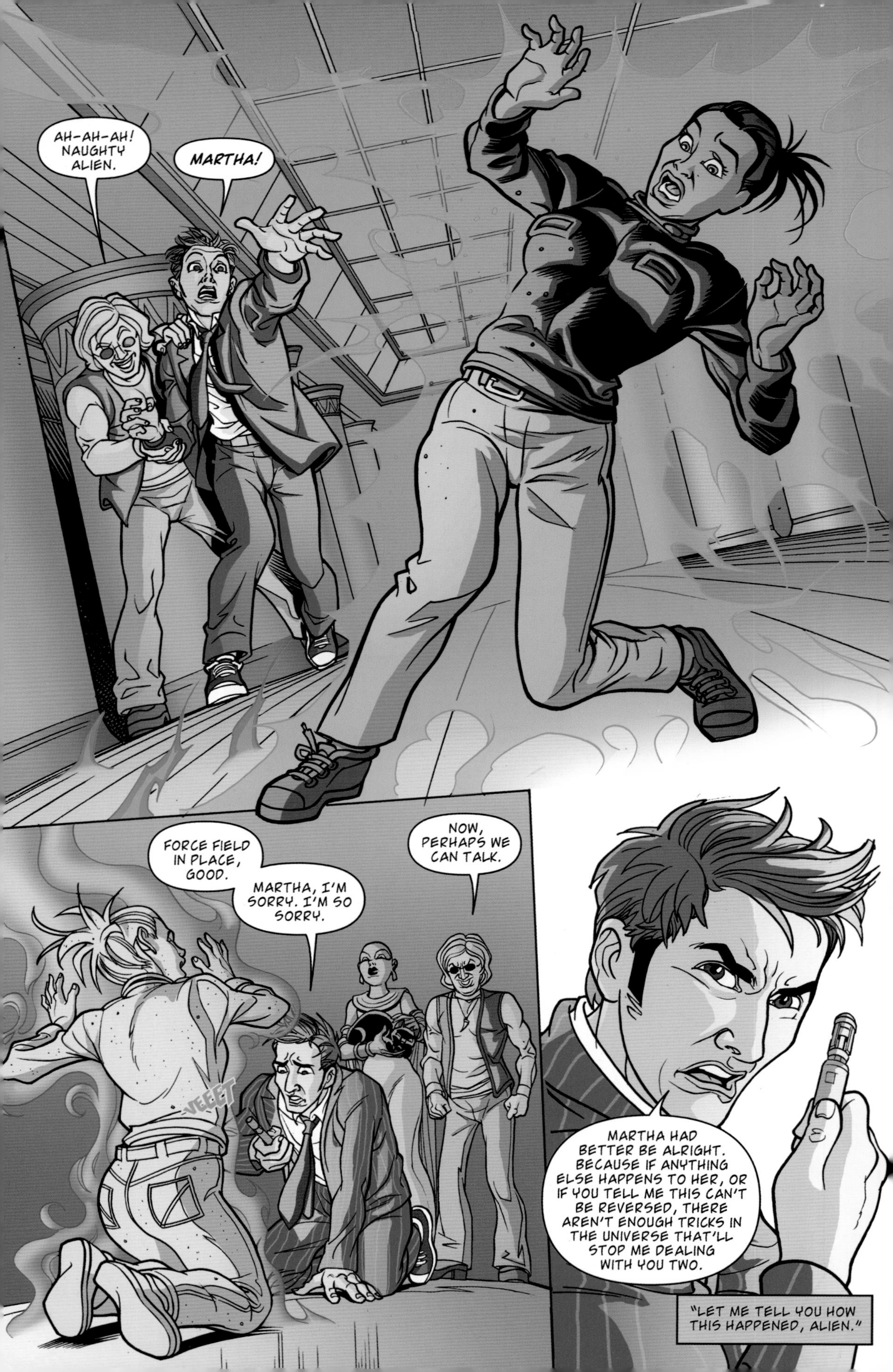
AH-AH-AH! NAUGHTY ALIEN.
MARTHA!
FORCE FIELD IN PLACE, GOOD.
MARTHA, I'M SORRY. I'M SO SORRY.
NOW, PERHAPS WE CAN TALK.
VEEET
MARTHA HAD BETTER BE ALRIGHT. BECAUSE IF ANYTHING ELSE HAPPENS TO HER, OR IF YOU TELL ME THIS CAN'T BE REVERSED, THERE AREN'T ENOUGH TRICKS IN THE UNIVERSE THAT'LL STOP ME DEALING WITH YOU TWO.
"LET ME TELL YOU HOW THIS HAPPENED, ALIEN."

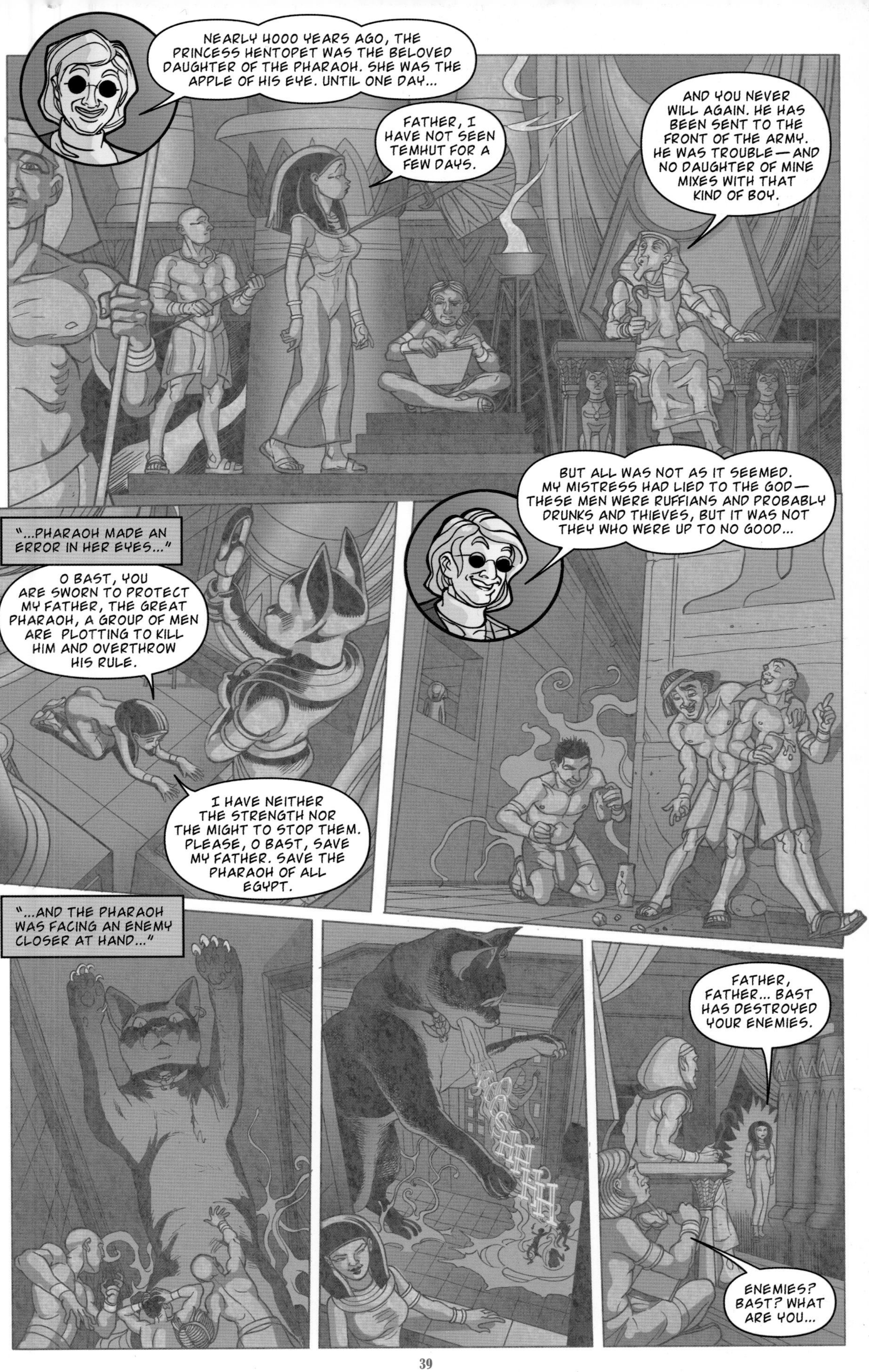
NEARLY 4000 YEARS AGO, THE PRINCESS HENTOPET WAS THE BELOVED DAUGHTER OF THE PHARAOH. SHE WAS THE APPLE OF HIS EYE. UNTIL ONE DAY...
FATHER, I HAVE NOT SEEN TEMHUT FOR A FEW DAYS.
AND YOU NEVER WILL AGAIN. HE HAS BEEN SENT TO THE FRONT OF THE ARMY. HE WAS TROUBLE—AND NO DAUGHTER OF MINE MIXES WITH THAT KIND OF BOY.
"...PHARAOH MADE AN ERROR IN HER EYES..."
O BAST, YOU ARE SWORN TO PROTECT MY FATHER, THE GREAT PHARAOH, A GROUP OF MEN ARE PLOTTING TO KILL HIM AND OVERTHROW HIS RULE.
I HAVE NEITHER THE STRENGTH NOR THE MIGHT TO STOP THEM. PLEASE, O BAST, SAVE MY FATHER. SAVE THE PHARAOH OF ALL EGYPT.
BUT ALL WAS NOT AS IT SEEMED. MY MISTRESS HAD LIED TO THE GOD—THESE MEN WERE RUFFIANS AND PROBABLY DRUNKS AND THIEVES, BUT IT WAS NOT THEY WHO WERE UP TO NO GOOD...
"...AND THE PHARAOH WAS FACING AN ENEMY CLOSER AT HAND..."
FATHER, FATHER... BAST HAS DESTROYED YOUR ENEMIES.
ENEMIES? BAST? WHAT ARE YOU...

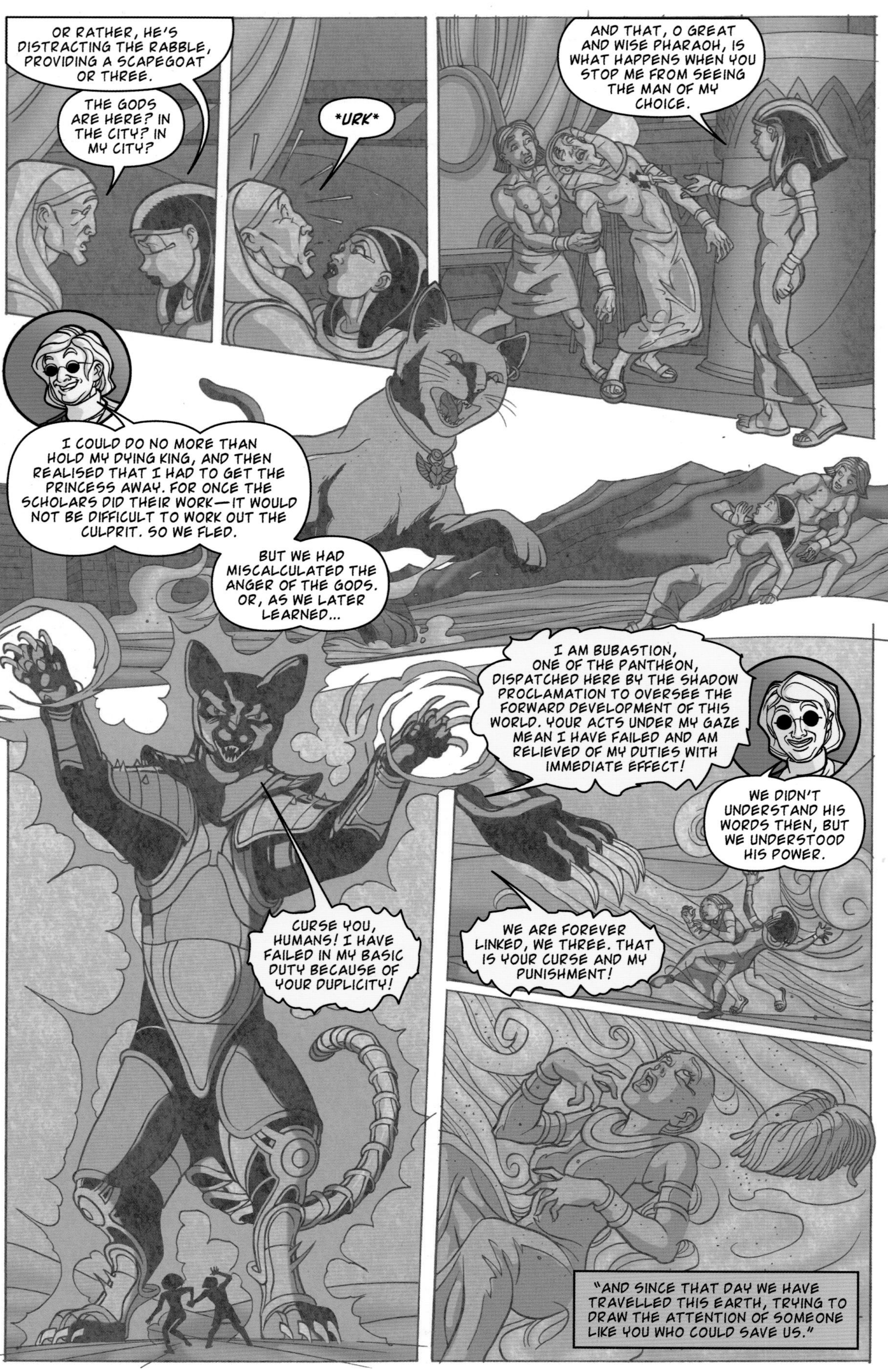
OR RATHER, HE'S DISTRACTING THE RABBLE, PROVIDING A SCAPEGOAT OR THREE.
THE GODS ARE HERE? IN THE CITY? IN MY CITY?
URK
AND THAT, O GREAT AND WISE PHARAOH, IS WHAT HAPPENS WHEN YOU STOP ME FROM SEEING THE MAN OF MY CHOICE.
I COULD DO NO MORE THAN HOLD MY DYING KING, AND THEN REALISED THAT I HAD TO GET THE PRINCESS AWAY. FOR ONCE THE SCHOLARS DID THEIR WORK—IT WOULD NOT BE DIFFICULT TO WORK OUT THE CULPRIT. SO WE FLED.
BUT WE HAD MISCALCULATED THE ANGER OF THE GODS. OR, AS WE LATER LEARNED...
I AM BUBASTION, ONE OF THE PANTHEON, DISPATCHED HERE BY THE SHADOW PROCLAMATION TO OVERSEE THE FORWARD DEVELOPMENT OF THIS WORLD. YOUR ACTS UNDER MY GAZE MEAN I HAVE FAILED AND AM RELIEVED OF MY DUTIES WITH IMMEDIATE EFFECT!
WE DIDN'T UNDERSTAND HIS WORDS THEN, BUT WE UNDERSTOOD HIS POWER.
CURSE YOU, HUMANS! I HAVE FAILED IN MY BASIC DUTY BECAUSE OF YOUR DUPLICITY!
WE ARE FOREVER LINKED, WE THREE. THAT IS YOUR CURSE AND MY PUNISHMENT!
"AND SINCE THAT DAY WE HAVE TRAVELLED THIS EARTH, TRYING TO DRAW THE ATTENTION OF SOMEONE LIKE YOU WHO COULD SAVE US."

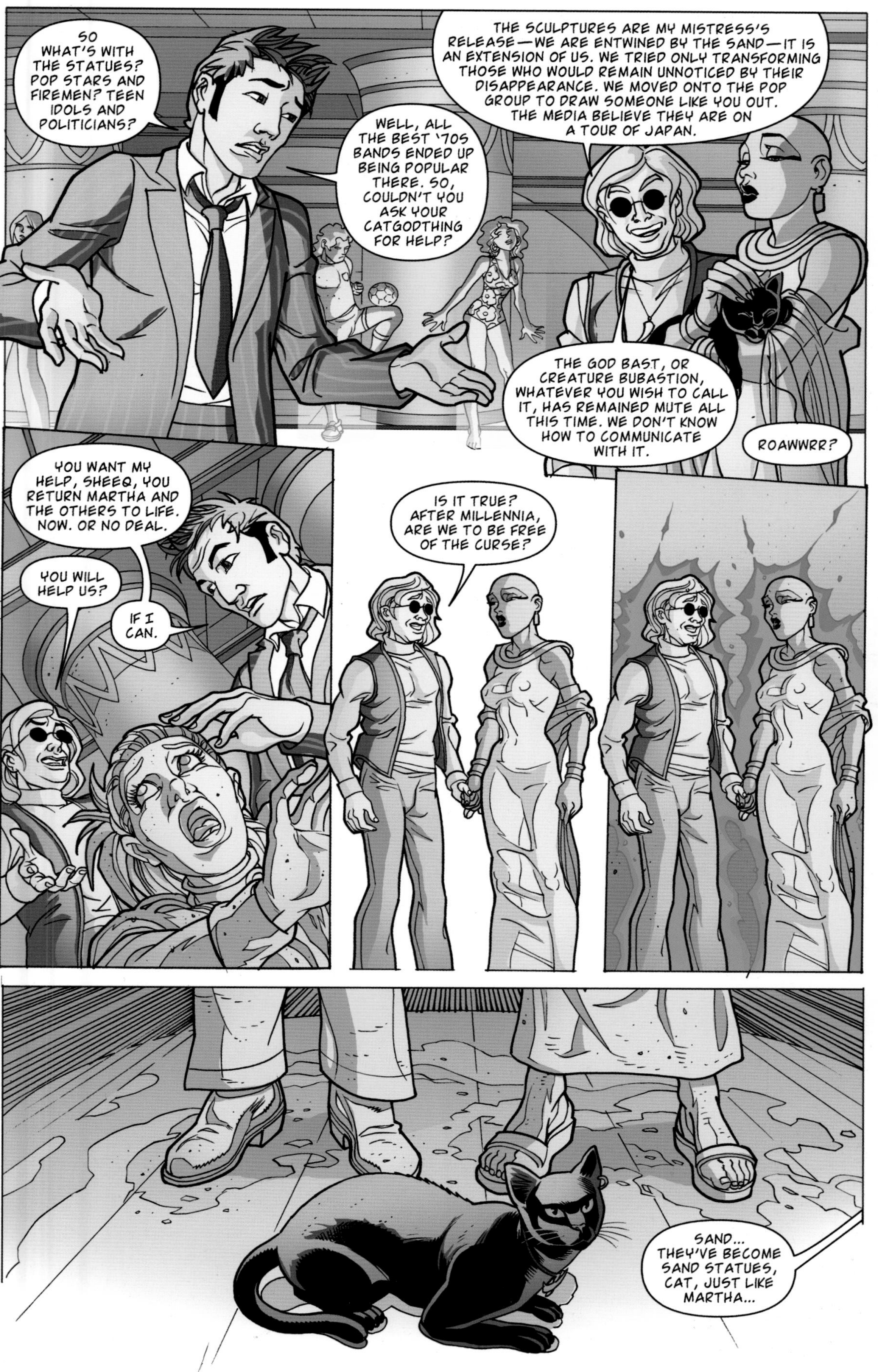
SO WHAT'S WITH THE STATUES? POP STARS AND FIREMEN? TEEN IDOLS AND POLITICIANS?
THE SCULPTURES ARE MY MISTRESS'S RELEASE—WE ARE ENTWINED BY THE SAND—IT IS AN EXTENSION OF US. WE TRIED ONLY TRANSFORMING THOSE WHO WOULD REMAIN UNNOTICED BY THEIR DISAPPEARANCE. WE MOVED ONTO THE POP GROUP TO DRAW SOMEONE LIKE YOU OUT. THE MEDIA BELIEVE THEY ARE ON A TOUR OF JAPAN.
WELL, ALL THE BEST '70S BANDS ENDED UP BEING POPULAR THERE. SO, COULDN'T YOU ASK YOUR CATGODTHING FOR HELP?
THE GOD BAST, OR CREATURE BUBASTION, WHATEVER YOU WISH TO CALL IT, HAS REMAINED MUTE ALL THIS TIME. WE DON'T KNOW HOW TO COMMUNICATE WITH IT.
ROAWWRR?
YOU WANT MY HELP, SHEEQ, YOU RETURN MARTHA AND THE OTHERS TO LIFE. NOW. OR NO DEAL.
YOU WILL HELP US?
IF I CAN.
IS IT TRUE? AFTER MILLENNIA, ARE WE TO BE FREE OF THE CURSE?
SAND... THEY'VE BECOME SAND STATUES, CAT, JUST LIKE MARTHA...

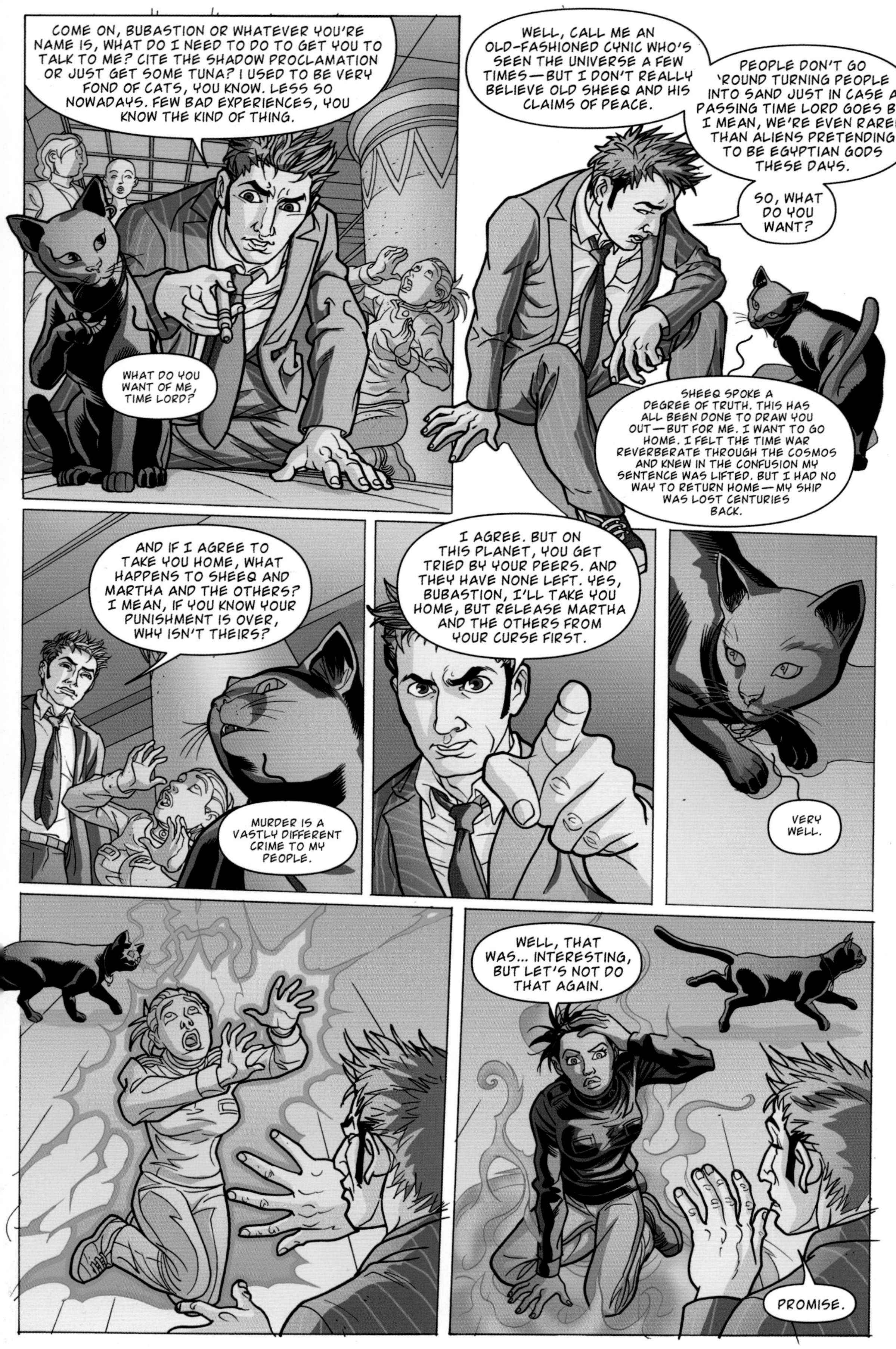

COME ON, BUBASTION OR WHATEVER YOU'RE NAME IS, WHAT DO I NEED TO DO TO GET YOU TO TALK TO ME? CITE THE SHADOW PROCLAMATION OR JUST GET SOME TUNA? I USED TO BE VERY FOND OF CATS, YOU KNOW. LESS SO NOWADAYS. FEW BAD EXPERIENCES, YOU KNOW THE KIND OF THING.
WHAT DO YOU WANT OF ME, TIME LORD?
WELL, CALL ME AN OLD-FASHIONED CYNIC WHO'S SEEN THE UNIVERSE A FEW TIMES—BUT I DON'T REALLY BELIEVE OLD SHEEQ AND HIS CLAIMS OF PEACE.
PEOPLE DON'T GO 'ROUND TURNING PEOPLE INTO SAND JUST IN CASE A PASSING TIME LORD GOES BY. I MEAN, WE'RE EVEN RARER THAN ALIENS PRETENDING TO BE EGYPTIAN GODS THESE DAYS.
SO, WHAT DO YOU WANT?
SHEEQ SPOKE A DEGREE OF TRUTH. THIS HAS ALL BEEN DONE TO DRAW YOU OUT—BUT FOR ME. I WANT TO GO HOME. I FELT THE TIME WAR REVERBERATE THROUGH THE COSMOS AND KNEW IN THE CONFUSION MY SENTENCE WAS LIFTED. BUT I HAD NO WAY TO RETURN HOME—MY SHIP WAS LOST CENTURIES BACK.
AND IF I AGREE TO TAKE YOU HOME, WHAT HAPPENS TO SHEEQ AND MARTHA AND THE OTHERS? I MEAN, IF YOU KNOW YOUR PUNISHMENT IS OVER, WHY ISN'T THEIRS?
MURDER IS A VASTLY DIFFERENT CRIME TO MY PEOPLE.
I AGREE. BUT ON THIS PLANET, YOU GET TRIED BY YOUR PEERS. AND THEY HAVE NONE LEFT. YES, BUBASTION, I'LL TAKE YOU HOME, BUT RELEASE MARTHA AND THE OTHERS FROM YOUR CURSE FIRST.
VERY WELL.
WELL, THAT WAS... INTERESTING, BUT LET'S NOT DO THAT AGAIN.
PROMISE.

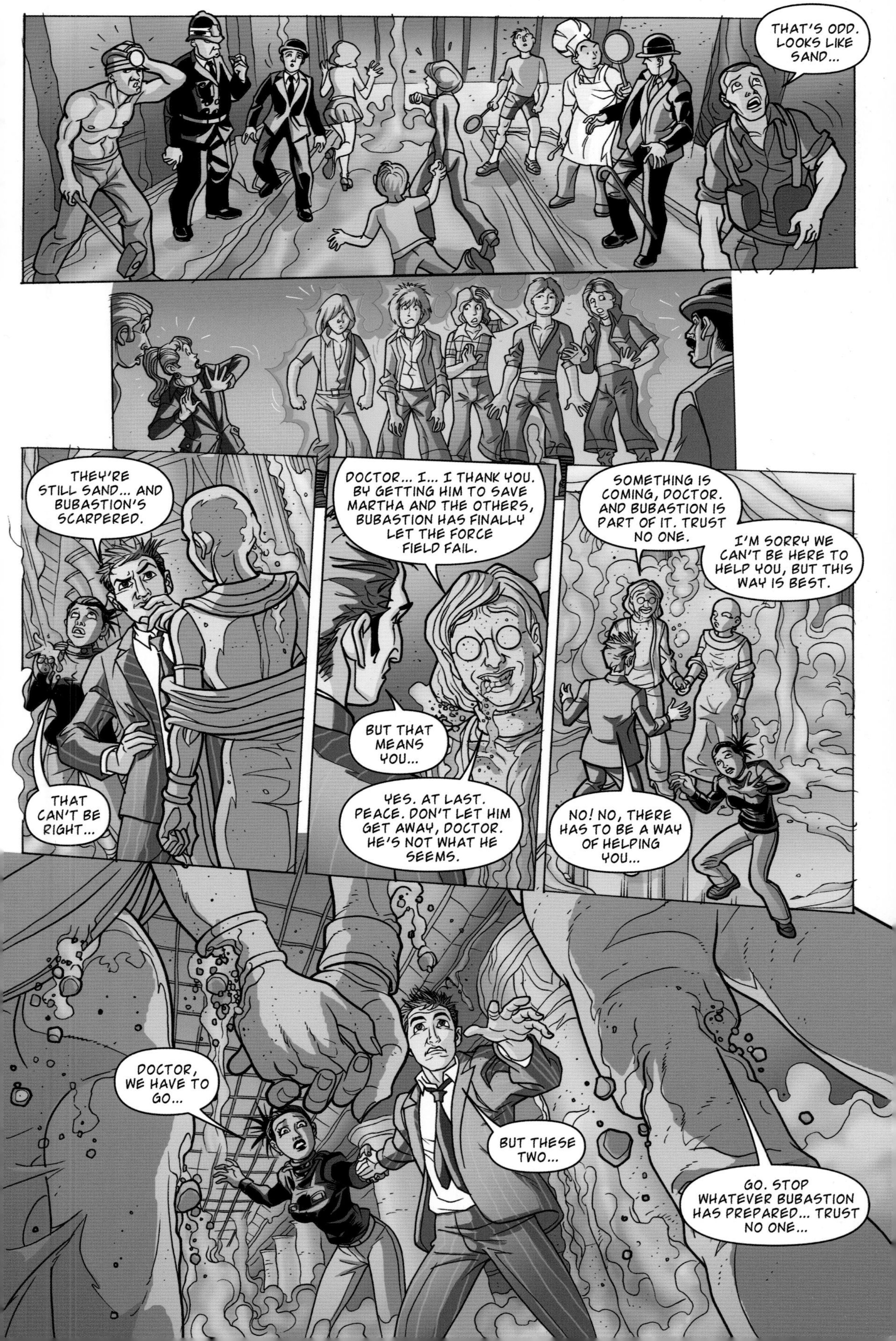
THAT'S ODD. LOOKS LIKE SAND...
THEY'RE STILL SAND... AND BUBASTION'S SCARPERED.
THAT CAN'T BE RIGHT...
DOCTOR... I... I THANK YOU. BY GETTING HIM TO SAVE MARTHA AND THE OTHERS, BUBASTION HAS FINALLY LET THE FORCE FIELD FAIL.
BUT THAT MEANS YOU...
YES. AT LAST. PEACE. DON'T LET HIM GET AWAY, DOCTOR. HE'S NOT WHAT HE SEEMS.
SOMETHING IS COMING, DOCTOR. AND BUBASTION IS PART OF IT. TRUST NO ONE.
I'M SORRY WE CAN'T BE HERE TO HELP YOU, BUT THIS WAY IS BEST.
NO! NO, THERE HAS TO BE A WAY OF HELPING YOU...
DOCTOR, WE HAVE TO GO...
BUT THESE TWO...
GO. STOP WHATEVER BUBASTION HAS PREPARED... TRUST NO ONE...

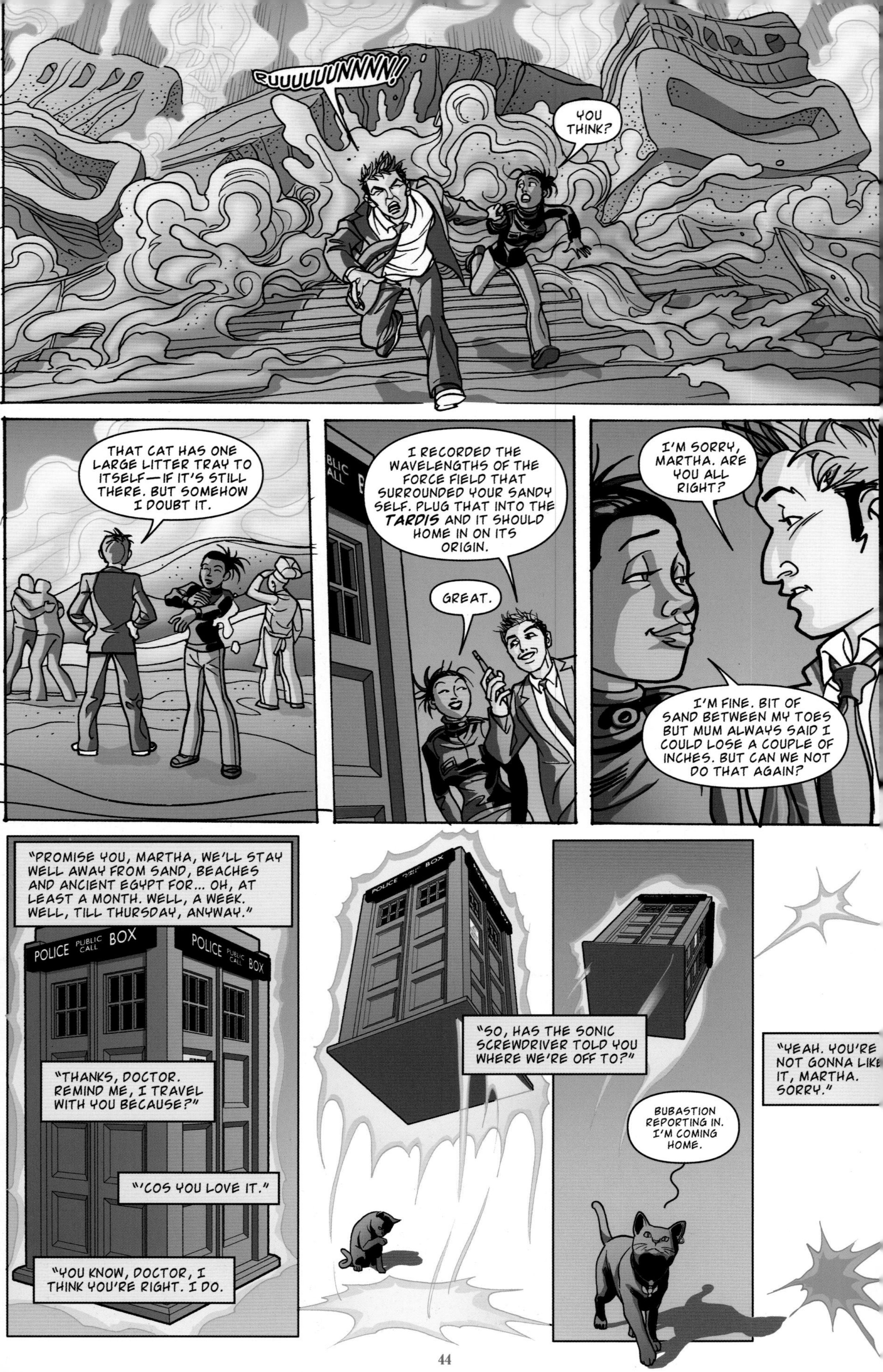
RUUUUUUNNNN!
YOU THINK?
THAT CAT HAS ONE LARGE LITTER TRAY TO ITSELF—IF IT'S STILL THERE. BUT SOMEHOW I DOUBT IT.
I RECORDED THE WAVELENGTHS OF THE FORCE FIELD THAT SURROUNDED YOUR SANDY SELF. PLUG THAT INTO THE TARDIS AND IT SHOULD HOME IN ON ITS ORIGIN.
GREAT.
I'M SORRY, MARTHA. ARE YOU ALL RIGHT?
I'M FINE. BIT OF SAND BETWEEN MY TOES BUT MUM ALWAYS SAID I COULD LOSE A COUPLE OF INCHES. BUT CAN WE NOT DO THAT AGAIN?
"PROMISE YOU, MARTHA, WE'LL STAY WELL AWAY FROM SAND, BEACHES AND ANCIENT EGYPT FOR... OH, AT LEAST A MONTH. WELL, A WEEK. WELL, TILL THURSDAY, ANYWAY."
POLICE PUBLIC CALL BOX
"THANKS, DOCTOR. REMIND ME, I TRAVEL WITH YOU BECAUSE?"
"'COS YOU LOVE IT."
"YOU KNOW, DOCTOR, I THINK YOU'RE RIGHT. I DO.
POLICE PUBLIC CALL BOX
"SO, HAS THE SONIC SCREWDRIVER TOLD YOU WHERE WE'RE OFF TO?"
BUBASTION REPORTING IN. I'M COMING HOME.
"YEAH. YOU'RE NOT GONNA LIKE IT, MARTHA. SORRY."

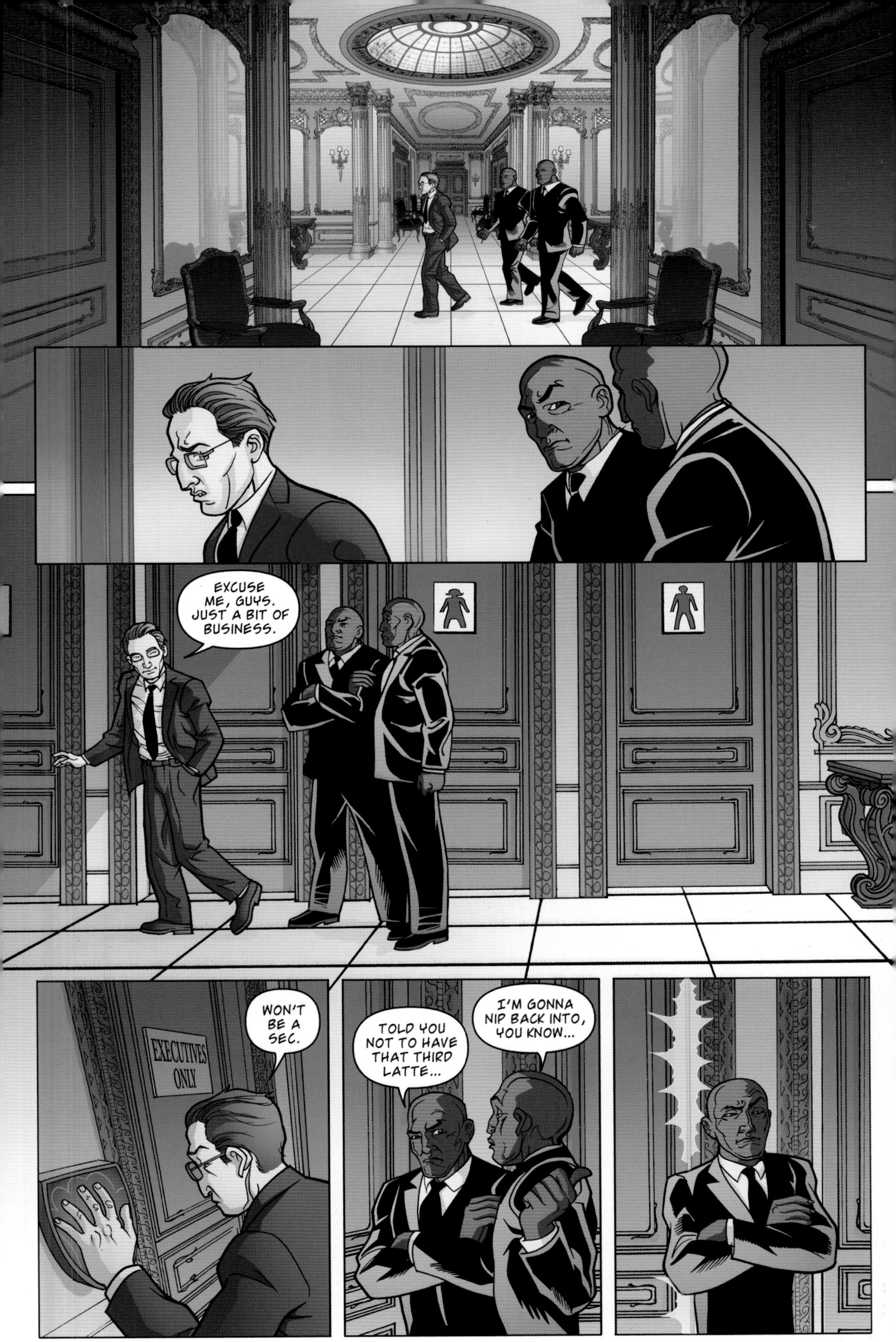
EXCUSE ME, GUYS. JUST A BIT OF BUSINESS.
EXECUTIVES ONLY
WON'T BE A SEC.
TOLD YOU NOT TO HAVE THAT THIRD LATTE...
I'M GONNA NIP BACK INTO, YOU KNOW...

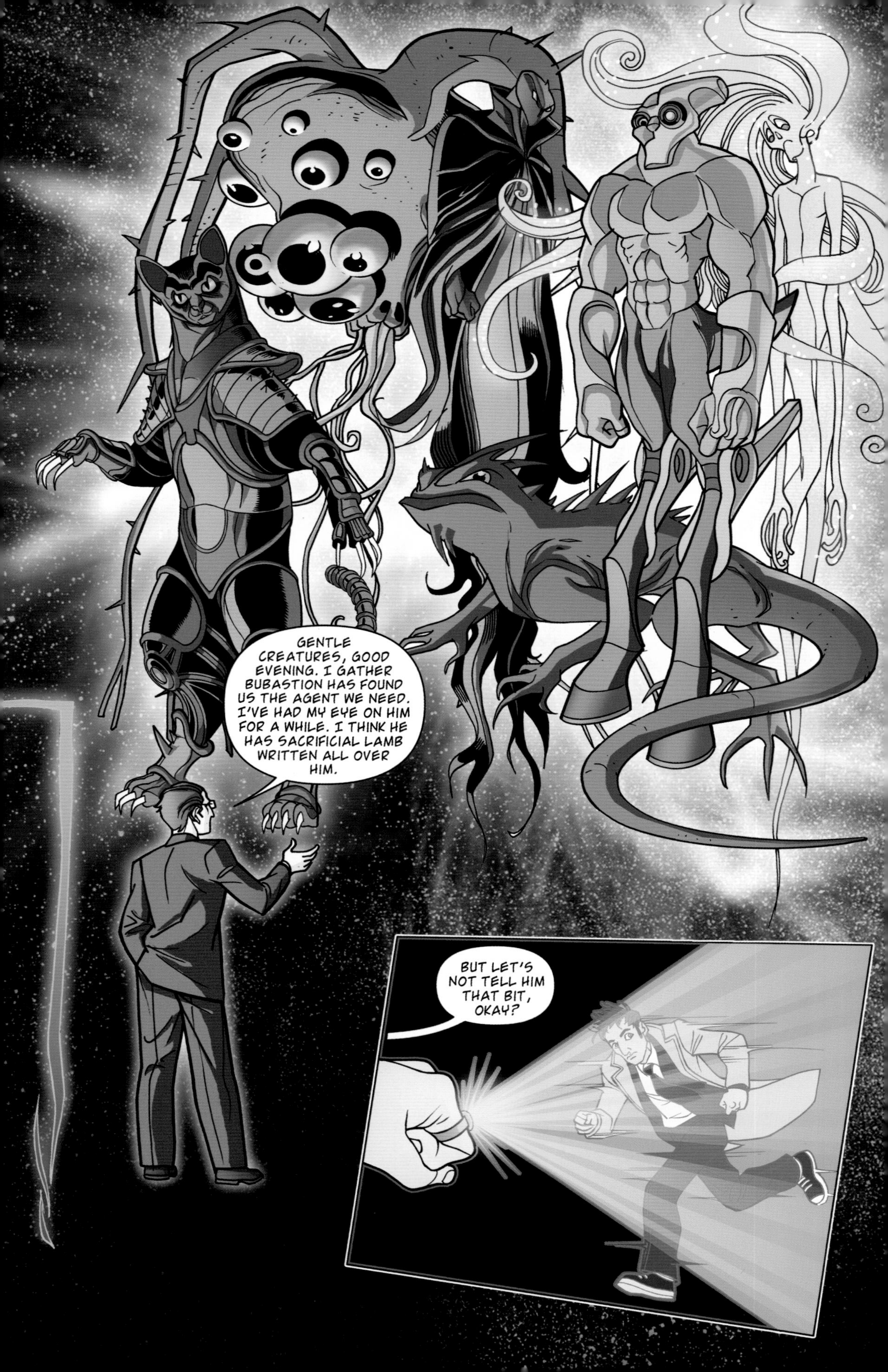
GENTLE CREATURES, GOOD EVENING. I GATHER BUBASTION HAS FOUND US THE AGENT WE NEED. I'VE HAD MY EYE ON HIM FOR A WHILE. I THINK HE HAS SACRIFICIAL LAMB WRITTEN ALL OVER HIM.
BUT LET'S NOT TELL HIM THAT BIT, OKAY?

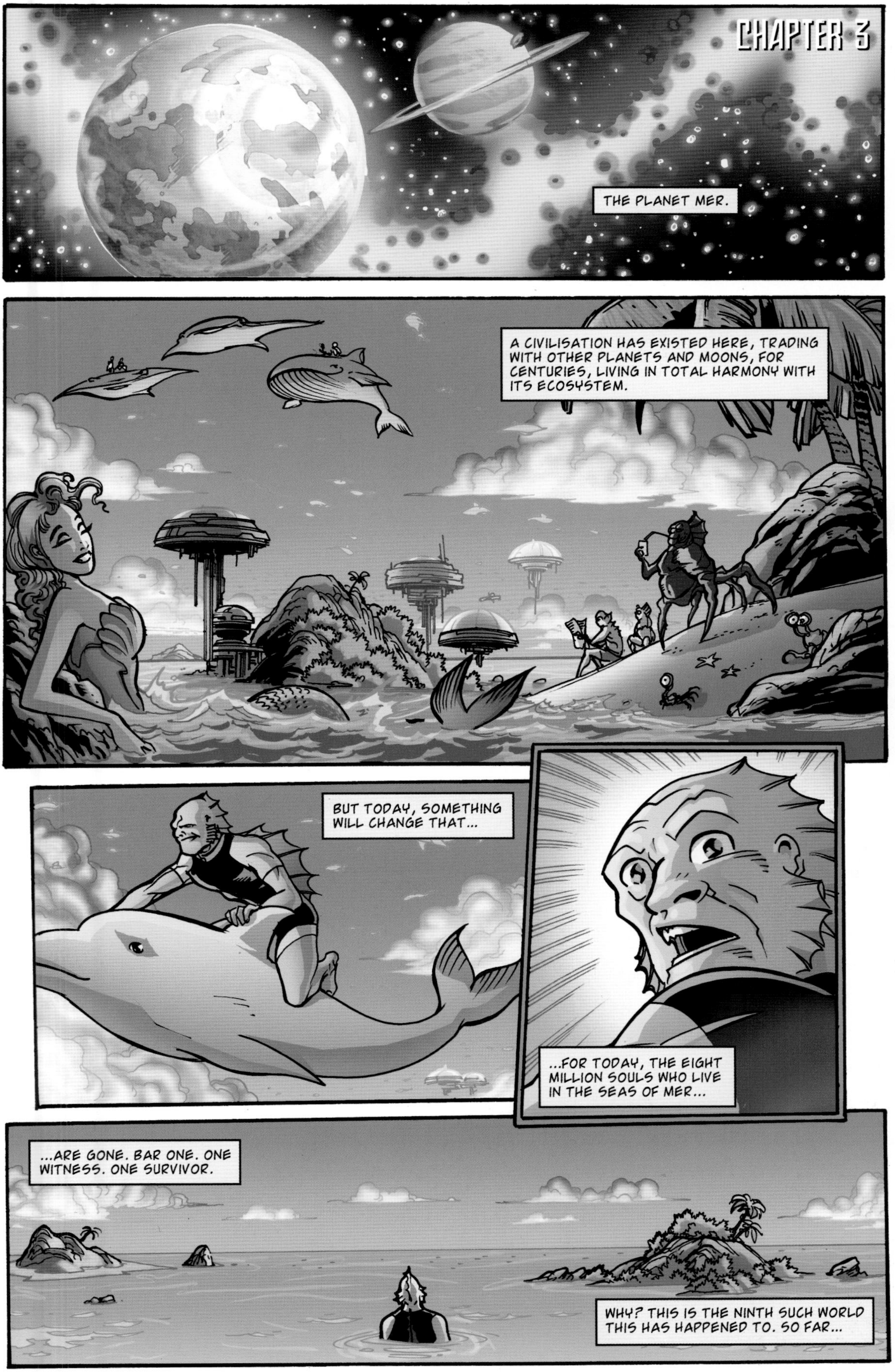
CHAPTER 3
THE PLANET MER.
A CIVILISATION HAS EXISTED HERE, TRADING WITH OTHER PLANETS AND MOONS, FOR CENTURIES, LIVING IN TOTAL HARMONY WITH ITS ECOSYSTEM.
BUT TODAY, SOMETHING WILL CHANGE THAT...
...FOR TODAY, THE EIGHT MILLION SOULS WHO LIVE IN THE SEAS OF MER...
...ARE GONE. BAR ONE. ONE WITNESS. ONE SURVIVOR.
WHY? THIS IS THE NINTH SUCH WORLD THIS HAS HAPPENED TO. SO FAR...

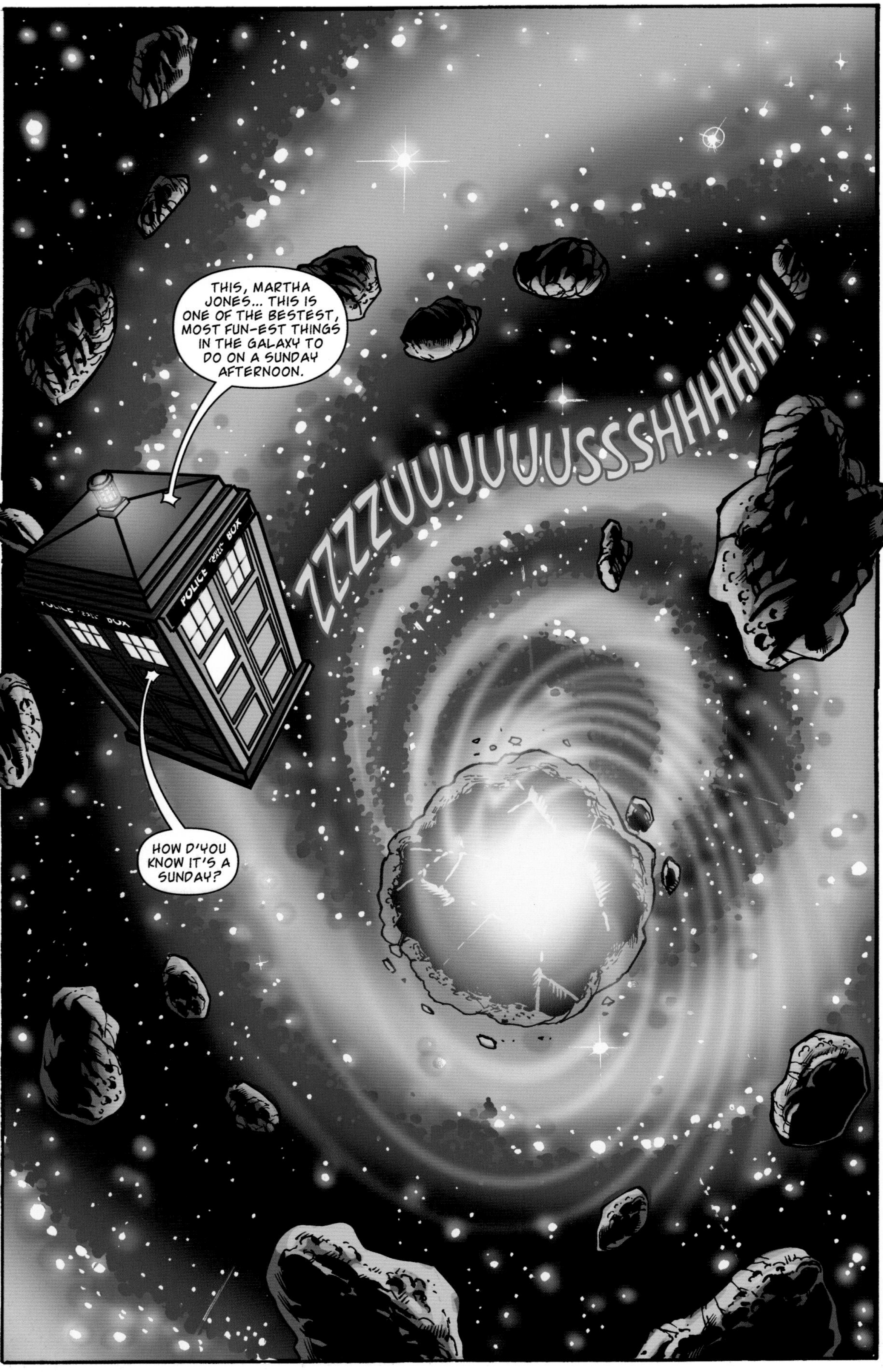
THIS, MARTHA JONES... THIS IS ONE OF THE BESTEST, MOST FUN-EST THINGS IN THE GALAXY TO DO ON A SUNDAY AFTERNOON.
HOW D'YOU KNOW IT'S A SUNDAY?
ZZZZUUUUUUUSSSHHHHHH
POLICE BOX

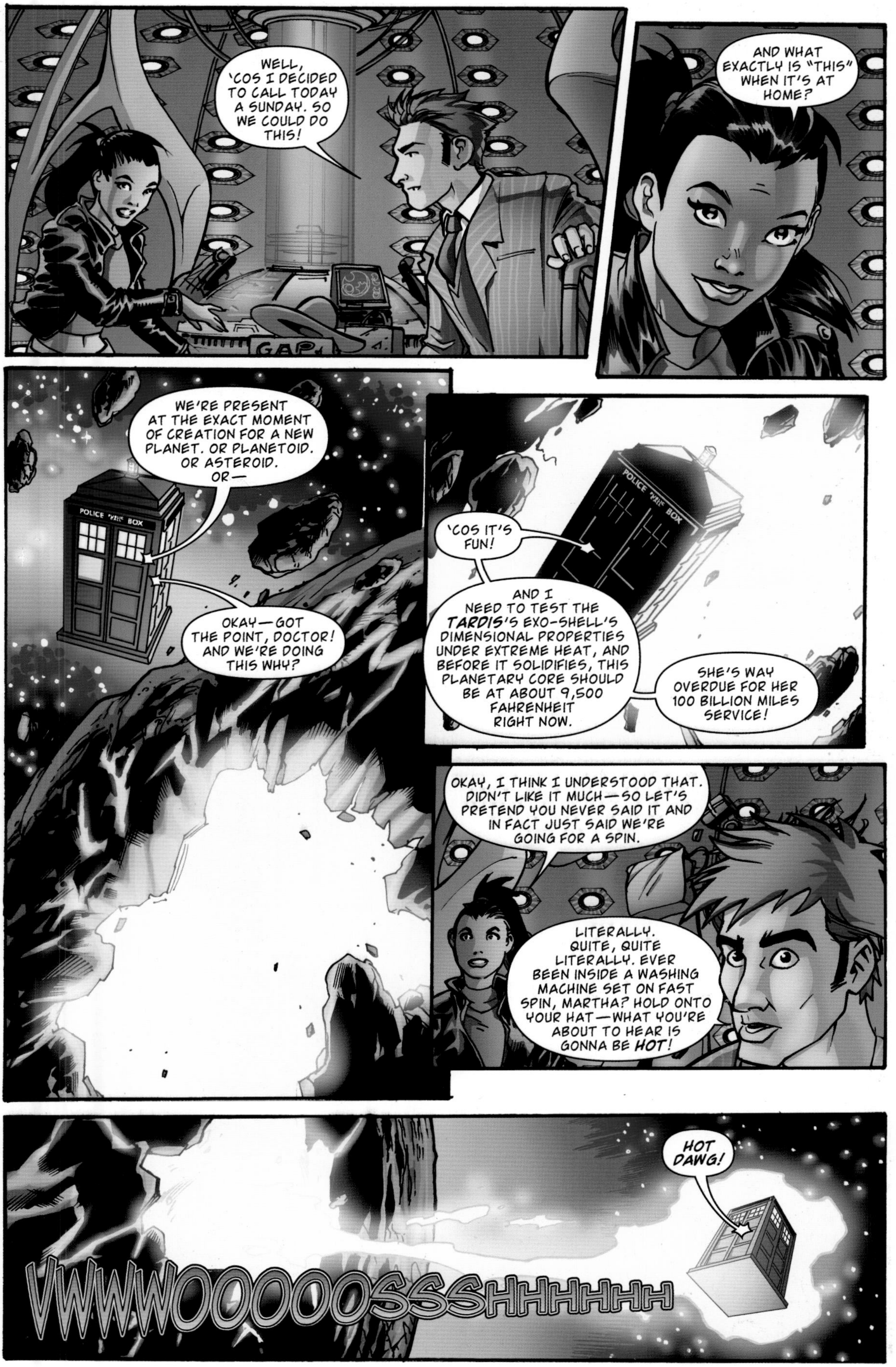
WELL, 'COS I DECIDED TO CALL TODAY A SUNDAY. SO WE COULD DO THIS!
AND WHAT EXACTLY IS "THIS" WHEN IT'S AT HOME?
WE'RE PRESENT AT THE EXACT MOMENT OF CREATION FOR A NEW PLANET. OR PLANETOID. OR ASTEROID. OR—
OKAY—GOT THE POINT, DOCTOR! AND WE'RE DOING THIS WHY?
'COS IT'S FUN!
AND I NEED TO TEST THE TARDIS'S EXO-SHELL'S DIMENSIONAL PROPERTIES UNDER EXTREME HEAT, AND BEFORE IT SOLIDIFIES, THIS PLANETARY CORE SHOULD BE AT ABOUT 9,500 FAHRENHEIT RIGHT NOW.
SHE'S WAY OVERDUE FOR HER 100 BILLION MILES SERVICE!
OKAY, I THINK I UNDERSTOOD THAT. DIDN'T LIKE IT MUCH—SO LET'S PRETEND YOU NEVER SAID IT AND IN FACT JUST SAID WE'RE GOING FOR A SPIN.
LITERALLY. QUITE, QUITE LITERALLY. EVER BEEN INSIDE A WASHING MACHINE SET ON FAST SPIN, MARTHA? HOLD ONTO YOUR HAT—WHAT YOU'RE ABOUT TO HEAR IS GONNA BE HOT!
HOT DAWG!
VWWWOOOOOOSSSHHHHHH

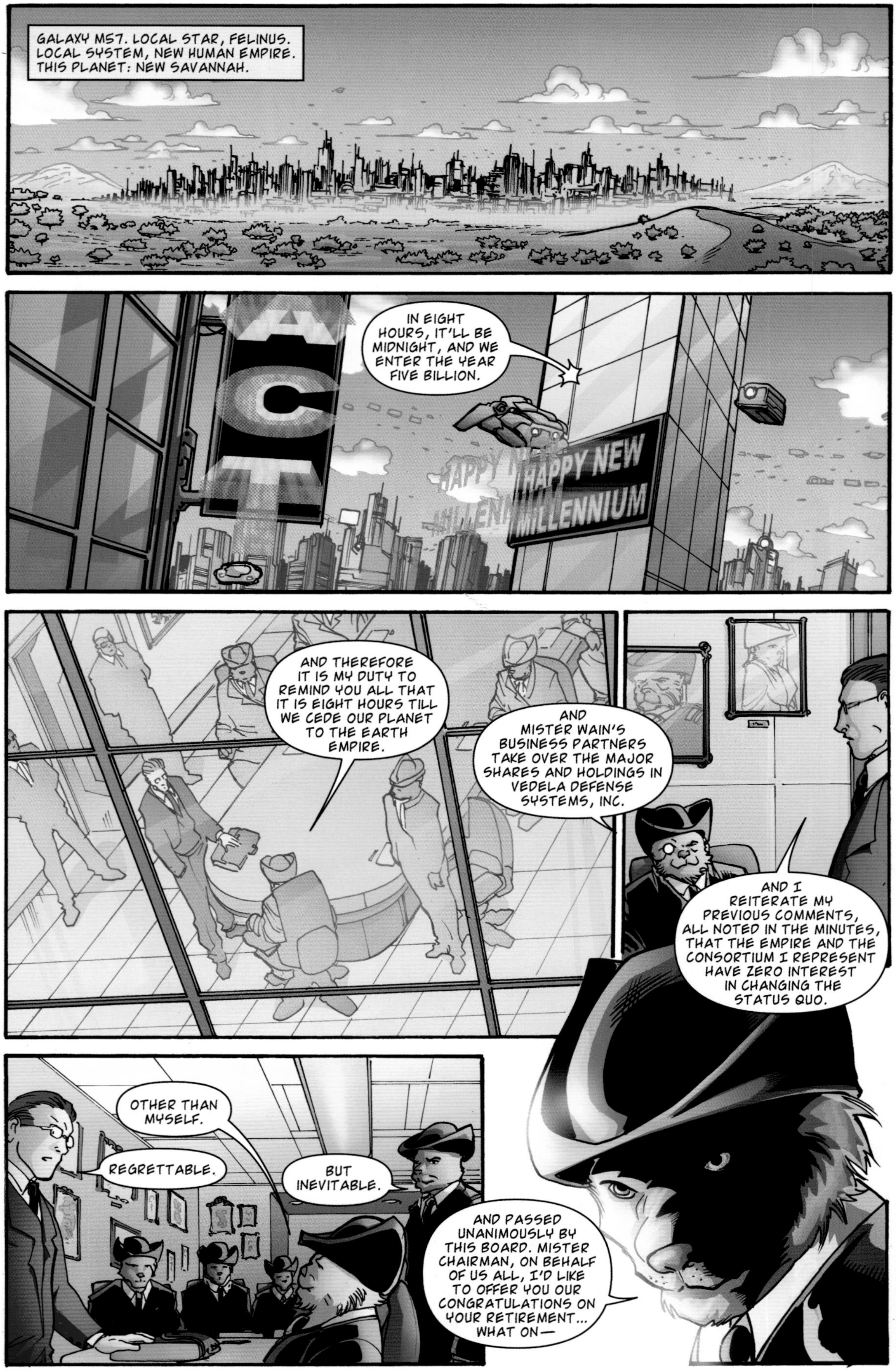
GALAXY M57. LOCAL STAR, FELINUS. LOCAL SYSTEM, NEW HUMAN EMPIRE. THIS PLANET: NEW SAVANNAH.
IN EIGHT HOURS, IT'LL BE MIDNIGHT, AND WE ENTER THE YEAR FIVE BILLION.
HAPPY NEW MILLENNIUM
AND THEREFORE IT IS MY DUTY TO REMIND YOU ALL THAT IT IS EIGHT HOURS TILL WE CEDE OUR PLANET TO THE EARTH EMPIRE.
AND MISTER WAIN'S BUSINESS PARTNERS TAKE OVER THE MAJOR SHARES AND HOLDINGS IN VEDELA DEFENSE SYSTEMS, INC.
AND I REITERATE MY PREVIOUS COMMENTS, ALL NOTED IN THE MINUTES, THAT THE EMPIRE AND THE CONSORTIUM I REPRESENT HAVE ZERO INTEREST IN CHANGING THE STATUS QUO.
OTHER THAN MYSELF.
REGRETTABLE.
BUT INEVITABLE.
AND PASSED UNANIMOUSLY BY THIS BOARD. MISTER CHAIRMAN, ON BEHALF OF US ALL, I'D LIKE TO OFFER YOU OUR CONGRATULATIONS ON YOUR RETIREMENT... WHAT ON—

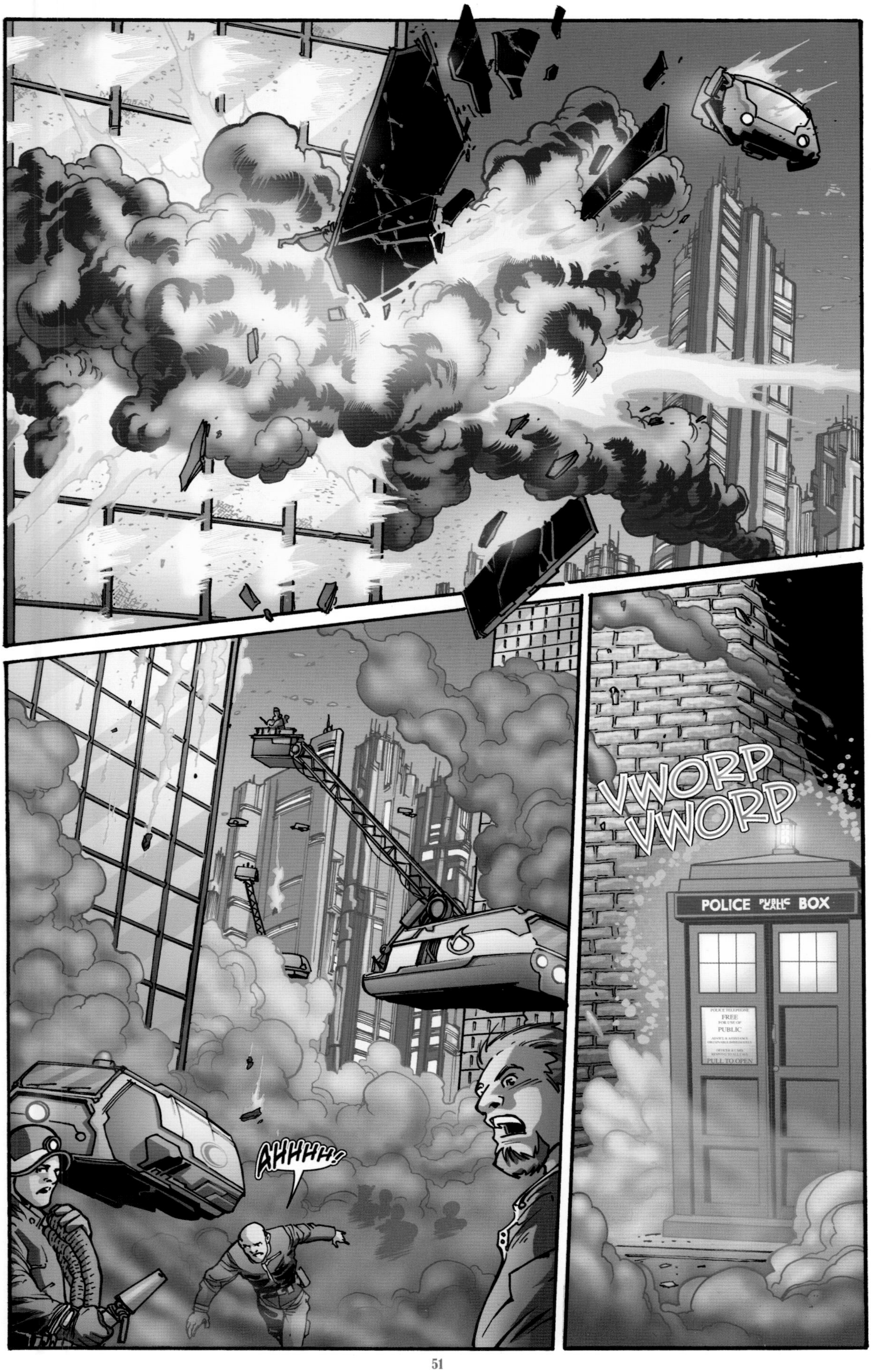
AHHHH!
VWORP VWORP
POLICE PUBLIC CALL BOX
POLICE TELEPHONE
FREE
FOR USE OF
PUBLIC
PULL TO OPEN

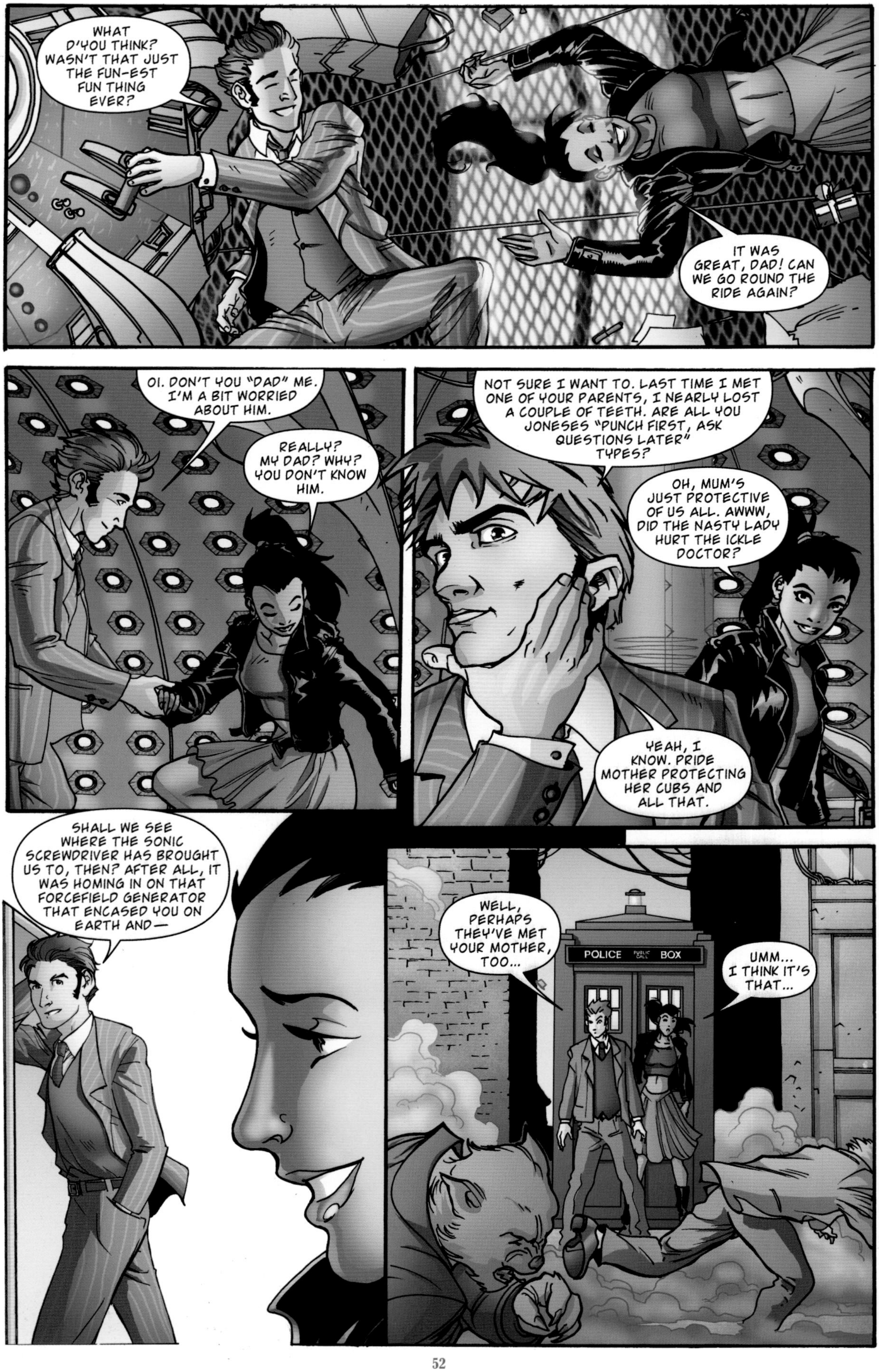
WHAT D'YOU THINK? WASN'T THAT JUST THE FUN-EST FUN THING EVER?
IT WAS GREAT, DAD! CAN WE GO ROUND THE RIDE AGAIN?
OI. DON'T YOU "DAD" ME. I'M A BIT WORRIED ABOUT HIM.
REALLY? MY DAD? WHY? YOU DON'T KNOW HIM.
NOT SURE I WANT TO. LAST TIME I MET ONE OF YOUR PARENTS, I NEARLY LOST A COUPLE OF TEETH. ARE ALL YOU JONESES "PUNCH FIRST, ASK QUESTIONS LATER" TYPES?
OH, MUM'S JUST PROTECTIVE OF US ALL. AWWW, DID THE NASTY LADY HURT THE ICKLE DOCTOR?
YEAH, I KNOW. PRIDE MOTHER PROTECTING HER CUBS AND ALL THAT.
SHALL WE SEE WHERE THE SONIC SCREWDRIVER HAS BROUGHT US TO, THEN? AFTER ALL, IT WAS HOMING IN ON THAT FORCEFIELD GENERATOR THAT ENCASED YOU ON EARTH AND—
WELL, PERHAPS THEY'VE MET YOUR MOTHER, TOO...
POLICE PUBLIC CALL BOX
UMM... I THINK IT'S THAT...

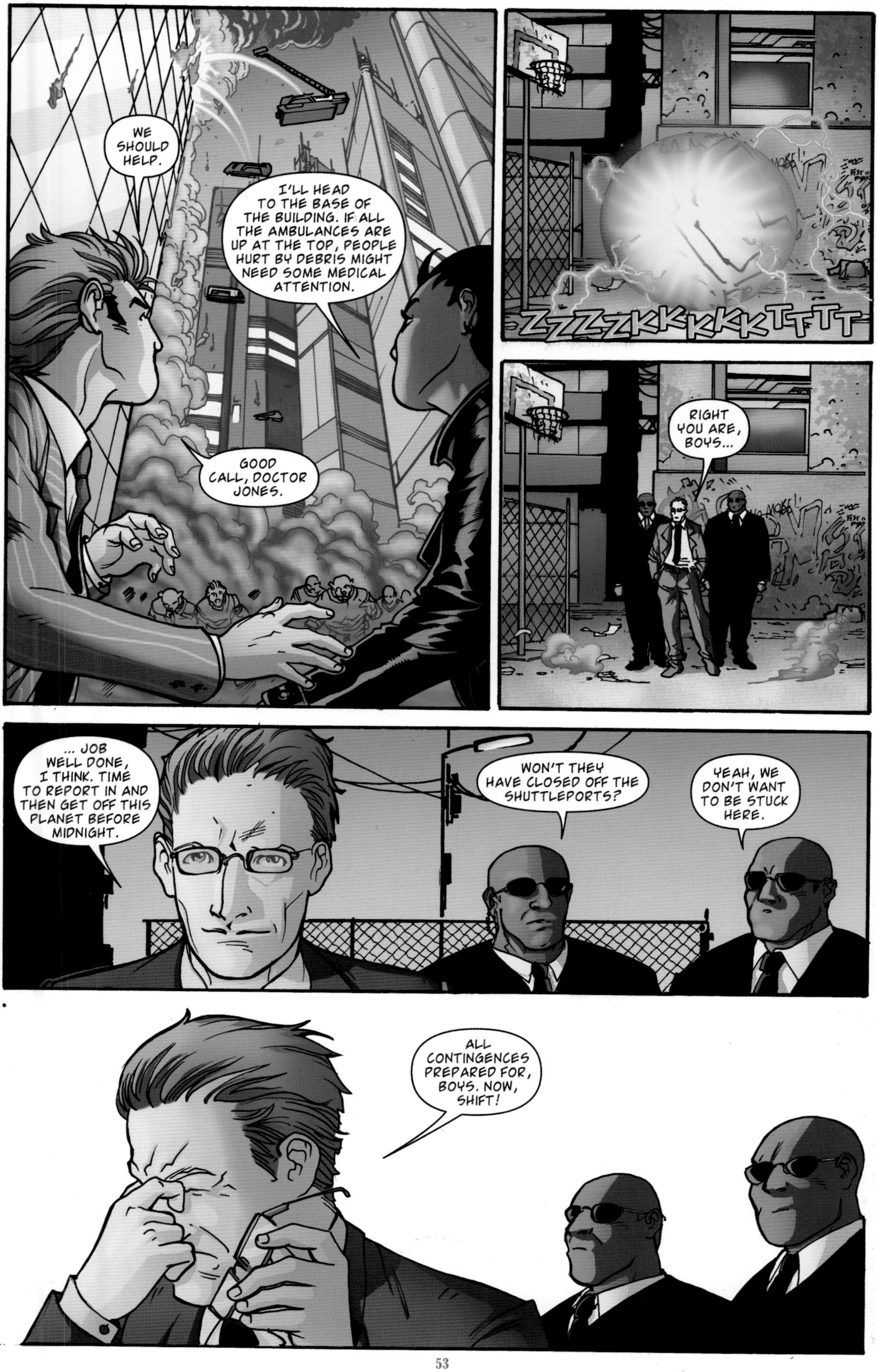
WE SHOULD HELP.
I'LL HEAD TO THE BASE OF THE BUILDING. IF ALL THE AMBULANCES ARE UP AT THE TOP, PEOPLE HURT BY DEBRIS MIGHT NEED SOME MEDICAL ATTENTION.
GOOD CALL, DOCTOR JONES.
ZZZZKKKKKKTTTT
RIGHT YOU ARE, BOYS...
... JOB WELL DONE, I THINK. TIME TO REPORT IN AND THEN GET OFF THIS PLANET BEFORE MIDNIGHT.
WON'T THEY HAVE CLOSED OFF THE SHUTTLEPORTS?
YEAH, WE DON'T WANT TO BE STUCK HERE.
ALL CONTINGENCES PREPARED FOR, BOYS. NOW, SHIFT!

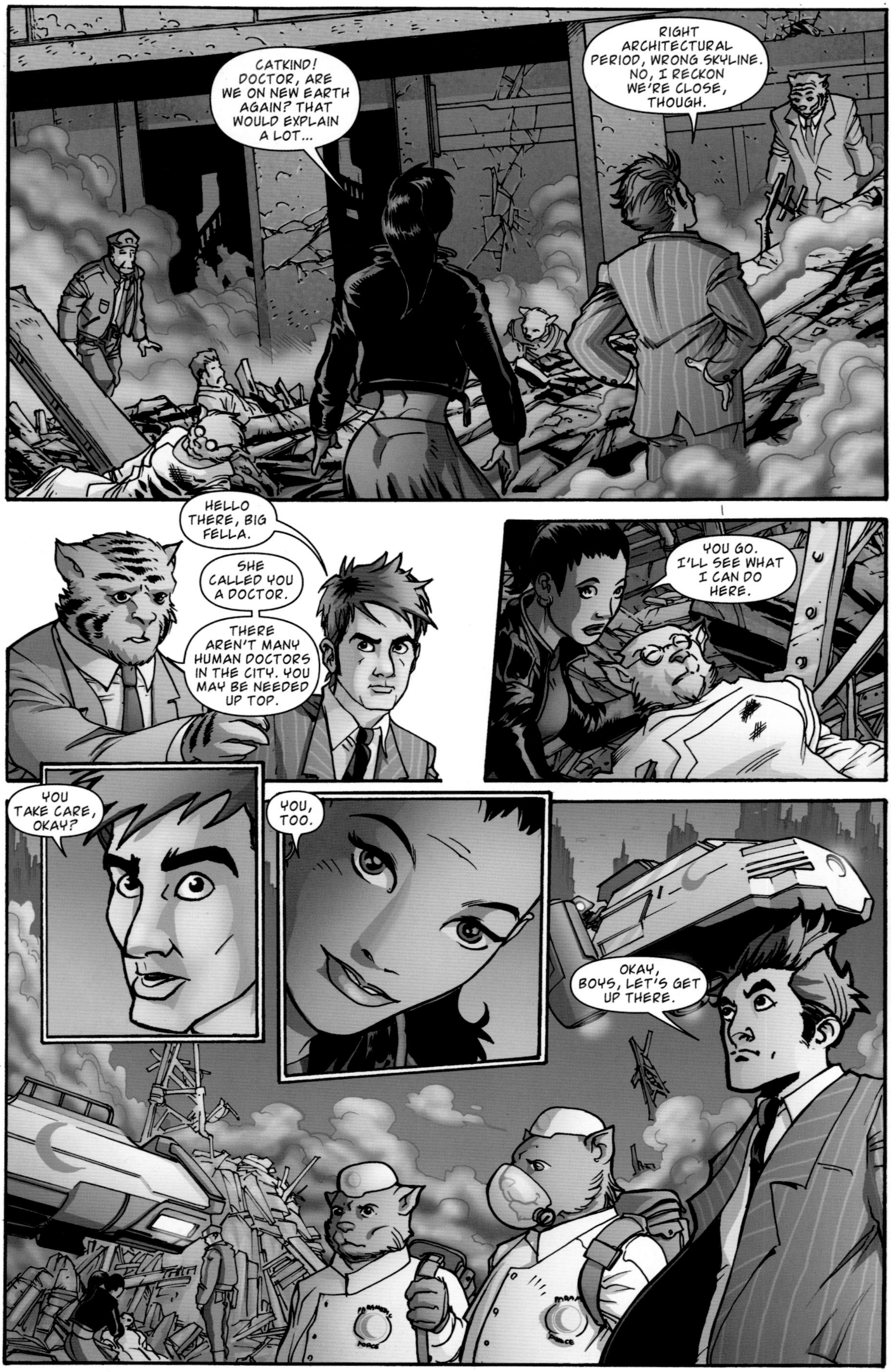

CATKIND! DOCTOR, ARE WE ON NEW EARTH AGAIN? THAT WOULD EXPLAIN A LOT...
RIGHT ARCHITECTURAL PERIOD, WRONG SKYLINE. NO, I RECKON WE'RE CLOSE, THOUGH.
HELLO THERE, BIG FELLA.
SHE CALLED YOU A DOCTOR.
THERE AREN'T MANY HUMAN DOCTORS IN THE CITY. YOU MAY BE NEEDED UP TOP.
YOU GO. I'LL SEE WHAT I CAN DO HERE.
YOU TAKE CARE, OKAY?
YOU, TOO.
OKAY, BOYS, LET'S GET UP THERE.

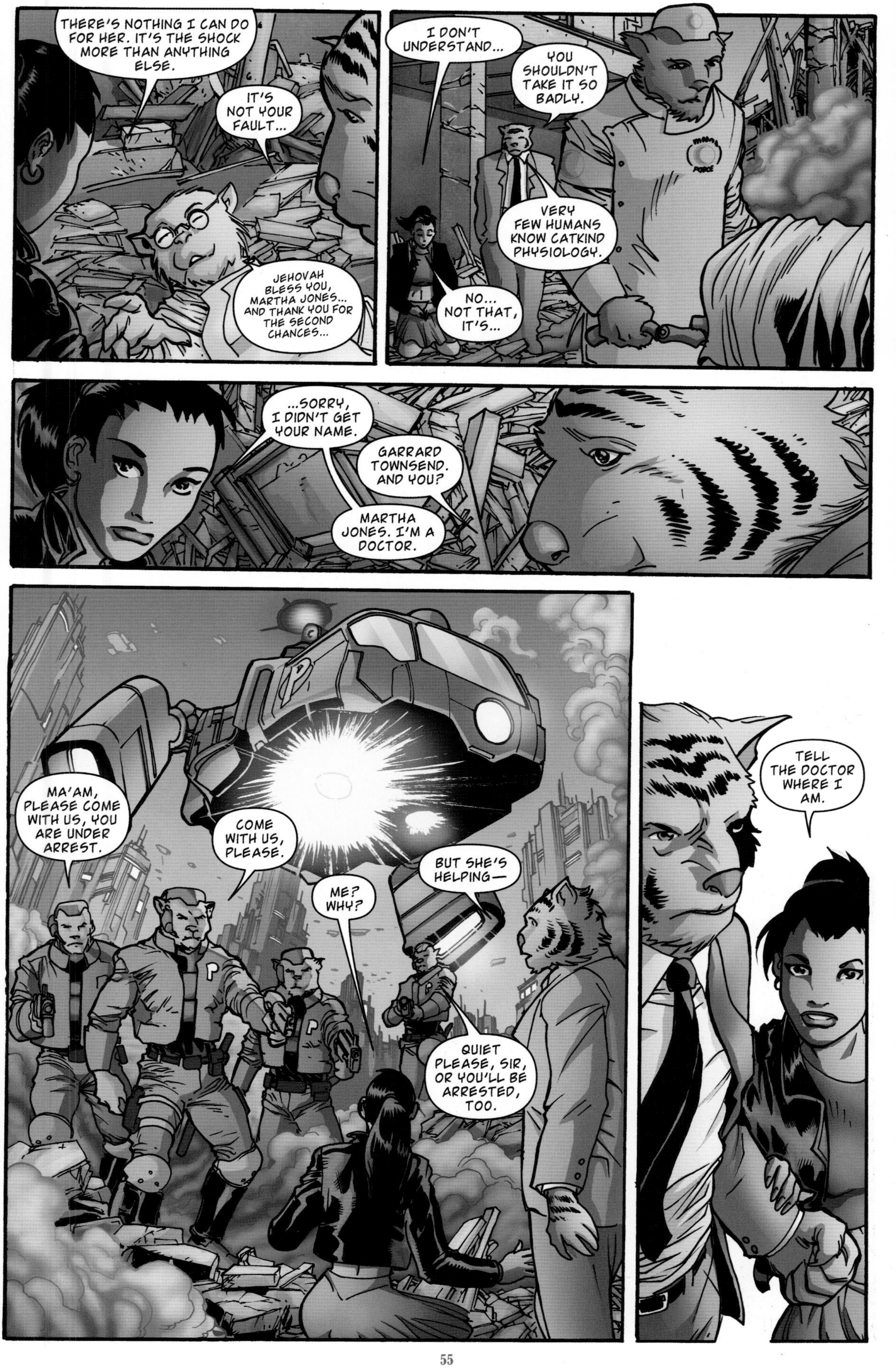
THERE'S NOTHING I CAN DO FOR HER. IT'S THE SHOCK MORE THAN ANYTHING ELSE.
IT'S NOT YOUR FAULT...
JEHOVAH BLESS YOU, MARTHA JONES... AND THANK YOU FOR THE SECOND CHANCES...
I DON'T UNDERSTAND...
YOU SHOULDN'T TAKE IT SO BADLY.
VERY FEW HUMANS KNOW CATKIND PHYSIOLOGY.
NO... NOT THAT, IT'S...
...SORRY, I DIDN'T GET YOUR NAME.
GARRARD TOWNSEND. AND YOU?
MARTHA JONES. I'M A DOCTOR.
MA'AM, PLEASE COME WITH US, YOU ARE UNDER ARREST.
COME WITH US, PLEASE.
ME? WHY?
BUT SHE'S HELPING—
QUIET PLEASE, SIR, OR YOU'LL BE ARRESTED, TOO.
TELL THE DOCTOR WHERE I AM.

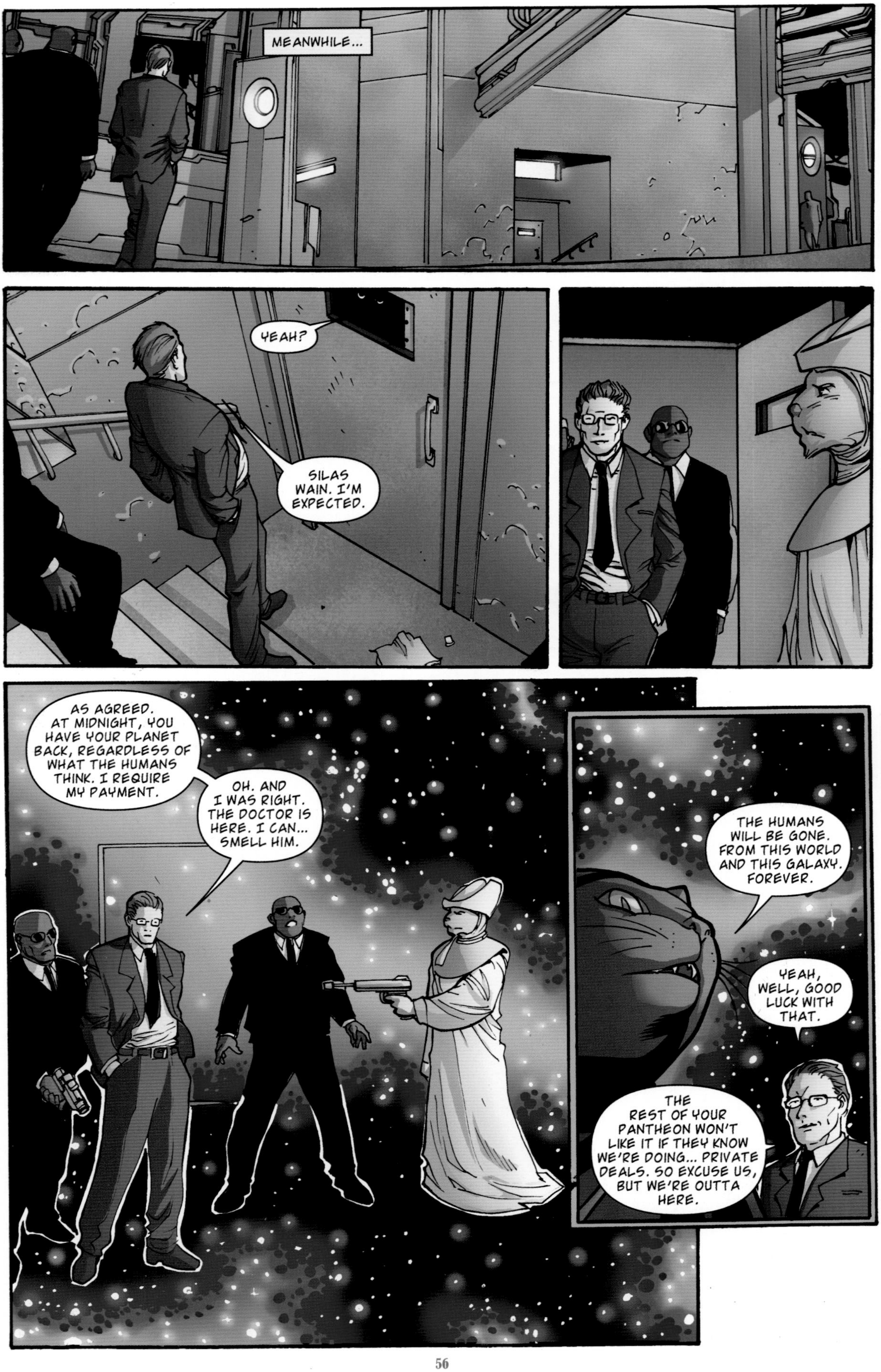
MEANWHILE...
YEAH?
SILAS WAIN. I'M EXPECTED.
AS AGREED. AT MIDNIGHT, YOU HAVE YOUR PLANET BACK, REGARDLESS OF WHAT THE HUMANS THINK. I REQUIRE MY PAYMENT.
OH. AND I WAS RIGHT. THE DOCTOR IS HERE. I CAN... SMELL HIM.
THE HUMANS WILL BE GONE. FROM THIS WORLD AND THIS GALAXY. FOREVER.
YEAH, WELL, GOOD LUCK WITH THAT.
THE REST OF YOUR PANTHEON WON'T LIKE IT IF THEY KNOW WE'RE DOING... PRIVATE DEALS. SO EXCUSE US, BUT WE'RE OUTTA HERE.

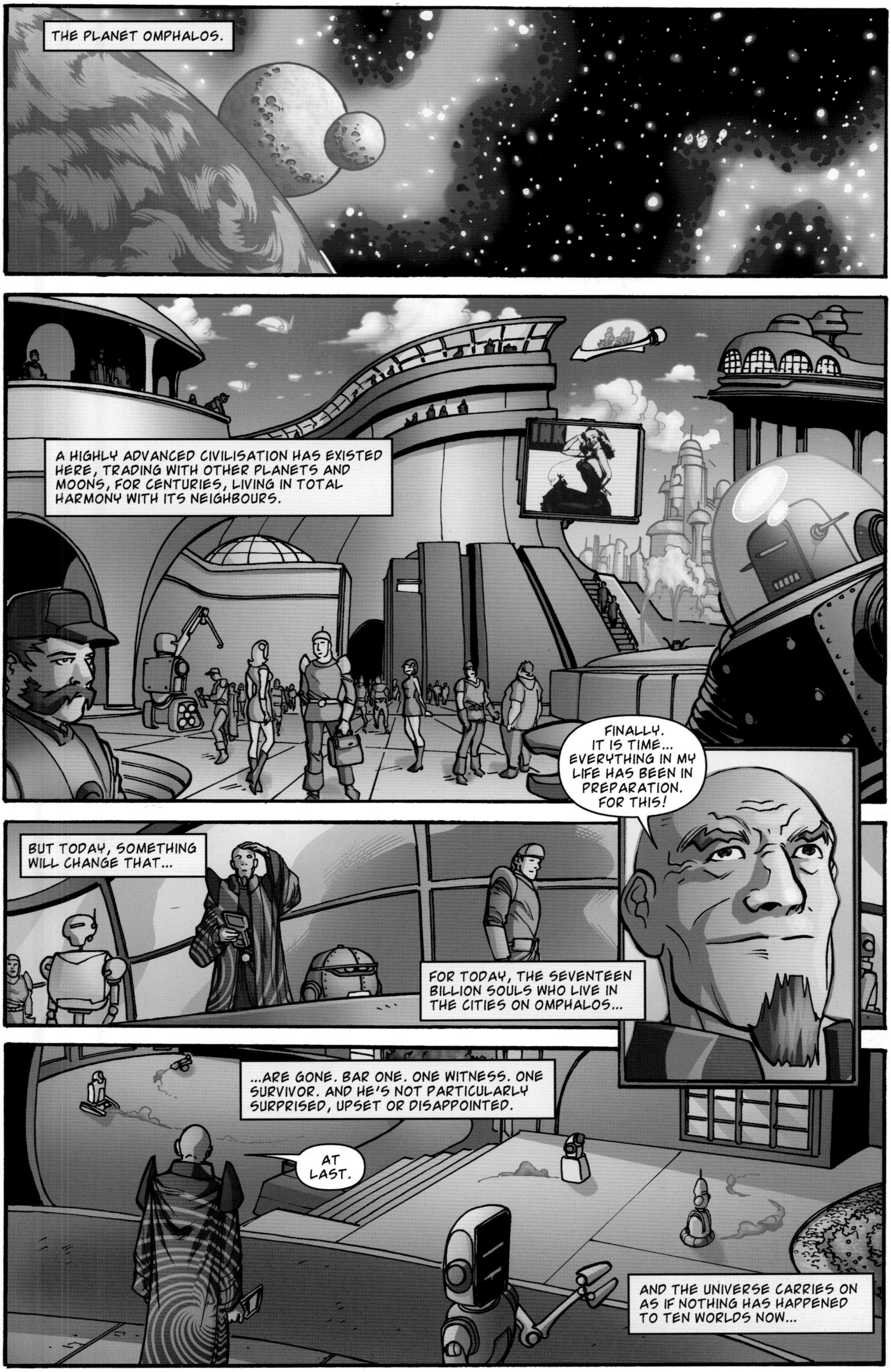
THE PLANET OMPHALOS.
A HIGHLY ADVANCED CIVILISATION HAS EXISTED HERE, TRADING WITH OTHER PLANETS AND MOONS, FOR CENTURIES, LIVING IN TOTAL HARMONY WITH ITS NEIGHBOURS.
INK
BUT TODAY, SOMETHING WILL CHANGE THAT...
FOR TODAY, THE SEVENTEEN BILLION SOULS WHO LIVE IN THE CITIES ON OMPHALOS...
FINALLY. IT IS TIME... EVERYTHING IN MY LIFE HAS BEEN IN PREPARATION. FOR THIS!
...ARE GONE. BAR ONE. ONE WITNESS. ONE SURVIVOR. AND HE'S NOT PARTICULARLY SURPRISED, UPSET OR DISAPPOINTED.
AT LAST.
AND THE UNIVERSE CARRIES ON AS IF NOTHING HAS HAPPENED TO TEN WORLDS NOW...

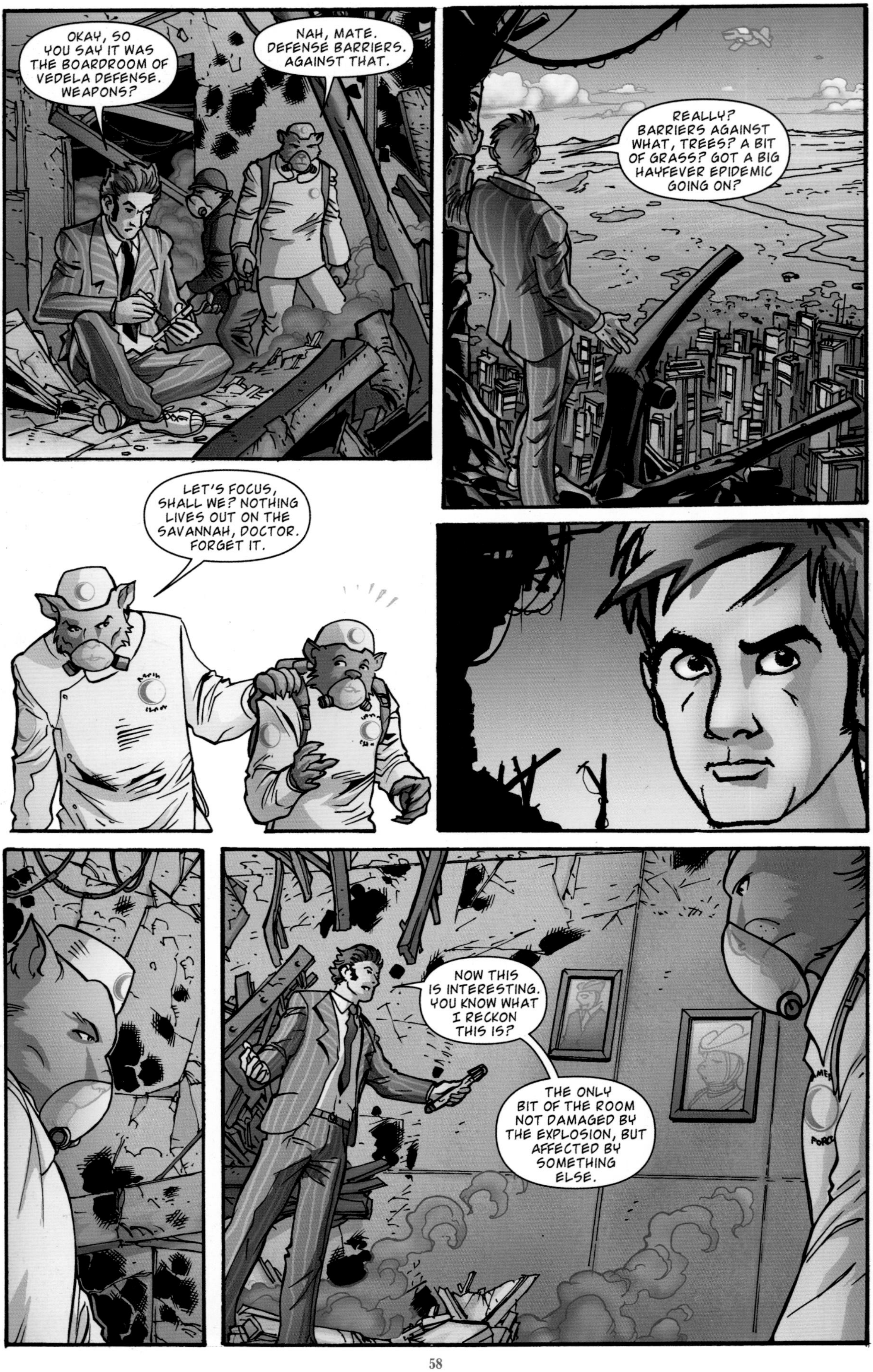
OKAY, SO YOU SAY IT WAS THE BOARDROOM OF VEDELA DEFENSE. WEAPONS?
NAH, MATE. DEFENSE BARRIERS. AGAINST THAT.
REALLY? BARRIERS AGAINST WHAT, TREES? A BIT OF GRASS? GOT A BIG HAYFEVER EPIDEMIC GOING ON?
LET'S FOCUS, SHALL WE? NOTHING LIVES OUT ON THE SAVANNAH, DOCTOR. FORGET IT.
NOW THIS IS INTERESTING. YOU KNOW WHAT I RECKON THIS IS?
THE ONLY BIT OF THE ROOM NOT DAMAGED BY THE EXPLOSION, BUT AFFECTED BY SOMETHING ELSE.

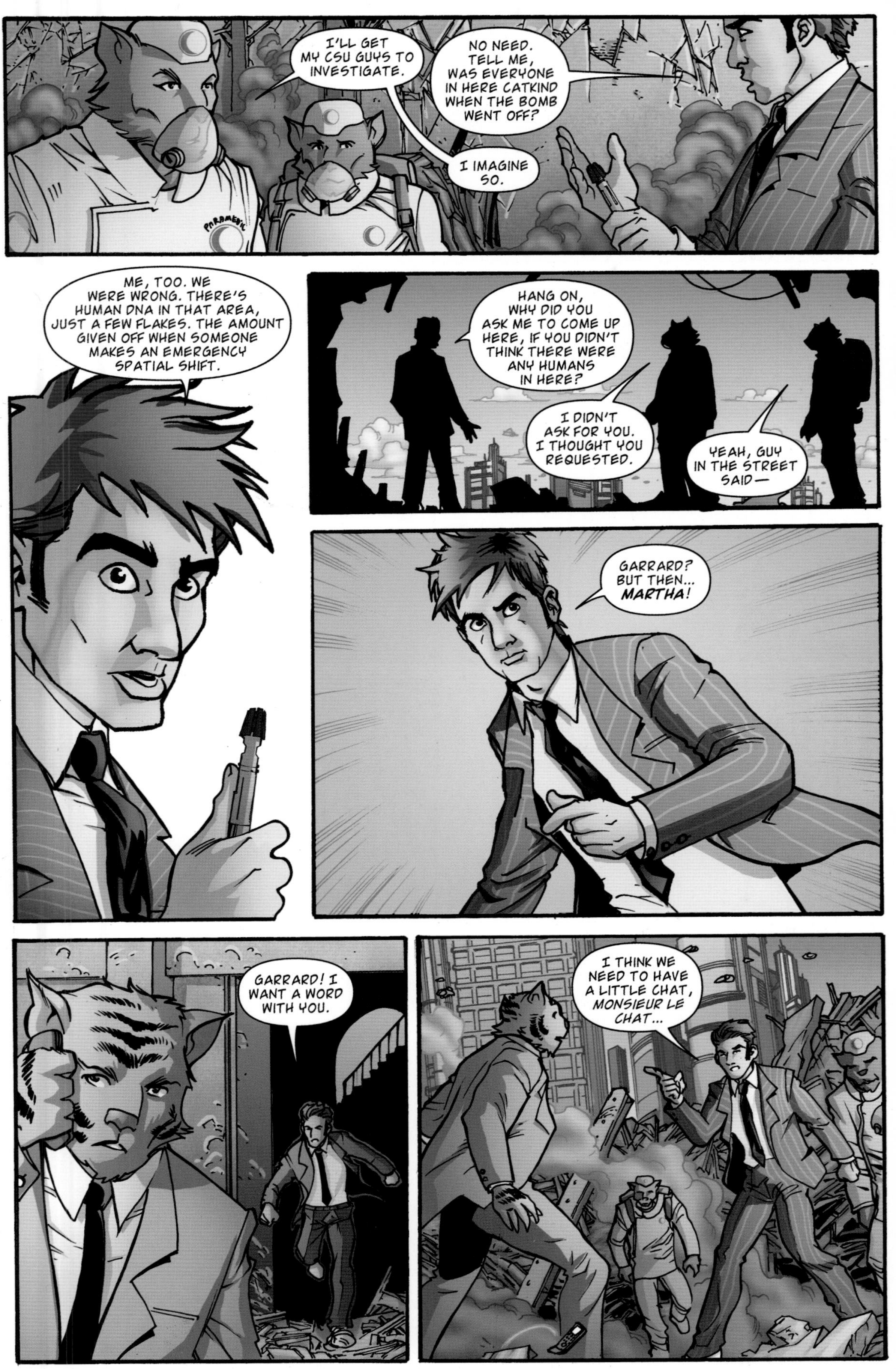
I'LL GET MY CSU GUYS TO INVESTIGATE.
NO NEED. TELL ME, WAS EVERYONE IN HERE CATKIND WHEN THE BOMB WENT OFF?
I IMAGINE SO.
PARAMEDIC
ME, TOO. WE WERE WRONG. THERE'S HUMAN DNA IN THAT AREA, JUST A FEW FLAKES. THE AMOUNT GIVEN OFF WHEN SOMEONE MAKES AN EMERGENCY SPATIAL SHIFT.
HANG ON, WHY DID YOU ASK ME TO COME UP HERE, IF YOU DIDN'T THINK THERE WERE ANY HUMANS IN HERE?
I DIDN'T ASK FOR YOU. I THOUGHT YOU REQUESTED.
YEAH, GUY IN THE STREET SAID—
GARRARD? BUT THEN... *MARTHA*!
GARRARD! I WANT A WORD WITH YOU.
I THINK WE NEED TO HAVE A LITTLE CHAT, *MONSIEUR LE CHAT*...

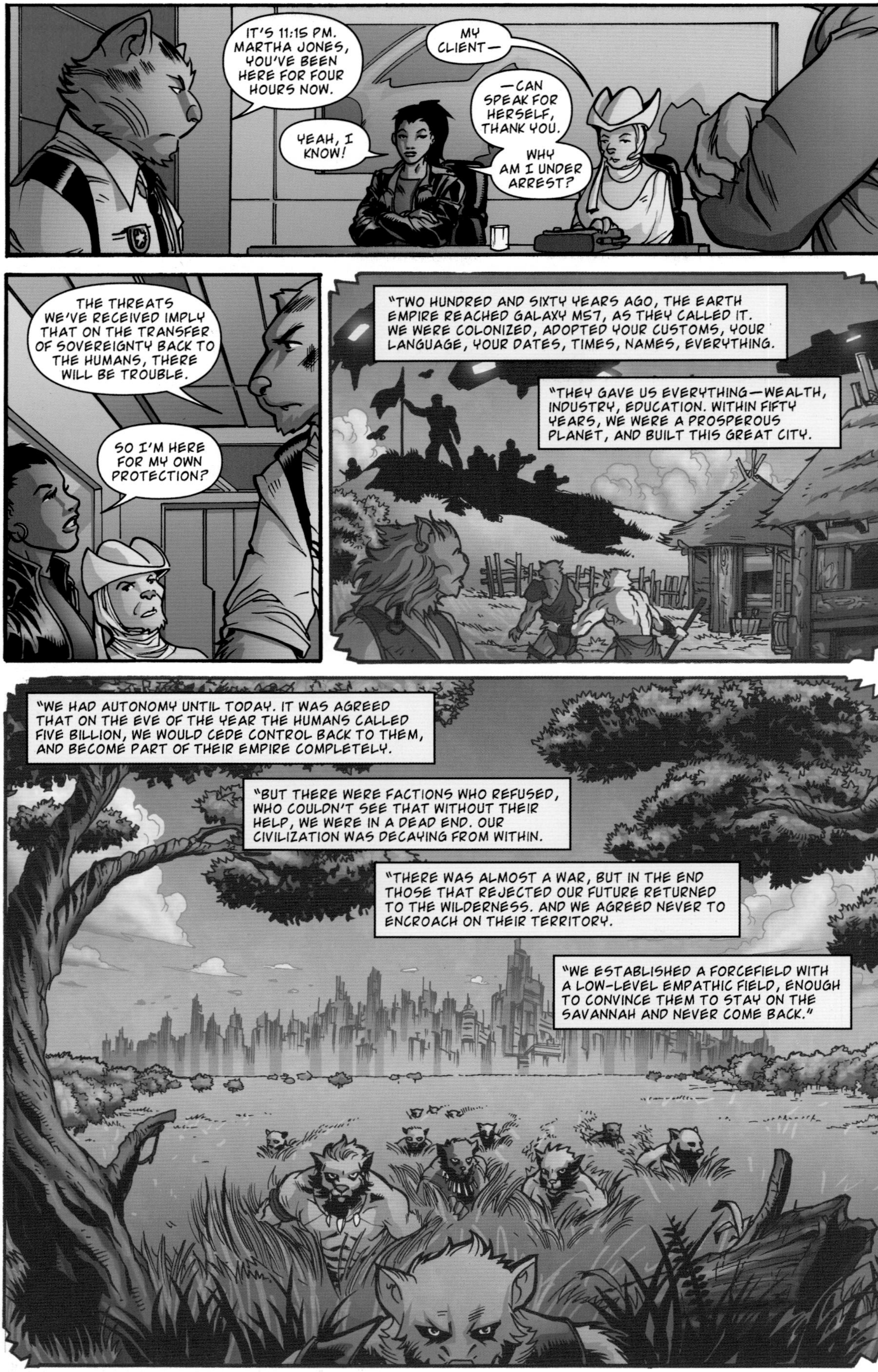
IT'S 11:15 PM. MARTHA JONES, YOU'VE BEEN HERE FOR FOUR HOURS NOW.
YEAH, I KNOW!
MY CLIENT—
—CAN SPEAK FOR HERSELF, THANK YOU.
WHY AM I UNDER ARREST?
THE THREATS WE'VE RECEIVED IMPLY THAT ON THE TRANSFER OF SOVEREIGNTY BACK TO THE HUMANS, THERE WILL BE TROUBLE.
SO I'M HERE FOR MY OWN PROTECTION?
"TWO HUNDRED AND SIXTY YEARS AGO, THE EARTH EMPIRE REACHED GALAXY M57, AS THEY CALLED IT. WE WERE COLONIZED, ADOPTED YOUR CUSTOMS, YOUR LANGUAGE, YOUR DATES, TIMES, NAMES, EVERYTHING.
"THEY GAVE US EVERYTHING—WEALTH, INDUSTRY, EDUCATION. WITHIN FIFTY YEARS, WE WERE A PROSPEROUS PLANET, AND BUILT THIS GREAT CITY.
"WE HAD AUTONOMY UNTIL TODAY. IT WAS AGREED THAT ON THE EVE OF THE YEAR THE HUMANS CALLED FIVE BILLION, WE WOULD CEDE CONTROL BACK TO THEM, AND BECOME PART OF THEIR EMPIRE COMPLETELY.
"BUT THERE WERE FACTIONS WHO REFUSED, WHO COULDN'T SEE THAT WITHOUT THEIR HELP, WE WERE IN A DEAD END. OUR CIVILIZATION WAS DECAYING FROM WITHIN.
"THERE WAS ALMOST A WAR, BUT IN THE END THOSE THAT REJECTED OUR FUTURE RETURNED TO THE WILDERNESS. AND WE AGREED NEVER TO ENCROACH ON THEIR TERRITORY.
"WE ESTABLISHED A FORCEFIELD WITH A LOW-LEVEL EMPATHIC FIELD, ENOUGH TO CONVINCE THEM TO STAY ON THE SAVANNAH AND NEVER COME BACK."

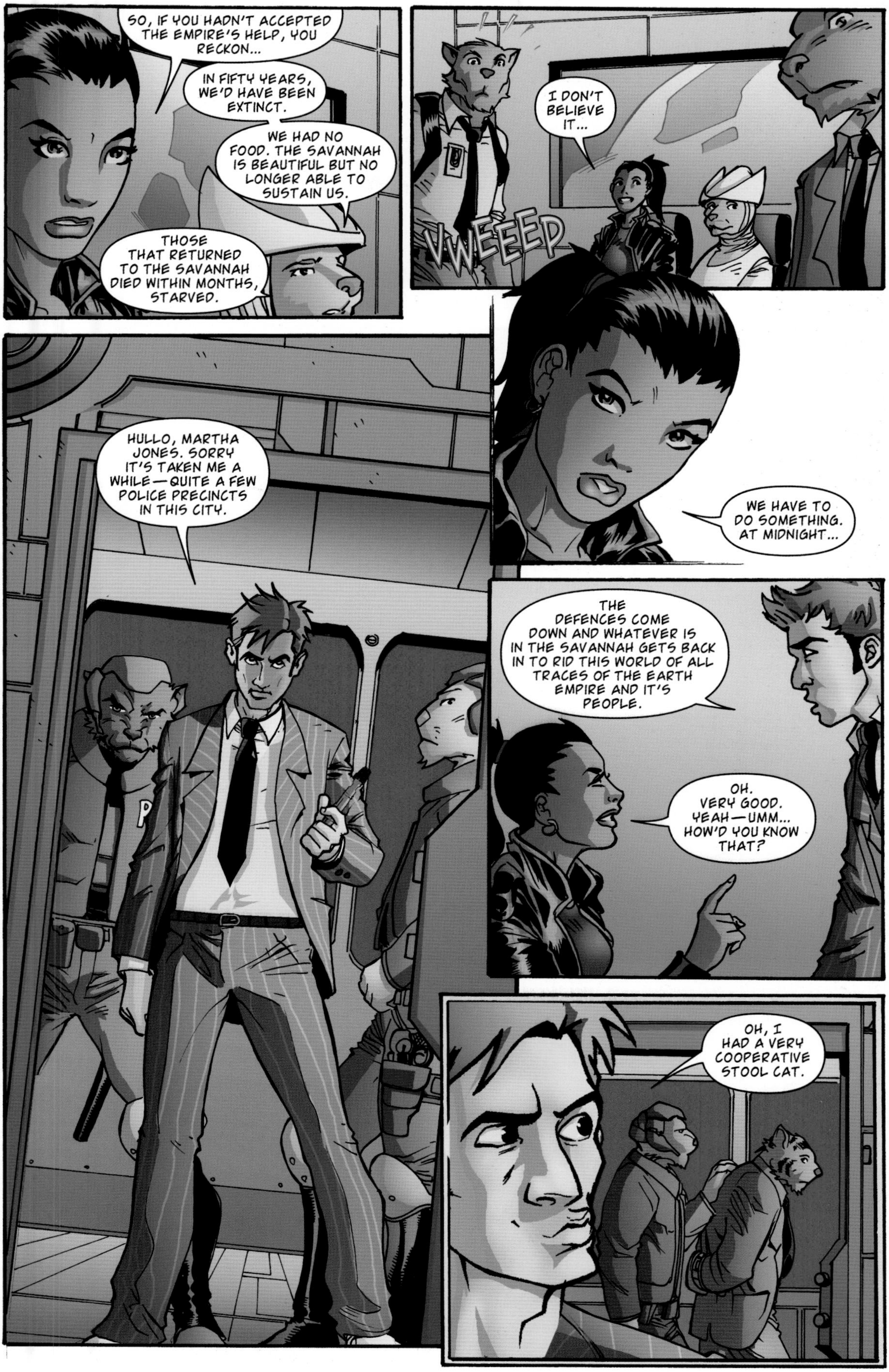

SO, IF YOU HADN'T ACCEPTED THE EMPIRE'S HELP, YOU RECKON...
IN FIFTY YEARS, WE'D HAVE BEEN EXTINCT.
WE HAD NO FOOD. THE SAVANNAH IS BEAUTIFUL BUT NO LONGER ABLE TO SUSTAIN US.
THOSE THAT RETURNED TO THE SAVANNAH DIED WITHIN MONTHS, STARVED.
I DON'T BELIEVE IT...
VWEEEP
HULLO, MARTHA JONES. SORRY IT'S TAKEN ME A WHILE—QUITE A FEW POLICE PRECINCTS IN THIS CITY.
WE HAVE TO DO SOMETHING. AT MIDNIGHT...
THE DEFENCES COME DOWN AND WHATEVER IS IN THE SAVANNAH GETS BACK IN TO RID THIS WORLD OF ALL TRACES OF THE EARTH EMPIRE AND IT'S PEOPLE.
OH. VERY GOOD. YEAH—UMM... HOW'D YOU KNOW THAT?
OH, I HAD A VERY COOPERATIVE STOOL CAT.

GARRARD, IT SEEMS, IS PART OF SOME ANTI-HUMAN CULT, DEDICATED TO OVERTHROWING THE EMPIRE. AND YOU KNOW ME, MARTHA, I'M ALL IN FAVOUR OF OVERTHROWING EVIL EMPIRES...

...BUT I'M NOT SURE AT THIS POINT, THE EARTH EMPIRE QUALIFIES.

AND ANYWAY, WE'VE BEEN TO THE FUTURE, WE KNOW IT WORKS.

OH, MARTHA JONES, YOU KNOW AS WELL AS I DO ALL THAT CAN COME UNRAVELLED IF...

YEAH, YEAH, INFINITE TEMPORAL FLUX, I REMEMBER.

YOU DO? OH. OH, GOOD. YEAH. WELL DONE.

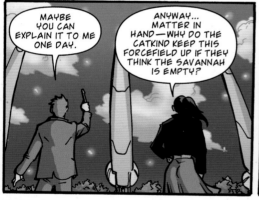

MAYBE YOU CAN EXPLAIN IT TO ME ONE DAY.

ANYWAY... MATTER IN HAND—WHY DO THE CATKIND KEEP THIS FORCEFIELD UP IF THEY THINK THE SAVANNAH IS EMPTY?

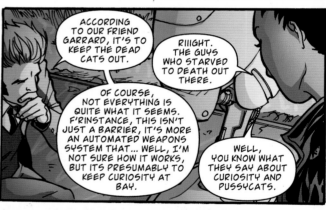

ACCORDING TO OUR FRIEND GARRARD, IT'S TO KEEP THE DEAD CATS OUT.

RIIIGHT. THE GUYS WHO STARVED TO DEATH OUT THERE.

OF COURSE, NOT EVERYTHING IS QUITE WHAT IT SEEMS. F'RINSTANCE, THIS ISN'T JUST A BARRIER, IT'S MORE AN AUTOMATED WEAPONS SYSTEM THAT... WELL, I'M NOT SURE HOW IT WORKS, BUT ITS PRESUMABLY TO KEEP CURIOSITY AT BAY.

WELL, YOU KNOW WHAT THEY SAY ABOUT CURIOSITY AND PUSSYCATS.

BACK ON YOUR PLANET, F'RINSTANCE, YOU HAVE STORIES OF A MONSTER IN A HUGE LAKE IN SCOTLAND. MIGHT BE A LOAD OF OLD TWADDLE, BUT YOU CAN NEVER BE QUITE SURE, AND IT'S OFTEN THAT LITTLE SEED OF DOUBT THAT STOPS PEOPLE SWIMMING IN DANGEROUS WATERS.

GO ON, NOW TELL ME THERE REALLY IS A LOCH NESS MONSTER THAT EATS SWIMMERS.

WELL. I DON'T THINK EITHER OF THEM ACTUALLY EATS PEOPLE.

EITHER...? OF...? THEM?

YUP. ONE'S A BIG CYBORG, THE OTHER'S A MUTATED DNA EXPERIMENT BETWEEN A VERY SILLY MAN AND AN INNOCENT SNAKE.

OF COURSE. TWO. WHY DIDN'T I GUESS THAT...?

"WHOEVER BLEW UP THAT OFFICE BLOCK DID IT TO GET HOLD OF THE MECHANISM TO LOWER THESE FORCEFIELDS. IN ABOUT FIVE MINUTES, MARTHA JONES, IF I'M RIGHT, THEY'LL GO DOWN AT THE STROKE OF MIDNIGHT."

"AND WHAT, DOCTOR, DO WE DO IF, YOU KNOW, WE GET ATTACKED BY FERAL GHOSTLY CATKIND FROM THE SAVANNAH?"

"RUN?"

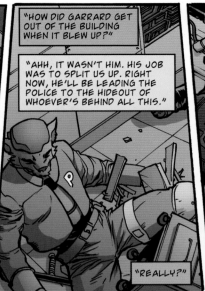

"HOW DID GARRARD GET OUT OF THE BUILDING WHEN IT BLEW UP?"

"AHH, IT WASN'T HIM. HIS JOB WAS TO SPLIT US UP. RIGHT NOW, HE'LL BE LEADING THE POLICE TO THE HIDEOUT OF WHOEVER'S BEHIND ALL THIS."

"REALLY?"

"I GAVE THE POLICE A TARDIS HOMING DEVICE TO PLANT ON HIM. THEY'RE FOLLOWING HIM RIGHT NOW."

SO IF I TRIANGULATE WITH THIS BETWEEN HERE, THE TARDIS AND THE HOMING DEVICE, WE SHOULD BE ABLE TO ASCERTAIN WHERE... OH...

OH? I DON'T LIKE "OH"...

"OH" USUALLY MEANS "THE PLAN'S GONE WRONG, MARTHA."

THE PLAN'S GONE WRONG, MAR—

WHY DO I THINK IT'S MIDNIGHT, DOCTOR?

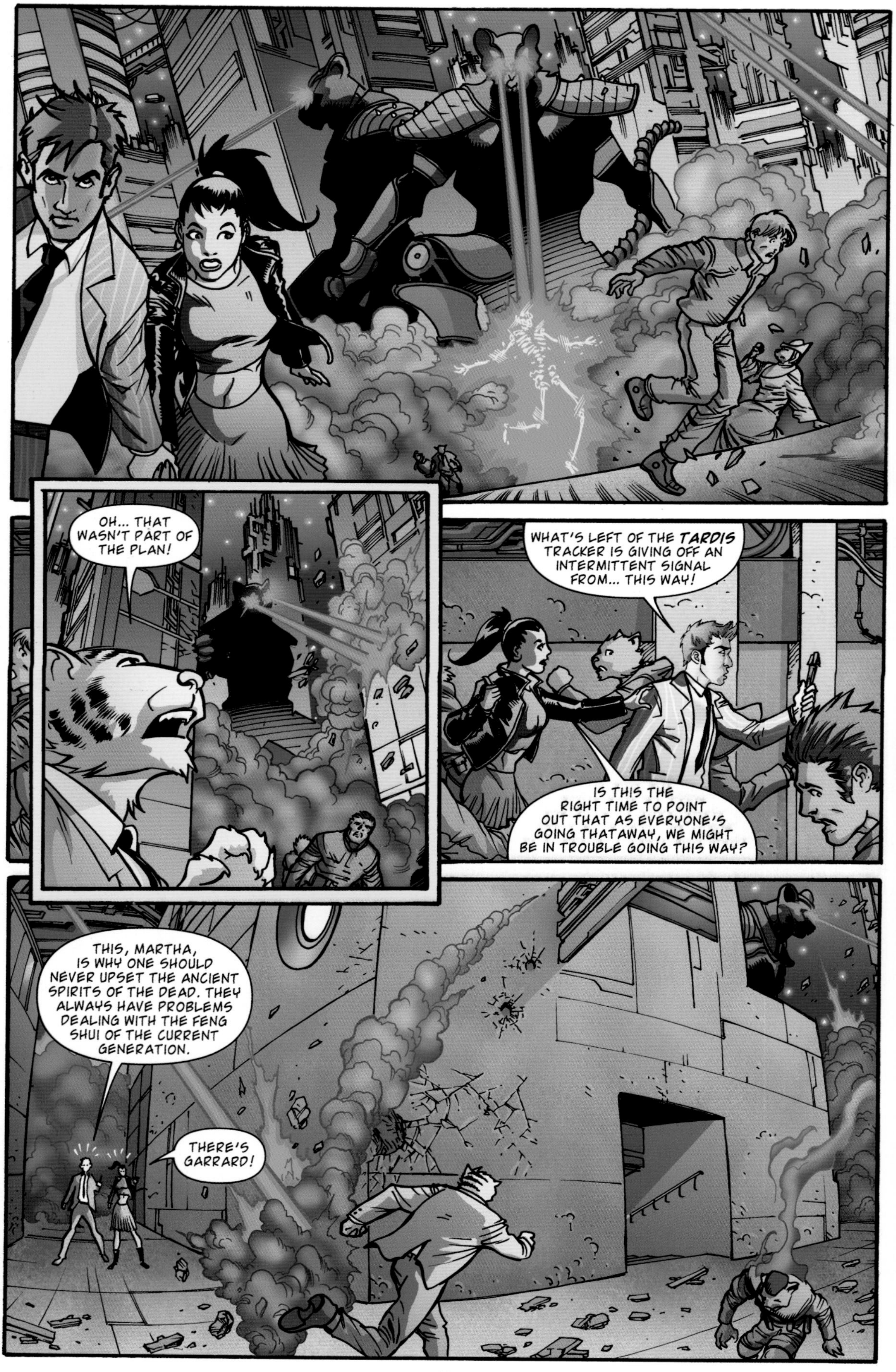
OH... THAT WASN'T PART OF THE PLAN!
WHAT'S LEFT OF THE *TARDIS* TRACKER IS GIVING OFF AN INTERMITTENT SIGNAL FROM... THIS WAY!
IS THIS THE RIGHT TIME TO POINT OUT THAT AS EVERYONE'S GOING THATAWAY, WE MIGHT BE IN TROUBLE GOING THIS WAY?
THIS, MARTHA, IS WHY ONE SHOULD NEVER UPSET THE ANCIENT SPIRITS OF THE DEAD. THEY ALWAYS HAVE PROBLEMS DEALING WITH THE FENG SHUI OF THE CURRENT GENERATION.
THERE'S GARRARD!

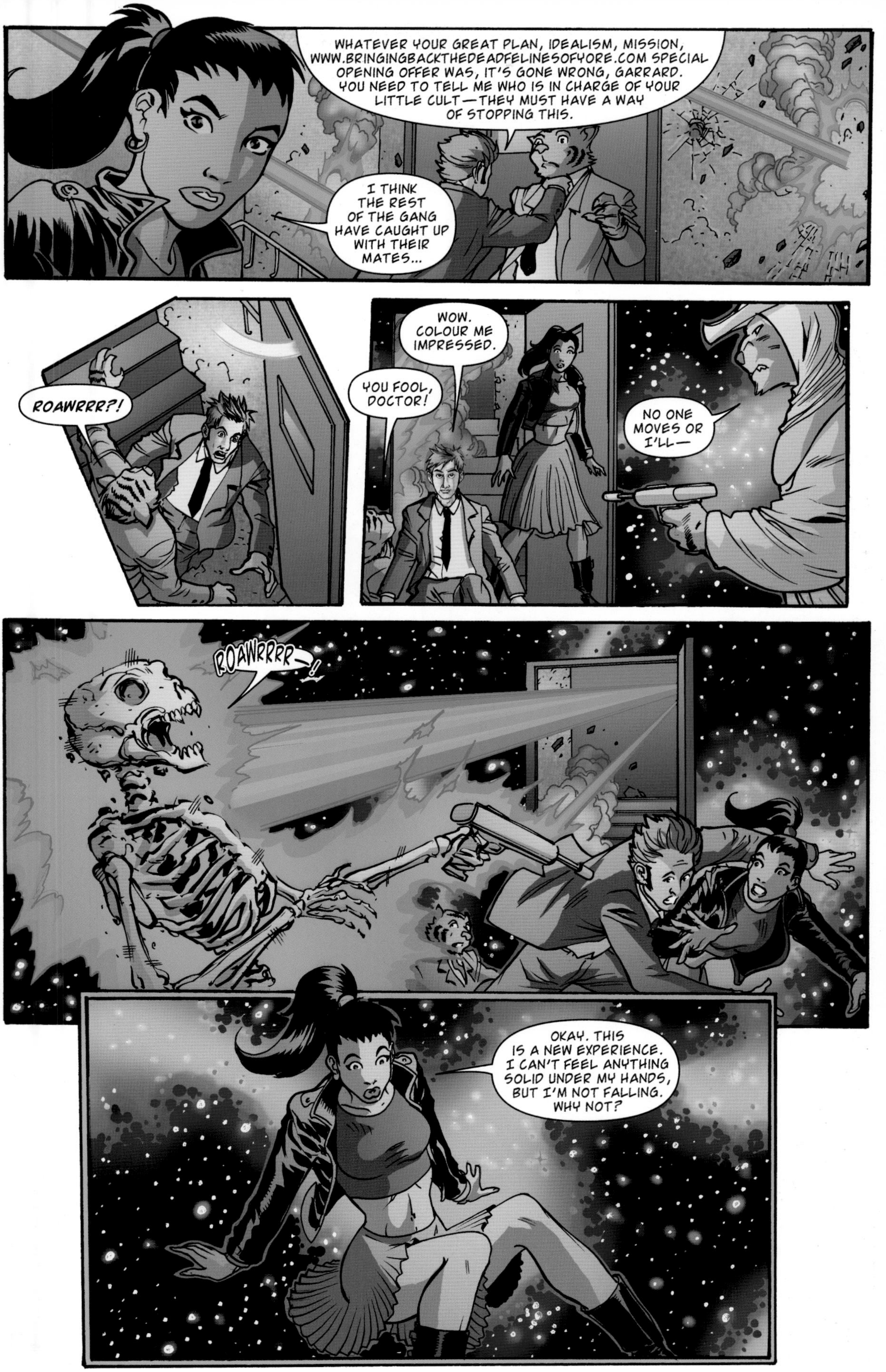
WHATEVER YOUR GREAT PLAN, IDEALISM, MISSION, WWW.BRINGINGBACKTHEDEADFELINESOFYORE.COM SPECIAL OPENING OFFER WAS, IT'S GONE WRONG, GARRARD. YOU NEED TO TELL ME WHO IS IN CHARGE OF YOUR LITTLE CULT—THEY MUST HAVE A WAY OF STOPPING THIS.
I THINK THE REST OF THE GANG HAVE CAUGHT UP WITH THEIR MATES...
ROAWRRR?!
WOW. COLOUR ME IMPRESSED.
YOU FOOL, DOCTOR!
NO ONE MOVES OR I'LL—
ROAWRRRR—!
OKAY. THIS IS A NEW EXPERIENCE. I CAN'T FEEL ANYTHING SOLID UNDER MY HANDS, BUT I'M NOT FALLING. WHY NOT?

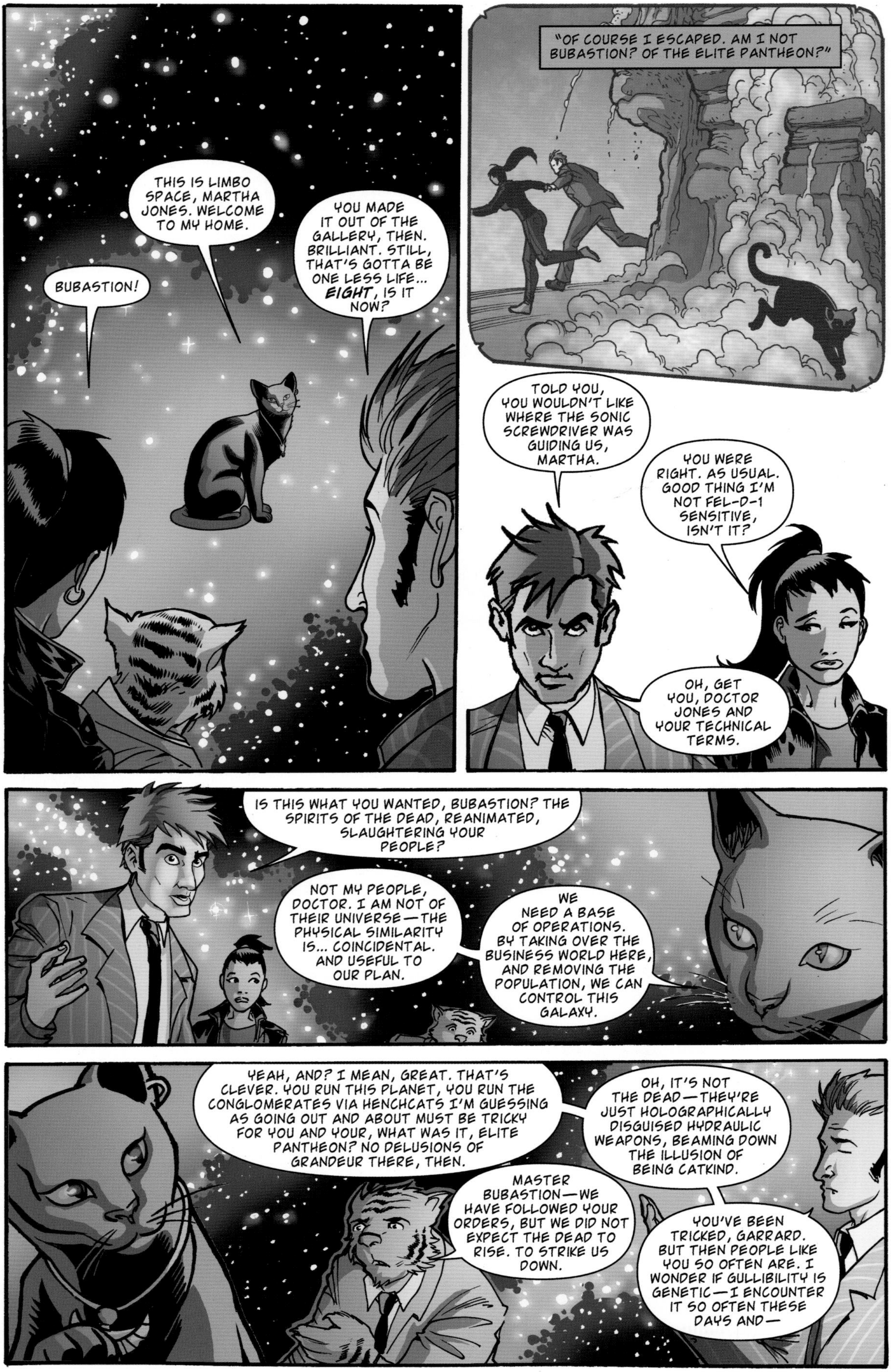
BUBASTION!
THIS IS LIMBO SPACE, MARTHA JONES. WELCOME TO MY HOME.
YOU MADE IT OUT OF THE GALLERY, THEN. BRILLIANT. STILL, THAT'S GOTTA BE ONE LESS LIFE... **EIGHT**, IS IT NOW?
"OF COURSE I ESCAPED. AM I NOT BUBASTION? OF THE ELITE PANTHEON?"
TOLD YOU, YOU WOULDN'T LIKE WHERE THE SONIC SCREWDRIVER WAS GUIDING US, MARTHA.
YOU WERE RIGHT. AS USUAL. GOOD THING I'M NOT FEL-D-1 SENSITIVE, ISN'T IT?
OH, GET YOU, DOCTOR JONES AND YOUR TECHNICAL TERMS.
IS THIS WHAT YOU WANTED, BUBASTION? THE SPIRITS OF THE DEAD, REANIMATED, SLAUGHTERING YOUR PEOPLE?
NOT MY PEOPLE, DOCTOR. I AM NOT OF THEIR UNIVERSE—THE PHYSICAL SIMILARITY IS... COINCIDENTAL. AND USEFUL TO OUR PLAN.
WE NEED A BASE OF OPERATIONS. BY TAKING OVER THE BUSINESS WORLD HERE, AND REMOVING THE POPULATION, WE CAN CONTROL THIS GALAXY.
YEAH, AND? I MEAN, GREAT. THAT'S CLEVER. YOU RUN THIS PLANET, YOU RUN THE CONGLOMERATES VIA HENCHCATS I'M GUESSING AS GOING OUT AND ABOUT MUST BE TRICKY FOR YOU AND YOUR, WHAT WAS IT, ELITE PANTHEON? NO DELUSIONS OF GRANDEUR THERE, THEN.
OH, IT'S NOT THE DEAD—THEY'RE JUST HOLOGRAPHICALLY DISGUISED HYDRAULIC WEAPONS, BEAMING DOWN THE ILLUSION OF BEING CATKIND.
MASTER BUBASTION—WE HAVE FOLLOWED YOUR ORDERS, BUT WE DID NOT EXPECT THE DEAD TO RISE. TO STRIKE US DOWN.
YOU'VE BEEN TRICKED, GARRARD. BUT THEN PEOPLE LIKE YOU SO OFTEN ARE. I WONDER IF GULLIBILITY IS GENETIC—I ENCOUNTER IT SO OFTEN THESE DAYS AND—

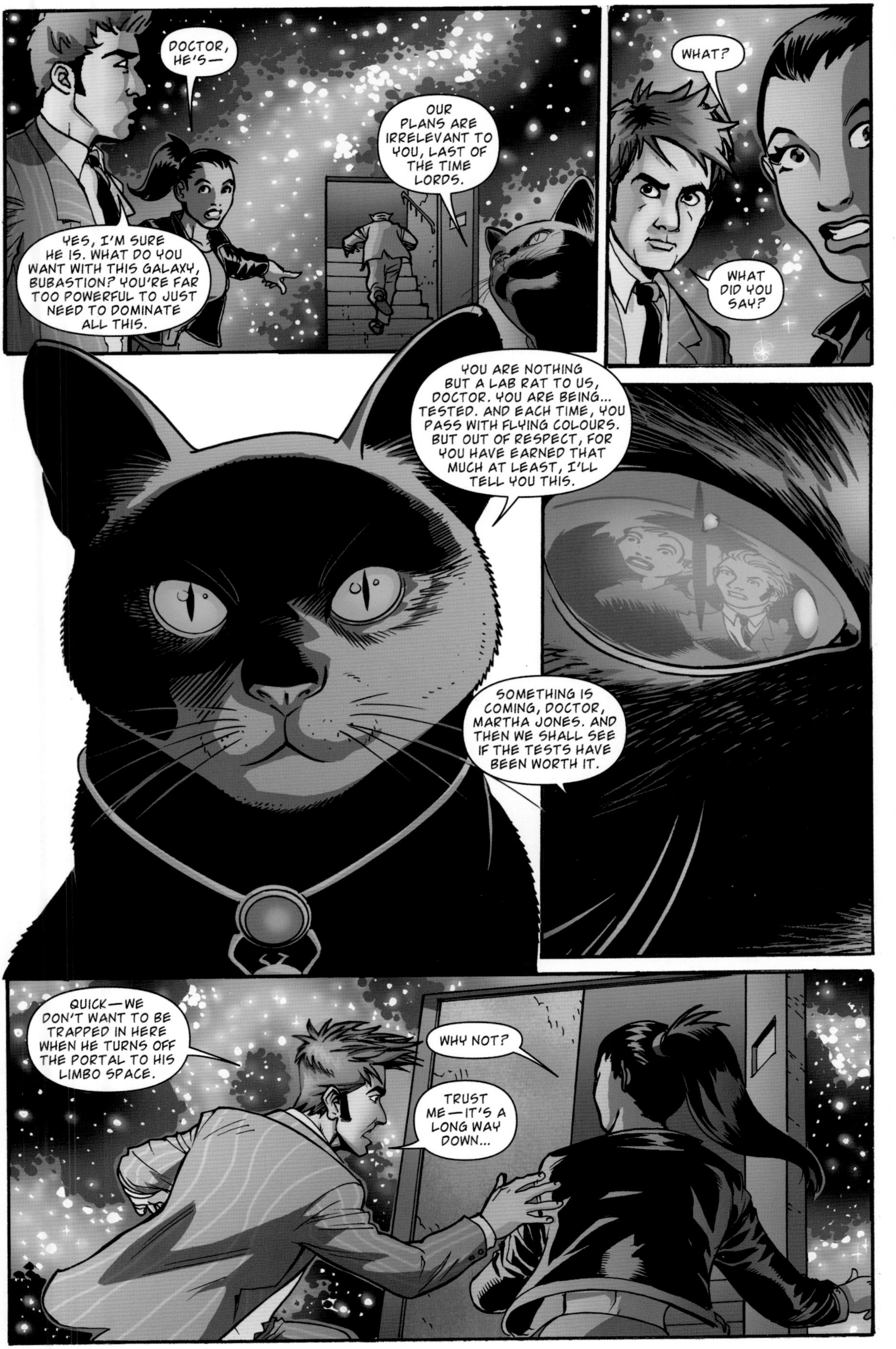
DOCTOR, HE'S—
OUR PLANS ARE IRRELEVANT TO YOU, LAST OF THE TIME LORDS.
YES, I'M SURE HE IS. WHAT DO YOU WANT WITH THIS GALAXY, BUBASTION? YOU'RE FAR TOO POWERFUL TO JUST NEED TO DOMINATE ALL THIS.
WHAT?
WHAT DID YOU SAY?
YOU ARE NOTHING BUT A LAB RAT TO US, DOCTOR. YOU ARE BEING... TESTED. AND EACH TIME, YOU PASS WITH FLYING COLOURS. BUT OUT OF RESPECT, FOR YOU HAVE EARNED THAT MUCH AT LEAST, I'LL TELL YOU THIS.
SOMETHING IS COMING, DOCTOR, MARTHA JONES. AND THEN WE SHALL SEE IF THE TESTS HAVE BEEN WORTH IT.
QUICK—WE DON'T WANT TO BE TRAPPED IN HERE WHEN HE TURNS OFF THE PORTAL TO HIS LIMBO SPACE.
WHY NOT?
TRUST ME—IT'S A LONG WAY DOWN...

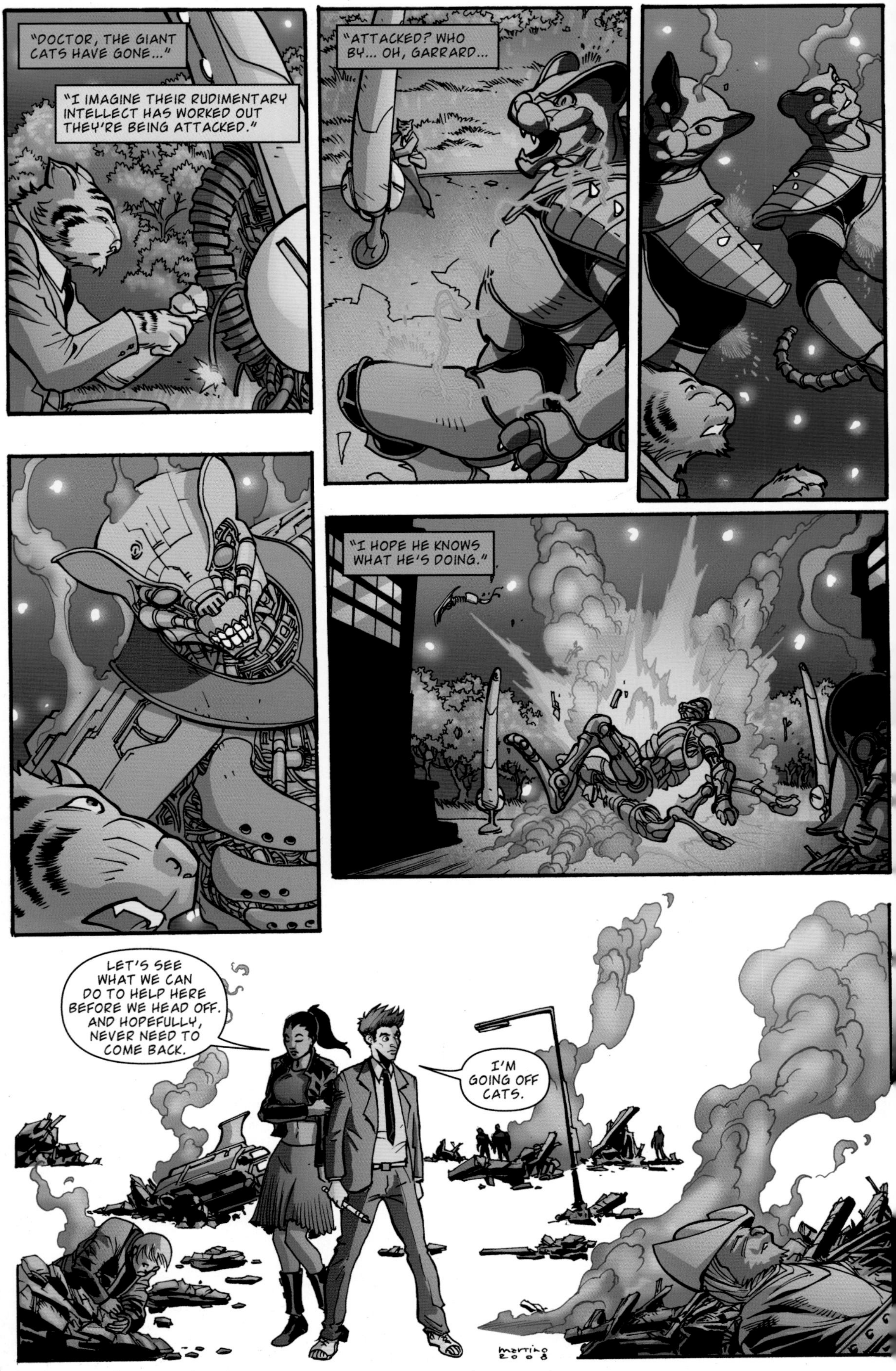
"DOCTOR, THE GIANT CATS HAVE GONE..."
"I IMAGINE THEIR RUDIMENTARY INTELLECT HAS WORKED OUT THEY'RE BEING ATTACKED."
"ATTACKED? WHO BY... OH, GARRARD..."
"I HOPE HE KNOWS WHAT HE'S DOING."
LET'S SEE WHAT WE CAN DO TO HELP HERE BEFORE WE HEAD OFF. AND HOPEFULLY, NEVER NEED TO COME BACK.
I'M GOING OFF CATS.
MARTINO 2008

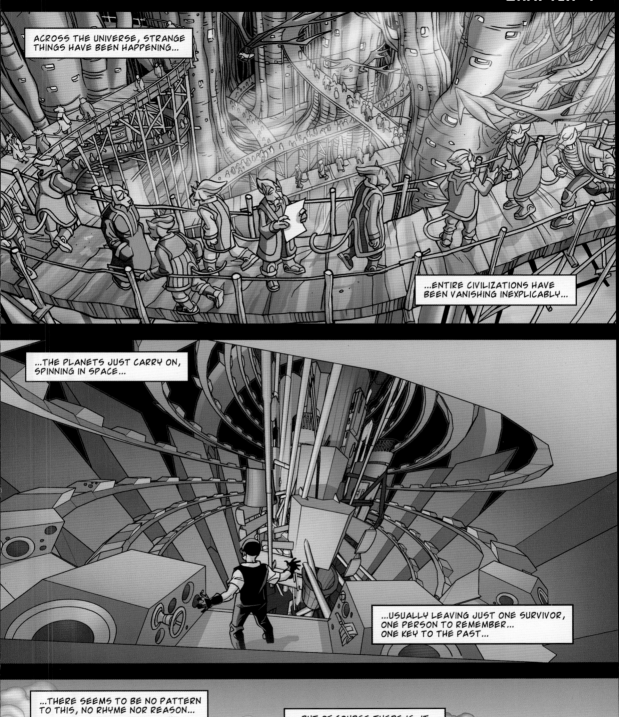

CHAPTER 4

ACROSS THE UNIVERSE, STRANGE THINGS HAVE BEEN HAPPENING...

...ENTIRE CIVILIZATIONS HAVE BEEN VANISHING INEXPLICABLY...

...THE PLANETS JUST CARRY ON, SPINNING IN SPACE...

...USUALLY LEAVING JUST ONE SURVIVOR, ONE PERSON TO REMEMBER... ONE KEY TO THE PAST...

...THERE SEEMS TO BE NO PATTERN TO THIS, NO RHYME NOR REASON...

...BUT OF COURSE THERE IS. IT JUST NEEDS SOMEONE TO COME ALONG AND WORK IT ALL OUT.

WONDER WHO THAT MIGHT BE...

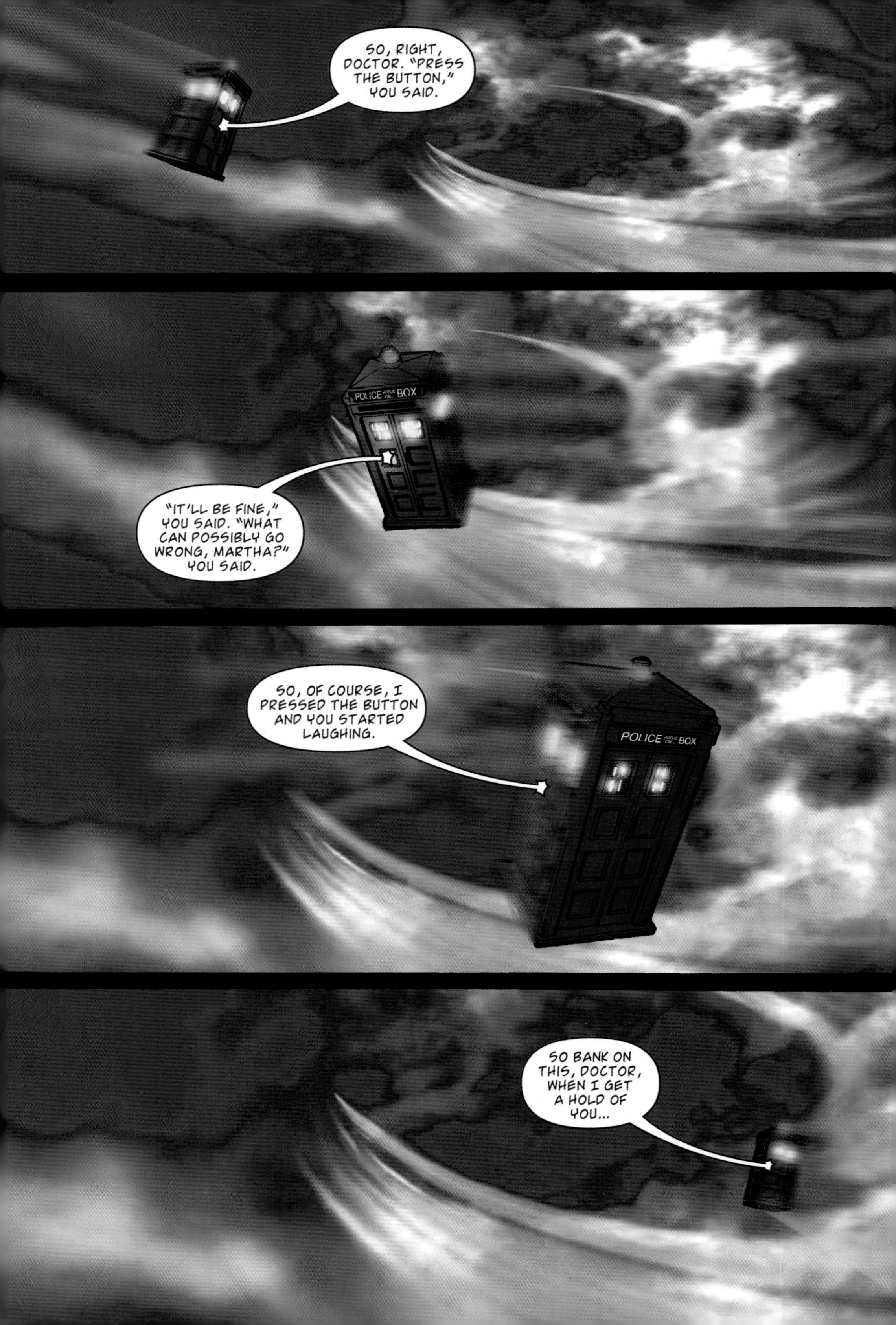
SO, RIGHT, DOCTOR. "PRESS THE BUTTON," YOU SAID.
"IT'LL BE FINE," YOU SAID. "WHAT CAN POSSIBLY GO WRONG, MARTHA?" YOU SAID.
POLICE PUBLIC CALL BOX
SO, OF COURSE, I PRESSED THE BUTTON AND YOU STARTED LAUGHING.
POLICE PUBLIC CALL BOX
SO BANK ON THIS, DOCTOR, WHEN I GET A HOLD OF YOU...

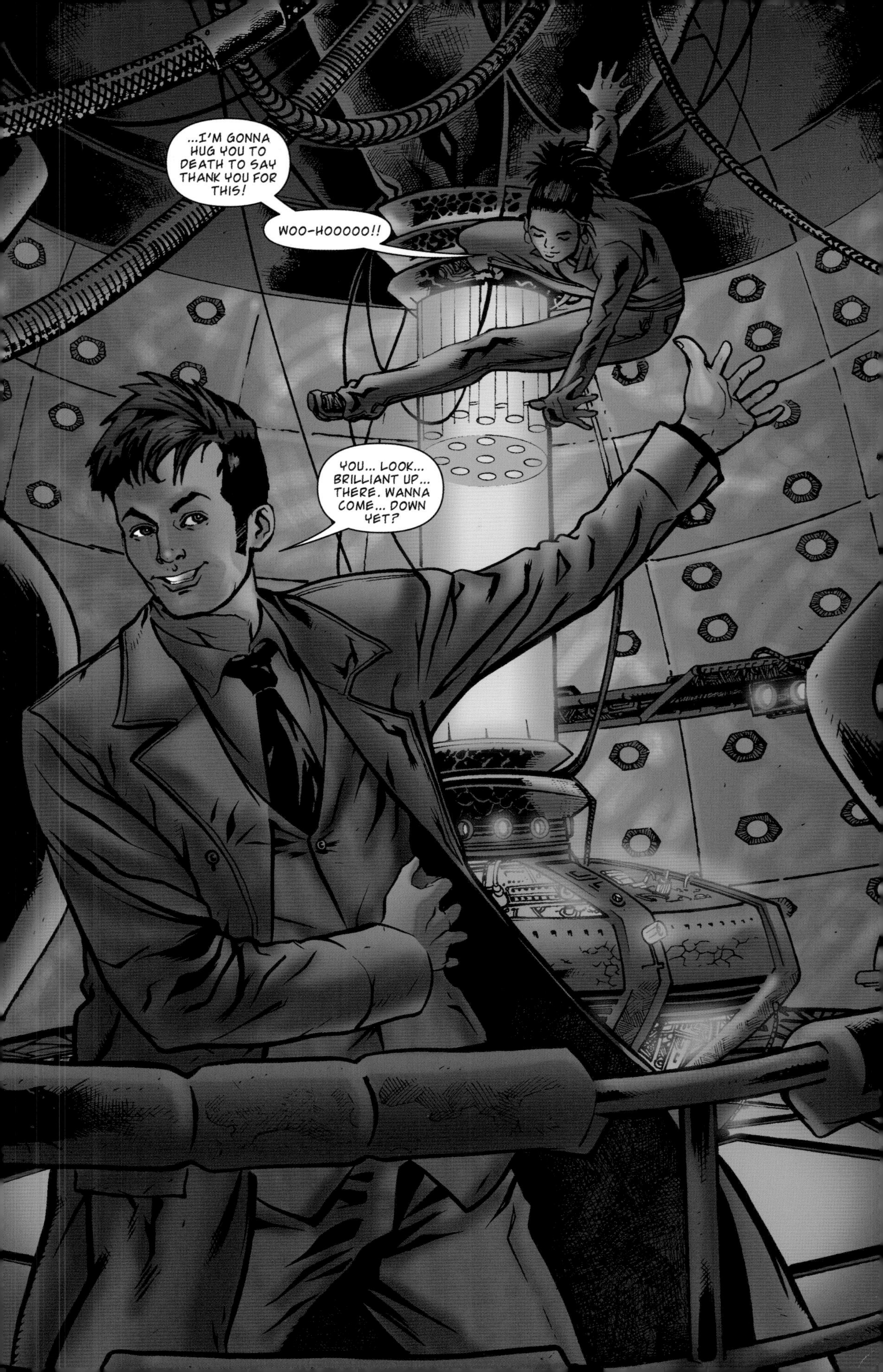
...I'M GONNA HUG YOU TO DEATH TO SAY THANK YOU FOR THIS!
WOO-HOOOOO!!
YOU... LOOK... BRILLIANT UP... THERE. WANNA COME... DOWN YET?

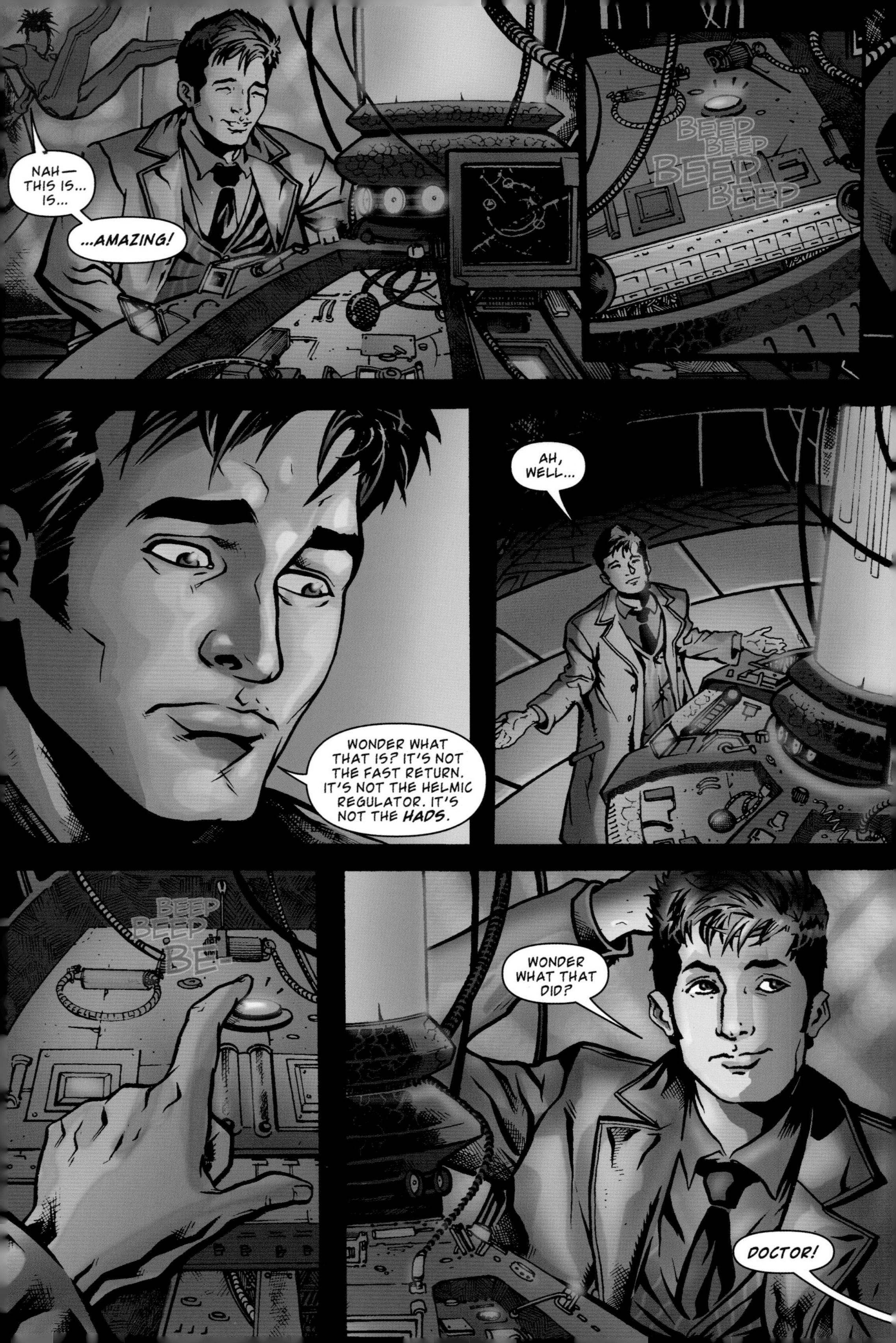
NAH— THIS IS... IS...
...AMAZING!
BEEP BEEP BEEP BEEP
WONDER WHAT THAT IS? IT'S NOT THE FAST RETURN. IT'S NOT THE HELMIC REGULATOR. IT'S NOT THE HADS.
AH, WELL...
BEEP BEEP BE-
WONDER WHAT THAT DID?
DOCTOR!

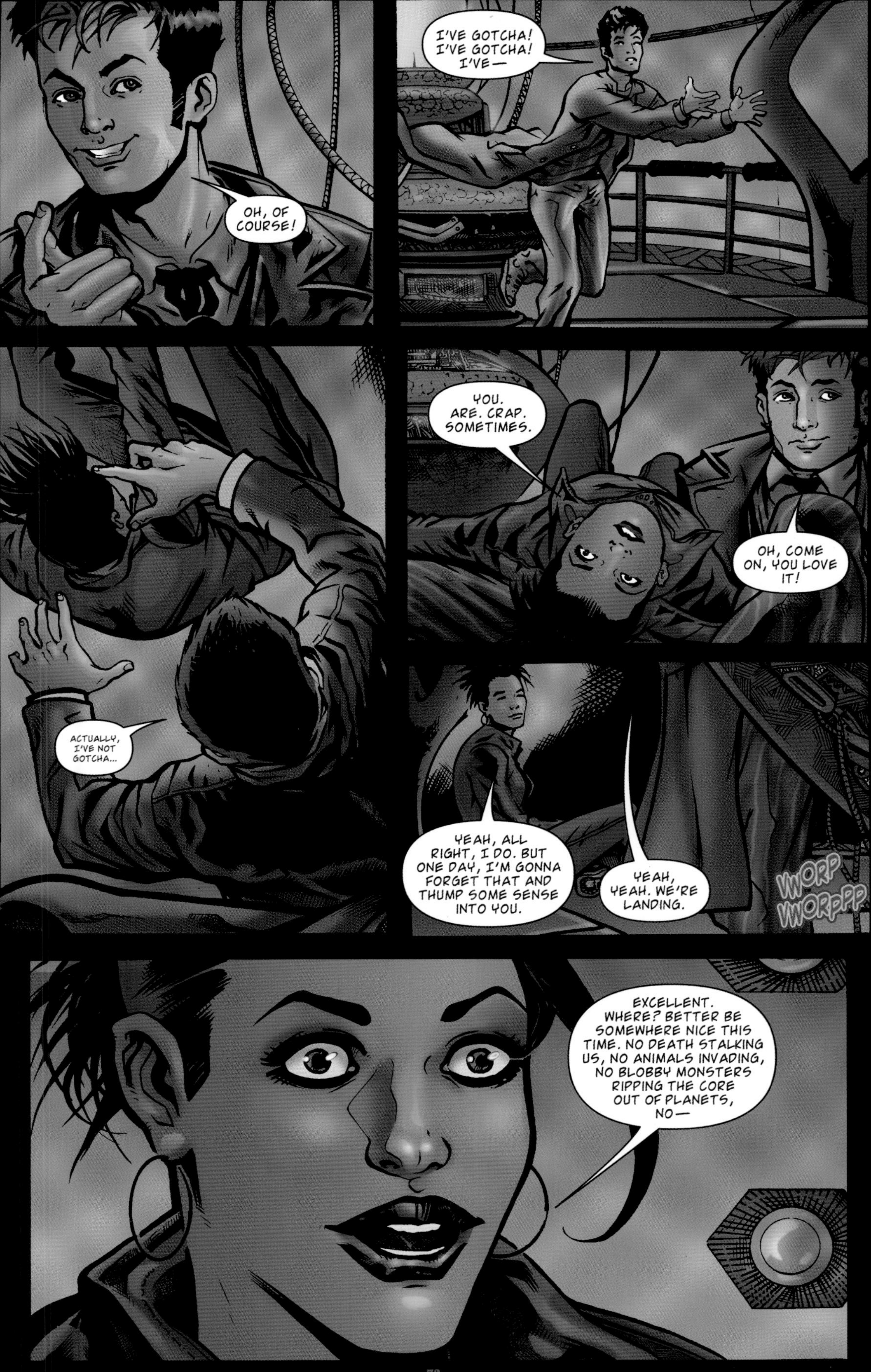
OH, OF COURSE!
I'VE GOTCHA! I'VE GOTCHA! I'VE—
ACTUALLY, I'VE NOT GOTCHA...
YOU. ARE. CRAP. SOMETIMES.
OH, COME ON, YOU LOVE IT!
YEAH, ALL RIGHT, I DO. BUT ONE DAY, I'M GONNA FORGET THAT AND THUMP SOME SENSE INTO YOU.
YEAH, YEAH. WE'RE LANDING.
VWORP VWORPPP
EXCELLENT. WHERE? BETTER BE SOMEWHERE NICE THIS TIME. NO DEATH STALKING US, NO ANIMALS INVADING, NO BLOBBY MONSTERS RIPPING THE CORE OUT OF PLANETS, NO—

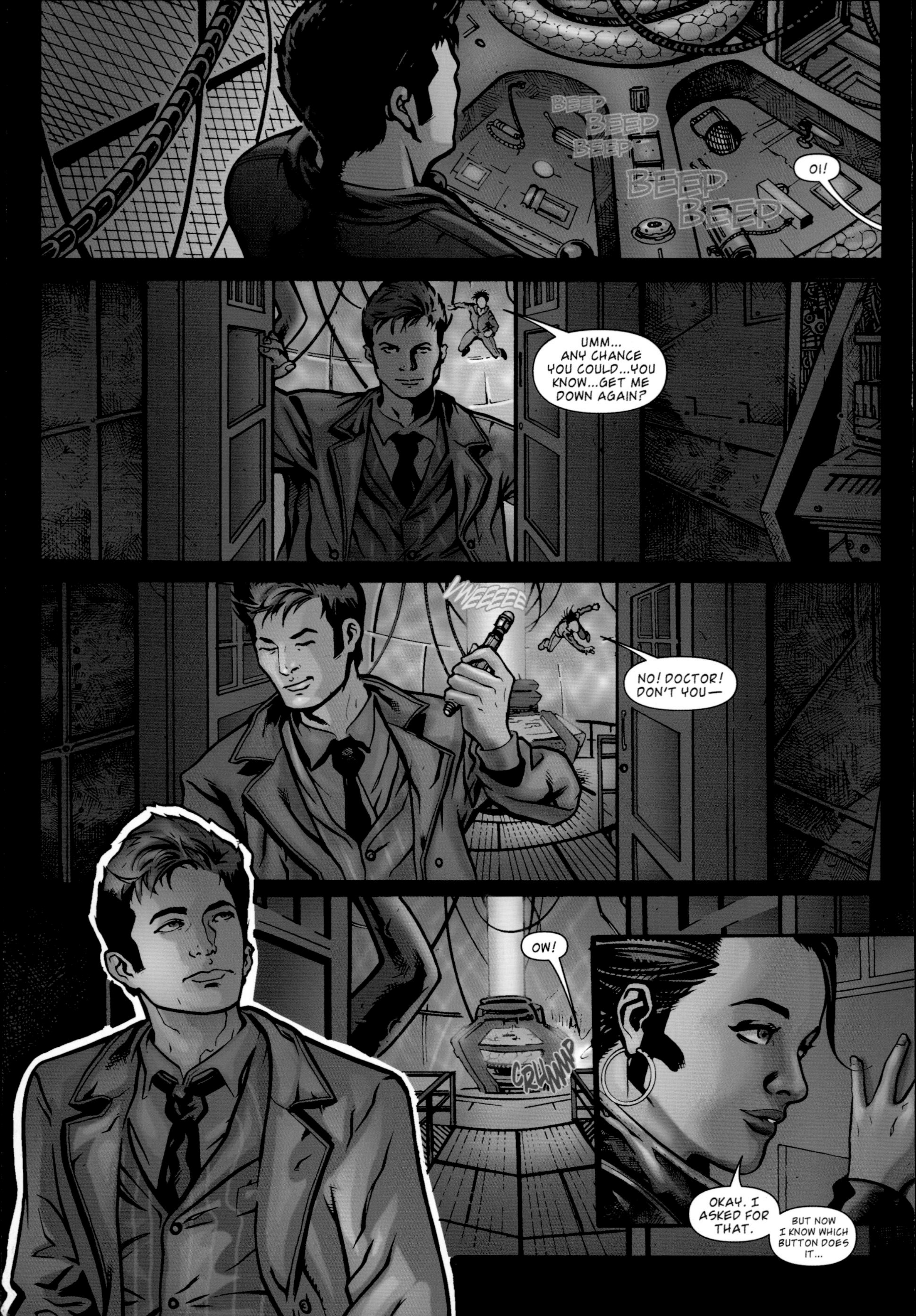
BEEP BEEP BEEP BEEP BEEP
OI!
UMM... ANY CHANCE YOU COULD...YOU KNOW...GET ME DOWN AGAIN?
VWEEEEE
NO! DOCTOR! DON'T YOU—
OW!
CRUMMP
OKAY. I ASKED FOR THAT.
BUT NOW I KNOW WHICH BUTTON DOES IT...

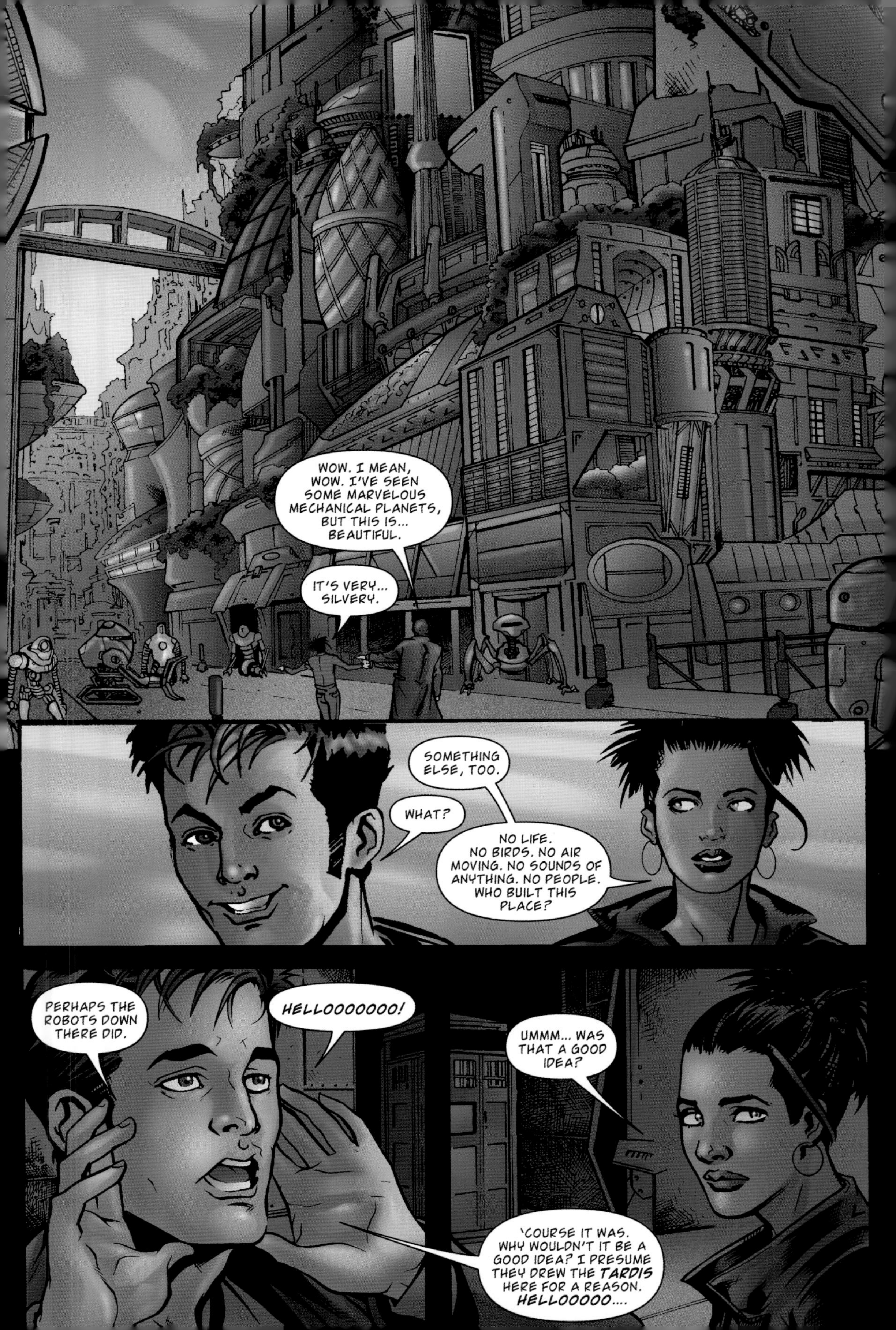
WOW. I MEAN, WOW. I'VE SEEN SOME MARVELOUS MECHANICAL PLANETS, BUT THIS IS... BEAUTIFUL.
IT'S VERY... SILVERY.
SOMETHING ELSE, TOO.
WHAT?
NO LIFE. NO BIRDS. NO AIR MOVING. NO SOUNDS OF ANYTHING. NO PEOPLE. WHO BUILT THIS PLACE?
PERHAPS THE ROBOTS DOWN THERE DID.
HELLOOOOOOO!
UMMM... WAS THAT A GOOD IDEA?
'COURSE IT WAS. WHY WOULDN'T IT BE A GOOD IDEA? I PRESUME THEY DREW THE TARDIS HERE FOR A REASON. HELLOOOOO....

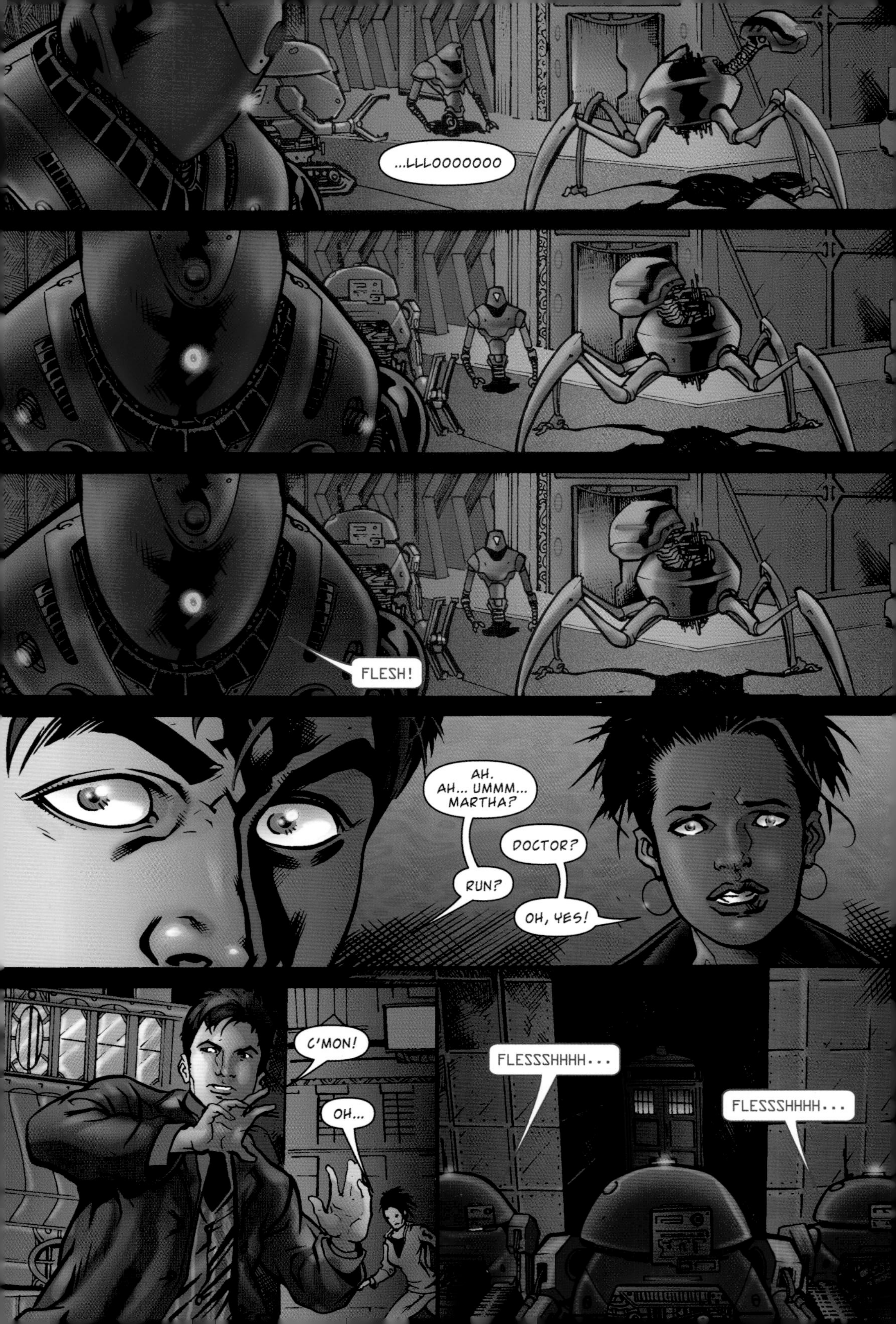
...LLLOOOOOOO
FLESH!
AH.
AH... UMMM... MARTHA?
DOCTOR?
RUN?
OH, YES!
C'MON!
OH...
FLESSSHHHH...
FLESSSHHHH...

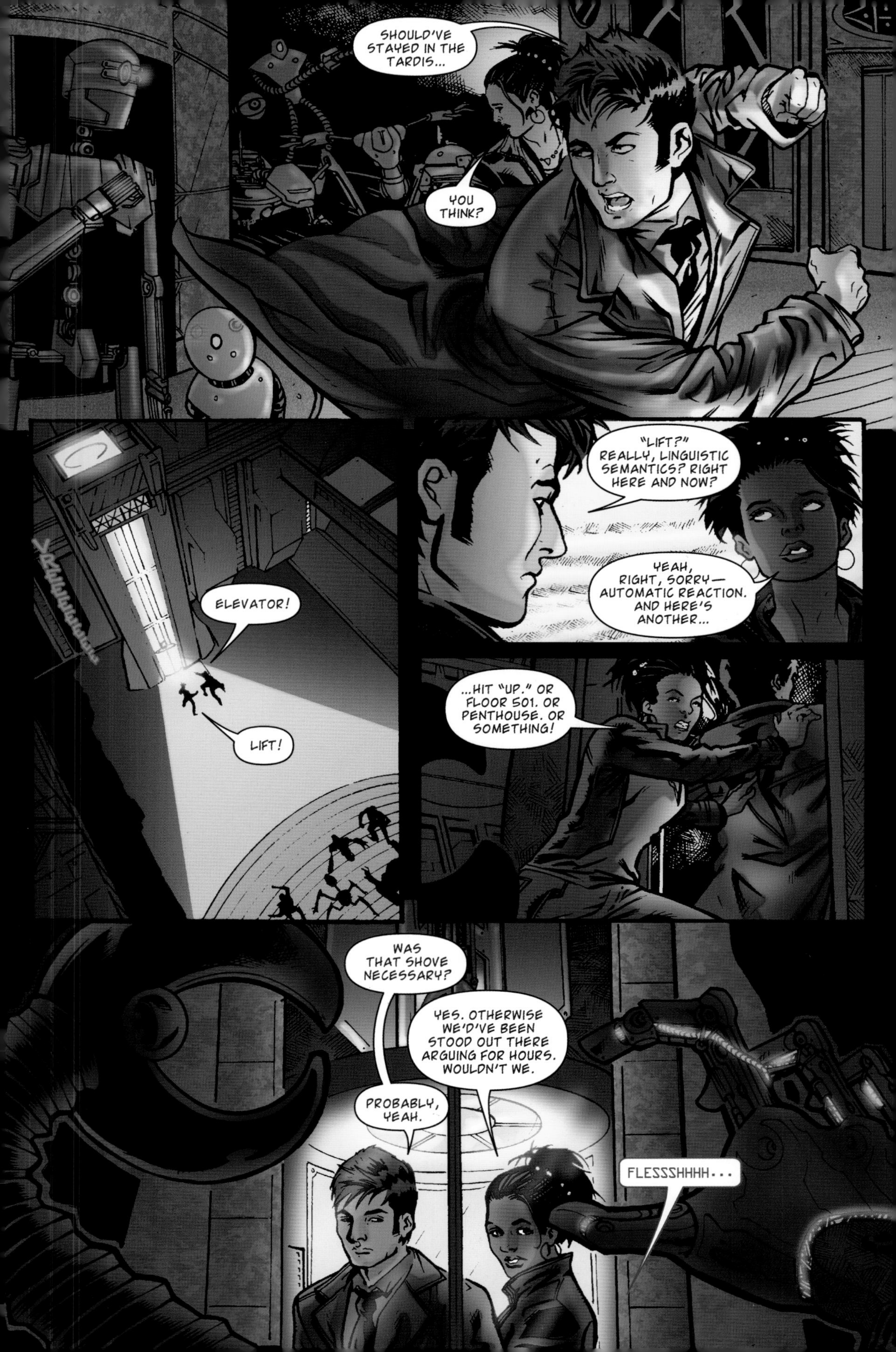
SHOULD'VE STAYED IN THE TARDIS...
YOU THINK?
ELEVATOR!
LIFT!
"LIFT?" REALLY, LINGUISTIC SEMANTICS? RIGHT HERE AND NOW?
YEAH, RIGHT, SORRY— AUTOMATIC REACTION. AND HERE'S ANOTHER...
...HIT "UP." OR FLOOR 501. OR PENTHOUSE. OR SOMETHING!
WAS THAT SHOVE NECESSARY?
YES. OTHERWISE WE'D'VE BEEN STOOD OUT THERE ARGUING FOR HOURS. WOULDN'T WE.
PROBABLY, YEAH.
FLESSSHHHH...

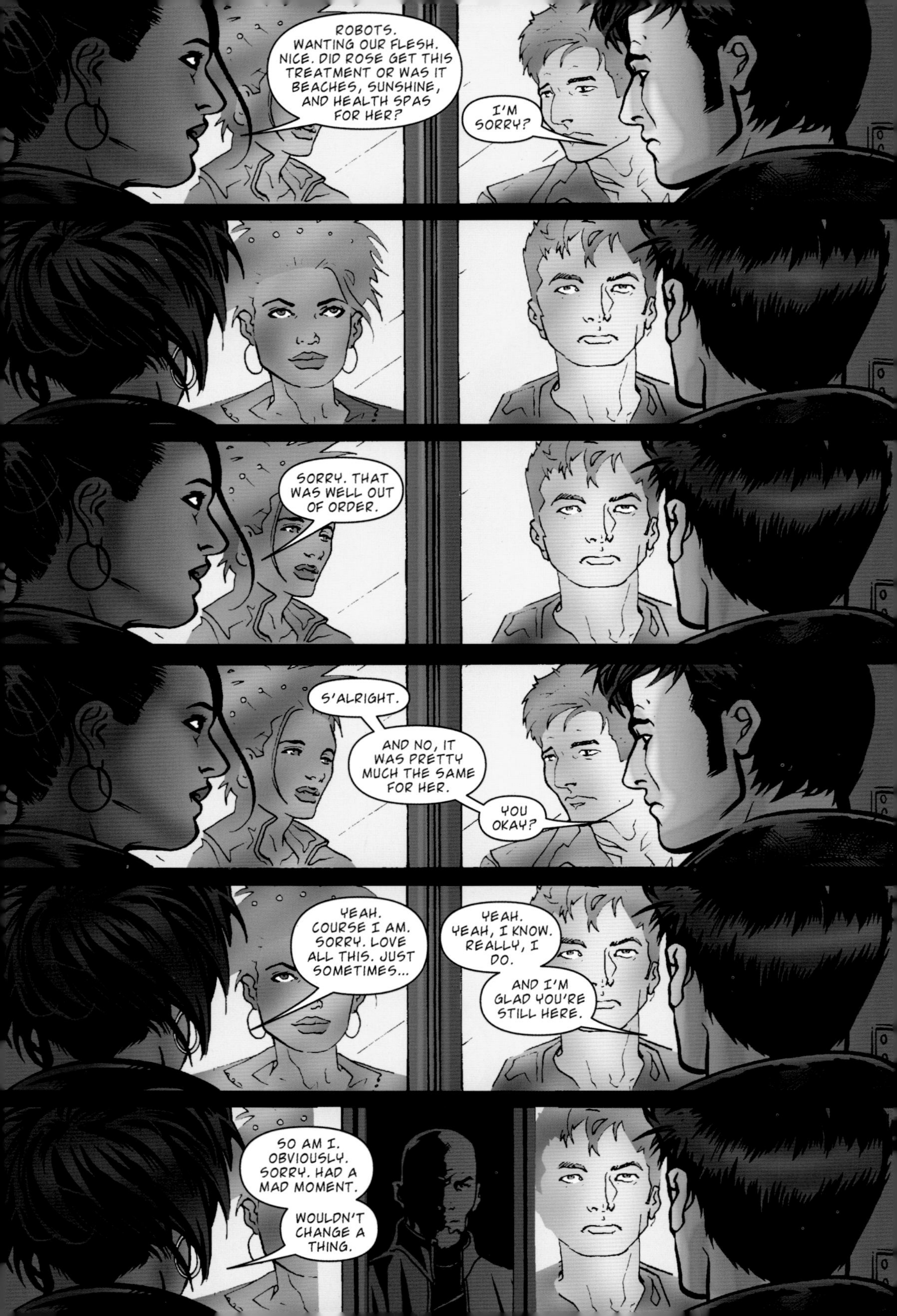
ROBOTS. WANTING OUR FLESH. NICE. DID ROSE GET THIS TREATMENT OR WAS IT BEACHES, SUNSHINE, AND HEALTH SPAS FOR HER?
I'M SORRY?
SORRY. THAT WAS WELL OUT OF ORDER.
S'ALRIGHT.
AND NO, IT WAS PRETTY MUCH THE SAME FOR HER.
YOU OKAY?
YEAH. COURSE I AM. SORRY. LOVE ALL THIS. JUST SOMETIMES...
YEAH. YEAH, I KNOW. REALLY, I DO.
AND I'M GLAD YOU'RE STILL HERE.
SO AM I. OBVIOUSLY. SORRY. HAD A MAD MOMENT.
WOULDN'T CHANGE A THING.

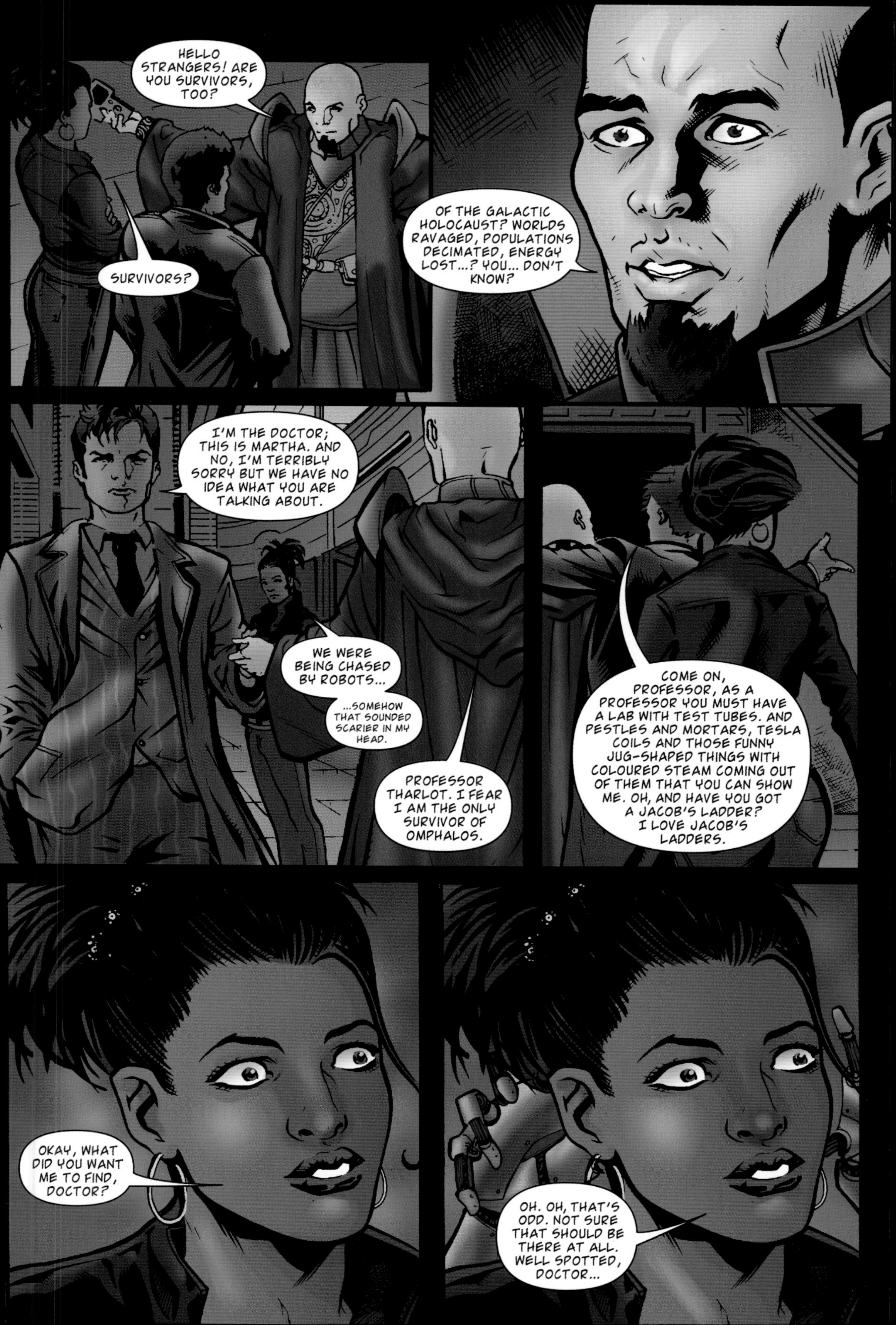
HELLO STRANGERS! ARE YOU SURVIVORS, TOO?
SURVIVORS?
OF THE GALACTIC HOLOCAUST? WORLDS RAVAGED, POPULATIONS DECIMATED, ENERGY LOST...? YOU... DON'T KNOW?
I'M THE DOCTOR; THIS IS MARTHA. AND NO, I'M TERRIBLY SORRY BUT WE HAVE NO IDEA WHAT YOU ARE TALKING ABOUT.
WE WERE BEING CHASED BY ROBOTS...
...SOMEHOW THAT SOUNDED SCARIER IN MY HEAD.
PROFESSOR THARLOT. I FEAR I AM THE ONLY SURVIVOR OF OMPHALOS.
COME ON, PROFESSOR, AS A PROFESSOR YOU MUST HAVE A LAB WITH TEST TUBES. AND PESTLES AND MORTARS, TESLA COILS AND THOSE FUNNY JUG-SHAPED THINGS WITH COLOURED STEAM COMING OUT OF THEM THAT YOU CAN SHOW ME. OH, AND HAVE YOU GOT A JACOB'S LADDER? I LOVE JACOB'S LADDERS.
OKAY, WHAT DID YOU WANT ME TO FIND, DOCTOR?
OH. OH, THAT'S ODD. NOT SURE THAT SHOULD BE THERE AT ALL. WELL SPOTTED, DOCTOR...

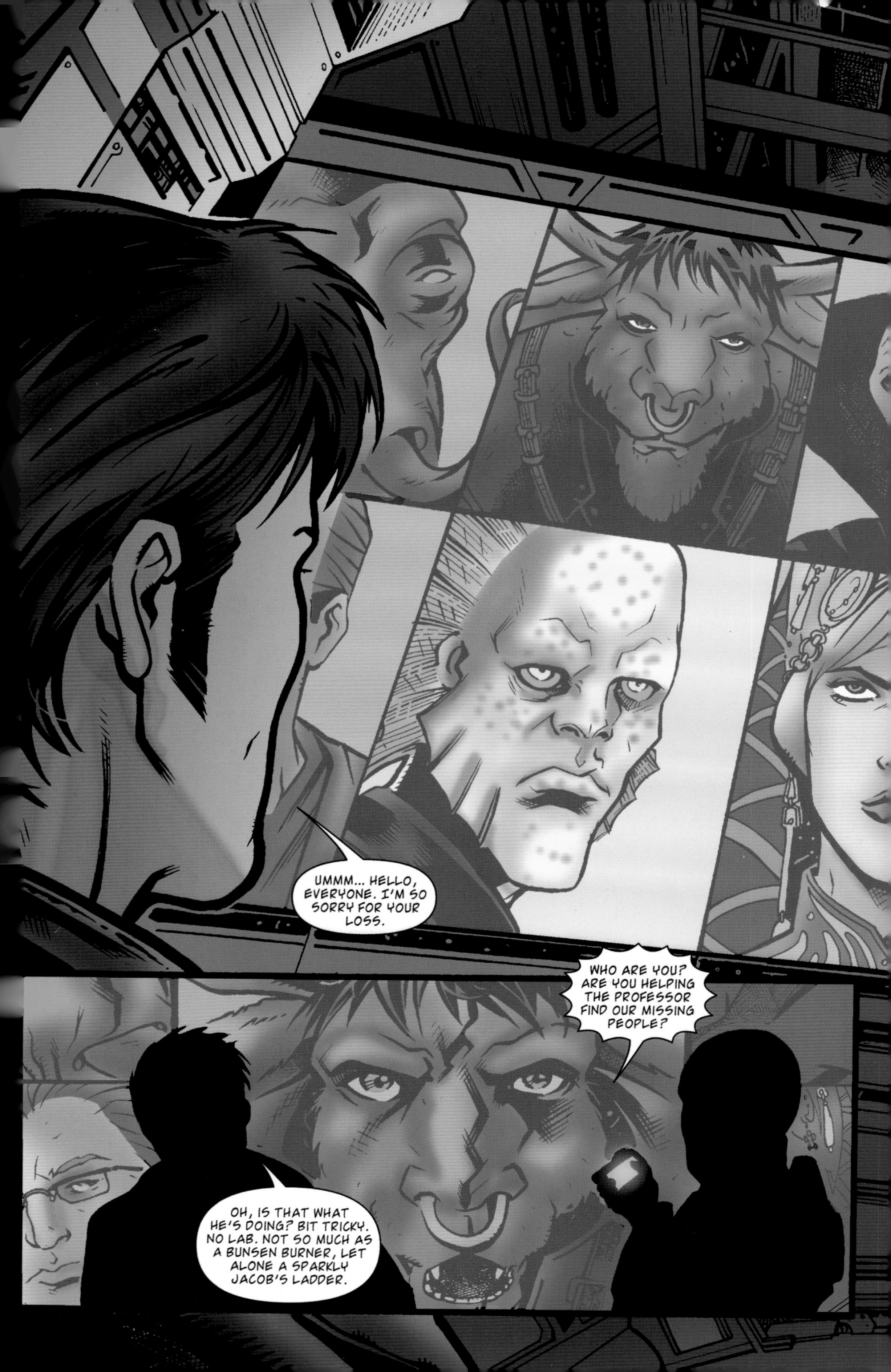
UMMM... HELLO, EVERYONE. I'M SO SORRY FOR YOUR LOSS.
WHO ARE YOU? ARE YOU HELPING THE PROFESSOR FIND OUR MISSING PEOPLE?
OH, IS THAT WHAT HE'S DOING? BIT TRICKY. NO LAB. NOT SO MUCH AS A BUNSEN BURNER, LET ALONE A SPARKLY JACOB'S LADDER.

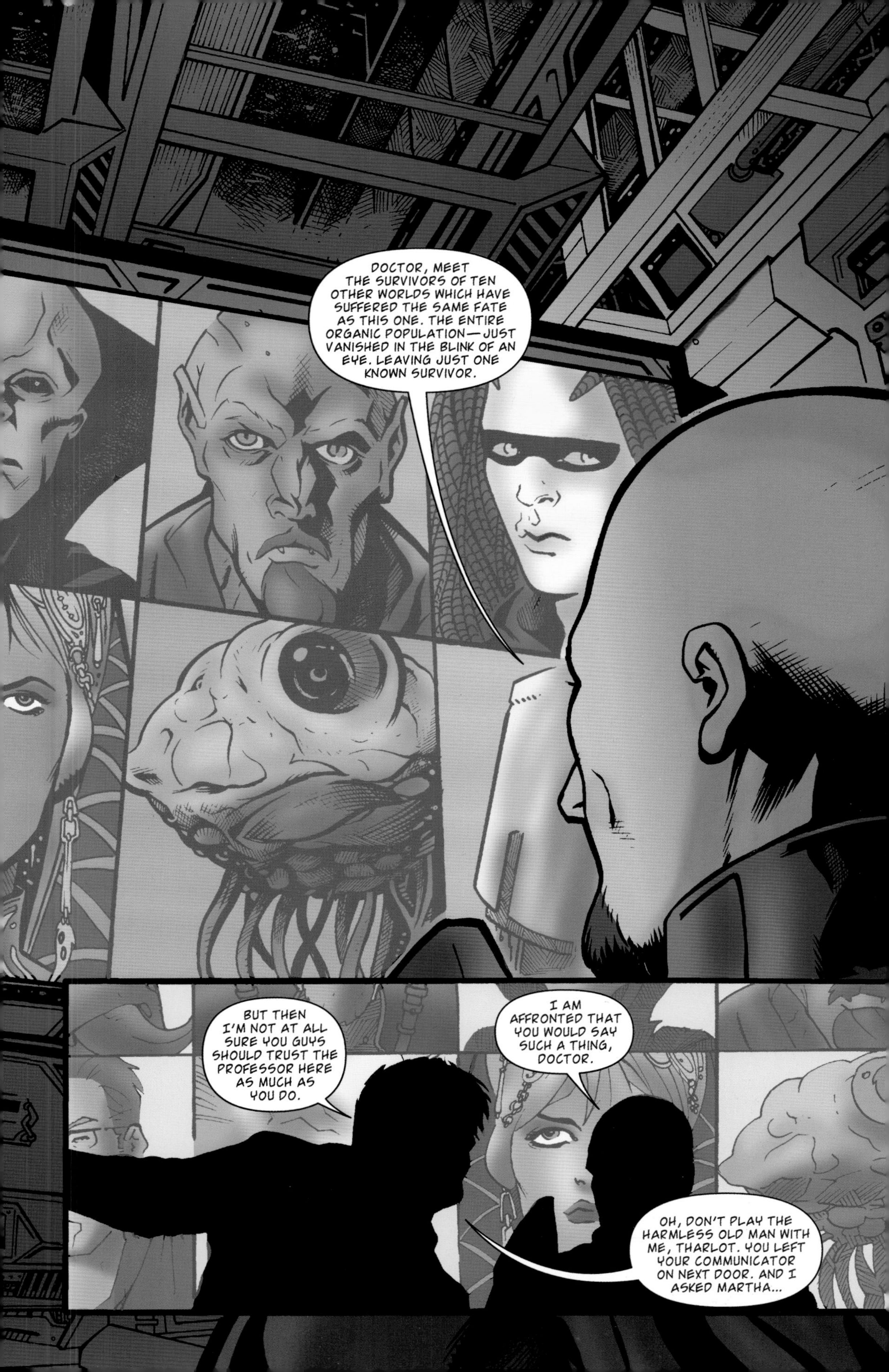
DOCTOR, MEET THE SURVIVORS OF TEN OTHER WORLDS WHICH HAVE SUFFERED THE SAME FATE AS THIS ONE. THE ENTIRE ORGANIC POPULATION— JUST VANISHED IN THE BLINK OF AN EYE. LEAVING JUST ONE KNOWN SURVIVOR.
BUT THEN I'M NOT AT ALL SURE YOU GUYS SHOULD TRUST THE PROFESSOR HERE AS MUCH AS YOU DO.
I AM AFFRONTED THAT YOU WOULD SAY SUCH A THING, DOCTOR.
OH, DON'T PLAY THE HARMLESS OLD MAN WITH ME, THARLOT. YOU LEFT YOUR COMMUNICATOR ON NEXT DOOR. AND I ASKED MARTHA...

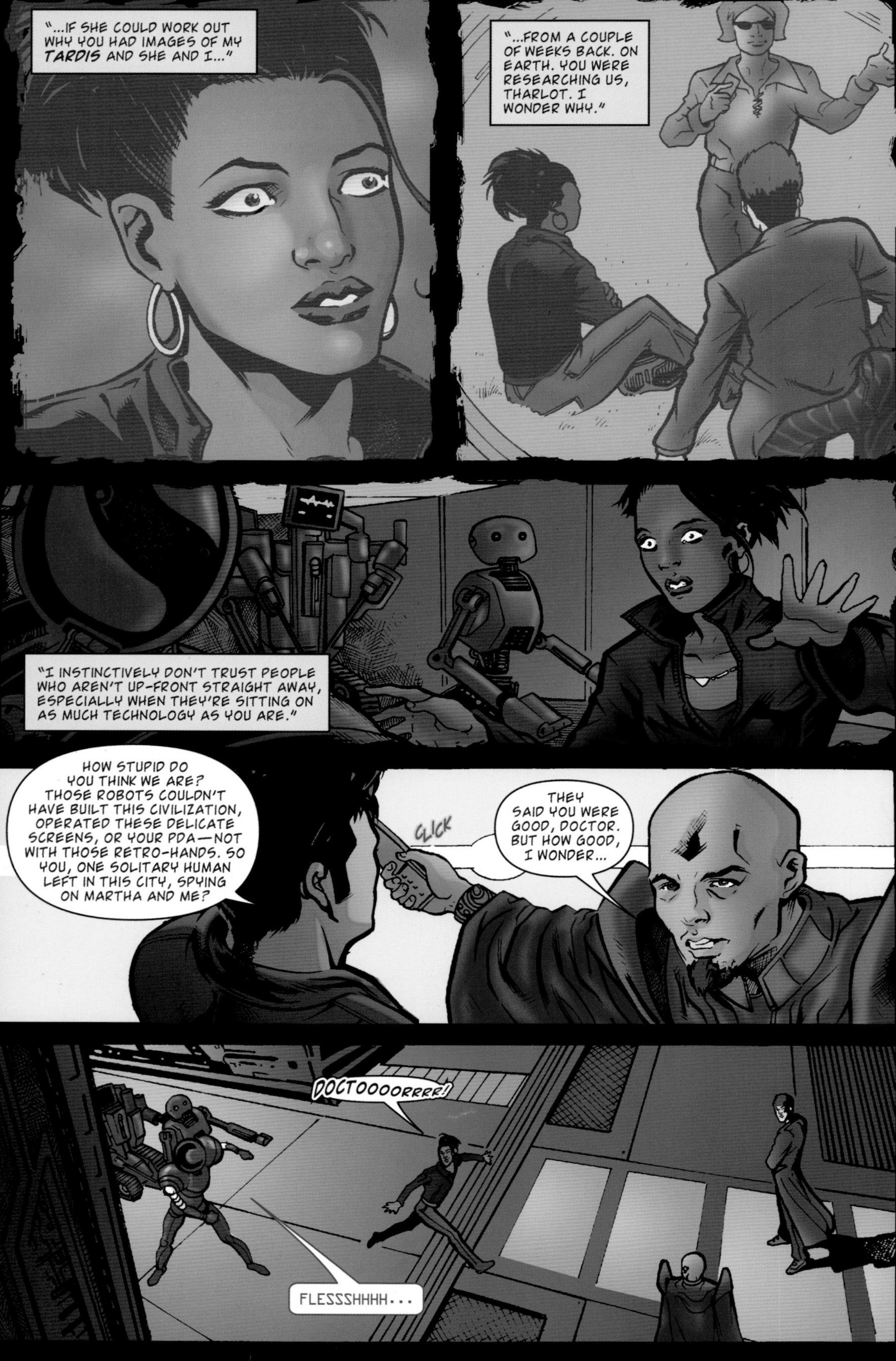
"...IF SHE COULD WORK OUT WHY YOU HAD IMAGES OF MY *TARDIS* AND SHE AND I..."
"...FROM A COUPLE OF WEEKS BACK. ON EARTH. YOU WERE RESEARCHING US, THARLOT. I WONDER WHY."
"I INSTINCTIVELY DON'T TRUST PEOPLE WHO AREN'T UP-FRONT STRAIGHT AWAY, ESPECIALLY WHEN THEY'RE SITTING ON AS MUCH TECHNOLOGY AS YOU ARE."
HOW STUPID DO YOU THINK WE ARE? THOSE ROBOTS COULDN'T HAVE BUILT THIS CIVILIZATION, OPERATED THESE DELICATE SCREENS, OR YOUR PDA—NOT WITH THOSE RETRO-HANDS. SO YOU, ONE SOLITARY HUMAN LEFT IN THIS CITY, SPYING ON MARTHA AND ME?
CLICK
THEY SAID YOU WERE GOOD, DOCTOR. BUT HOW GOOD, I WONDER...
DOCTOOOORRRR!
FLESSSHHHH...

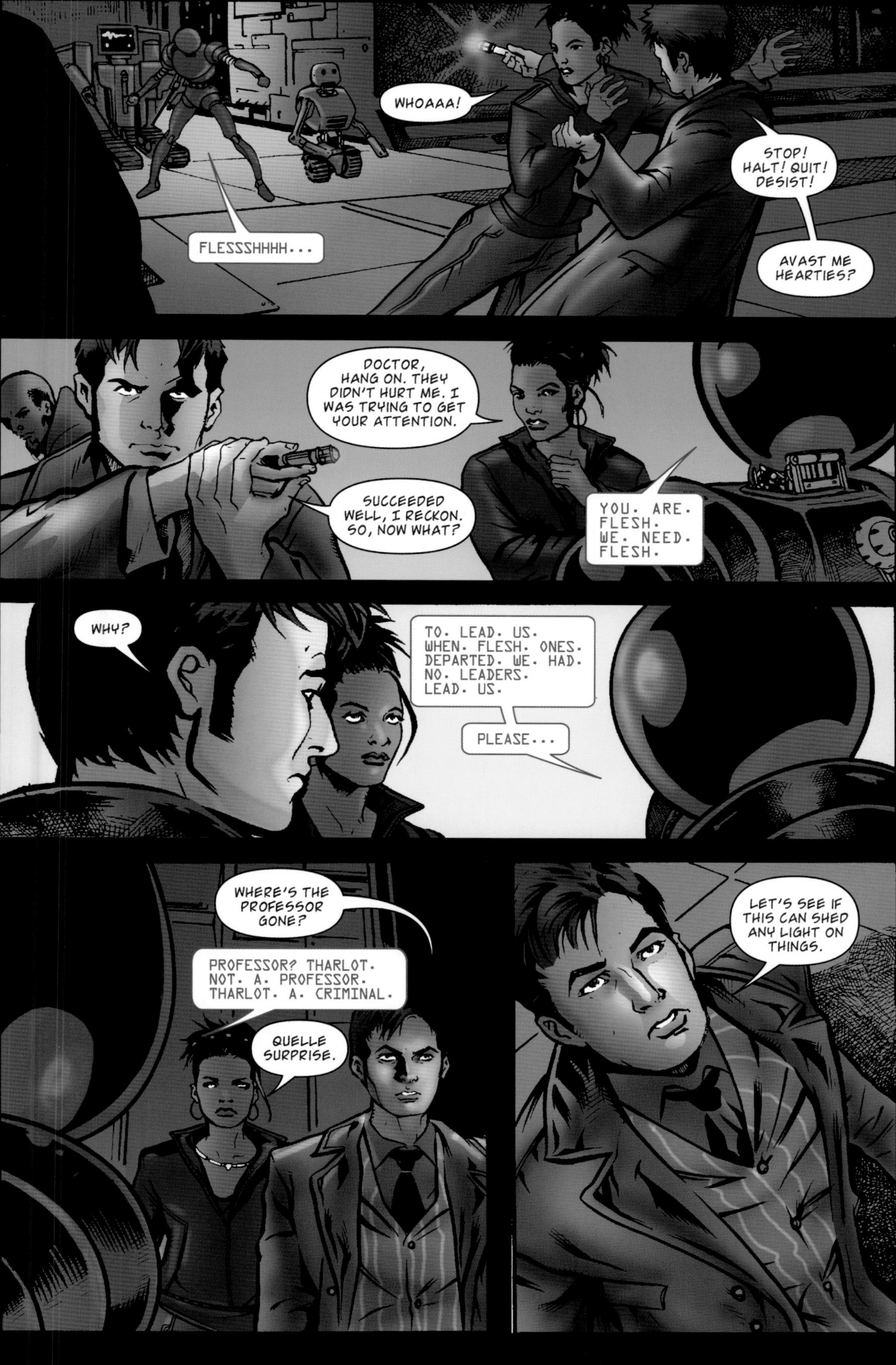
WHOAAA!
FLESSSHHHH...
STOP! HALT! QUIT! DESIST!
AVAST ME HEARTIES?
DOCTOR, HANG ON. THEY DIDN'T HURT ME. I WAS TRYING TO GET YOUR ATTENTION.
SUCCEEDED WELL, I RECKON. SO, NOW WHAT?
YOU. ARE. FLESH. WE. NEED. FLESH.
WHY?
TO. LEAD. US. WHEN. FLESH. ONES. DEPARTED. WE. HAD. NO. LEADERS. LEAD. US.
PLEASE...
WHERE'S THE PROFESSOR GONE?
PROFESSOR? THARLOT. NOT. A. PROFESSOR. THARLOT. A. CRIMINAL.
QUELLE SURPRISE.
LET'S SEE IF THIS CAN SHED ANY LIGHT ON THINGS.

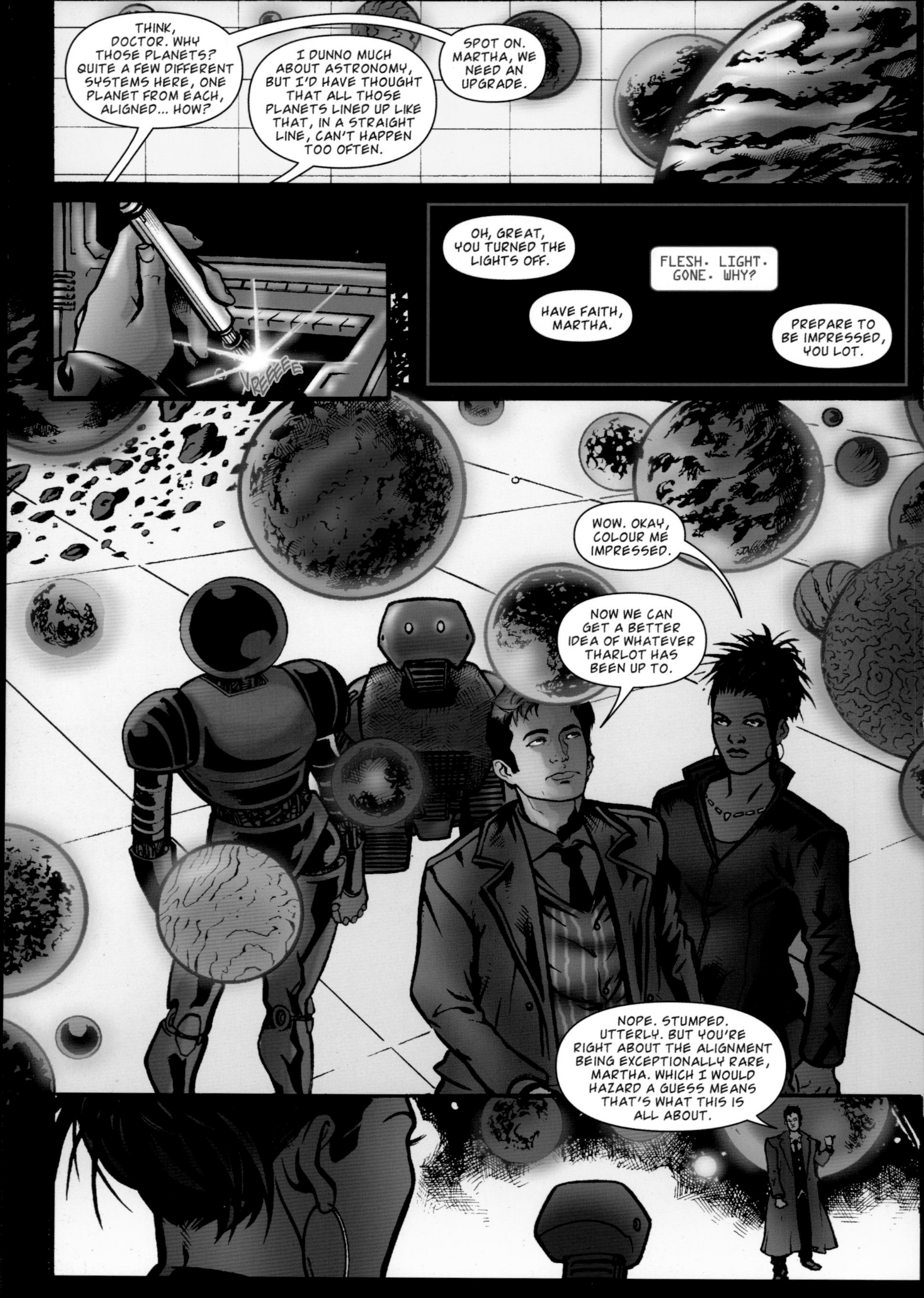
THINK, DOCTOR. WHY THOSE PLANETS? QUITE A FEW DIFFERENT SYSTEMS HERE, ONE PLANET FROM EACH, ALIGNED... HOW?
I DUNNO MUCH ABOUT ASTRONOMY, BUT I'D HAVE THOUGHT THAT ALL THOSE PLANETS LINED UP LIKE THAT, IN A STRAIGHT LINE, CAN'T HAPPEN TOO OFTEN.
SPOT ON. MARTHA, WE NEED AN UPGRADE.
VREEEEE
OH, GREAT, YOU TURNED THE LIGHTS OFF.
FLESH. LIGHT. GONE. WHY?
HAVE FAITH, MARTHA.
PREPARE TO BE IMPRESSED, YOU LOT.
WOW. OKAY, COLOUR ME IMPRESSED.
NOW WE CAN GET A BETTER IDEA OF WHATEVER THARLOT HAS BEEN UP TO.
NOPE. STUMPED. UTTERLY. BUT YOU'RE RIGHT ABOUT THE ALIGNMENT BEING EXCEPTIONALLY RARE, MARTHA. WHICH I WOULD HAZARD A GUESS MEANS THAT'S WHAT THIS IS ALL ABOUT.

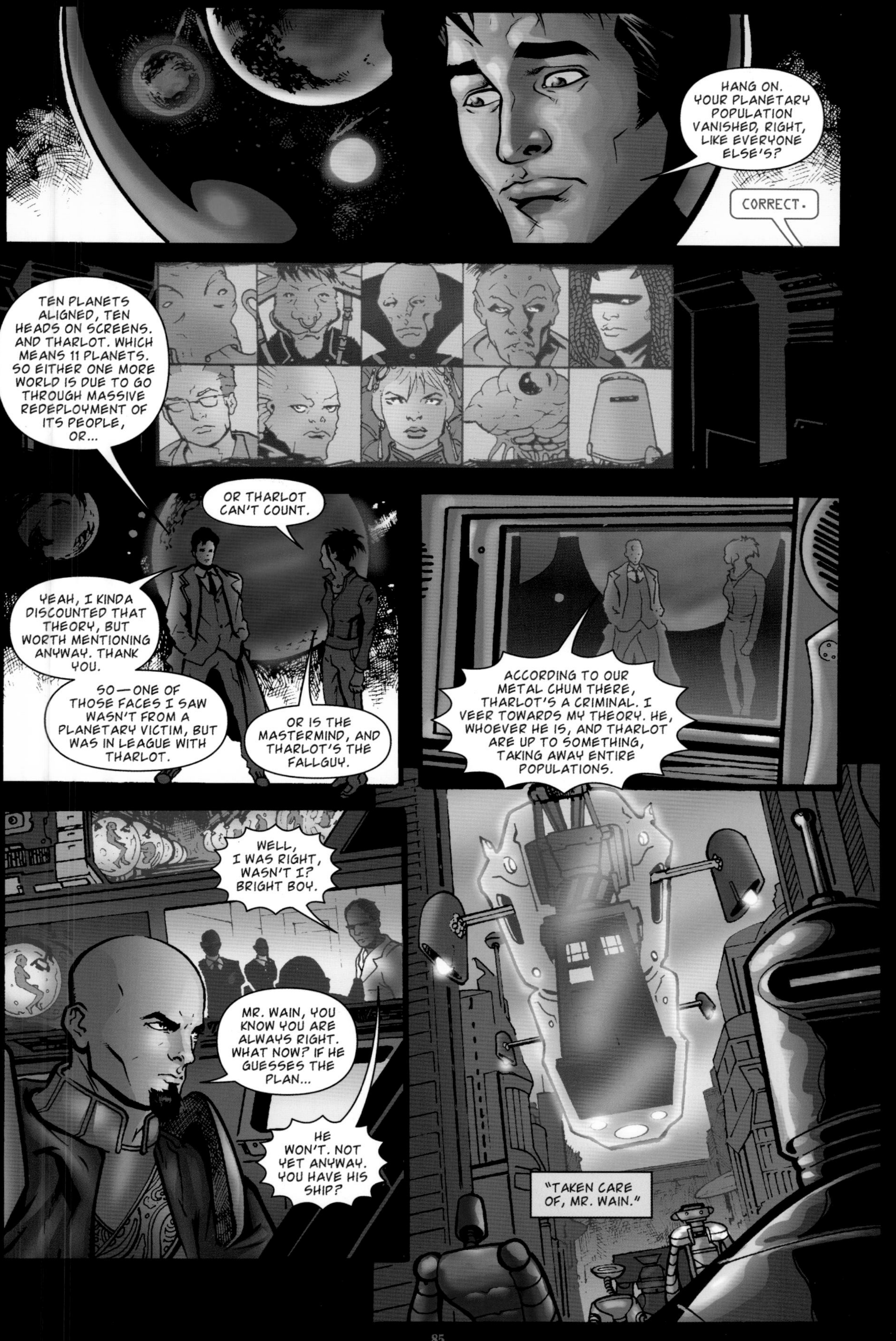
HANG ON. YOUR PLANETARY POPULATION VANISHED, RIGHT, LIKE EVERYONE ELSE'S?
CORRECT.
TEN PLANETS ALIGNED, TEN HEADS ON SCREENS. AND THARLOT. WHICH MEANS 11 PLANETS. SO EITHER ONE MORE WORLD IS DUE TO GO THROUGH MASSIVE REDEPLOYMENT OF ITS PEOPLE, OR...
OR THARLOT CAN'T COUNT.
YEAH, I KINDA DISCOUNTED THAT THEORY, BUT WORTH MENTIONING ANYWAY. THANK YOU.
SO—ONE OF THOSE FACES I SAW WASN'T FROM A PLANETARY VICTIM, BUT WAS IN LEAGUE WITH THARLOT.
OR IS THE MASTERMIND, AND THARLOT'S THE FALLGUY.
ACCORDING TO OUR METAL CHUM THERE, THARLOT'S A CRIMINAL. I VEER TOWARDS MY THEORY. HE, WHOEVER HE IS, AND THARLOT ARE UP TO SOMETHING, TAKING AWAY ENTIRE POPULATIONS.
WELL, I WAS RIGHT, WASN'T I? BRIGHT BOY.
MR. WAIN, YOU KNOW YOU ARE ALWAYS RIGHT. WHAT NOW? IF HE GUESSES THE PLAN...
HE WON'T. NOT YET ANYWAY. YOU HAVE HIS SHIP?
"TAKEN CARE OF, MR. WAIN."

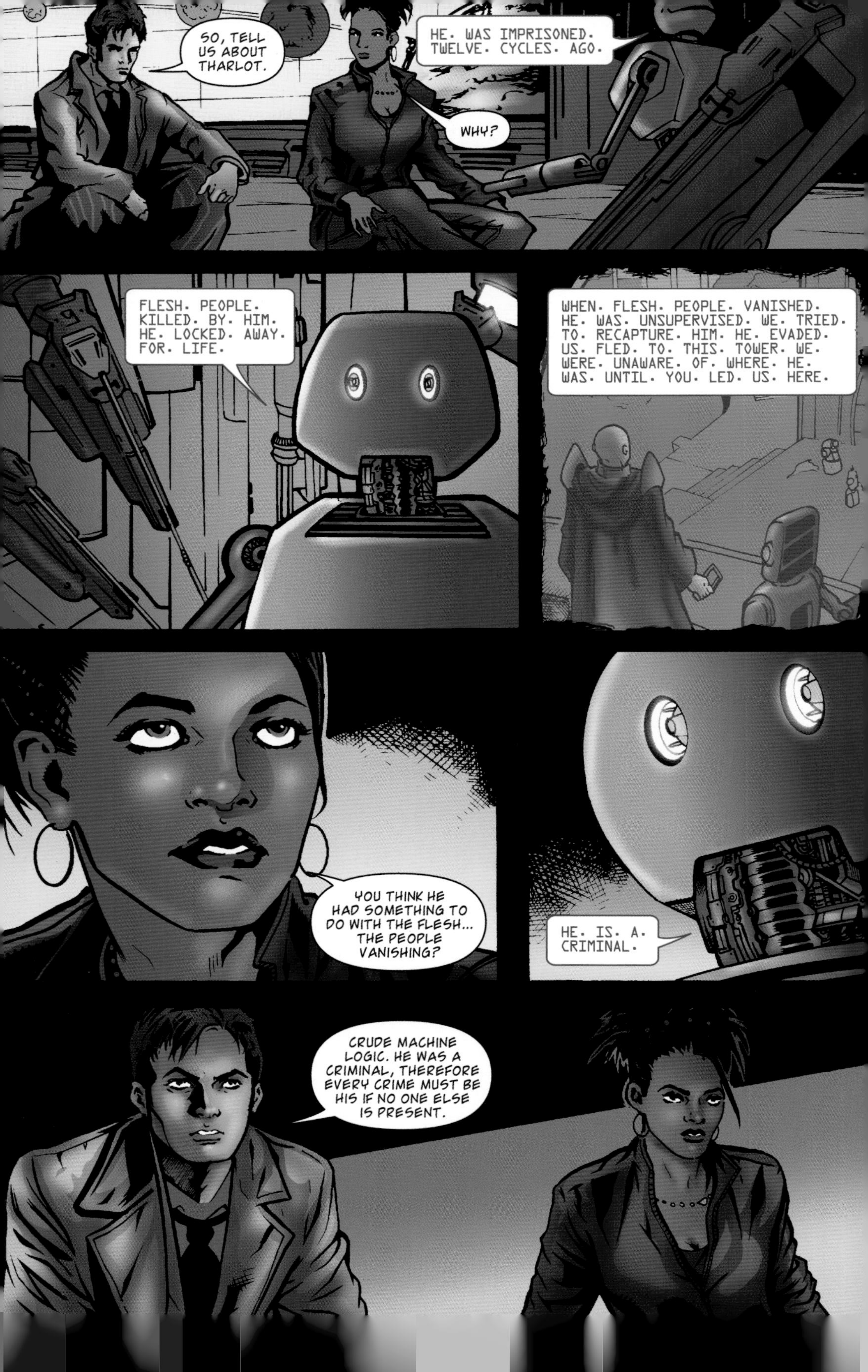
SO, TELL US ABOUT THARLOT.
HE. WAS IMPRISONED. TWELVE. CYCLES. AGO.
WHY?
FLESH. PEOPLE. KILLED. BY. HIM. HE. LOCKED. AWAY. FOR. LIFE.
WHEN. FLESH. PEOPLE. VANISHED. HE. WAS. UNSUPERVISED. WE. TRIED. TO. RECAPTURE. HIM. HE. EVADED. US. FLED. TO. THIS. TOWER. WE. WERE. UNAWARE. OF. WHERE. HE. WAS. UNTIL. YOU. LED. US. HERE.
YOU THINK HE HAD SOMETHING TO DO WITH THE FLESH... THE PEOPLE VANISHING?
HE. IS. A. CRIMINAL.
CRUDE MACHINE LOGIC. HE WAS A CRIMINAL, THEREFORE EVERY CRIME MUST BE HIS IF NO ONE ELSE IS PRESENT.

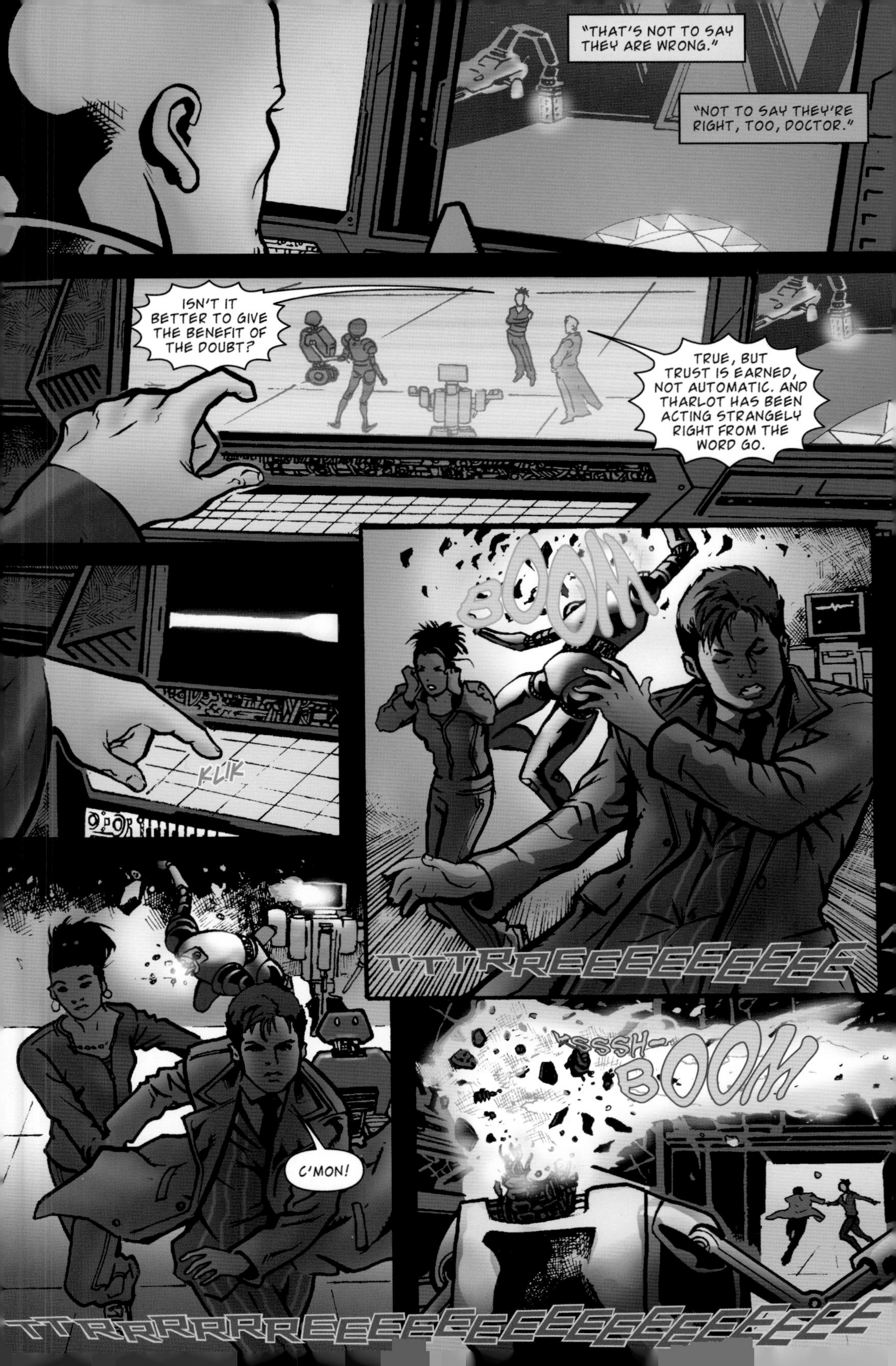
"THAT'S NOT TO SAY THEY ARE WRONG."
"NOT TO SAY THEY'RE RIGHT, TOO, DOCTOR."
ISN'T IT BETTER TO GIVE THE BENEFIT OF THE DOUBT?
TRUE, BUT TRUST IS EARNED, NOT AUTOMATIC. AND THARLOT HAS BEEN ACTING STRANGELY RIGHT FROM THE WORD GO.
KLIK
BOOM
TTTRREEEEEEEEEE
C'MON!
KSSSH-BOOM
TTRRRRRRREEEEEEEEEEEEEEEEEEEE

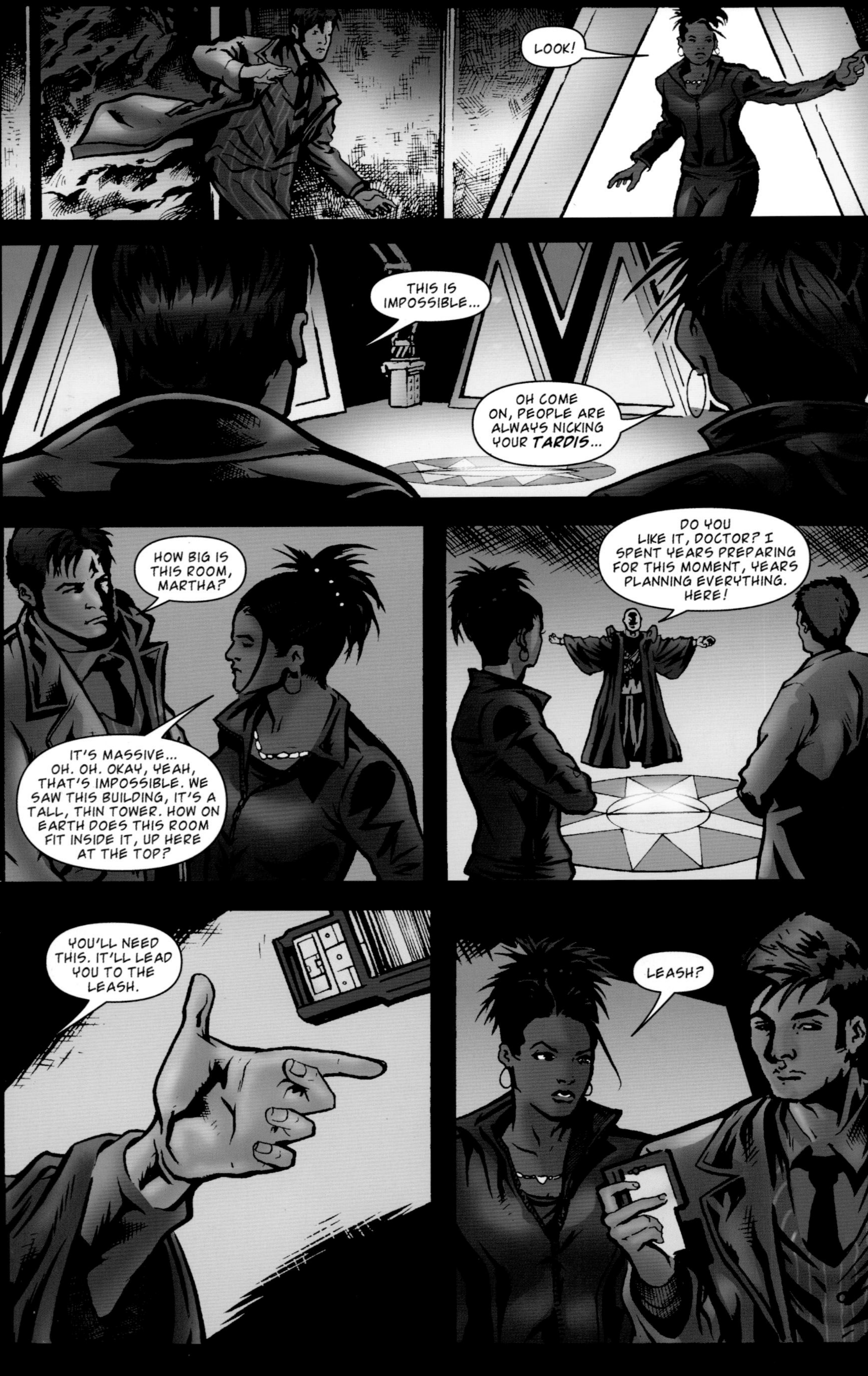
LOOK!
THIS IS IMPOSSIBLE...
OH COME ON, PEOPLE ARE ALWAYS NICKING YOUR TARDIS...
HOW BIG IS THIS ROOM, MARTHA?
IT'S MASSIVE... OH. OH. OKAY, YEAH, THAT'S IMPOSSIBLE. WE SAW THIS BUILDING, IT'S A TALL, THIN TOWER. HOW ON EARTH DOES THIS ROOM FIT INSIDE IT, UP HERE AT THE TOP?
DO YOU LIKE IT, DOCTOR? I SPENT YEARS PREPARING FOR THIS MOMENT, YEARS PLANNING EVERYTHING. HERE!
YOU'LL NEED THIS. IT'LL LEAD YOU TO THE LEASH.
LEASH?

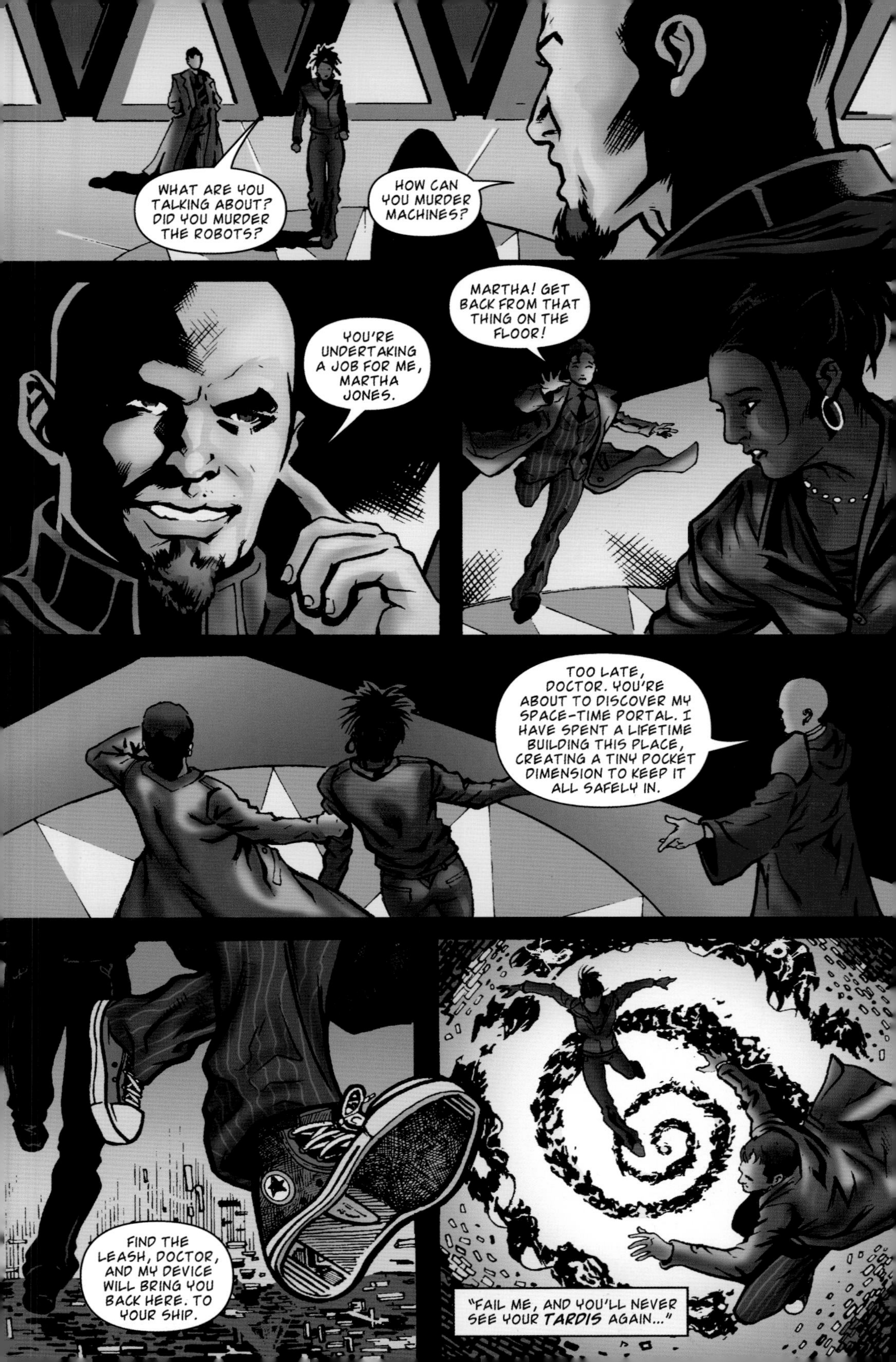
WHAT ARE YOU TALKING ABOUT? DID YOU MURDER THE ROBOTS?
HOW CAN YOU MURDER MACHINES?
YOU'RE UNDERTAKING A JOB FOR ME, MARTHA JONES.
MARTHA! GET BACK FROM THAT THING ON THE FLOOR!
TOO LATE, DOCTOR. YOU'RE ABOUT TO DISCOVER MY SPACE-TIME PORTAL. I HAVE SPENT A LIFETIME BUILDING THIS PLACE, CREATING A TINY POCKET DIMENSION TO KEEP IT ALL SAFELY IN.
FIND THE LEASH, DOCTOR, AND MY DEVICE WILL BRING YOU BACK HERE. TO YOUR SHIP.
"FAIL ME, AND YOU'LL NEVER SEE YOUR *TARDIS* AGAIN..."

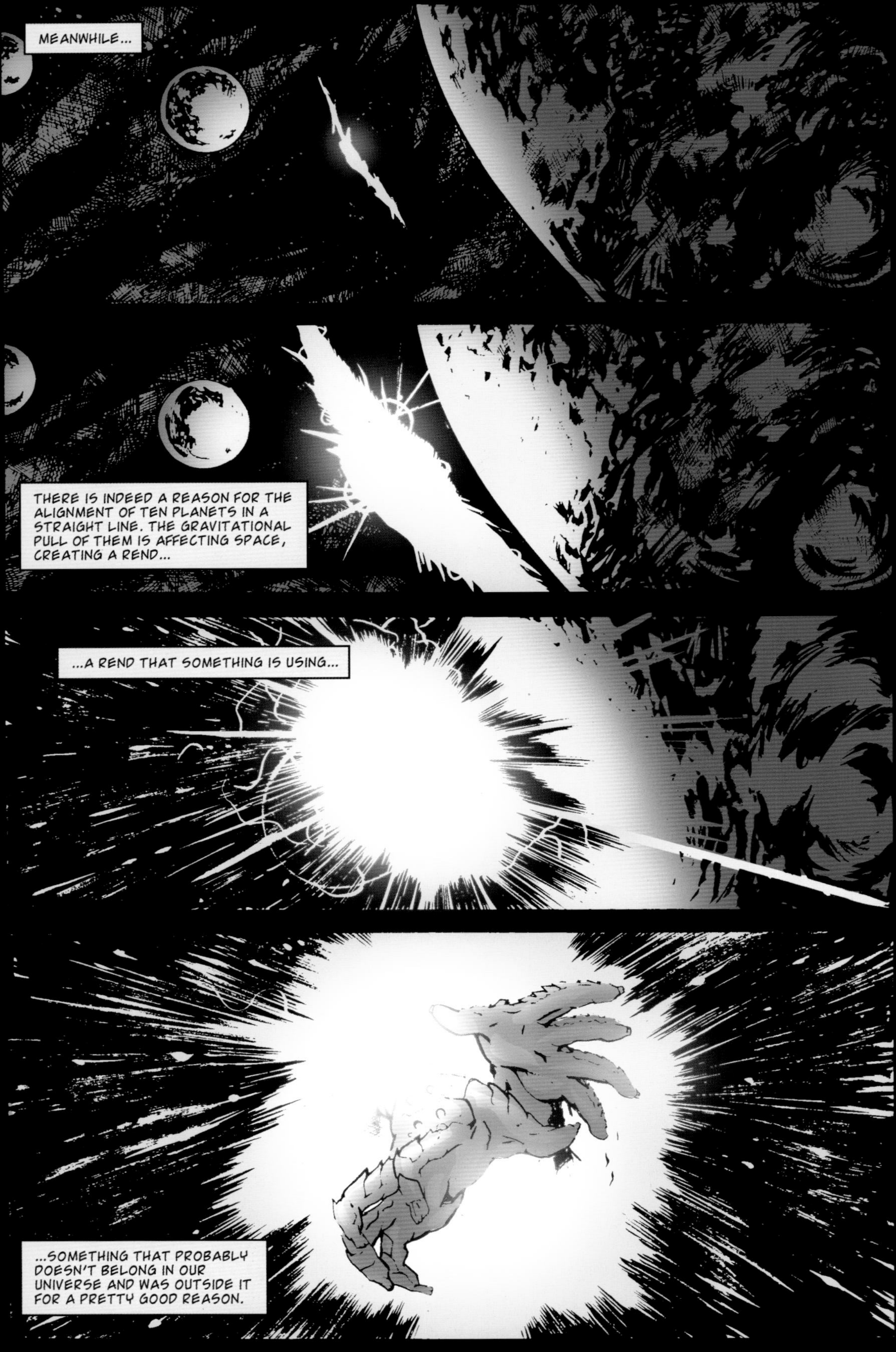
MEANWHILE...
THERE IS INDEED A REASON FOR THE ALIGNMENT OF TEN PLANETS IN A STRAIGHT LINE. THE GRAVITATIONAL PULL OF THEM IS AFFECTING SPACE, CREATING A REND...
...A REND THAT SOMETHING IS USING...
...SOMETHING THAT PROBABLY DOESN'T BELONG IN OUR UNIVERSE AND WAS OUTSIDE IT FOR A PRETTY GOOD REASON.

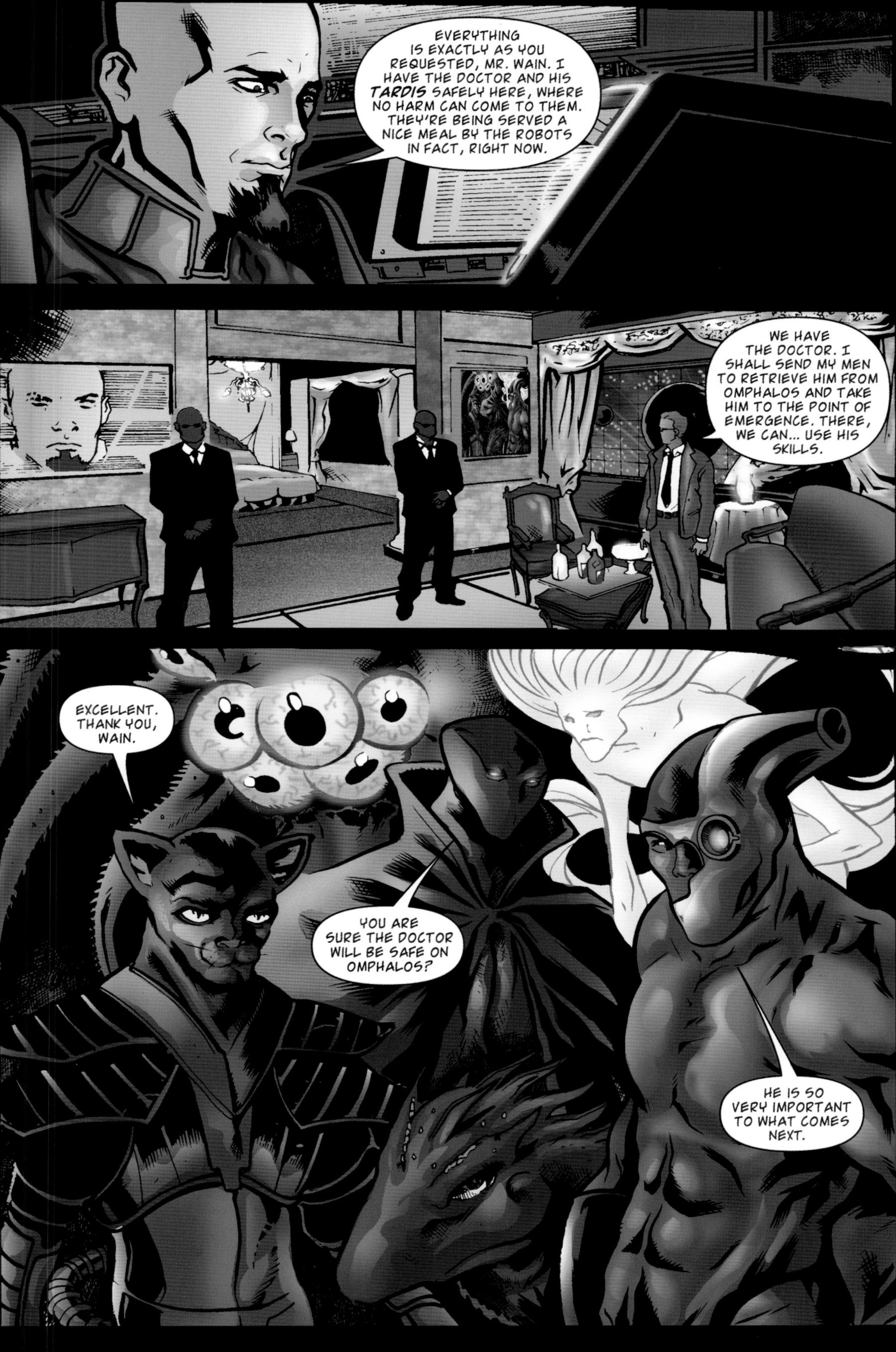
EVERYTHING IS EXACTLY AS YOU REQUESTED, MR. WAIN. I HAVE THE DOCTOR AND HIS TARDIS SAFELY HERE, WHERE NO HARM CAN COME TO THEM. THEY'RE BEING SERVED A NICE MEAL BY THE ROBOTS IN FACT, RIGHT NOW.
WE HAVE THE DOCTOR. I SHALL SEND MY MEN TO RETRIEVE HIM FROM OMPHALOS AND TAKE HIM TO THE POINT OF EMERGENCE. THERE, WE CAN... USE HIS SKILLS.
EXCELLENT. THANK YOU, WAIN.
YOU ARE SURE THE DOCTOR WILL BE SAFE ON OMPHALOS?
HE IS SO VERY IMPORTANT TO WHAT COMES NEXT.

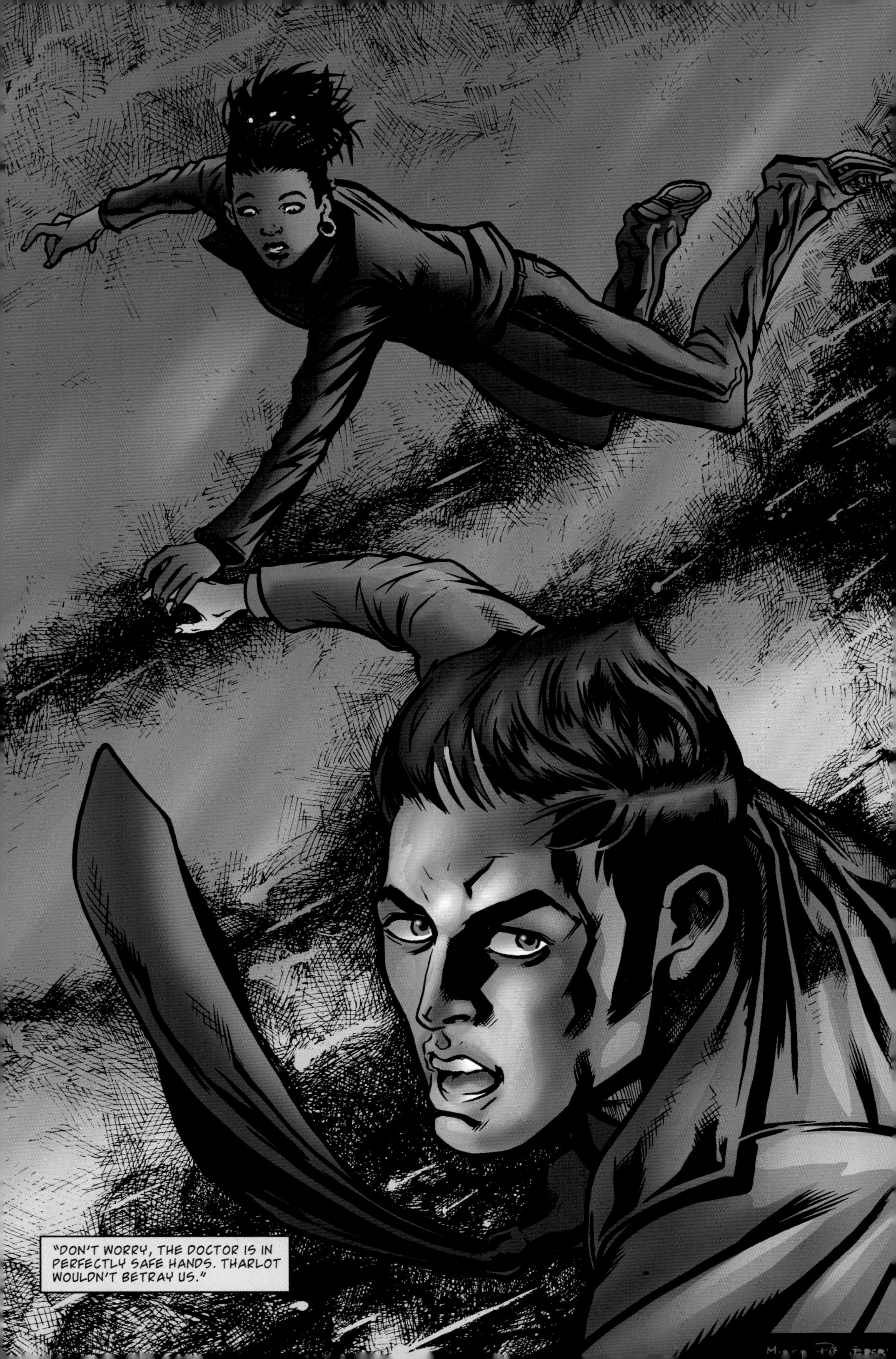
"DON'T WORRY, THE DOCTOR IS IN PERFECTLY SAFE HANDS. THARLOT WOULDN'T BETRAY US."

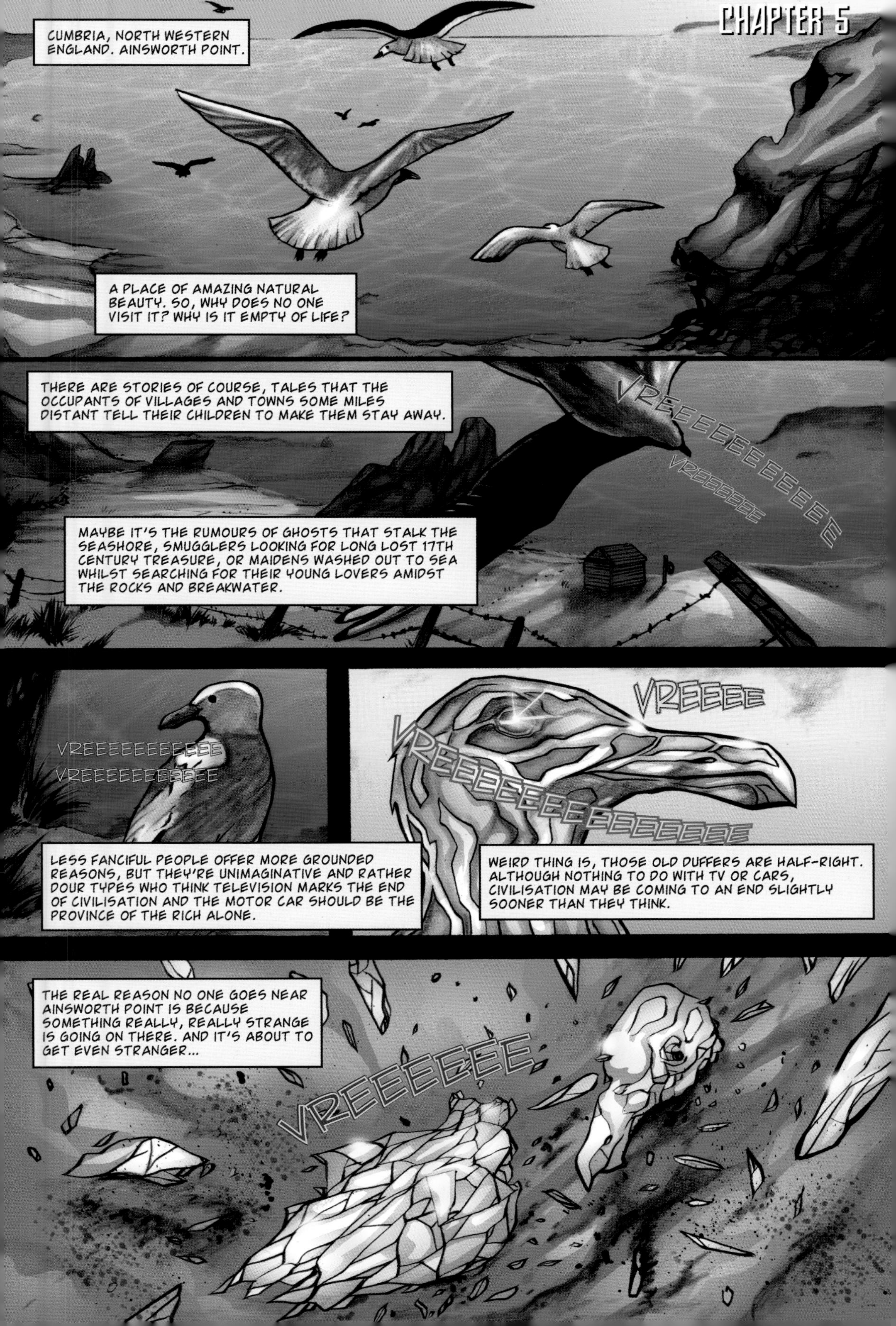
CHAPTER 5
CUMBRIA, NORTH WESTERN ENGLAND. AINSWORTH POINT.
A PLACE OF AMAZING NATURAL BEAUTY. SO, WHY DOES NO ONE VISIT IT? WHY IS IT EMPTY OF LIFE?
THERE ARE STORIES OF COURSE, TALES THAT THE OCCUPANTS OF VILLAGES AND TOWNS SOME MILES DISTANT TELL THEIR CHILDREN TO MAKE THEM STAY AWAY.
VREEEEEEEEEEEEE
VREEEEEEE
MAYBE IT'S THE RUMOURS OF GHOSTS THAT STALK THE SEASHORE, SMUGGLERS LOOKING FOR LONG LOST 17TH CENTURY TREASURE, OR MAIDENS WASHED OUT TO SEA WHILST SEARCHING FOR THEIR YOUNG LOVERS AMIDST THE ROCKS AND BREAKWATER.
VREEEEEEEEEEEE
VREEEEEEEEEEEE
LESS FANCIFUL PEOPLE OFFER MORE GROUNDED REASONS, BUT THEY'RE UNIMAGINATIVE AND RATHER DOUR TYPES WHO THINK TELEVISION MARKS THE END OF CIVILISATION AND THE MOTOR CAR SHOULD BE THE PROVINCE OF THE RICH ALONE.
VREEEEE
VREEEEEEEEEEEEEEEEEEE
WEIRD THING IS, THOSE OLD DUFFERS ARE HALF-RIGHT. ALTHOUGH NOTHING TO DO WITH TV OR CARS, CIVILISATION MAY BE COMING TO AN END SLIGHTLY SOONER THAN THEY THINK.
THE REAL REASON NO ONE GOES NEAR AINSWORTH POINT IS BECAUSE SOMETHING REALLY, REALLY STRANGE IS GOING ON THERE. AND IT'S ABOUT TO GET EVEN STRANGER...
VREEEEEEEE

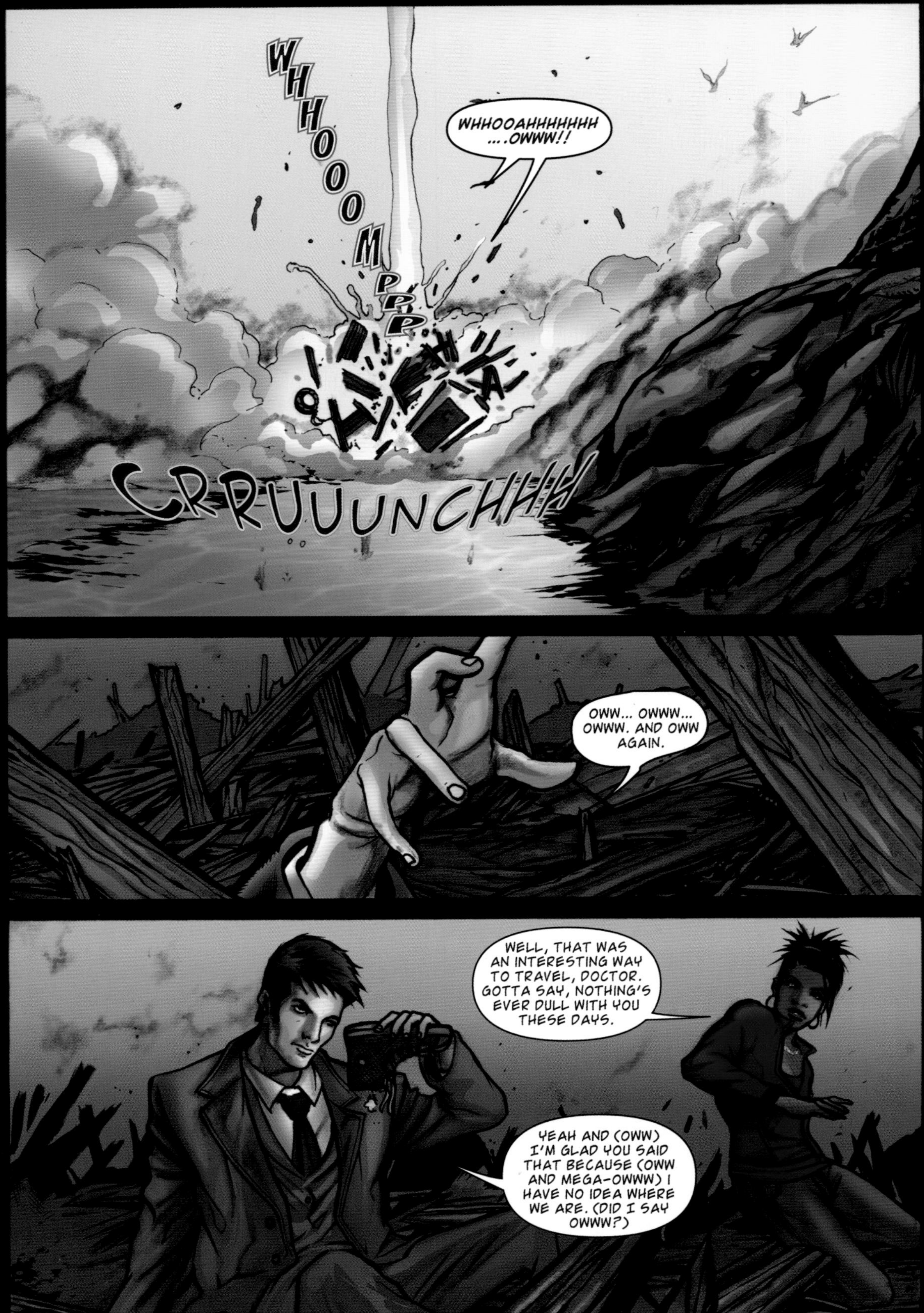
WHHOOOMPPP
WHHOOAHHHHHHH ....OWWW!!
CRRUUUNCHHH
OWW... OWWW... OWWW. AND OWW AGAIN.
WELL, THAT WAS AN INTERESTING WAY TO TRAVEL, DOCTOR. GOTTA SAY, NOTHING'S EVER DULL WITH YOU THESE DAYS.
YEAH AND (OWW) I'M GLAD YOU SAID THAT BECAUSE (OWW AND MEGA-OWWW) I HAVE NO IDEA WHERE WE ARE. (DID I SAY OWWW?)

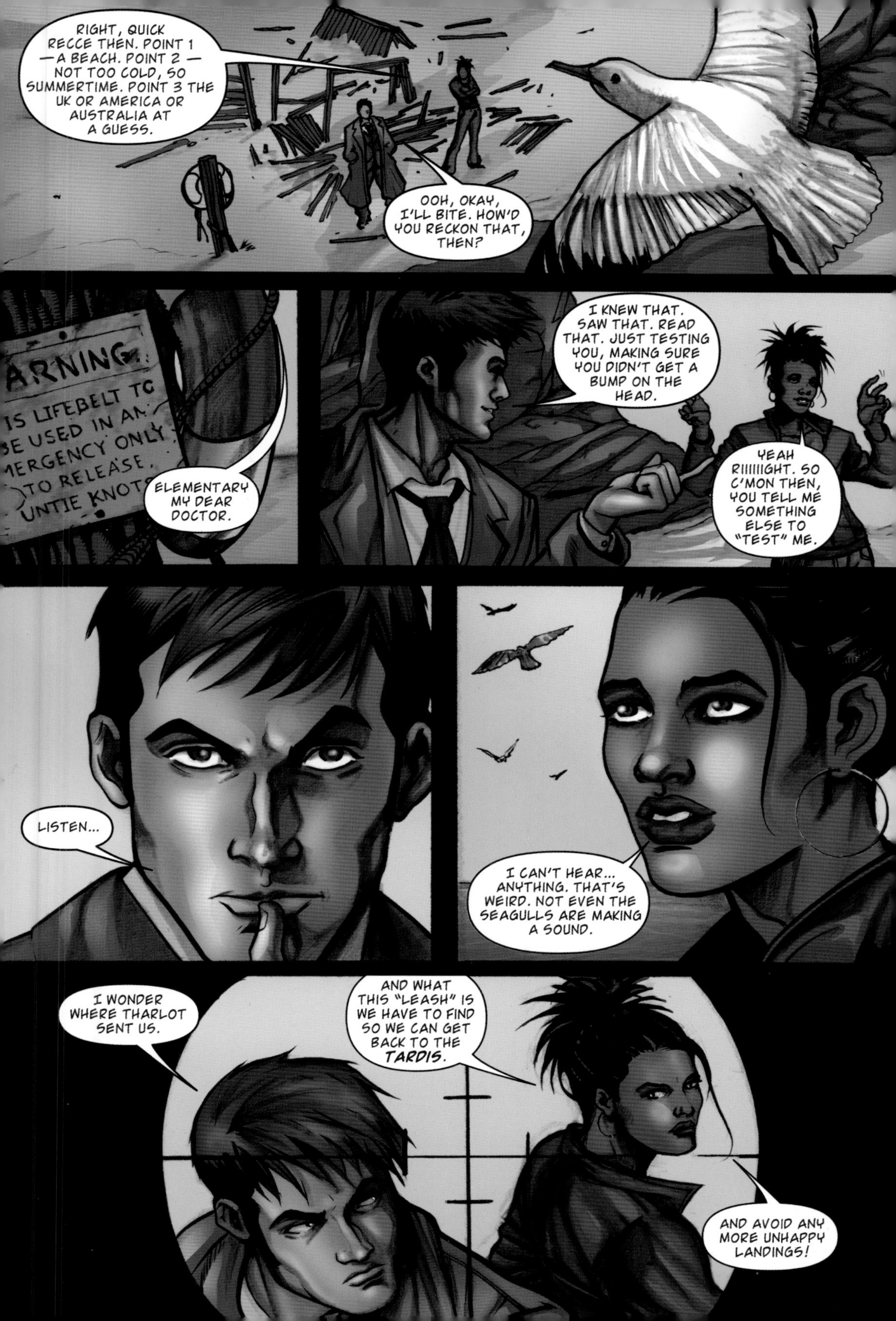
RIGHT, QUICK RECCE THEN. POINT 1 —A BEACH. POINT 2 — NOT TOO COLD, SO SUMMERTIME. POINT 3 THE UK OR AMERICA OR AUSTRALIA AT A GUESS.
OOH, OKAY, I'LL BITE. HOW'D YOU RECKON THAT, THEN?
ELEMENTARY MY DEAR DOCTOR.
I KNEW THAT. SAW THAT. READ THAT. JUST TESTING YOU, MAKING SURE YOU DIDN'T GET A BUMP ON THE HEAD.
YEAH RIIIIIIGHT. SO C'MON THEN, YOU TELL ME SOMETHING ELSE TO "TEST" ME.
LISTEN...
I CAN'T HEAR... ANYTHING. THAT'S WEIRD. NOT EVEN THE SEAGULLS ARE MAKING A SOUND.
I WONDER WHERE THARLOT SENT US.
AND WHAT THIS "LEASH" IS WE HAVE TO FIND SO WE CAN GET BACK TO THE *TARDIS*.
AND AVOID ANY MORE UNHAPPY LANDINGS!

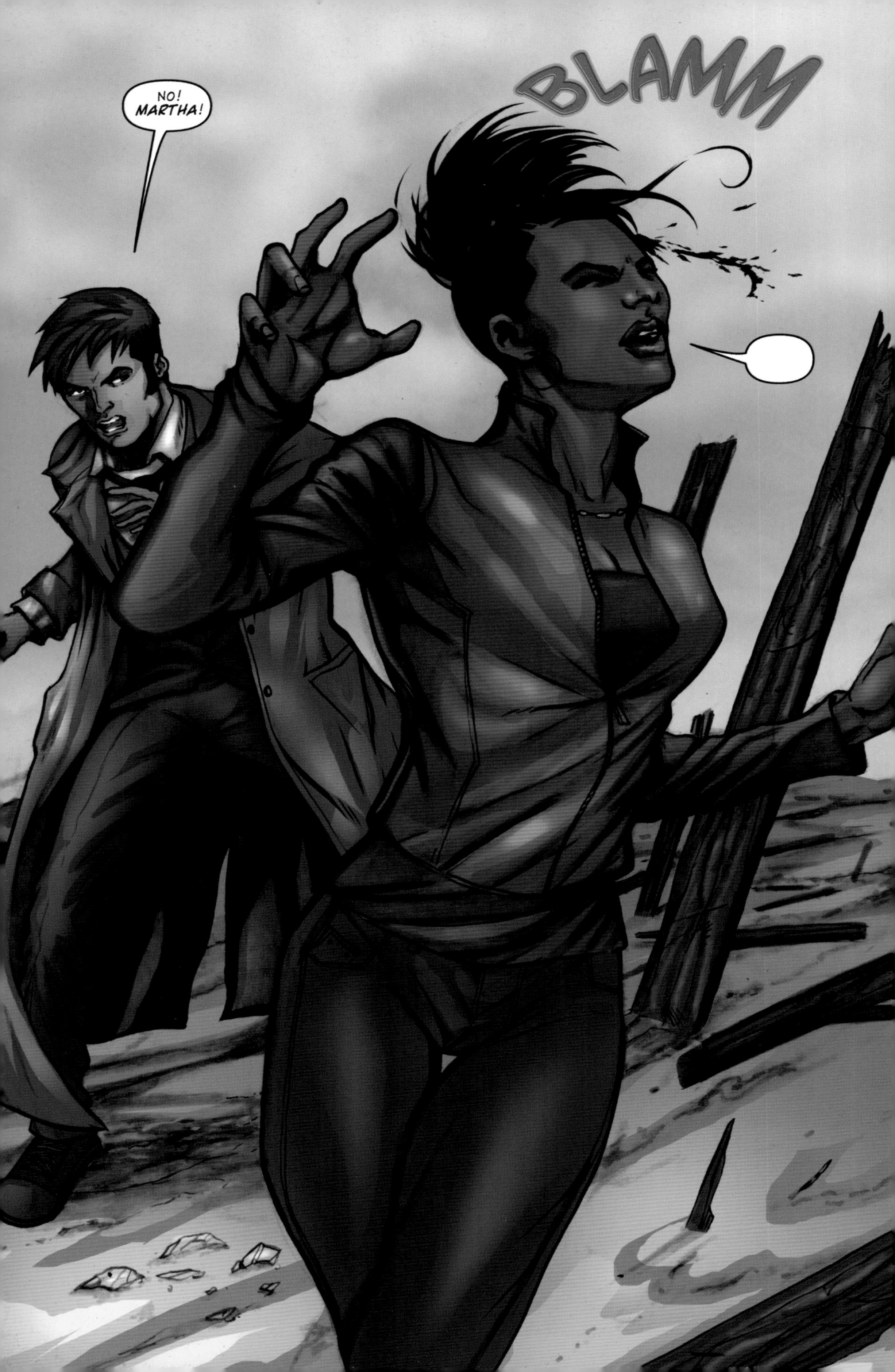
NO! MARTHA!
BLAMM

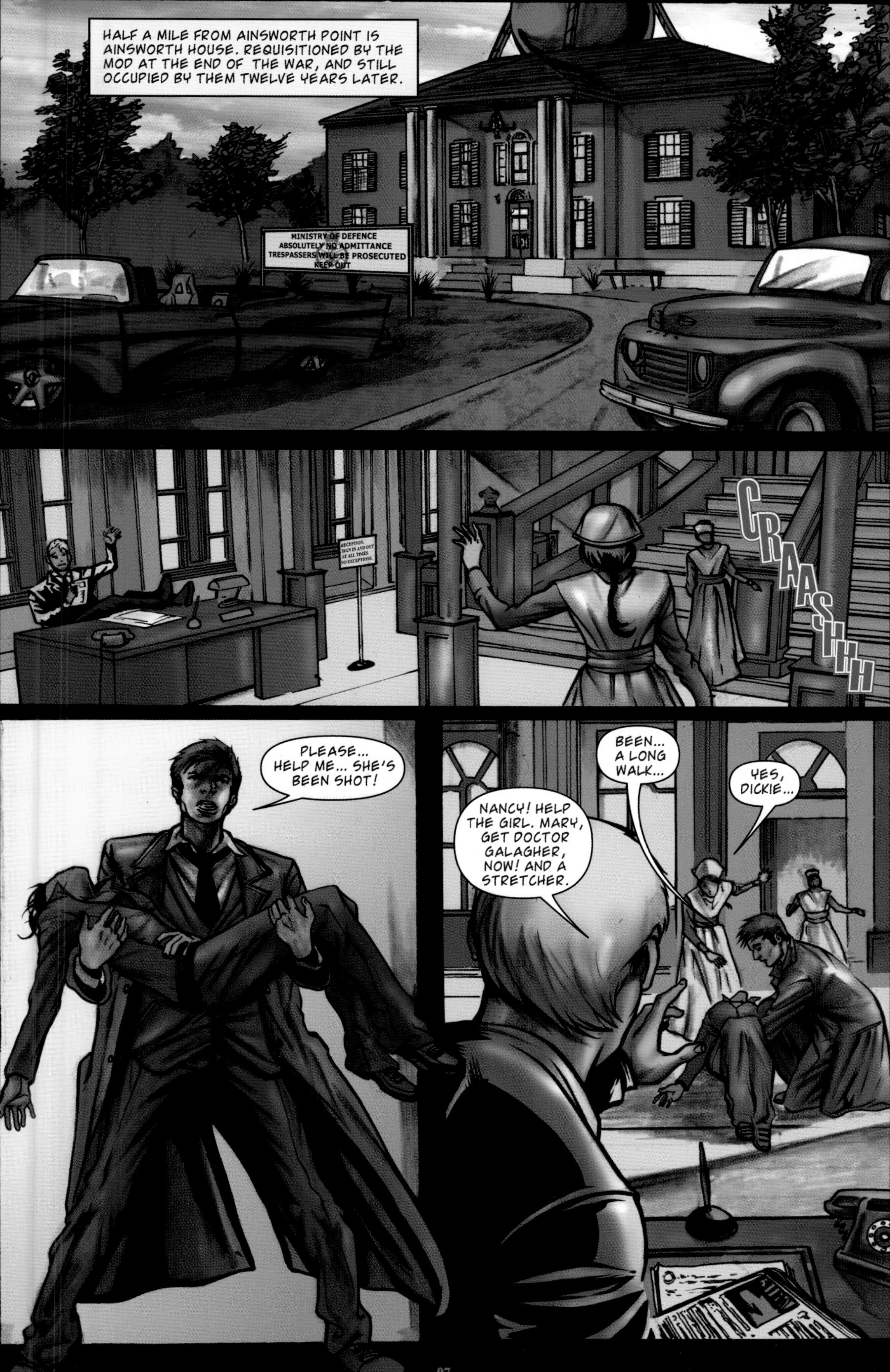
HALF A MILE FROM AINSWORTH POINT IS AINSWORTH HOUSE. REQUISITIONED BY THE MOD AT THE END OF THE WAR, AND STILL OCCUPIED BY THEM TWELVE YEARS LATER.
MINISTRY OF DEFENCE
ABSOLUTELY NO ADMITTANCE
TRESPASSERS WILL BE PROSECUTED
KEEP OUT
RECEPTION. SIGN IN AND OUT AT ALL TIMES. NO EXCEPTIONS.
CRAAASHHH
PLEASE... HELP ME... SHE'S BEEN SHOT!
NANCY! HELP THE GIRL. MARY, GET DOCTOR GALAGHER, NOW! AND A STRETCHER.
BEEN... A LONG WALK...
YES, DICKIE...

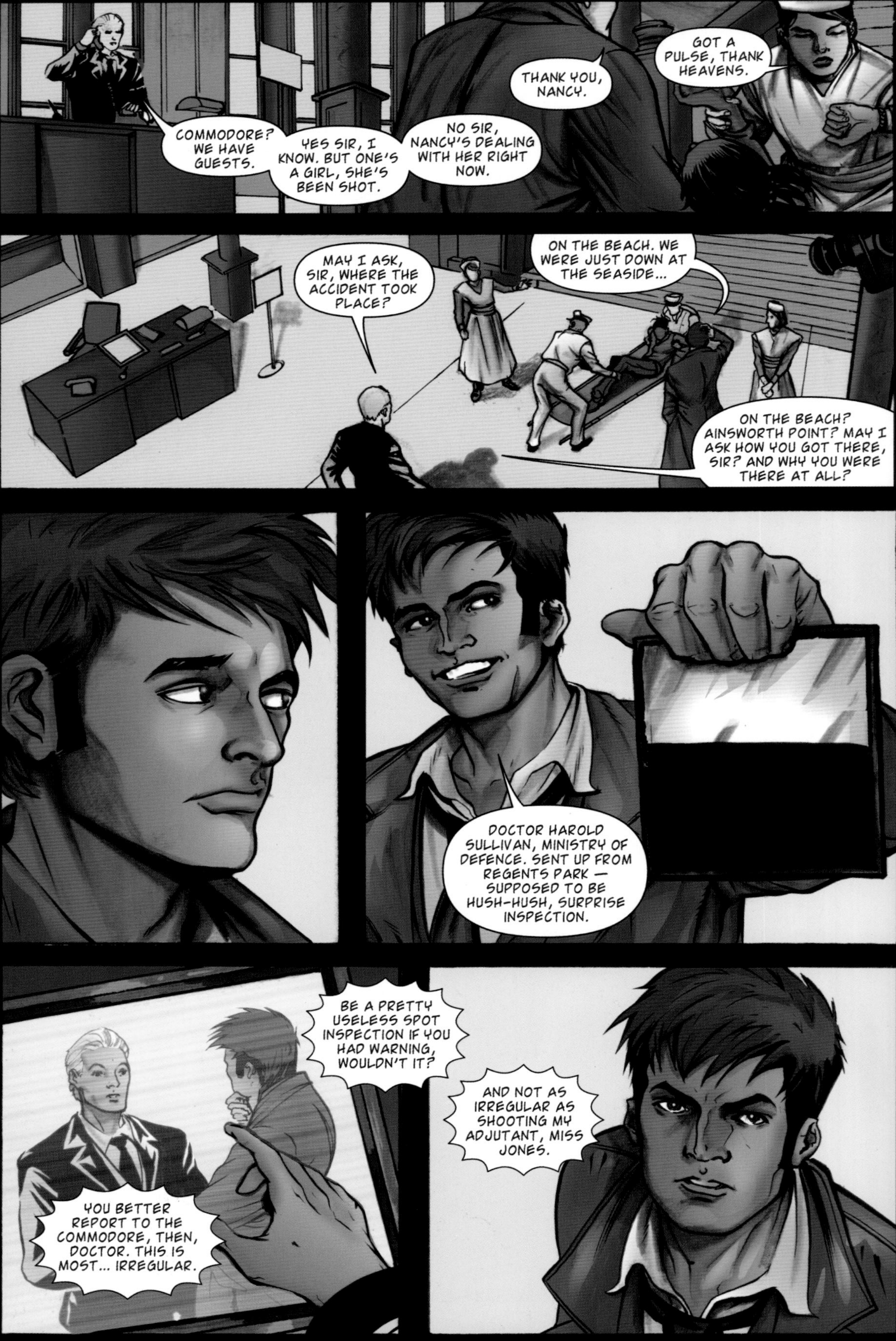
COMMODORE? WE HAVE GUESTS.
YES SIR, I KNOW. BUT ONE'S A GIRL, SHE'S BEEN SHOT.
NO SIR, NANCY'S DEALING WITH HER RIGHT NOW.
THANK YOU, NANCY.
GOT A PULSE, THANK HEAVENS.
MAY I ASK, SIR, WHERE THE ACCIDENT TOOK PLACE?
ON THE BEACH. WE WERE JUST DOWN AT THE SEASIDE...
ON THE BEACH? AINSWORTH POINT? MAY I ASK HOW YOU GOT THERE, SIR? AND WHY YOU WERE THERE AT ALL?
DOCTOR HAROLD SULLIVAN, MINISTRY OF DEFENCE. SENT UP FROM REGENTS PARK — SUPPOSED TO BE HUSH-HUSH, SURPRISE INSPECTION.
YOU BETTER REPORT TO THE COMMODORE, THEN, DOCTOR. THIS IS MOST... IRREGULAR.
BE A PRETTY USELESS SPOT INSPECTION IF YOU HAD WARNING, WOULDN'T IT?
AND NOT AS IRREGULAR AS SHOOTING MY ADJUTANT, MISS JONES.

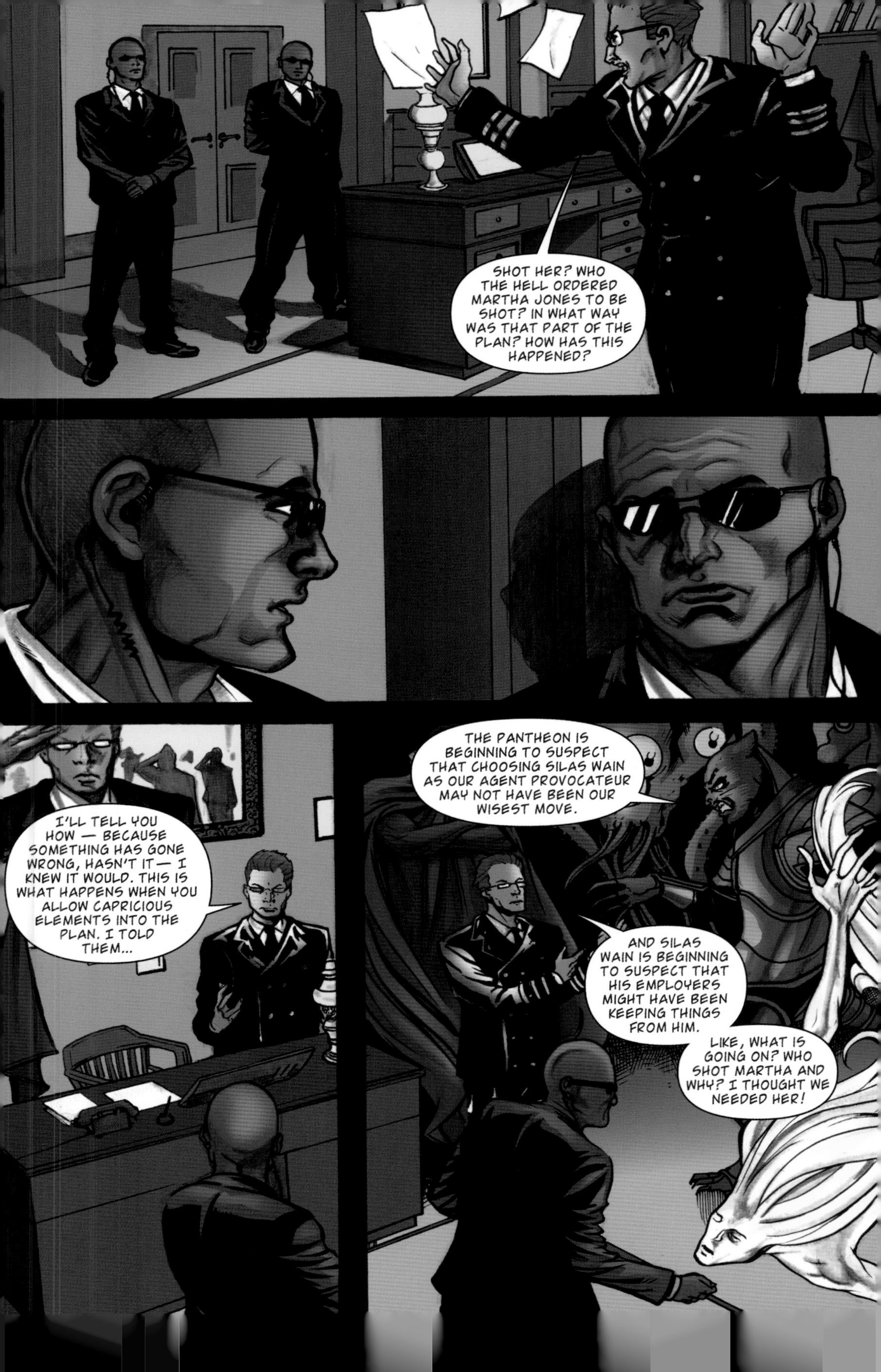
SHOT HER? WHO THE HELL ORDERED MARTHA JONES TO BE SHOT? IN WHAT WAY WAS THAT PART OF THE PLAN? HOW HAS THIS HAPPENED?
I'LL TELL YOU HOW — BECAUSE SOMETHING HAS GONE WRONG, HASN'T IT — I KNEW IT WOULD. THIS IS WHAT HAPPENS WHEN YOU ALLOW CAPRICIOUS ELEMENTS INTO THE PLAN. I TOLD THEM...
THE PANTHEON IS BEGINNING TO SUSPECT THAT CHOOSING SILAS WAIN AS OUR AGENT PROVOCATEUR MAY NOT HAVE BEEN OUR WISEST MOVE.
AND SILAS WAIN IS BEGINNING TO SUSPECT THAT HIS EMPLOYERS MIGHT HAVE BEEN KEEPING THINGS FROM HIM.
LIKE, WHAT IS GOING ON? WHO SHOT MARTHA AND WHY? I THOUGHT WE NEEDED HER!

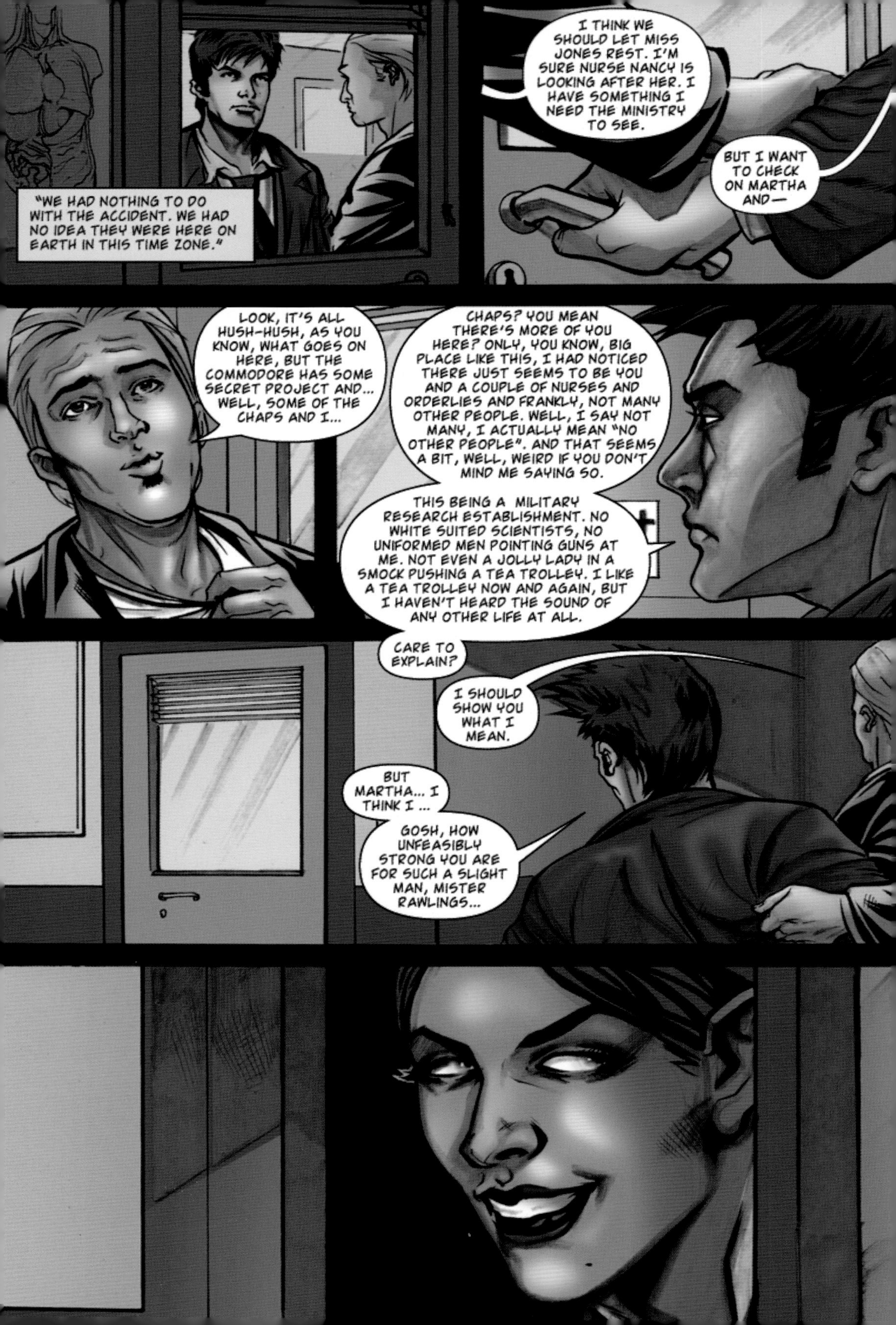

"WE HAD NOTHING TO DO WITH THE ACCIDENT. WE HAD NO IDEA THEY WERE HERE ON EARTH IN THIS TIME ZONE."
I THINK WE SHOULD LET MISS JONES REST. I'M SURE NURSE NANCY IS LOOKING AFTER HER. I HAVE SOMETHING I NEED THE MINISTRY TO SEE.
BUT I WANT TO CHECK ON MARTHA AND—
LOOK, IT'S ALL HUSH-HUSH, AS YOU KNOW, WHAT GOES ON HERE, BUT THE COMMODORE HAS SOME SECRET PROJECT AND... WELL, SOME OF THE CHAPS AND I...
CHAPS? YOU MEAN THERE'S MORE OF YOU HERE? ONLY, YOU KNOW, BIG PLACE LIKE THIS, I HAD NOTICED THERE JUST SEEMS TO BE YOU AND A COUPLE OF NURSES AND ORDERLIES AND FRANKLY, NOT MANY OTHER PEOPLE. WELL, I SAY NOT MANY, I ACTUALLY MEAN "NO OTHER PEOPLE". AND THAT SEEMS A BIT, WELL, WEIRD IF YOU DON'T MIND ME SAYING SO.
THIS BEING A MILITARY RESEARCH ESTABLISHMENT. NO WHITE SUITED SCIENTISTS, NO UNIFORMED MEN POINTING GUNS AT ME. NOT EVEN A JOLLY LADY IN A SMOCK PUSHING A TEA TROLLEY. I LIKE A TEA TROLLEY NOW AND AGAIN, BUT I HAVEN'T HEARD THE SOUND OF ANY OTHER LIFE AT ALL.
CARE TO EXPLAIN?
I SHOULD SHOW YOU WHAT I MEAN.
BUT MARTHA... I THINK I ...
GOSH, HOW UNFEASIBLY STRONG YOU ARE FOR SUCH A SLIGHT MAN, MISTER RAWLINGS...

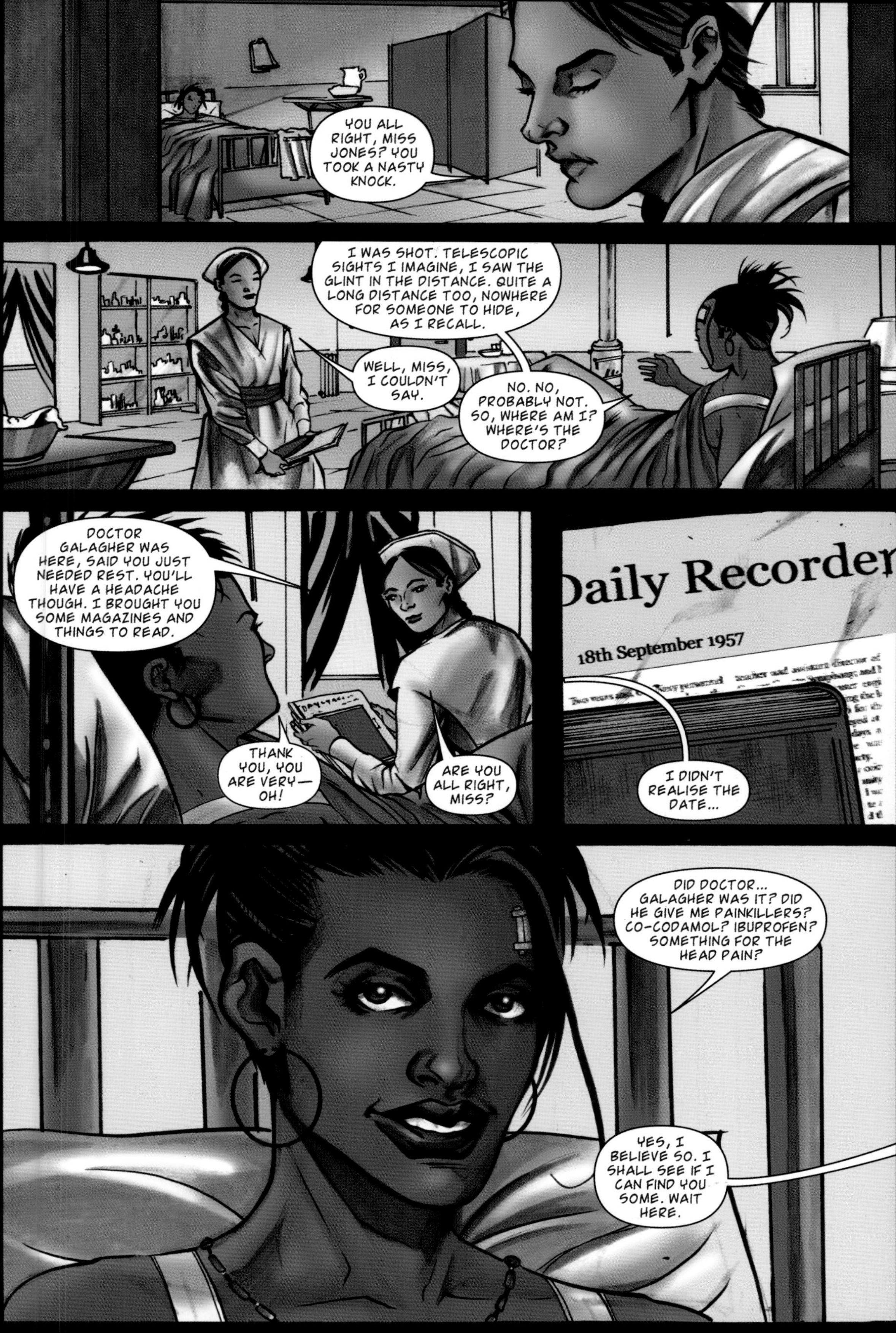
YOU ALL RIGHT, MISS JONES? YOU TOOK A NASTY KNOCK.
I WAS SHOT. TELESCOPIC SIGHTS I IMAGINE, I SAW THE GLINT IN THE DISTANCE. QUITE A LONG DISTANCE TOO, NOWHERE FOR SOMEONE TO HIDE, AS I RECALL.
WELL, MISS, I COULDN'T SAY.
NO. NO, PROBABLY NOT. SO, WHERE AM I? WHERE'S THE DOCTOR?
DOCTOR GALAGHER WAS HERE, SAID YOU JUST NEEDED REST. YOU'LL HAVE A HEADACHE THOUGH. I BROUGHT YOU SOME MAGAZINES AND THINGS TO READ.
THANK YOU, YOU ARE VERY— OH!
ARE YOU ALL RIGHT, MISS?
Daily Recorder
18th September 1957
I DIDN'T REALISE THE DATE...
DID DOCTOR... GALAGHER WAS IT? DID HE GIVE ME PAINKILLERS? CO-CODAMOL? IBUPROFEN? SOMETHING FOR THE HEAD PAIN?
YES, I BELIEVE SO. I SHALL SEE IF I CAN FIND YOU SOME. WAIT HERE.

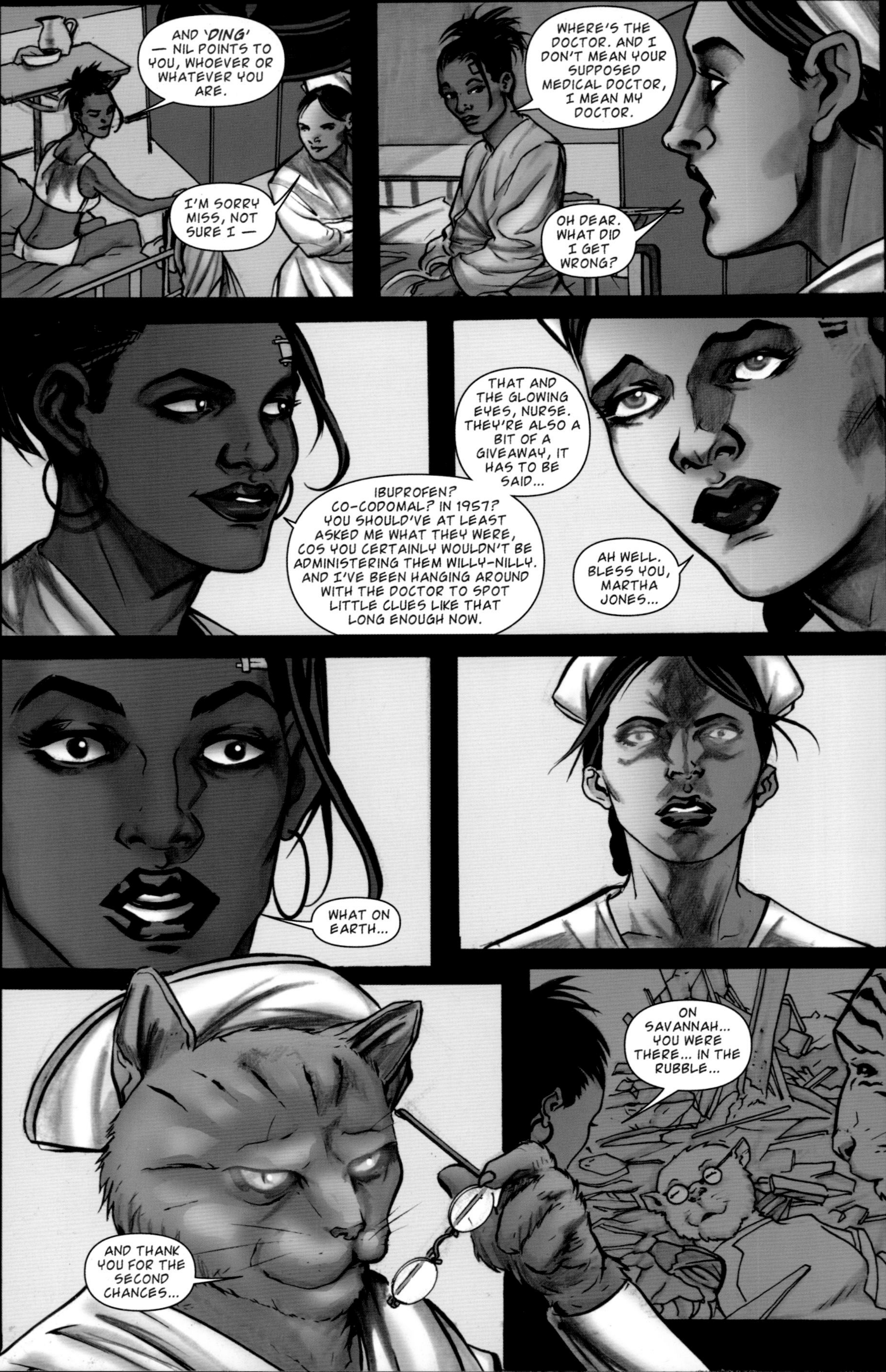
AND 'DING' — NIL POINTS TO YOU, WHOEVER OR WHATEVER YOU ARE.
I'M SORRY MISS, NOT SURE I —
WHERE'S THE DOCTOR. AND I DON'T MEAN YOUR SUPPOSED MEDICAL DOCTOR, I MEAN MY DOCTOR.
OH DEAR. WHAT DID I GET WRONG?
IBUPROFEN? CO-CODOMAL? IN 1957? YOU SHOULD'VE AT LEAST ASKED ME WHAT THEY WERE, COS YOU CERTAINLY WOULDN'T BE ADMINISTERING THEM WILLY-NILLY. AND I'VE BEEN HANGING AROUND WITH THE DOCTOR TO SPOT LITTLE CLUES LIKE THAT LONG ENOUGH NOW.
THAT AND THE GLOWING EYES, NURSE. THEY'RE ALSO A BIT OF A GIVEAWAY, IT HAS TO BE SAID...
AH WELL. BLESS YOU, MARTHA JONES...
WHAT ON EARTH...
AND THANK YOU FOR THE SECOND CHANCES...
ON SAVANNAH... YOU WERE THERE... IN THE RUBBLE...

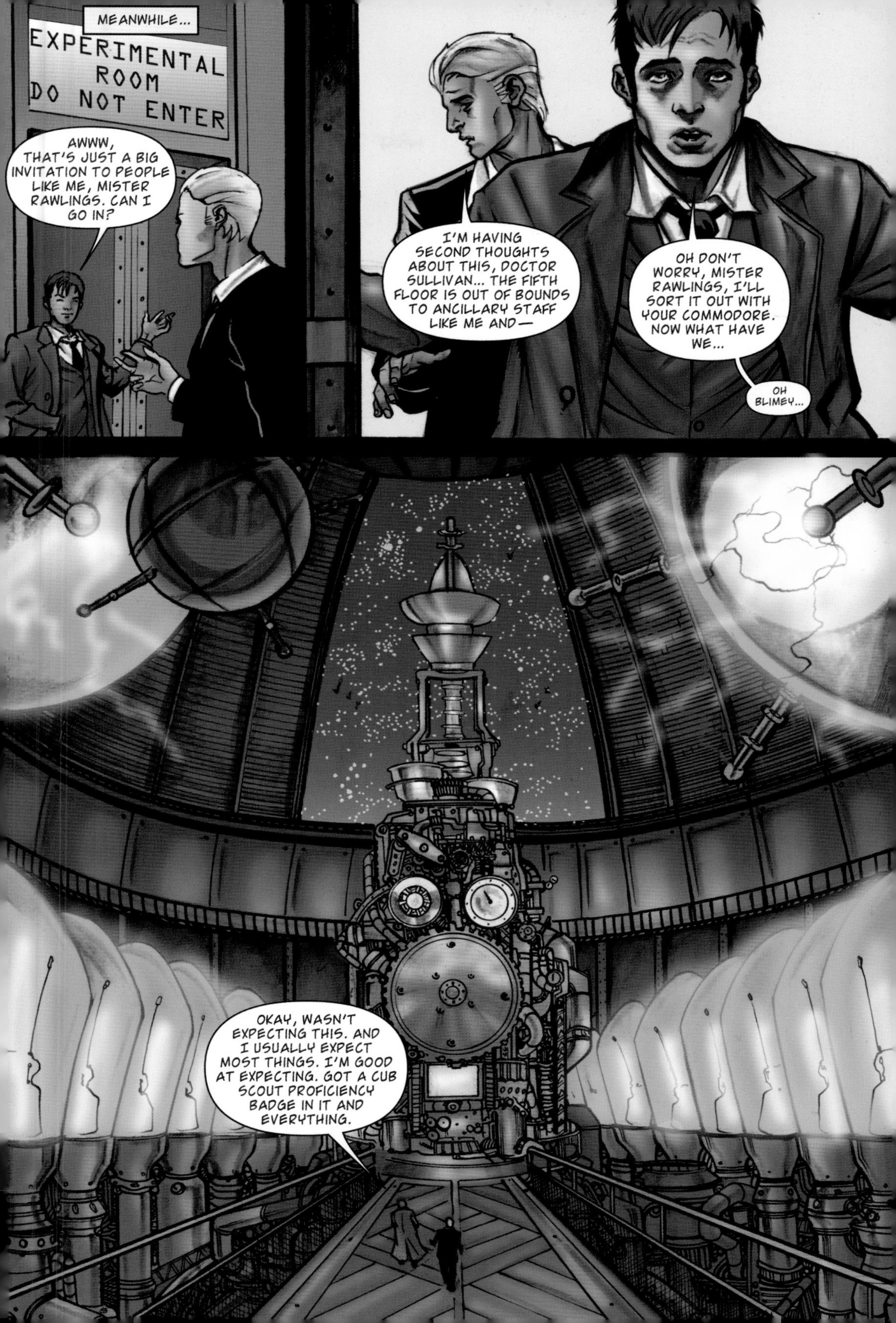
MEANWHILE...
EXPERIMENTAL ROOM DO NOT ENTER
AWWW, THAT'S JUST A BIG INVITATION TO PEOPLE LIKE ME, MISTER RAWLINGS. CAN I GO IN?
I'M HAVING SECOND THOUGHTS ABOUT THIS, DOCTOR SULLIVAN... THE FIFTH FLOOR IS OUT OF BOUNDS TO ANCILLARY STAFF LIKE ME AND—
OH DON'T WORRY, MISTER RAWLINGS, I'LL SORT IT OUT WITH YOUR COMMODORE. NOW WHAT HAVE WE...
OH BLIMEY...
OKAY, WASN'T EXPECTING THIS. AND I USUALLY EXPECT MOST THINGS. I'M GOOD AT EXPECTING. GOT A CUB SCOUT PROFICIENCY BADGE IN IT AND EVERYTHING.

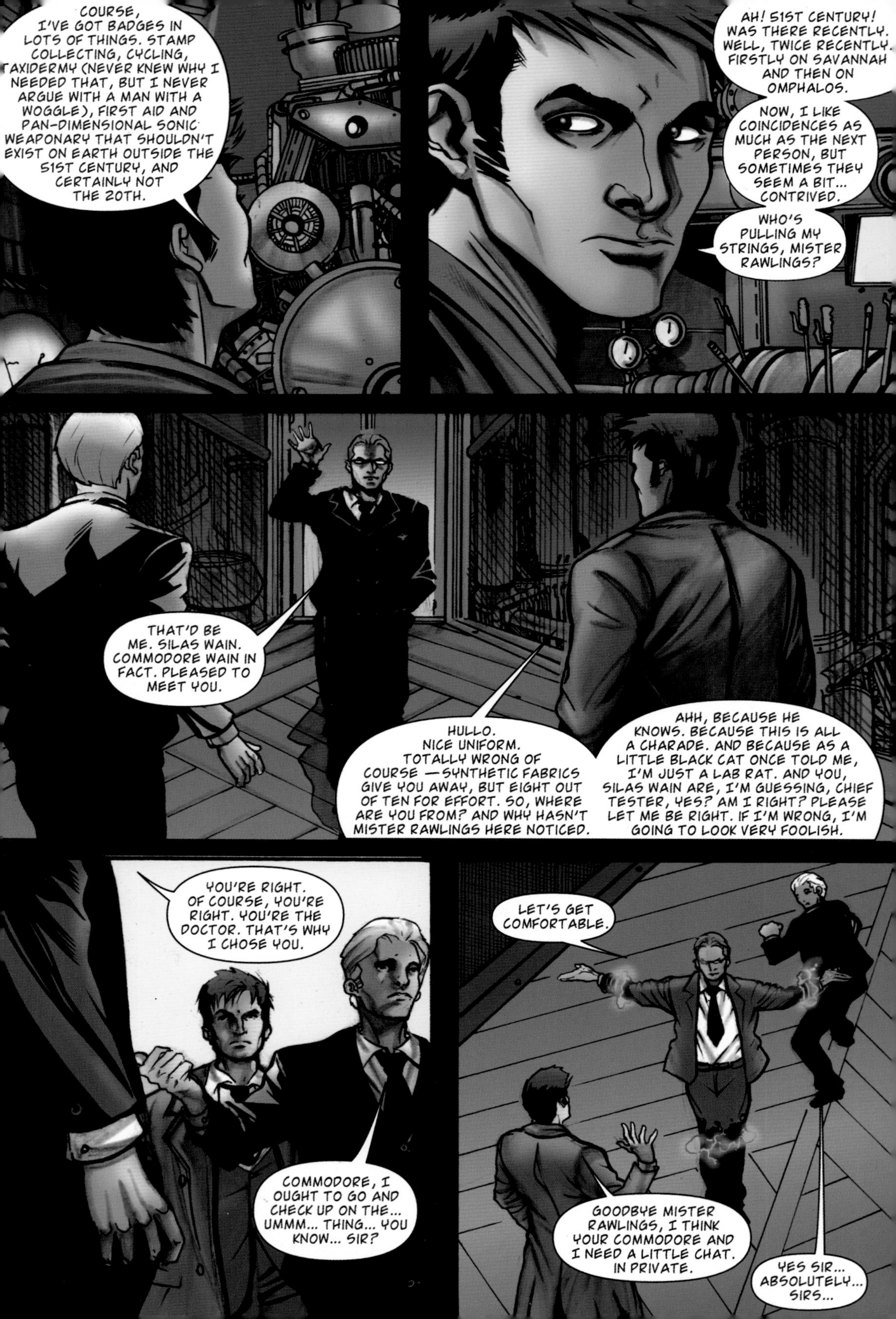
COURSE, I'VE GOT BADGES IN LOTS OF THINGS. STAMP COLLECTING, CYCLING, TAXIDERMY (NEVER KNEW WHY I NEEDED THAT, BUT I NEVER ARGUE WITH A MAN WITH A WOGGLE), FIRST AID AND PAN-DIMENSIONAL SONIC WEAPONARY THAT SHOULDN'T EXIST ON EARTH OUTSIDE THE 51ST CENTURY, AND CERTAINLY NOT THE 20TH.
AH! 51ST CENTURY! WAS THERE RECENTLY. WELL, TWICE RECENTLY. FIRSTLY ON SAVANNAH AND THEN ON OMPHALOS.
NOW, I LIKE COINCIDENCES AS MUCH AS THE NEXT PERSON, BUT SOMETIMES THEY SEEM A BIT... CONTRIVED.
WHO'S PULLING MY STRINGS, MISTER RAWLINGS?
THAT'D BE ME. SILAS WAIN. COMMODORE WAIN IN FACT. PLEASED TO MEET YOU.
HULLO. NICE UNIFORM. TOTALLY WRONG OF COURSE —SYNTHETIC FABRICS GIVE YOU AWAY, BUT EIGHT OUT OF TEN FOR EFFORT. SO, WHERE ARE YOU FROM? AND WHY HASN'T MISTER RAWLINGS HERE NOTICED.
AHH, BECAUSE HE KNOWS. BECAUSE THIS IS ALL A CHARADE. AND BECAUSE AS A LITTLE BLACK CAT ONCE TOLD ME, I'M JUST A LAB RAT. AND YOU, SILAS WAIN ARE, I'M GUESSING, CHIEF TESTER, YES? AM I RIGHT? PLEASE LET ME BE RIGHT. IF I'M WRONG, I'M GOING TO LOOK VERY FOOLISH.
YOU'RE RIGHT. OF COURSE, YOU'RE RIGHT. YOU'RE THE DOCTOR. THAT'S WHY I CHOSE YOU.
COMMODORE, I OUGHT TO GO AND CHECK UP ON THE... UMMM... THING... YOU KNOW... SIR?
LET'S GET COMFORTABLE.
GOODBYE MISTER RAWLINGS, I THINK YOUR COMMODORE AND I NEED A LITTLE CHAT. IN PRIVATE.
YES SIR... ABSOLUTELY... SIRS...

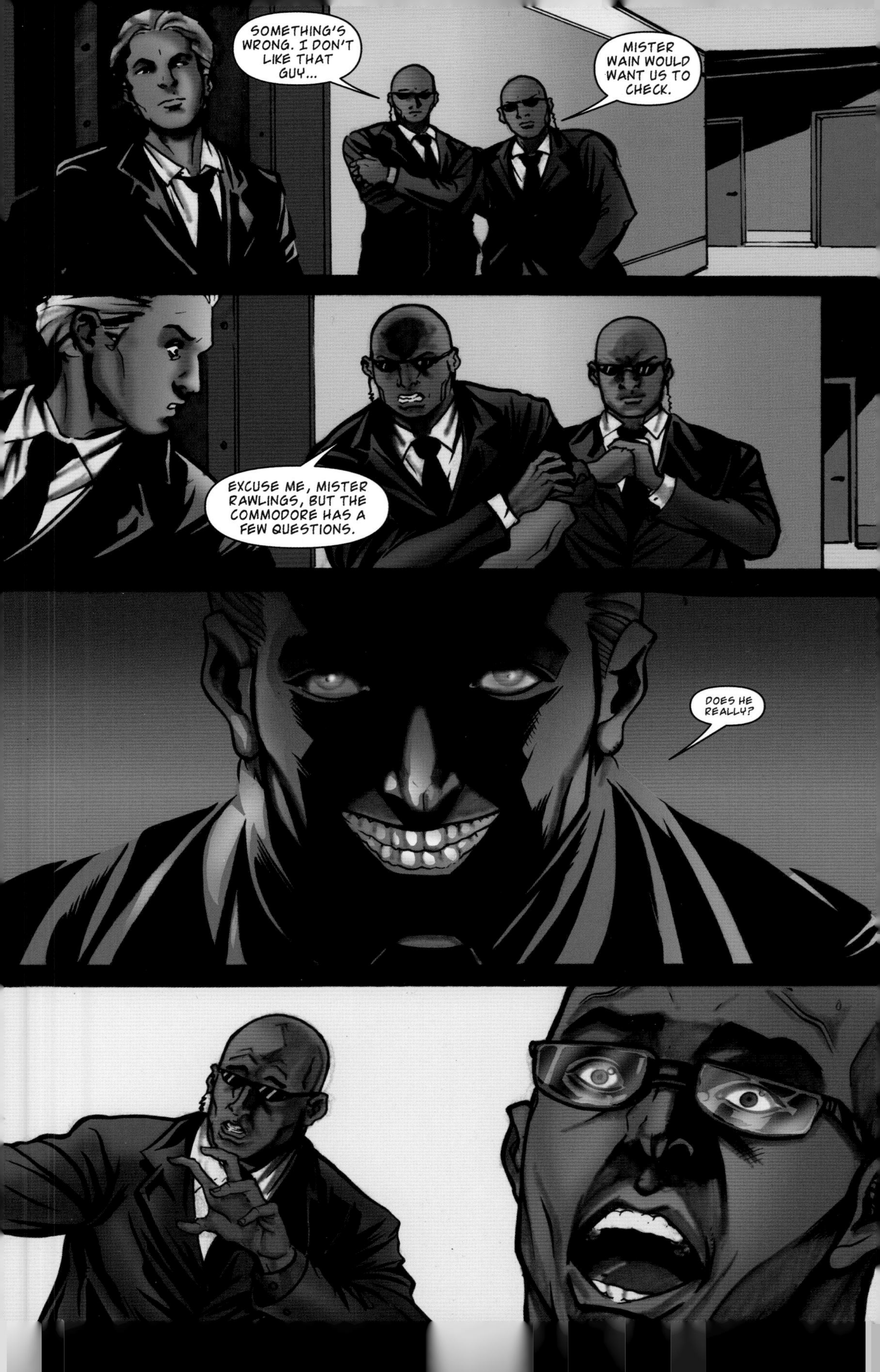
SOMETHING'S WRONG. I DON'T LIKE THAT GUY...
MISTER WAIN WOULD WANT US TO CHECK.
EXCUSE ME, MISTER RAWLINGS, BUT THE COMMODORE HAS A FEW QUESTIONS.
DOES HE REALLY?

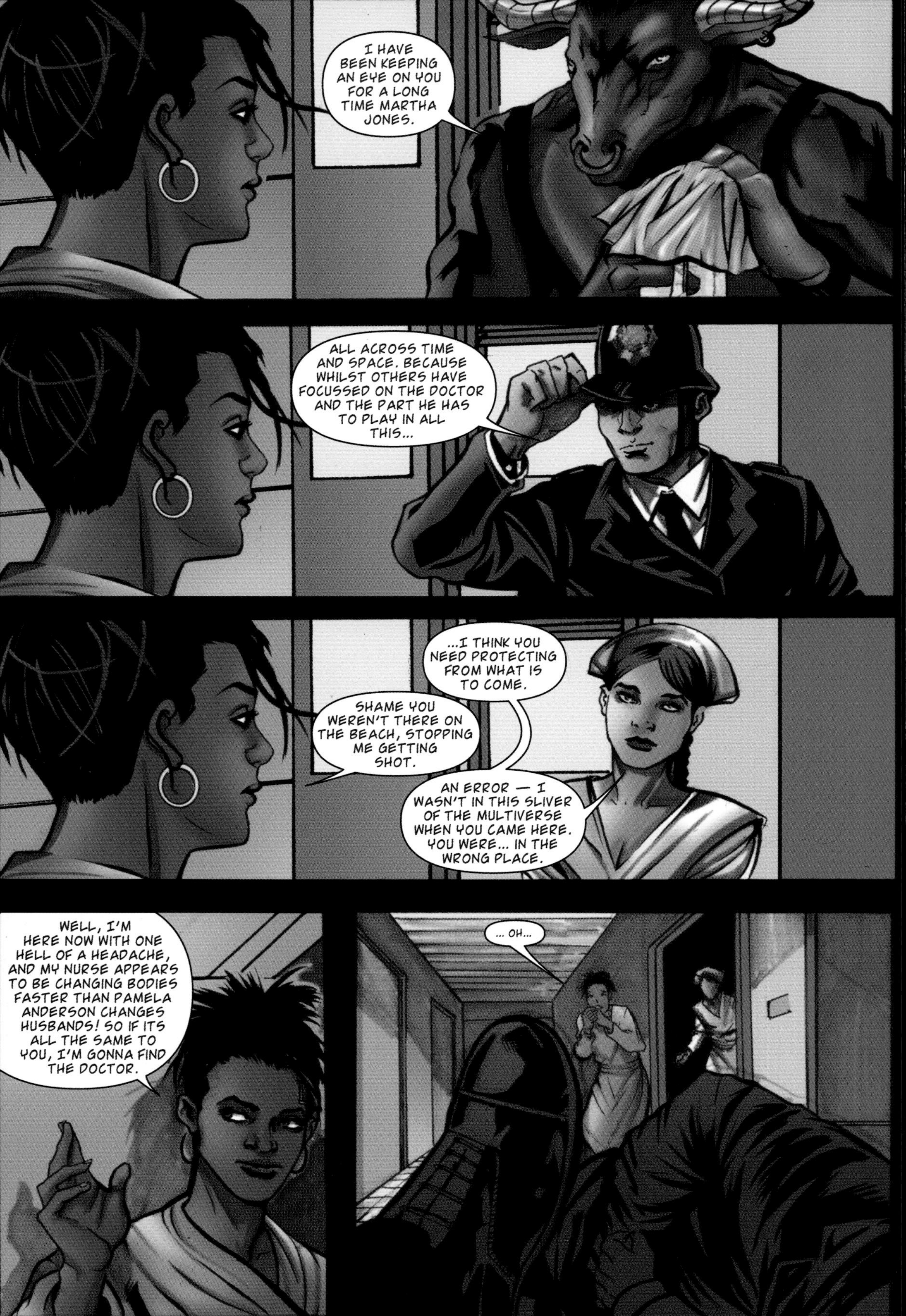
I HAVE BEEN KEEPING AN EYE ON YOU FOR A LONG TIME MARTHA JONES.
ALL ACROSS TIME AND SPACE. BECAUSE WHILST OTHERS HAVE FOCUSSED ON THE DOCTOR AND THE PART HE HAS TO PLAY IN ALL THIS...
...I THINK YOU NEED PROTECTING FROM WHAT IS TO COME.
SHAME YOU WEREN'T THERE ON THE BEACH, STOPPING ME GETTING SHOT.
AN ERROR — I WASN'T IN THIS SLIVER OF THE MULTIVERSE WHEN YOU CAME HERE. YOU WERE... IN THE WRONG PLACE.
WELL, I'M HERE NOW WITH ONE HELL OF A HEADACHE, AND MY NURSE APPEARS TO BE CHANGING BODIES FASTER THAN PAMELA ANDERSON CHANGES HUSBANDS! SO IF ITS ALL THE SAME TO YOU, I'M GONNA FIND THE DOCTOR.
... OH...

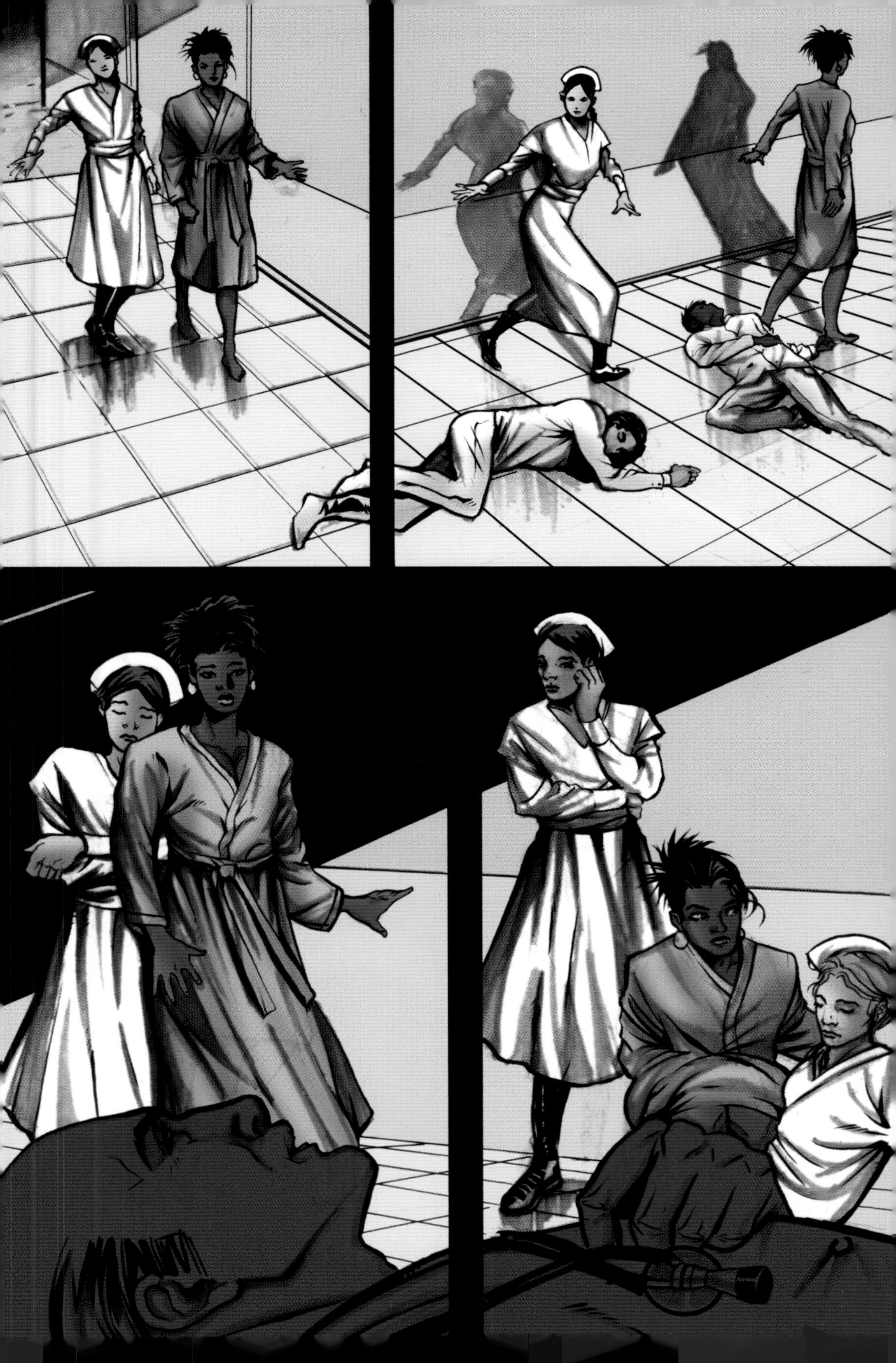

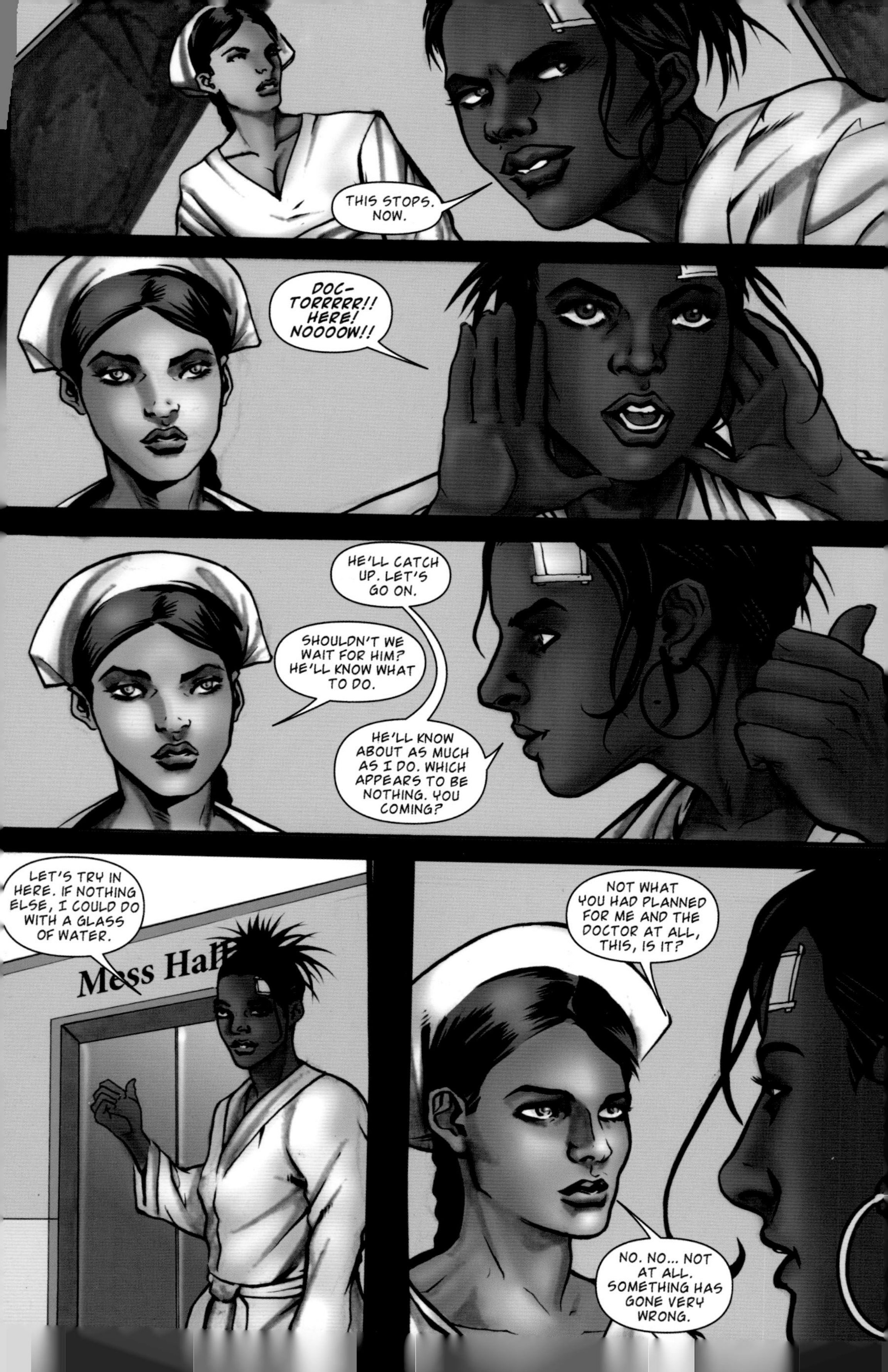
THIS STOPS. NOW.
DOC-TORRRRR!! HERE! NOOOOW!!
HE'LL CATCH UP. LET'S GO ON.
SHOULDN'T WE WAIT FOR HIM? HE'LL KNOW WHAT TO DO.
HE'LL KNOW ABOUT AS MUCH AS I DO. WHICH APPEARS TO BE NOTHING. YOU COMING?
LET'S TRY IN HERE. IF NOTHING ELSE, I COULD DO WITH A GLASS OF WATER.
Mess Hall
NOT WHAT YOU HAD PLANNED FOR ME AND THE DOCTOR AT ALL, THIS, IS IT?
NO. NO... NOT AT ALL. SOMETHING HAS GONE VERY WRONG.

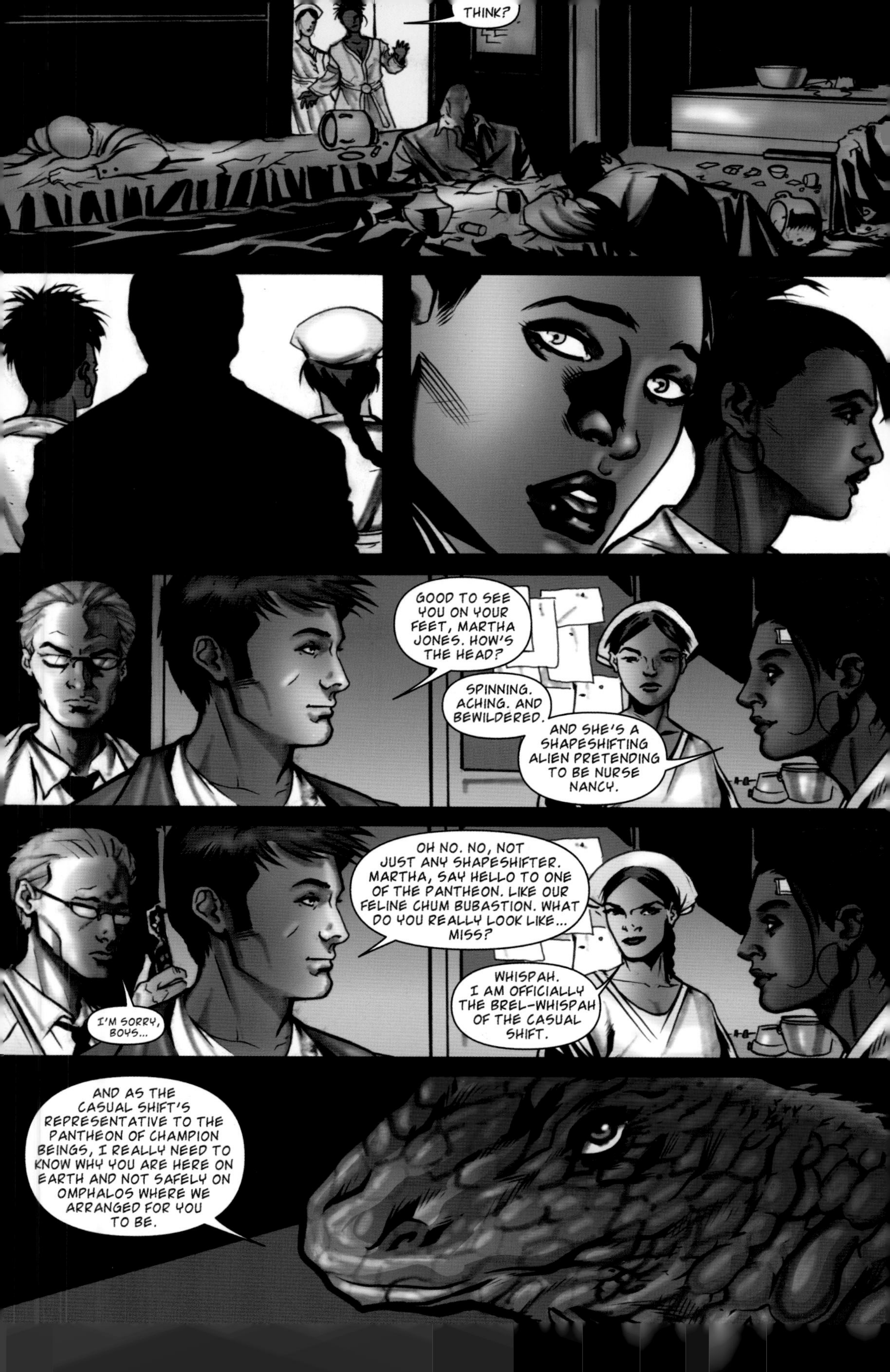

THINK?
GOOD TO SEE YOU ON YOUR FEET, MARTHA JONES. HOW'S THE HEAD?
SPINNING. ACHING. AND BEWILDERED.
AND SHE'S A SHAPESHIFTING ALIEN PRETENDING TO BE NURSE NANCY.
OH NO. NO, NOT JUST ANY SHAPESHIFTER. MARTHA, SAY HELLO TO ONE OF THE PANTHEON. LIKE OUR FELINE CHUM BUBASTION. WHAT DO YOU REALLY LOOK LIKE... MISS?
I'M SORRY, BOYS...
WHISPAH. I AM OFFICIALLY THE BREL-WHISPAH OF THE CASUAL SHIFT.
AND AS THE CASUAL SHIFT'S REPRESENTATIVE TO THE PANTHEON OF CHAMPION BEINGS, I REALLY NEED TO KNOW WHY YOU ARE HERE ON EARTH AND NOT SAFELY ON OMPHALOS WHERE WE ARRANGED FOR YOU TO BE.

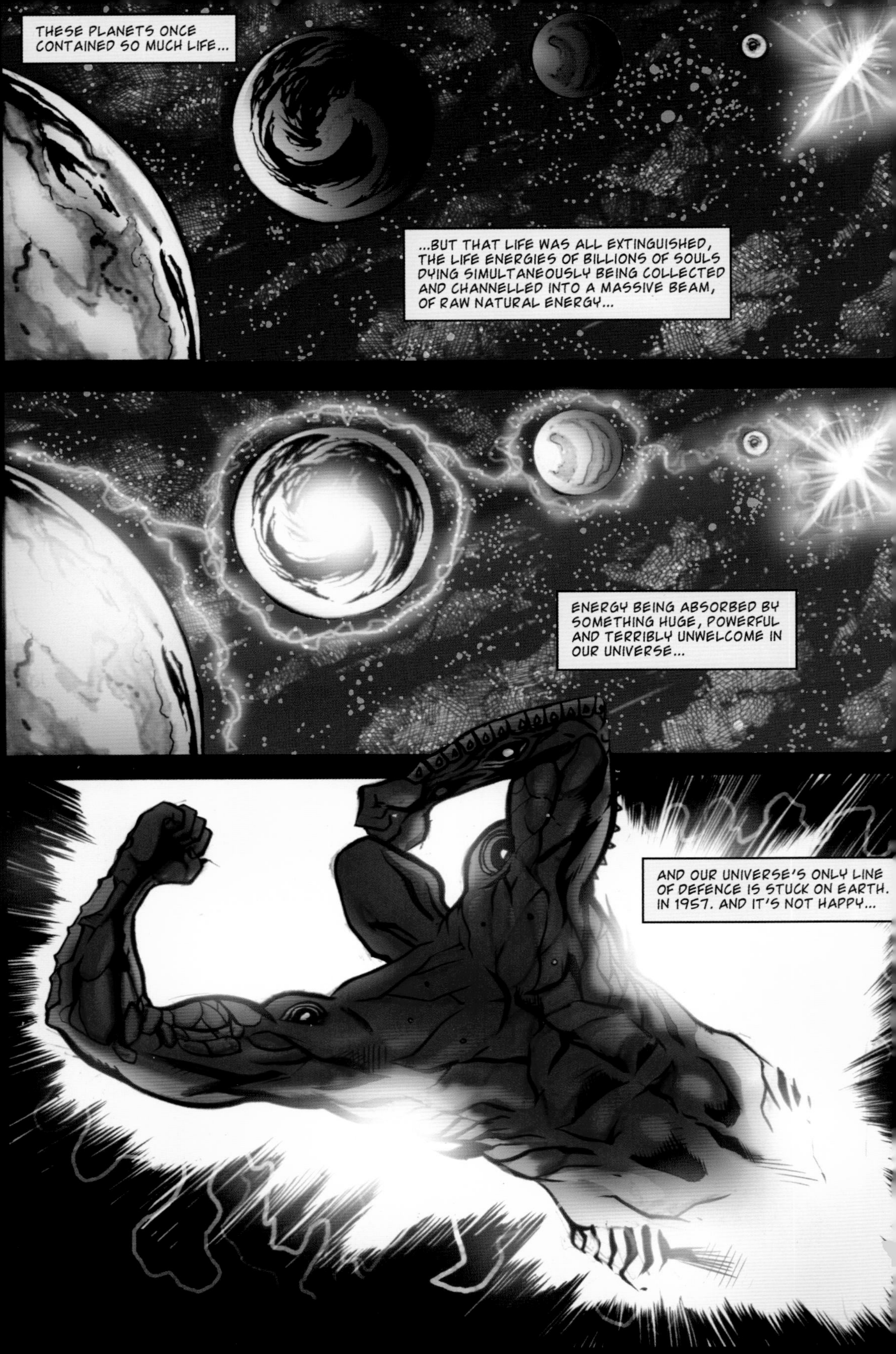
THESE PLANETS ONCE CONTAINED SO MUCH LIFE...
...BUT THAT LIFE WAS ALL EXTINGUISHED, THE LIFE ENERGIES OF BILLIONS OF SOULS DYING SIMULTANEOUSLY BEING COLLECTED AND CHANNELLED INTO A MASSIVE BEAM, OF RAW NATURAL ENERGY...
ENERGY BEING ABSORBED BY SOMETHING HUGE, POWERFUL AND TERRIBLY UNWELCOME IN OUR UNIVERSE...
AND OUR UNIVERSE'S ONLY LINE OF DEFENCE IS STUCK ON EARTH. IN 1957. AND IT'S NOT HAPPY...

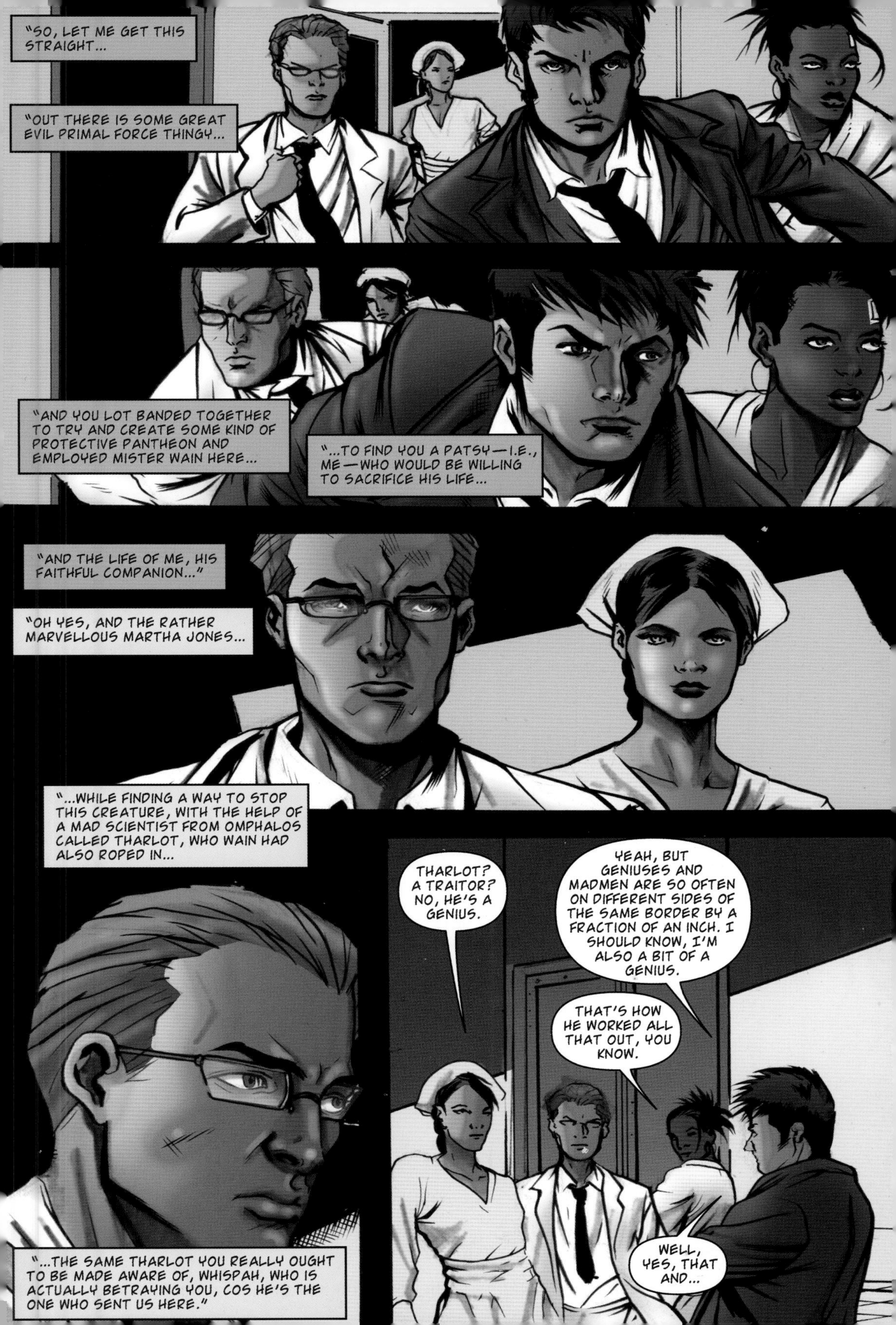
"SO, LET ME GET THIS STRAIGHT...
"OUT THERE IS SOME GREAT EVIL PRIMAL FORCE THINGY...
"AND YOU LOT BANDED TOGETHER TO TRY AND CREATE SOME KIND OF PROTECTIVE PANTHEON AND EMPLOYED MISTER WAIN HERE...
"...TO FIND YOU A PATSY—I.E., ME—WHO WOULD BE WILLING TO SACRIFICE HIS LIFE...
"AND THE LIFE OF ME, HIS FAITHFUL COMPANION..."
"OH YES, AND THE RATHER MARVELLOUS MARTHA JONES...
"...WHILE FINDING A WAY TO STOP THIS CREATURE, WITH THE HELP OF A MAD SCIENTIST FROM OMPHALOS CALLED THARLOT, WHO WAIN HAD ALSO ROPED IN...
"...THE SAME THARLOT YOU REALLY OUGHT TO BE MADE AWARE OF, WHISPAH, WHO IS ACTUALLY BETRAYING YOU, COS HE'S THE ONE WHO SENT US HERE."
THARLOT? A TRAITOR? NO, HE'S A GENIUS.
YEAH, BUT GENIUSES AND MADMEN ARE SO OFTEN ON DIFFERENT SIDES OF THE SAME BORDER BY A FRACTION OF AN INCH. I SHOULD KNOW, I'M ALSO A BIT OF A GENIUS.
THAT'S HOW HE WORKED ALL THAT OUT, YOU KNOW.
WELL, YES, THAT AND...

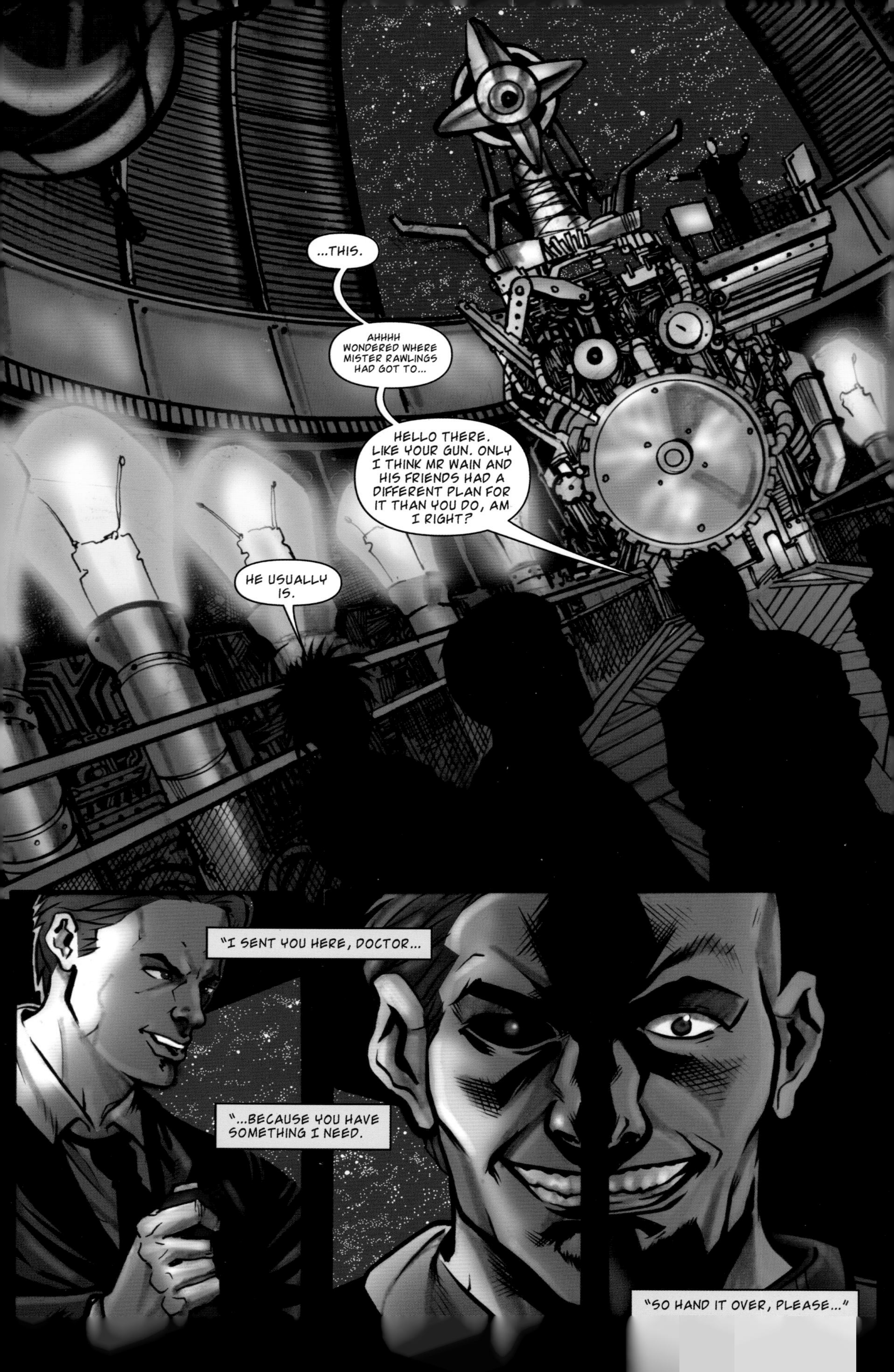
...THIS.
AHHHH WONDERED WHERE MISTER RAWLINGS HAD GOT TO...
HELLO THERE. LIKE YOUR GUN. ONLY I THINK MR WAIN AND HIS FRIENDS HAD A DIFFERENT PLAN FOR IT THAN YOU DO, AM I RIGHT?
HE USUALLY IS.
"I SENT YOU HERE, DOCTOR...
"...BECAUSE YOU HAVE SOMETHING I NEED.
"SO HAND IT OVER, PLEASE..."

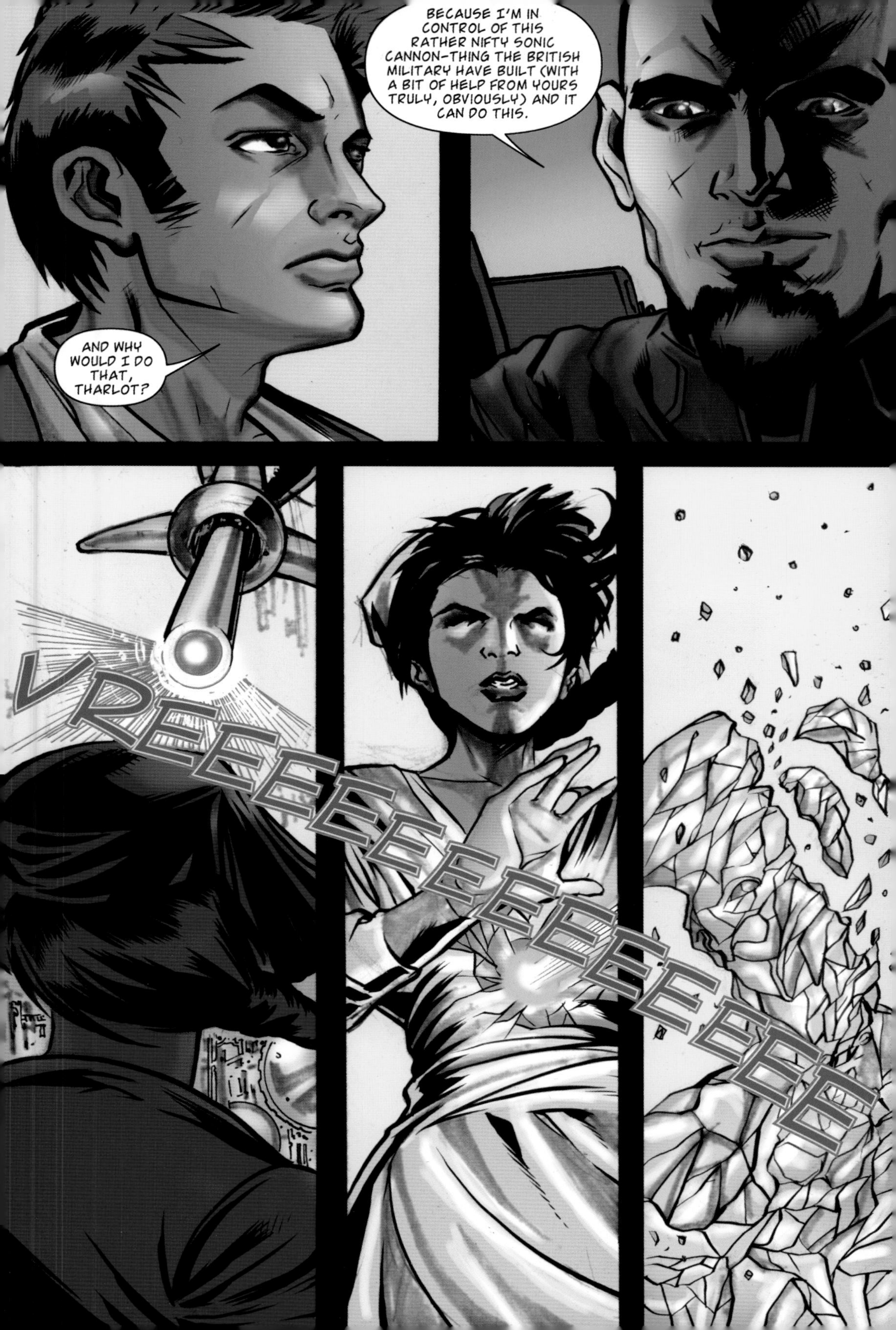
AND WHY WOULD I DO THAT, THARLOT?
BECAUSE I'M IN CONTROL OF THIS RATHER NIFTY SONIC CANNON-THING THE BRITISH MILITARY HAVE BUILT (WITH A BIT OF HELP FROM YOURS TRULY, OBVIOUSLY) AND IT CAN DO THIS.
VREEEEEEEEEEEEEEEEE

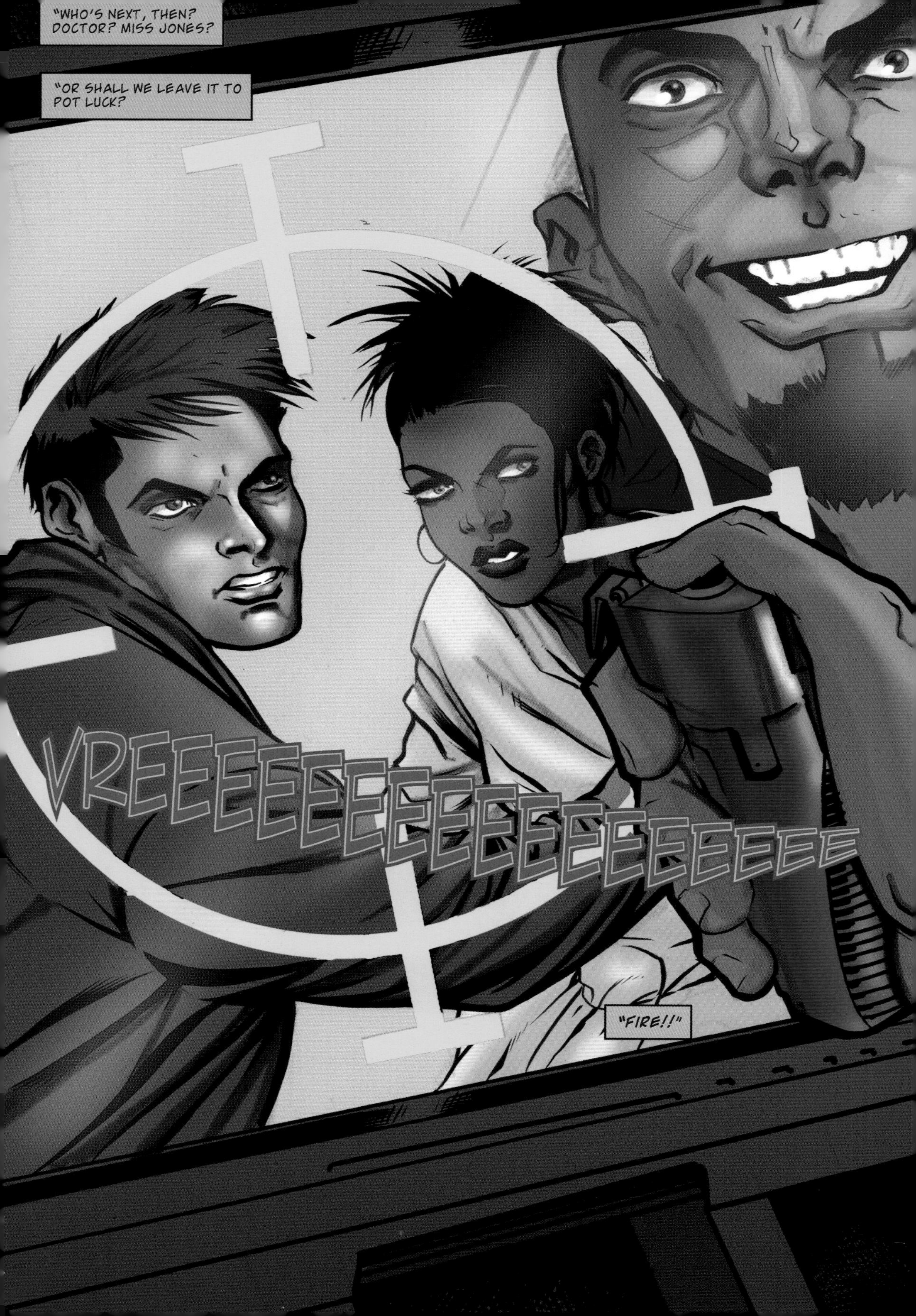
"WHO'S NEXT, THEN? DOCTOR? MISS JONES?
"OR SHALL WE LEAVE IT TO POT LUCK?
VREEEEEEEEEEEEEEEEEEEEEEEE
"FIRE!!"

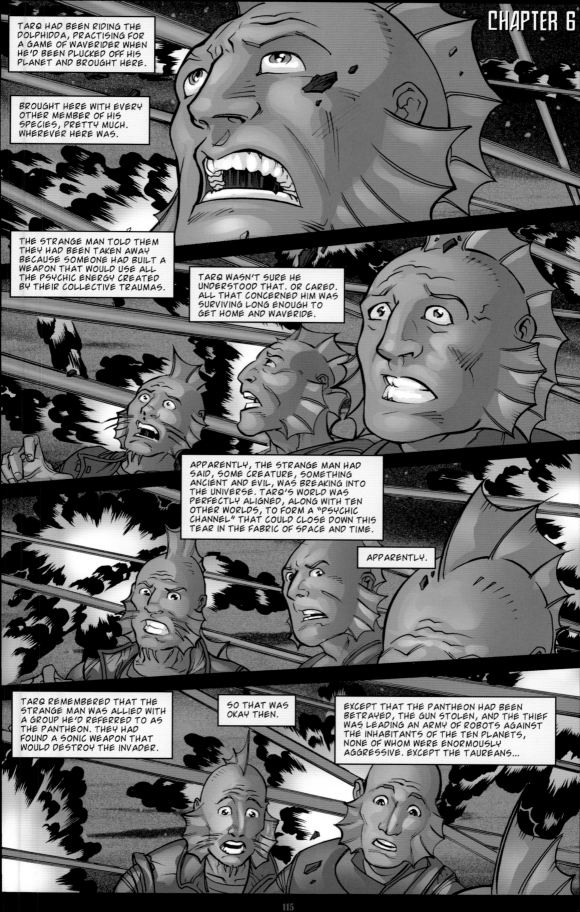

CHAPTER 6

TARQ HAD BEEN RIDING THE DOLPHIDDA, PRACTISING FOR A GAME OF WAVERIDER WHEN HE'D BEEN PLUCKED OFF HIS PLANET AND BROUGHT HERE.

BROUGHT HERE WITH EVERY OTHER MEMBER OF HIS SPECIES, PRETTY MUCH. WHEREVER HERE WAS.

THE STRANGE MAN TOLD THEM THEY HAD BEEN TAKEN AWAY BECAUSE SOMEONE HAD BUILT A WEAPON THAT WOULD USE ALL THE PSYCHIC ENERGY CREATED BY THEIR COLLECTIVE TRAUMAS.

TARQ WASN'T SURE HE UNDERSTOOD THAT. OR CARED. ALL THAT CONCERNED HIM WAS SURVIVING LONG ENOUGH TO GET HOME AND WAVERIDE.

APPARENTLY, THE STRANGE MAN HAD SAID, SOME CREATURE, SOMETHING ANCIENT AND EVIL, WAS BREAKING INTO THE UNIVERSE. TARQ'S WORLD WAS PERFECTLY ALIGNED, ALONG WITH TEN OTHER WORLDS, TO FORM A "PSYCHIC CHANNEL" THAT COULD CLOSE DOWN THIS TEAR IN THE FABRIC OF SPACE AND TIME.

APPARENTLY.

TARQ REMEMBERED THAT THE STRANGE MAN WAS ALLIED WITH A GROUP HE'D REFERRED TO AS THE PANTHEON. THEY HAD FOUND A SONIC WEAPON THAT WOULD DESTROY THE INVADER.

SO THAT WAS OKAY THEN.

EXCEPT THAT THE PANTHEON HAD BEEN BETRAYED, THE GUN STOLEN, AND THE THIEF WAS LEADING AN ARMY OF ROBOTS AGAINST THE INHABITANTS OF THE TEN PLANETS, NONE OF WHOM WERE ENORMOUSLY AGGRESSIVE. EXCEPT THE TAUREANS...

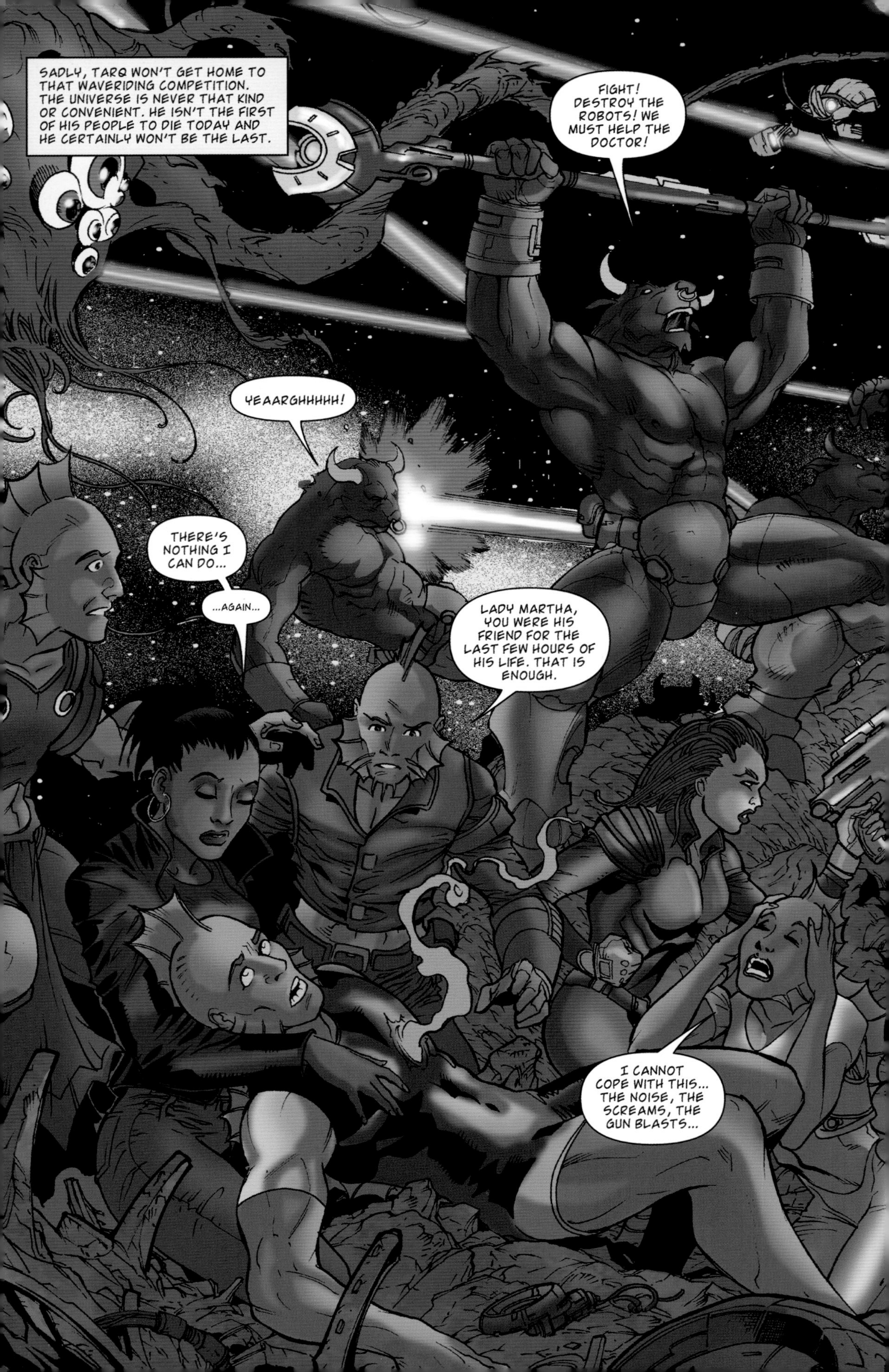
SADLY, TARQ WON'T GET HOME TO THAT WAVERIDING COMPETITION. THE UNIVERSE IS NEVER THAT KIND OR CONVENIENT. HE ISN'T THE FIRST OF HIS PEOPLE TO DIE TODAY AND HE CERTAINLY WON'T BE THE LAST.
FIGHT! DESTROY THE ROBOTS! WE MUST HELP THE DOCTOR!
YEAARGHHHHH!
THERE'S NOTHING I CAN DO...
...AGAIN...
LADY MARTHA, YOU WERE HIS FRIEND FOR THE LAST FEW HOURS OF HIS LIFE. THAT IS ENOUGH.
I CANNOT COPE WITH THIS... THE NOISE, THE SCREAMS, THE GUN BLASTS...

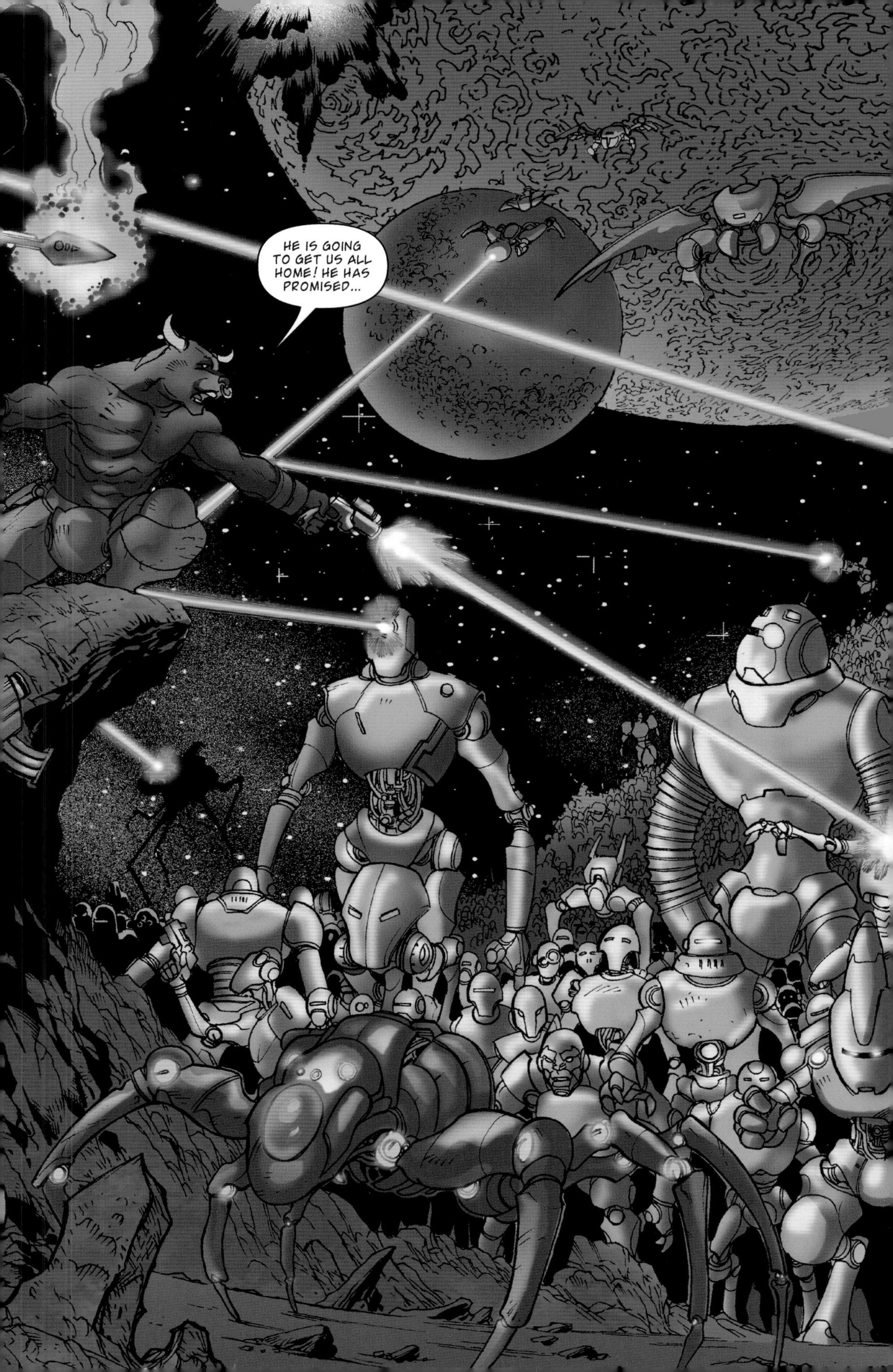
HE IS GOING TO GET US ALL HOME! HE HAS PROMISED...

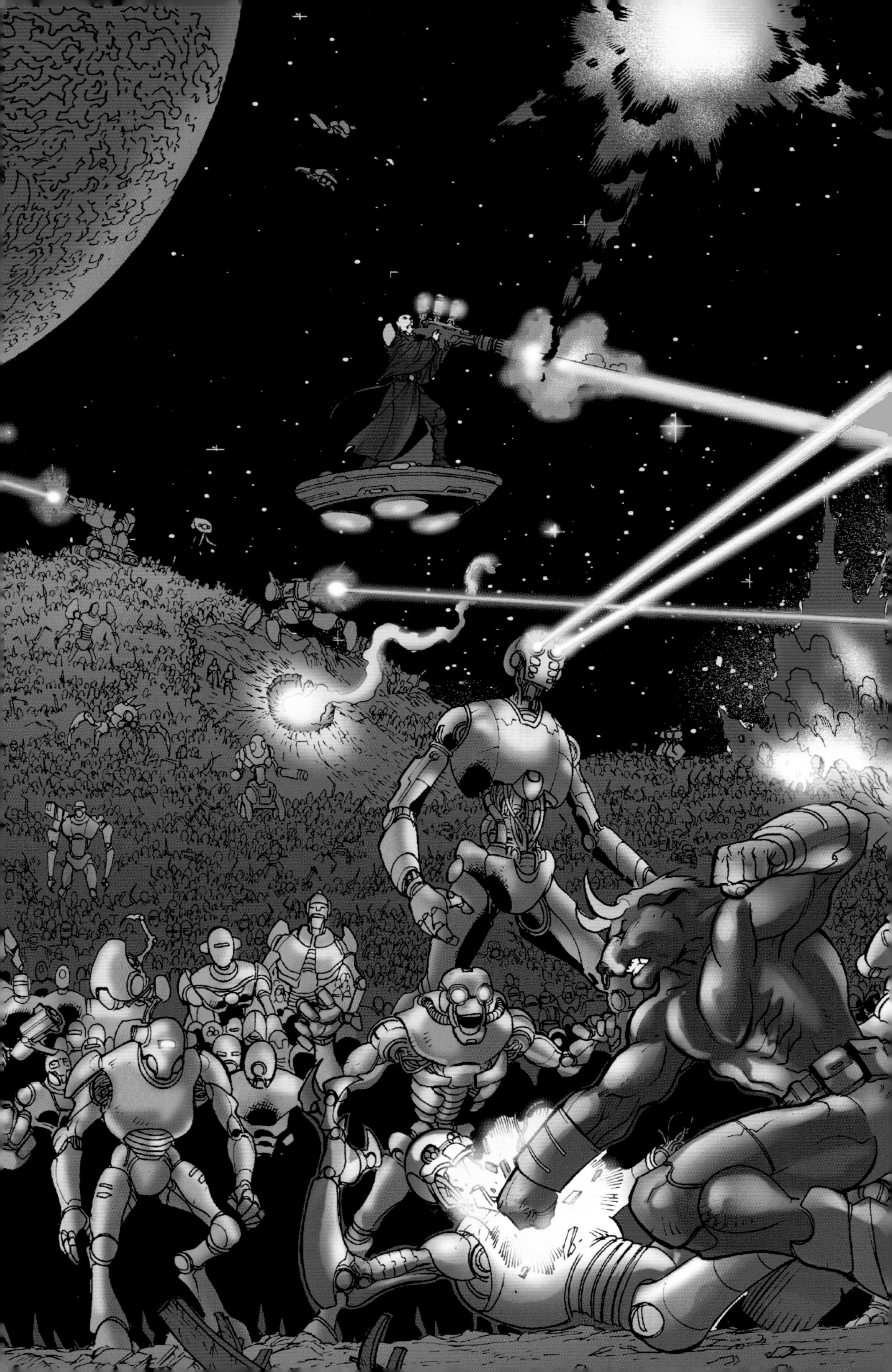

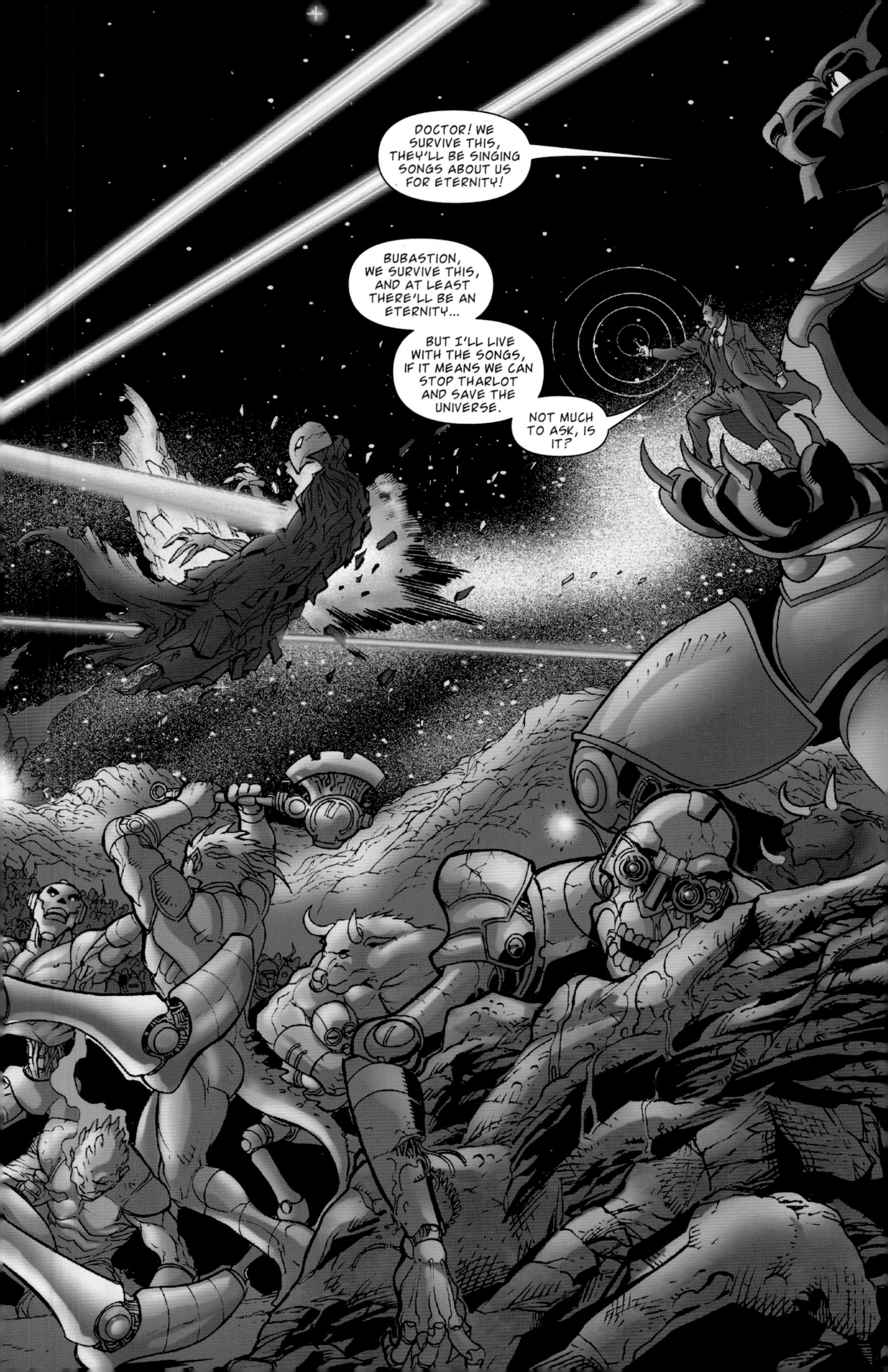
DOCTOR! WE SURVIVE THIS, THEY'LL BE SINGING SONGS ABOUT US FOR ETERNITY!
BUBASTION, WE SURVIVE THIS, AND AT LEAST THERE'LL BE AN ETERNITY...
BUT I'LL LIVE WITH THE SONGS, IF IT MEANS WE CAN STOP THARLOT AND SAVE THE UNIVERSE.
NOT MUCH TO ASK, IS IT?

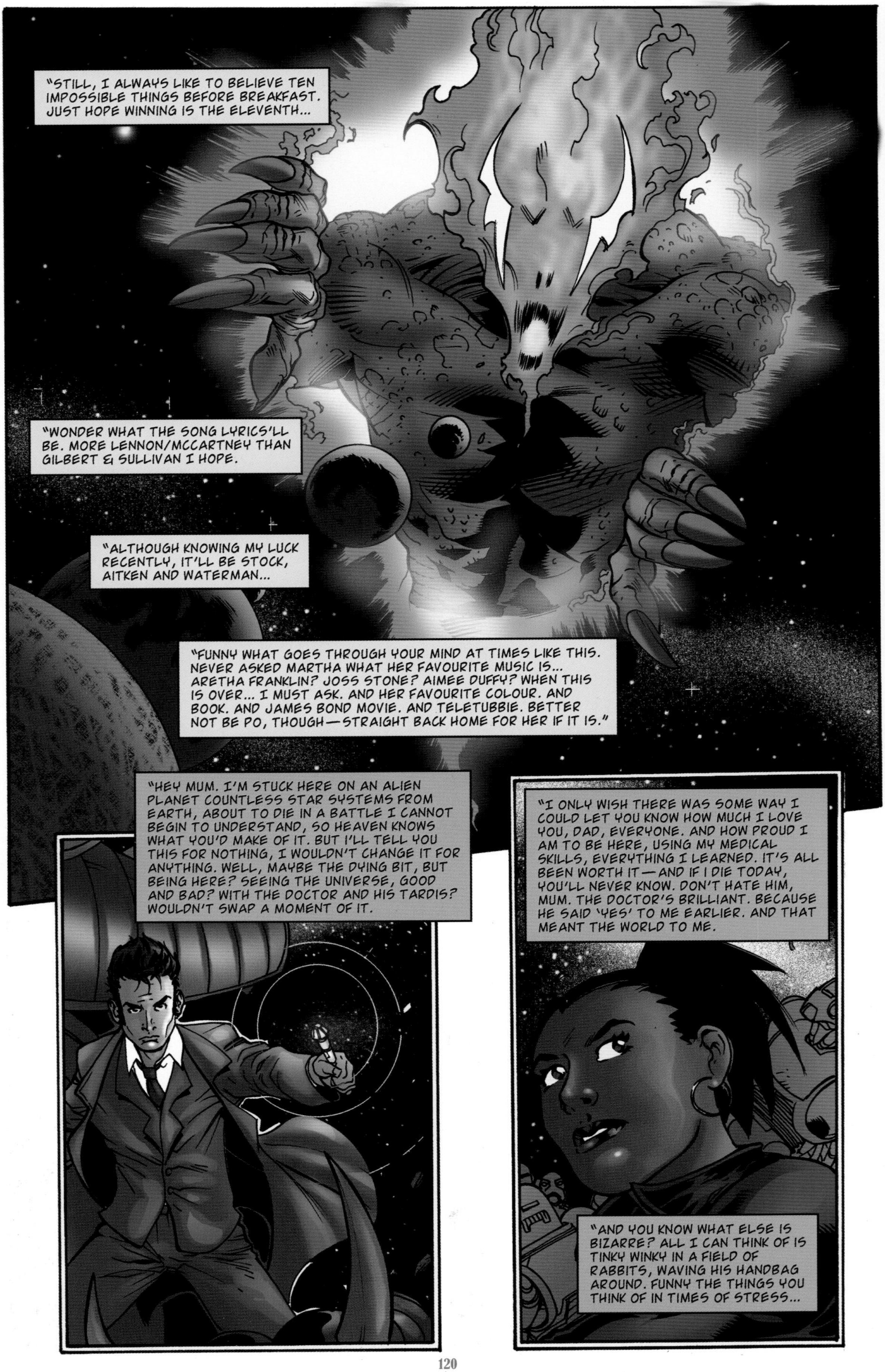
"STILL, I ALWAYS LIKE TO BELIEVE TEN IMPOSSIBLE THINGS BEFORE BREAKFAST. JUST HOPE WINNING IS THE ELEVENTH...
"WONDER WHAT THE SONG LYRICS'LL BE. MORE LENNON/MCCARTNEY THAN GILBERT & SULLIVAN I HOPE.
"ALTHOUGH KNOWING MY LUCK RECENTLY, IT'LL BE STOCK, AITKEN AND WATERMAN...
"FUNNY WHAT GOES THROUGH YOUR MIND AT TIMES LIKE THIS. NEVER ASKED MARTHA WHAT HER FAVOURITE MUSIC IS... ARETHA FRANKLIN? JOSS STONE? AIMEE DUFFY? WHEN THIS IS OVER... I MUST ASK. AND HER FAVOURITE COLOUR. AND BOOK. AND JAMES BOND MOVIE. AND TELETUBBIE. BETTER NOT BE PO, THOUGH—STRAIGHT BACK HOME FOR HER IF IT IS."
"HEY MUM. I'M STUCK HERE ON AN ALIEN PLANET COUNTLESS STAR SYSTEMS FROM EARTH, ABOUT TO DIE IN A BATTLE I CANNOT BEGIN TO UNDERSTAND, SO HEAVEN KNOWS WHAT YOU'D MAKE OF IT. BUT I'LL TELL YOU THIS FOR NOTHING, I WOULDN'T CHANGE IT FOR ANYTHING. WELL, MAYBE THE DYING BIT, BUT BEING HERE? SEEING THE UNIVERSE, GOOD AND BAD? WITH THE DOCTOR AND HIS TARDIS? WOULDN'T SWAP A MOMENT OF IT.
"I ONLY WISH THERE WAS SOME WAY I COULD LET YOU KNOW HOW MUCH I LOVE YOU, DAD, EVERYONE. AND HOW PROUD I AM TO BE HERE, USING MY MEDICAL SKILLS, EVERYTHING I LEARNED. IT'S ALL BEEN WORTH IT—AND IF I DIE TODAY, YOU'LL NEVER KNOW. DON'T HATE HIM, MUM. THE DOCTOR'S BRILLIANT. BECAUSE HE SAID 'YES' TO ME EARLIER. AND THAT MEANT THE WORLD TO ME.
"AND YOU KNOW WHAT ELSE IS BIZARRE? ALL I CAN THINK OF IS TINKY WINKY IN A FIELD OF RABBITS, WAVING HIS HANDBAG AROUND. FUNNY THE THINGS YOU THINK OF IN TIMES OF STRESS...

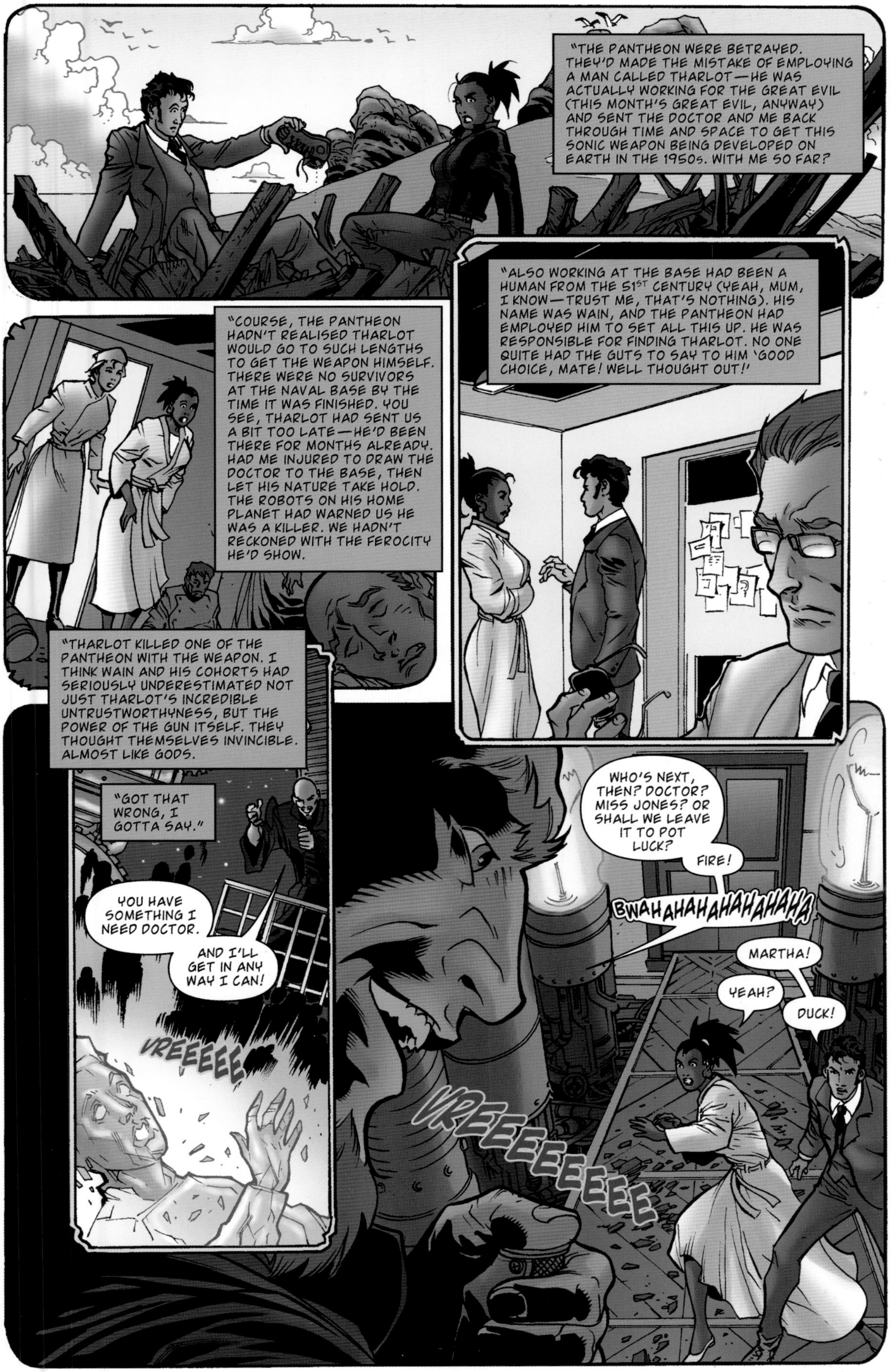
"THE PANTHEON WERE BETRAYED. THEY'D MADE THE MISTAKE OF EMPLOYING A MAN CALLED THARLOT—HE WAS ACTUALLY WORKING FOR THE GREAT EVIL (THIS MONTH'S GREAT EVIL, ANYWAY) AND SENT THE DOCTOR AND ME BACK THROUGH TIME AND SPACE TO GET THIS SONIC WEAPON BEING DEVELOPED ON EARTH IN THE 1950s. WITH ME SO FAR?
"COURSE, THE PANTHEON HADN'T REALISED THARLOT WOULD GO TO SUCH LENGTHS TO GET THE WEAPON HIMSELF. THERE WERE NO SURVIVORS AT THE NAVAL BASE BY THE TIME IT WAS FINISHED. YOU SEE, THARLOT HAD SENT US A BIT TOO LATE—HE'D BEEN THERE FOR MONTHS ALREADY. HAD ME INJURED TO DRAW THE DOCTOR TO THE BASE, THEN LET HIS NATURE TAKE HOLD. THE ROBOTS ON HIS HOME PLANET HAD WARNED US HE WAS A KILLER. WE HADN'T RECKONED WITH THE FEROCITY HE'D SHOW.
"ALSO WORKING AT THE BASE HAD BEEN A HUMAN FROM THE 51ST CENTURY (YEAH, MUM, I KNOW—TRUST ME, THAT'S NOTHING). HIS NAME WAS WAIN, AND THE PANTHEON HAD EMPLOYED HIM TO SET ALL THIS UP. HE WAS RESPONSIBLE FOR FINDING THARLOT. NO ONE QUITE HAD THE GUTS TO SAY TO HIM 'GOOD CHOICE, MATE! WELL THOUGHT OUT!'
"THARLOT KILLED ONE OF THE PANTHEON WITH THE WEAPON. I THINK WAIN AND HIS COHORTS HAD SERIOUSLY UNDERESTIMATED NOT JUST THARLOT'S INCREDIBLE UNTRUSTWORTHYNESS, BUT THE POWER OF THE GUN ITSELF. THEY THOUGHT THEMSELVES INVINCIBLE. ALMOST LIKE GODS.
"GOT THAT WRONG, I GOTTA SAY."
YOU HAVE SOMETHING I NEED DOCTOR.
AND I'LL GET IN ANY WAY I CAN!
VREEEEEE
WHO'S NEXT, THEN? DOCTOR? MISS JONES? OR SHALL WE LEAVE IT TO POT LUCK?
FIRE!
BWAHAHAHAHAHAHAHA
MARTHA!
YEAH?
DUCK!
VREEEEEEEEEEEE

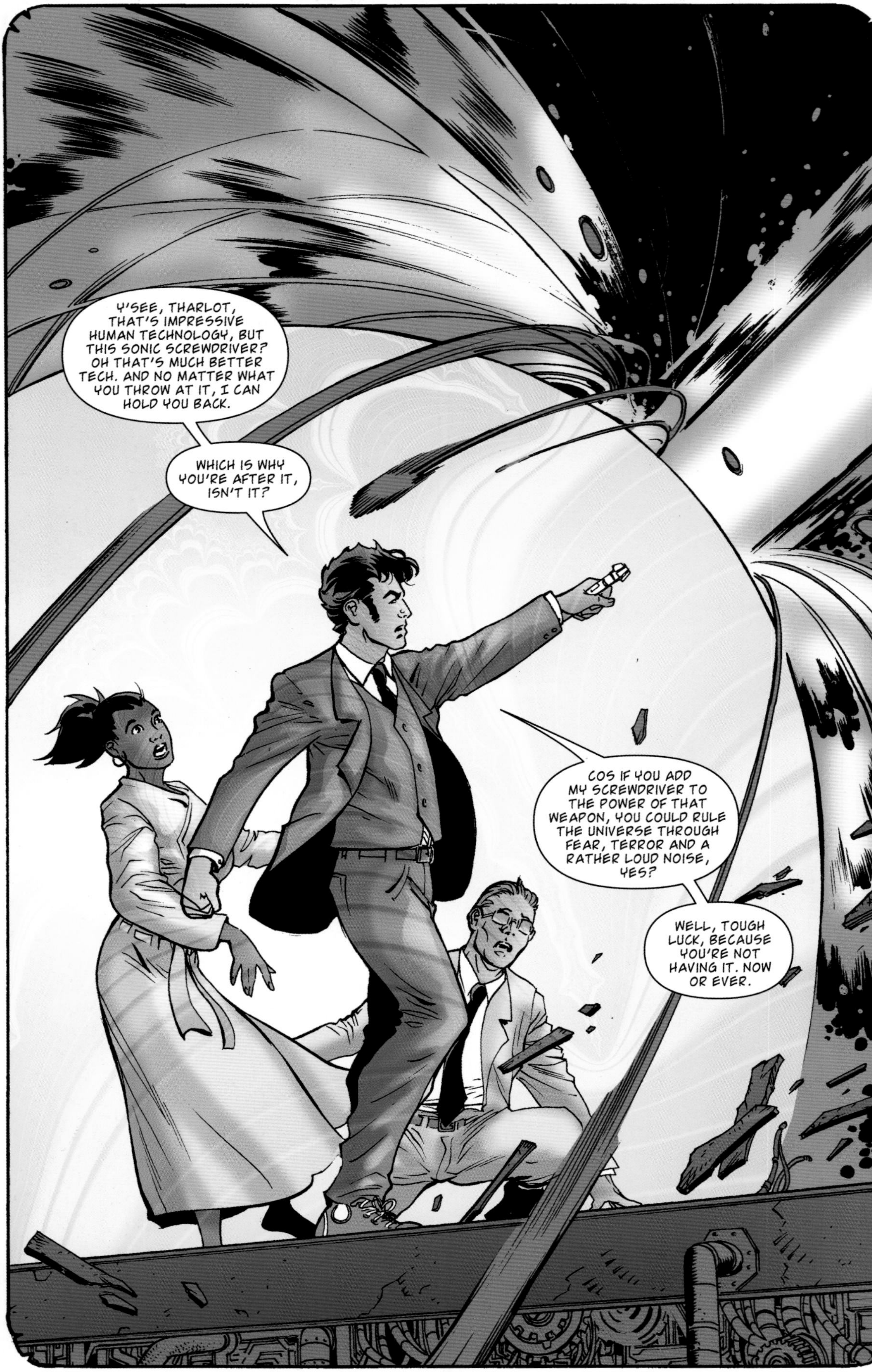
Y'SEE, THARLOT, THAT'S IMPRESSIVE HUMAN TECHNOLOGY, BUT THIS SONIC SCREWDRIVER? OH THAT'S MUCH BETTER TECH. AND NO MATTER WHAT YOU THROW AT IT, I CAN HOLD YOU BACK.
WHICH IS WHY YOU'RE AFTER IT, ISN'T IT?
COS IF YOU ADD MY SCREWDRIVER TO THE POWER OF THAT WEAPON, YOU COULD RULE THE UNIVERSE THROUGH FEAR, TERROR AND A RATHER LOUD NOISE, YES?
WELL, TOUGH LUCK, BECAUSE YOU'RE NOT HAVING IT. NOW OR EVER.

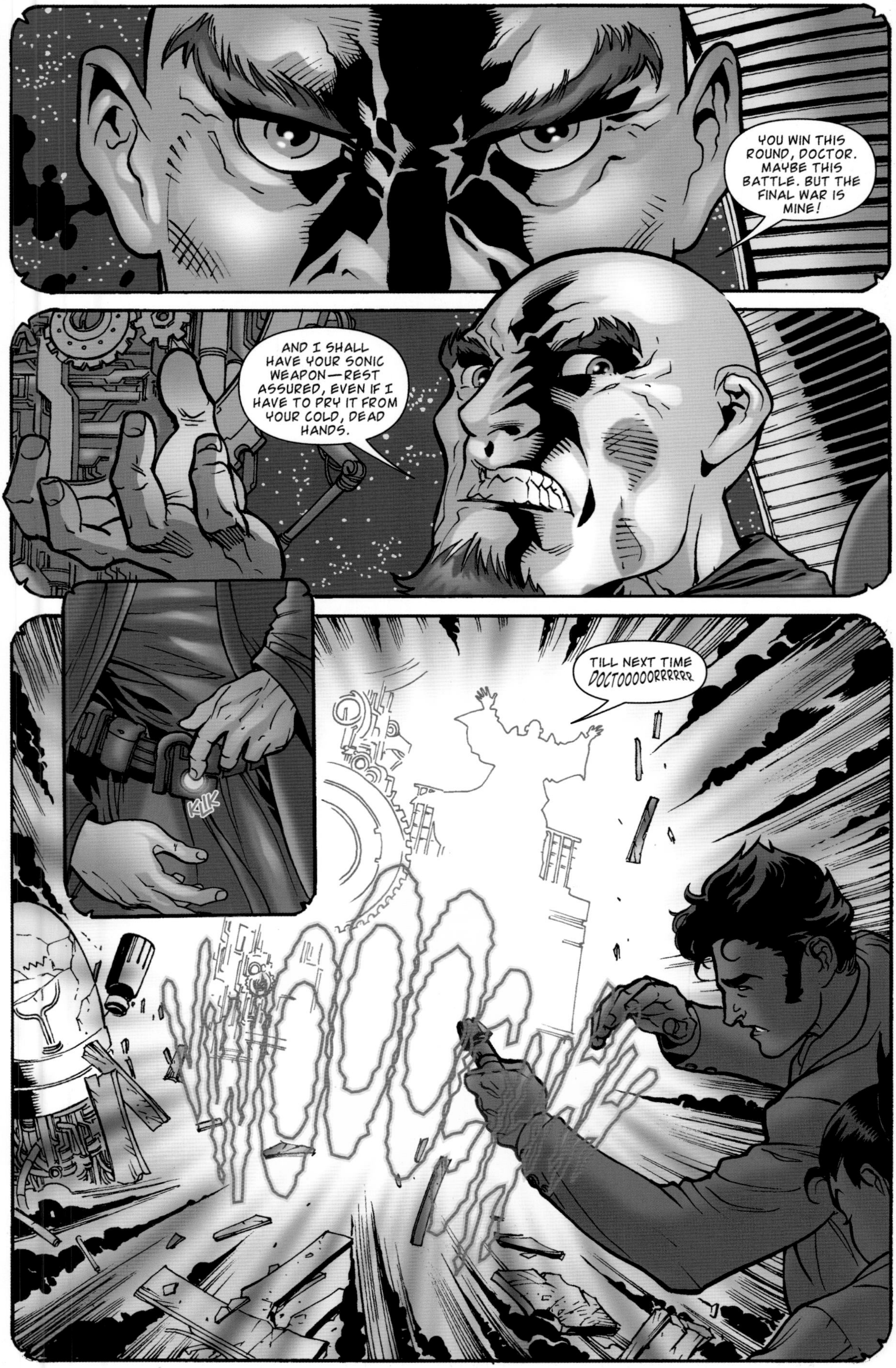
YOU WIN THIS ROUND, DOCTOR. MAYBE THIS BATTLE. BUT THE FINAL WAR IS MINE!
AND I SHALL HAVE YOUR SONIC WEAPON—REST ASSURED, EVEN IF I HAVE TO PRY IT FROM YOUR COLD, DEAD HANDS.
KLIK
TILL NEXT TIME DOCTOOOOORRRRRR

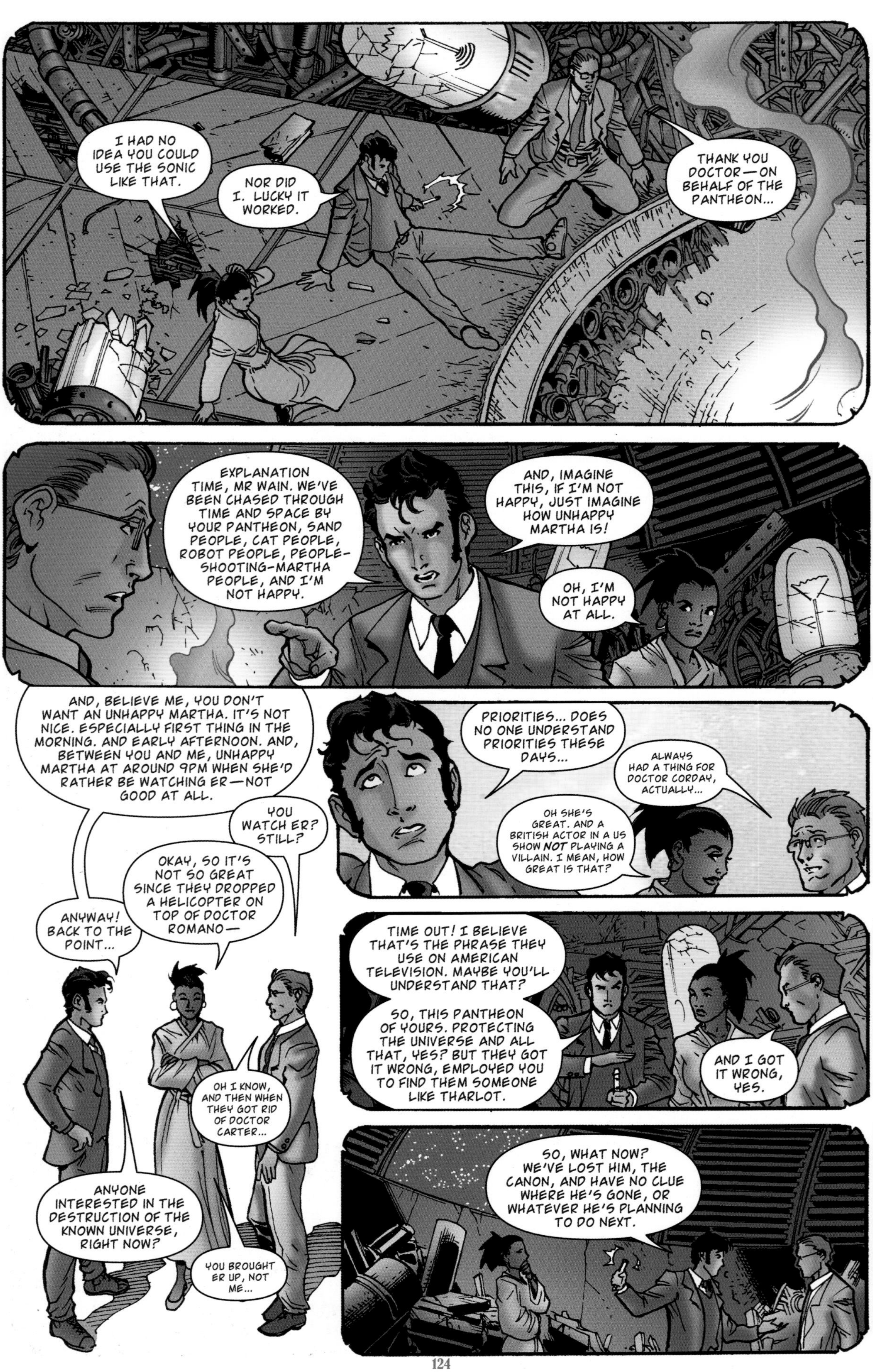
I HAD NO IDEA YOU COULD USE THE SONIC LIKE THAT.
NOR DID I. LUCKY IT WORKED.
THANK YOU DOCTOR—ON BEHALF OF THE PANTHEON...
EXPLANATION TIME, MR WAIN. WE'VE BEEN CHASED THROUGH TIME AND SPACE BY YOUR PANTHEON, SAND PEOPLE, CAT PEOPLE, ROBOT PEOPLE, PEOPLE-SHOOTING-MARTHA PEOPLE, AND I'M NOT HAPPY.
AND, IMAGINE THIS, IF I'M NOT HAPPY, JUST IMAGINE HOW UNHAPPY MARTHA IS!
OH, I'M NOT HAPPY AT ALL.
AND, BELIEVE ME, YOU DON'T WANT AN UNHAPPY MARTHA. IT'S NOT NICE. ESPECIALLY FIRST THING IN THE MORNING. AND EARLY AFTERNOON. AND, BETWEEN YOU AND ME, UNHAPPY MARTHA AT AROUND 9PM WHEN SHE'D RATHER BE WATCHING ER—NOT GOOD AT ALL.
YOU WATCH ER? STILL?
OKAY, SO IT'S NOT SO GREAT SINCE THEY DROPPED A HELICOPTER ON TOP OF DOCTOR ROMANO—
ANYWAY! BACK TO THE POINT...
OH I KNOW, AND THEN WHEN THEY GOT RID OF DOCTOR CARTER...
ANYONE INTERESTED IN THE DESTRUCTION OF THE KNOWN UNIVERSE, RIGHT NOW?
YOU BROUGHT ER UP, NOT ME...
PRIORITIES... DOES NO ONE UNDERSTAND PRIORITIES THESE DAYS...
ALWAYS HAD A THING FOR DOCTOR CORDAY, ACTUALLY...
OH SHE'S GREAT. AND A BRITISH ACTOR IN A US SHOW NOT PLAYING A VILLAIN. I MEAN, HOW GREAT IS THAT?
TIME OUT! I BELIEVE THAT'S THE PHRASE THEY USE ON AMERICAN TELEVISION. MAYBE YOU'LL UNDERSTAND THAT?
SO, THIS PANTHEON OF YOURS. PROTECTING THE UNIVERSE AND ALL THAT, YES? BUT THEY GOT IT WRONG, EMPLOYED YOU TO FIND THEM SOMEONE LIKE THARLOT.
AND I GOT IT WRONG, YES.
SO, WHAT NOW? WE'VE LOST HIM, THE CANON, AND HAVE NO CLUE WHERE HE'S GONE, OR WHATEVER HE'S PLANNING TO DO NEXT.

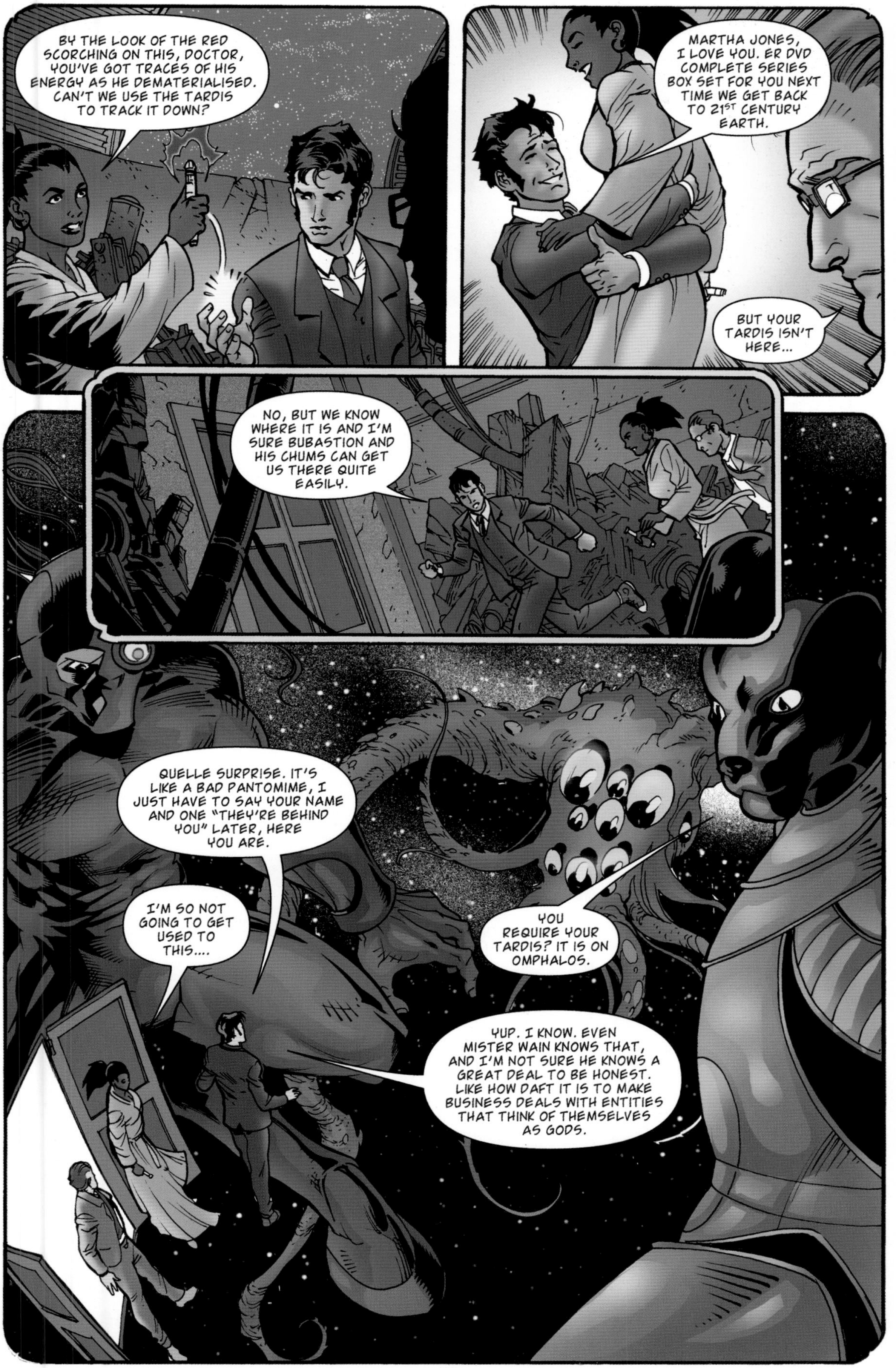
BY THE LOOK OF THE RED SCORCHING ON THIS, DOCTOR, YOU'VE GOT TRACES OF HIS ENERGY AS HE DEMATERIALISED. CAN'T WE USE THE TARDIS TO TRACK IT DOWN?
MARTHA JONES, I LOVE YOU. ER DVD COMPLETE SERIES BOX SET FOR YOU NEXT TIME WE GET BACK TO 21ST CENTURY EARTH.
BUT YOUR TARDIS ISN'T HERE...
NO, BUT WE KNOW WHERE IT IS AND I'M SURE BUBASTION AND HIS CHUMS CAN GET US THERE QUITE EASILY.
QUELLE SURPRISE. IT'S LIKE A BAD PANTOMIME, I JUST HAVE TO SAY YOUR NAME AND ONE "THEY'RE BEHIND YOU" LATER, HERE YOU ARE.
I'M SO NOT GOING TO GET USED TO THIS....
YOU REQUIRE YOUR TARDIS? IT IS ON OMPHALOS.
YUP. I KNOW. EVEN MISTER WAIN KNOWS THAT, AND I'M NOT SURE HE KNOWS A GREAT DEAL TO BE HONEST. LIKE HOW DAFT IT IS TO MAKE BUSINESS DEALS WITH ENTITIES THAT THINK OF THEMSELVES AS GODS.

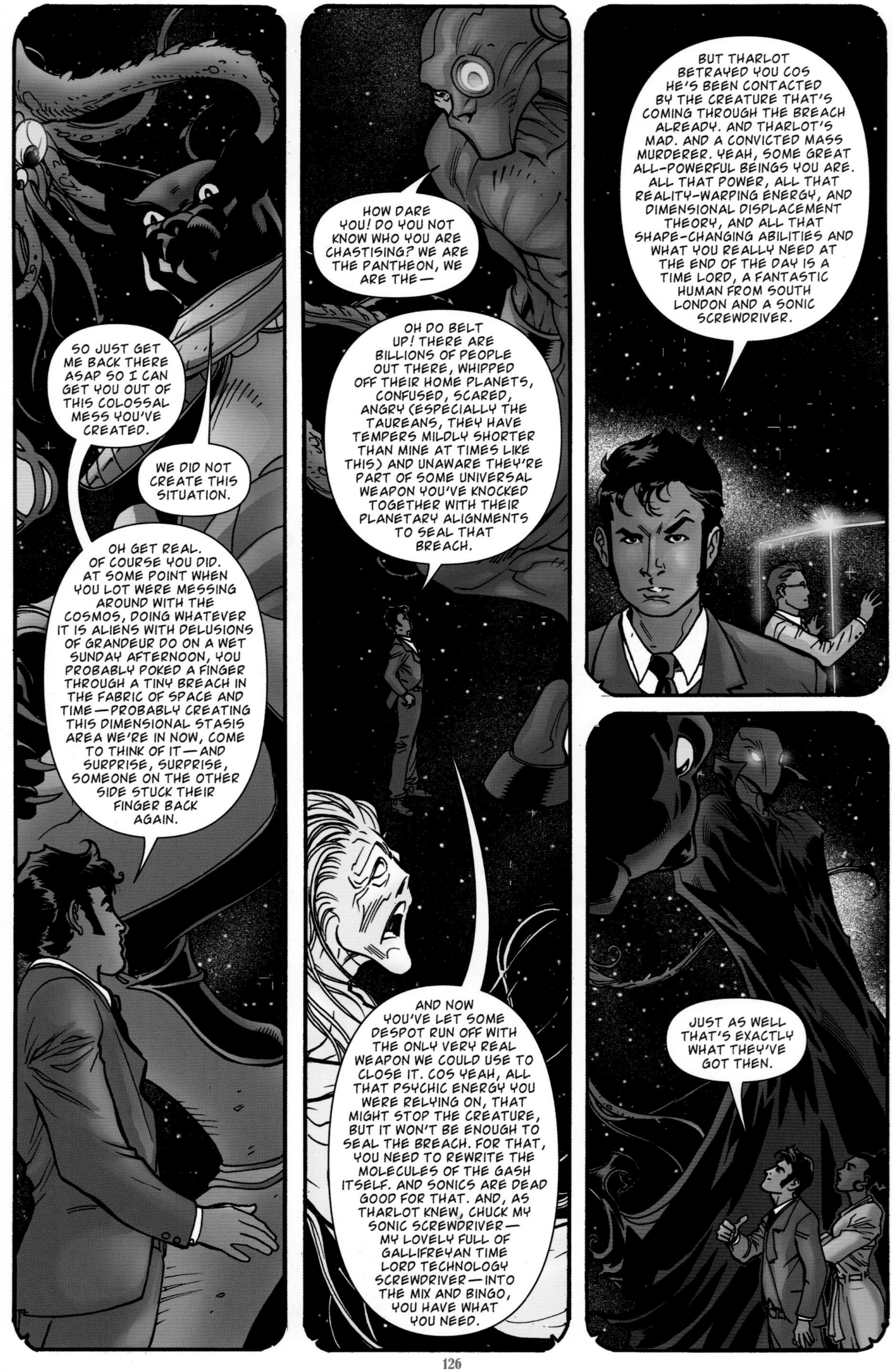
SO JUST GET ME BACK THERE ASAP SO I CAN GET YOU OUT OF THIS COLOSSAL MESS YOU'VE CREATED.
WE DID NOT CREATE THIS SITUATION.
OH GET REAL. OF COURSE YOU DID. AT SOME POINT WHEN YOU LOT WERE MESSING AROUND WITH THE COSMOS, DOING WHATEVER IT IS ALIENS WITH DELUSIONS OF GRANDEUR DO ON A WET SUNDAY AFTERNOON, YOU PROBABLY POKED A FINGER THROUGH A TINY BREACH IN THE FABRIC OF SPACE AND TIME—PROBABLY CREATING THIS DIMENSIONAL STASIS AREA WE'RE IN NOW, COME TO THINK OF IT—AND SURPRISE, SURPRISE, SOMEONE ON THE OTHER SIDE STUCK THEIR FINGER BACK AGAIN.
HOW DARE YOU! DO YOU NOT KNOW WHO YOU ARE CHASTISING? WE ARE THE PANTHEON, WE ARE THE—
OH DO BELT UP! THERE ARE BILLIONS OF PEOPLE OUT THERE, WHIPPED OFF THEIR HOME PLANETS, CONFUSED, SCARED, ANGRY (ESPECIALLY THE TAUREANS, THEY HAVE TEMPERS MILDLY SHORTER THAN MINE AT TIMES LIKE THIS) AND UNAWARE THEY'RE PART OF SOME UNIVERSAL WEAPON YOU'VE KNOCKED TOGETHER WITH THEIR PLANETARY ALIGNMENTS TO SEAL THAT BREACH.
AND NOW YOU'VE LET SOME DESPOT RUN OFF WITH THE ONLY VERY REAL WEAPON WE COULD USE TO CLOSE IT. COS YEAH, ALL THAT PSYCHIC ENERGY YOU WERE RELYING ON, THAT MIGHT STOP THE CREATURE, BUT IT WON'T BE ENOUGH TO SEAL THE BREACH. FOR THAT, YOU NEED TO REWRITE THE MOLECULES OF THE GASH ITSELF. AND SONICS ARE DEAD GOOD FOR THAT. AND, AS THARLOT KNEW, CHUCK MY SONIC SCREWDRIVER—MY LOVELY FULL OF GALLIFREYAN TIME LORD TECHNOLOGY SCREWDRIVER—INTO THE MIX AND BINGO, YOU HAVE WHAT YOU NEED.
BUT THARLOT BETRAYED YOU COS HE'S BEEN CONTACTED BY THE CREATURE THAT'S COMING THROUGH THE BREACH ALREADY. AND THARLOT'S MAD. AND A CONVICTED MASS MURDERER. YEAH, SOME GREAT ALL-POWERFUL BEINGS YOU ARE. ALL THAT POWER, ALL THAT REALITY-WARPING ENERGY, AND DIMENSIONAL DISPLACEMENT THEORY, AND ALL THAT SHAPE-CHANGING ABILITIES AND WHAT YOU REALLY NEED AT THE END OF THE DAY IS A TIME LORD, A FANTASTIC HUMAN FROM SOUTH LONDON AND A SONIC SCREWDRIVER.
JUST AS WELL THAT'S EXACTLY WHAT THEY'VE GOT THEN.

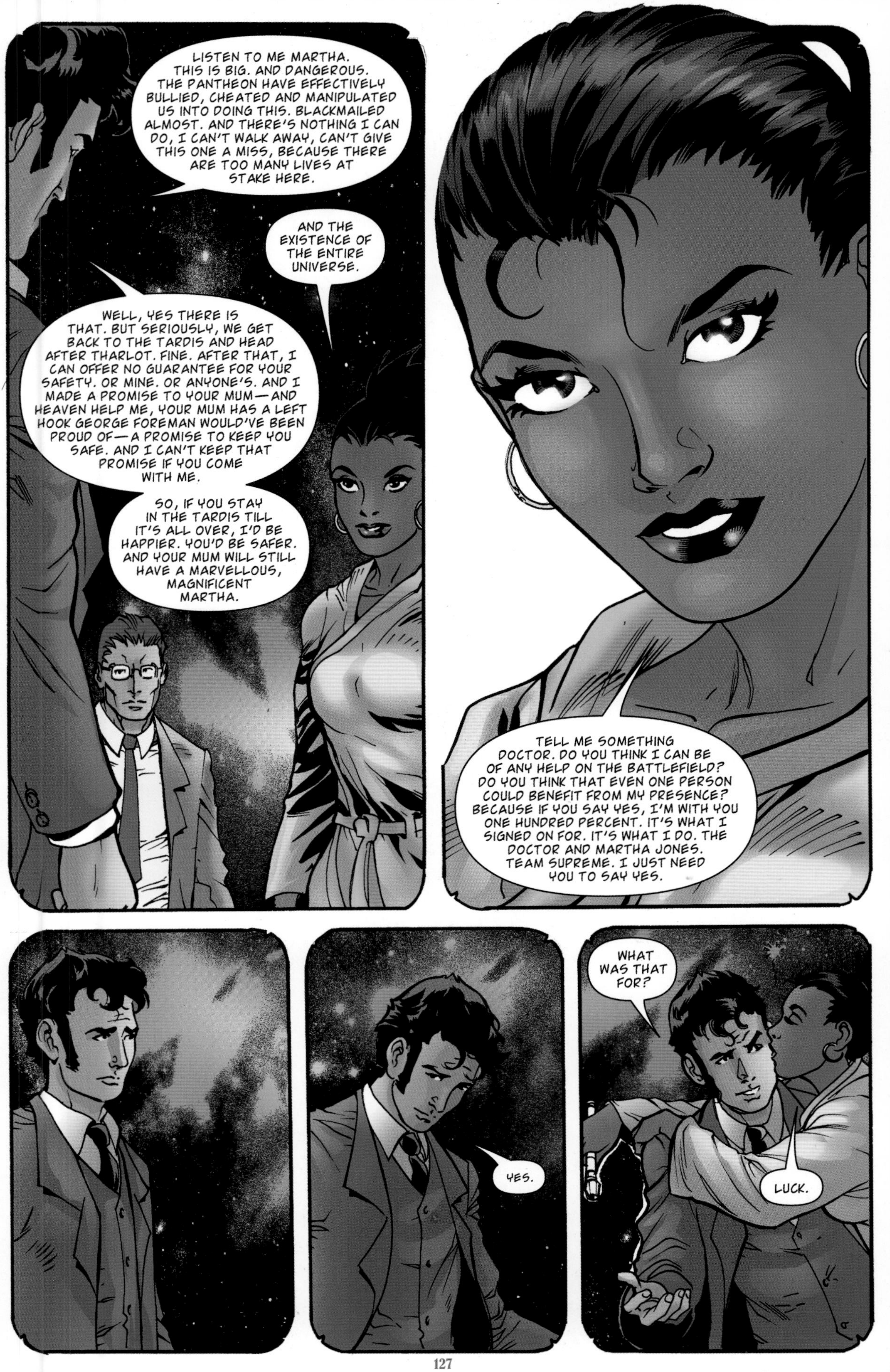
LISTEN TO ME MARTHA. THIS IS BIG. AND DANGEROUS. THE PANTHEON HAVE EFFECTIVELY BULLIED, CHEATED AND MANIPULATED US INTO DOING THIS. BLACKMAILED ALMOST. AND THERE'S NOTHING I CAN DO, I CAN'T WALK AWAY, CAN'T GIVE THIS ONE A MISS, BECAUSE THERE ARE TOO MANY LIVES AT STAKE HERE.
AND THE EXISTENCE OF THE ENTIRE UNIVERSE.
WELL, YES THERE IS THAT. BUT SERIOUSLY, WE GET BACK TO THE TARDIS AND HEAD AFTER THARLOT. FINE. AFTER THAT, I CAN OFFER NO GUARANTEE FOR YOUR SAFETY. OR MINE. OR ANYONE'S. AND I MADE A PROMISE TO YOUR MUM—AND HEAVEN HELP ME, YOUR MUM HAS A LEFT HOOK GEORGE FOREMAN WOULD'VE BEEN PROUD OF—A PROMISE TO KEEP YOU SAFE. AND I CAN'T KEEP THAT PROMISE IF YOU COME WITH ME.
SO, IF YOU STAY IN THE TARDIS TILL IT'S ALL OVER, I'D BE HAPPIER. YOU'D BE SAFER. AND YOUR MUM WILL STILL HAVE A MARVELLOUS, MAGNIFICENT MARTHA.
TELL ME SOMETHING DOCTOR. DO YOU THINK I CAN BE OF ANY HELP ON THE BATTLEFIELD? DO YOU THINK THAT EVEN ONE PERSON COULD BENEFIT FROM MY PRESENCE? BECAUSE IF YOU SAY YES, I'M WITH YOU ONE HUNDRED PERCENT. IT'S WHAT I SIGNED ON FOR. IT'S WHAT I DO. THE DOCTOR AND MARTHA JONES. TEAM SUPREME. I JUST NEED YOU TO SAY YES.
YES.
WHAT WAS THAT FOR?
LUCK.

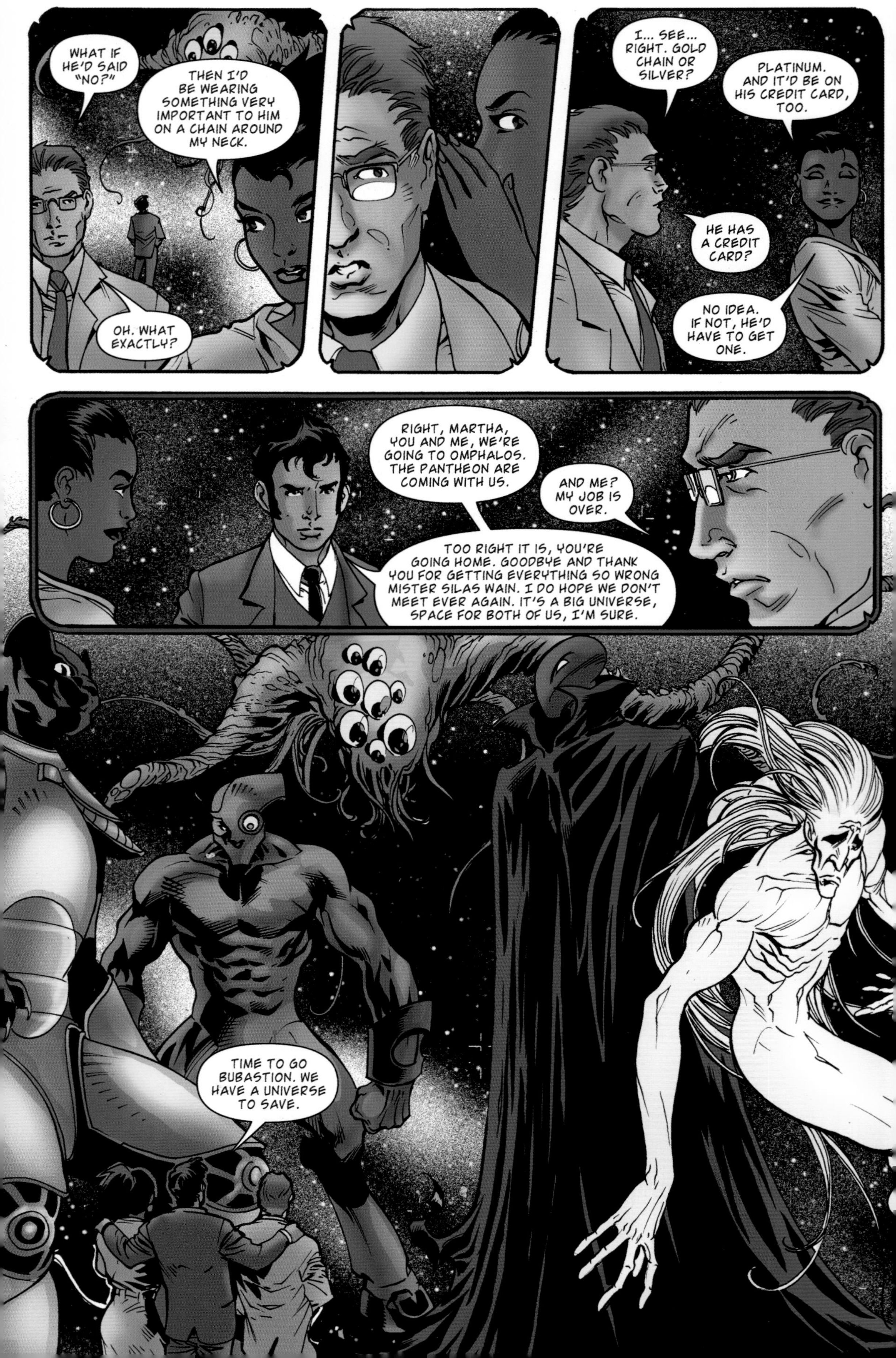
WHAT IF HE'D SAID "NO?"
THEN I'D BE WEARING SOMETHING VERY IMPORTANT TO HIM ON A CHAIN AROUND MY NECK.
OH. WHAT EXACTLY?
I... SEE... RIGHT. GOLD CHAIN OR SILVER?
PLATINUM. AND IT'D BE ON HIS CREDIT CARD, TOO.
HE HAS A CREDIT CARD?
NO IDEA. IF NOT, HE'D HAVE TO GET ONE.
RIGHT, MARTHA, YOU AND ME, WE'RE GOING TO OMPHALOS. THE PANTHEON ARE COMING WITH US.
AND ME? MY JOB IS OVER.
TOO RIGHT IT IS, YOU'RE GOING HOME. GOODBYE AND THANK YOU FOR GETTING EVERYTHING SO WRONG MISTER SILAS WAIN. I DO HOPE WE DON'T MEET EVER AGAIN. IT'S A BIG UNIVERSE, SPACE FOR BOTH OF US, I'M SURE.
TIME TO GO BUBASTION. WE HAVE A UNIVERSE TO SAVE.

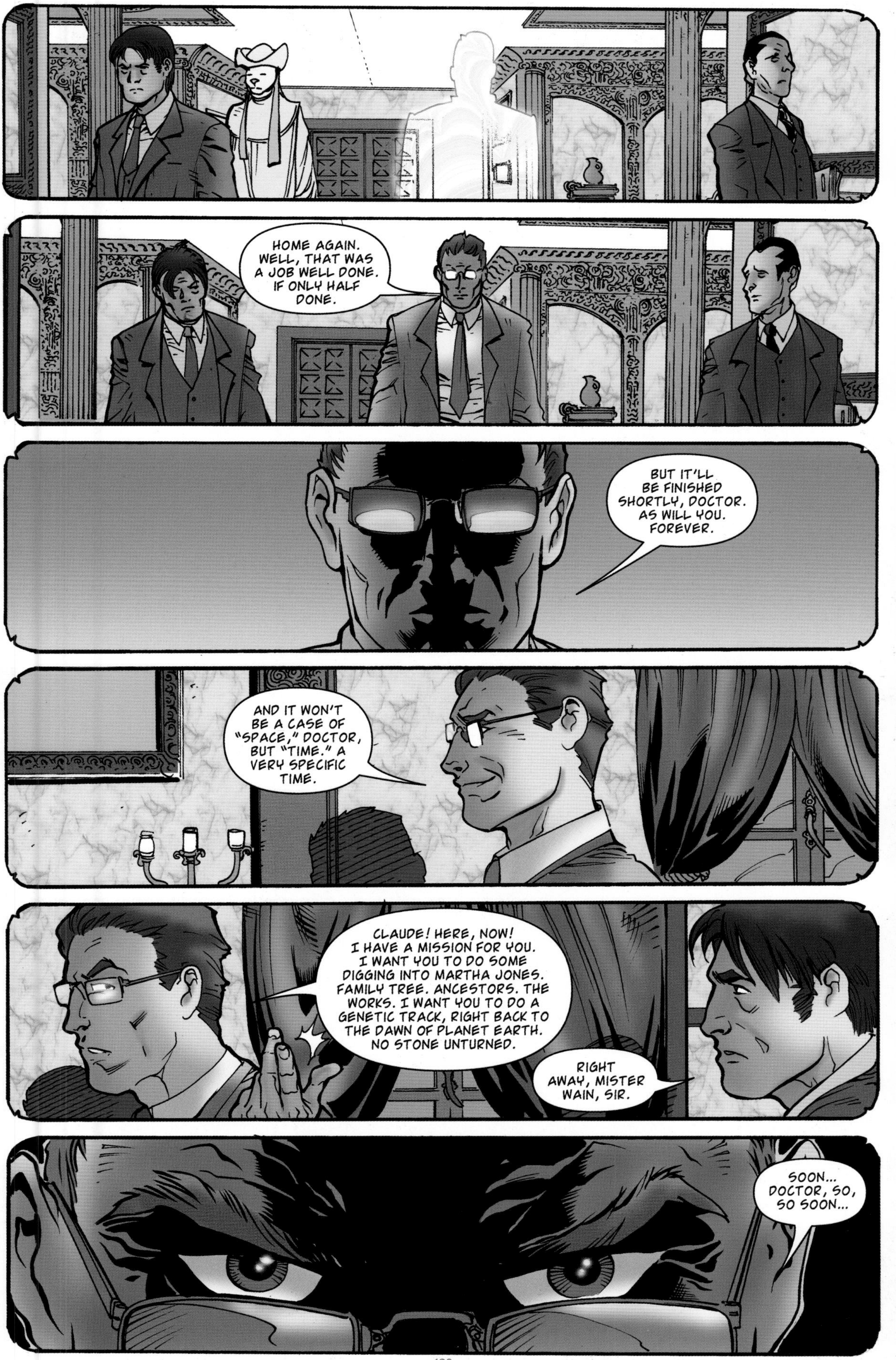
HOME AGAIN. WELL, THAT WAS A JOB WELL DONE. IF ONLY HALF DONE.
BUT IT'LL BE FINISHED SHORTLY, DOCTOR. AS WILL YOU. FOREVER.
AND IT WON'T BE A CASE OF "SPACE," DOCTOR, BUT "TIME." A VERY SPECIFIC TIME.
CLAUDE! HERE, NOW! I HAVE A MISSION FOR YOU. I WANT YOU TO DO SOME DIGGING INTO MARTHA JONES. FAMILY TREE. ANCESTORS. THE WORKS. I WANT YOU TO DO A GENETIC TRACK, RIGHT BACK TO THE DAWN OF PLANET EARTH. NO STONE UNTURNED.
RIGHT AWAY, MISTER WAIN, SIR.
SOON... DOCTOR, SO, SO SOON...

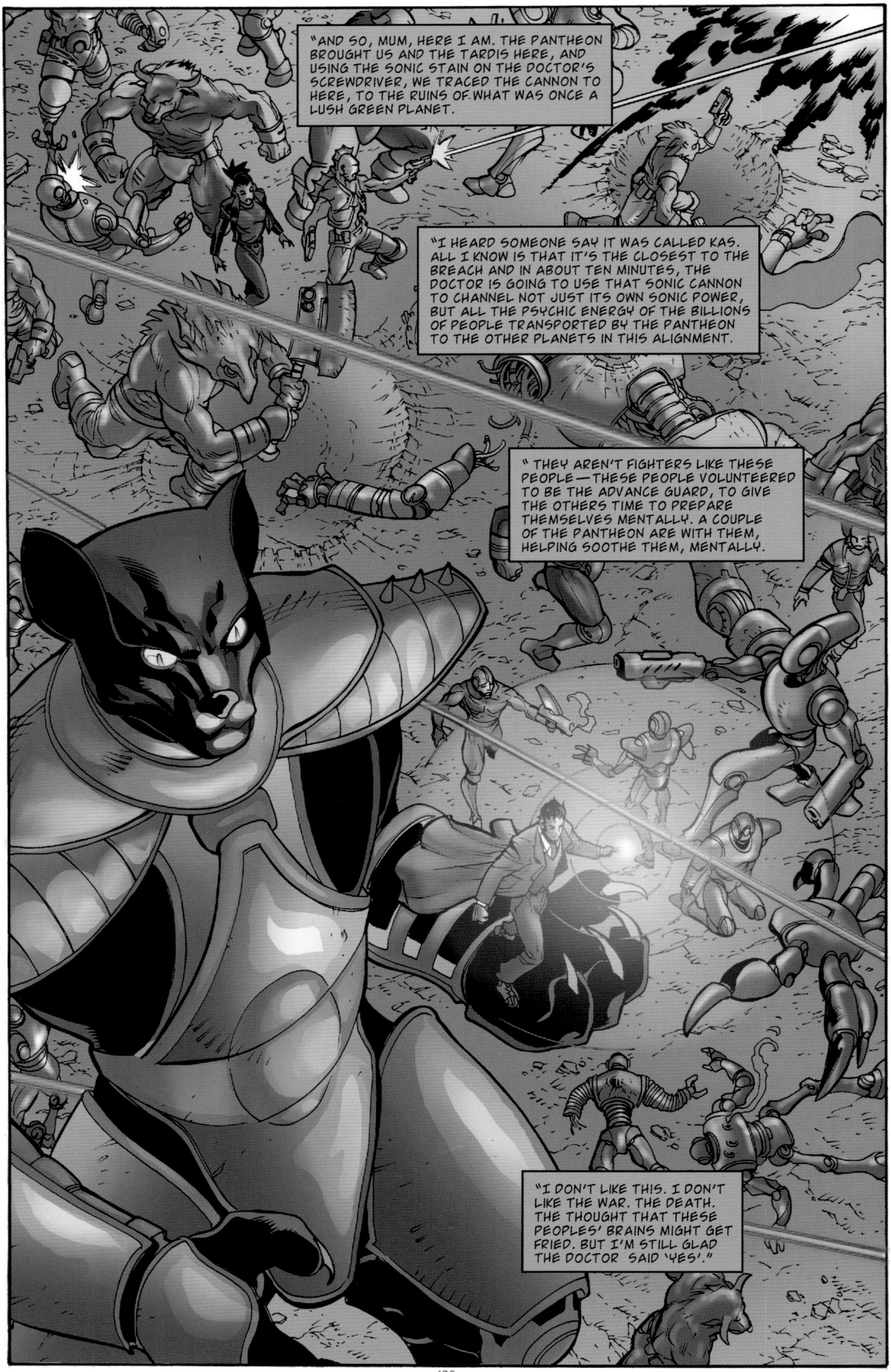
"AND SO, MUM, HERE I AM. THE PANTHEON BROUGHT US AND THE TARDIS HERE, AND USING THE SONIC STAIN ON THE DOCTOR'S SCREWDRIVER, WE TRACED THE CANNON TO HERE, TO THE RUINS OF WHAT WAS ONCE A LUSH GREEN PLANET.
"I HEARD SOMEONE SAY IT WAS CALLED KAS. ALL I KNOW IS THAT IT'S THE CLOSEST TO THE BREACH AND IN ABOUT TEN MINUTES, THE DOCTOR IS GOING TO USE THAT SONIC CANNON TO CHANNEL NOT JUST ITS OWN SONIC POWER, BUT ALL THE PSYCHIC ENERGY OF THE BILLIONS OF PEOPLE TRANSPORTED BY THE PANTHEON TO THE OTHER PLANETS IN THIS ALIGNMENT.
" THEY AREN'T FIGHTERS LIKE THESE PEOPLE—THESE PEOPLE VOLUNTEERED TO BE THE ADVANCE GUARD, TO GIVE THE OTHERS TIME TO PREPARE THEMSELVES MENTALLY. A COUPLE OF THE PANTHEON ARE WITH THEM, HELPING SOOTHE THEM, MENTALLY.
"I DON'T LIKE THIS. I DON'T LIKE THE WAR. THE DEATH. THE THOUGHT THAT THESE PEOPLES' BRAINS MIGHT GET FRIED. BUT I'M STILL GLAD THE DOCTOR SAID 'YES'."

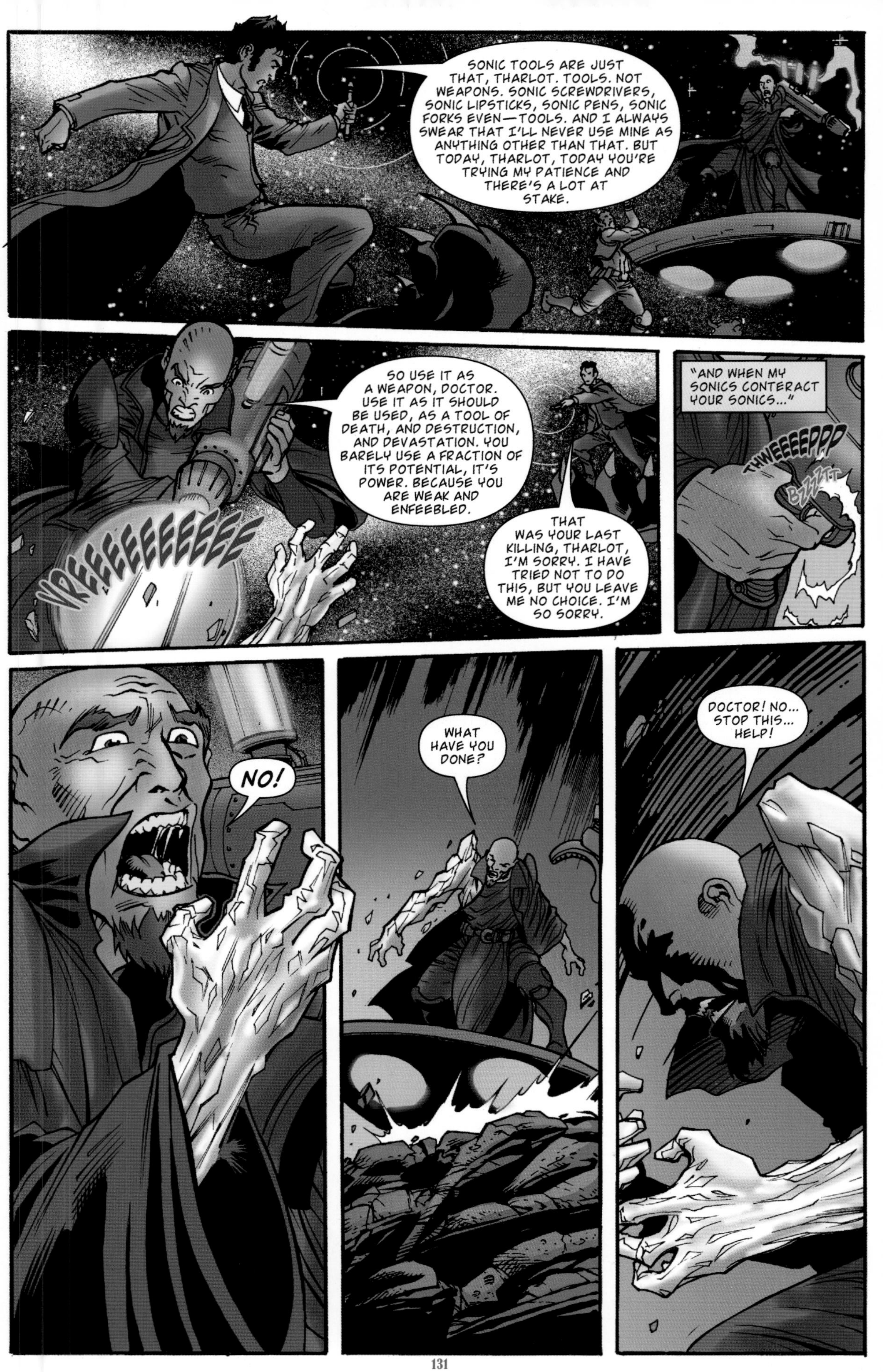

SONIC TOOLS ARE JUST THAT, THARLOT. TOOLS. NOT WEAPONS. SONIC SCREWDRIVERS, SONIC LIPSTICKS, SONIC PENS, SONIC FORKS EVEN—TOOLS. AND I ALWAYS SWEAR THAT I'LL NEVER USE MINE AS ANYTHING OTHER THAN THAT. BUT TODAY, THARLOT, TODAY YOU'RE TRYING MY PATIENCE AND THERE'S A LOT AT STAKE.
SO USE IT AS A WEAPON, DOCTOR. USE IT AS IT SHOULD BE USED, AS A TOOL OF DEATH, AND DESTRUCTION, AND DEVASTATION. YOU BARELY USE A FRACTION OF ITS POTENTIAL, IT'S POWER. BECAUSE YOU ARE WEAK AND ENFEEBLED.
VREEEEEEEEEE
THAT WAS YOUR LAST KILLING, THARLOT, I'M SORRY. I HAVE TRIED NOT TO DO THIS, BUT YOU LEAVE ME NO CHOICE. I'M SO SORRY.
"AND WHEN MY SONICS CONTERACT YOUR SONICS..."
THWEEEEPPP
BZZTT
NO!
WHAT HAVE YOU DONE?
DOCTOR! NO... STOP THIS... HELP!

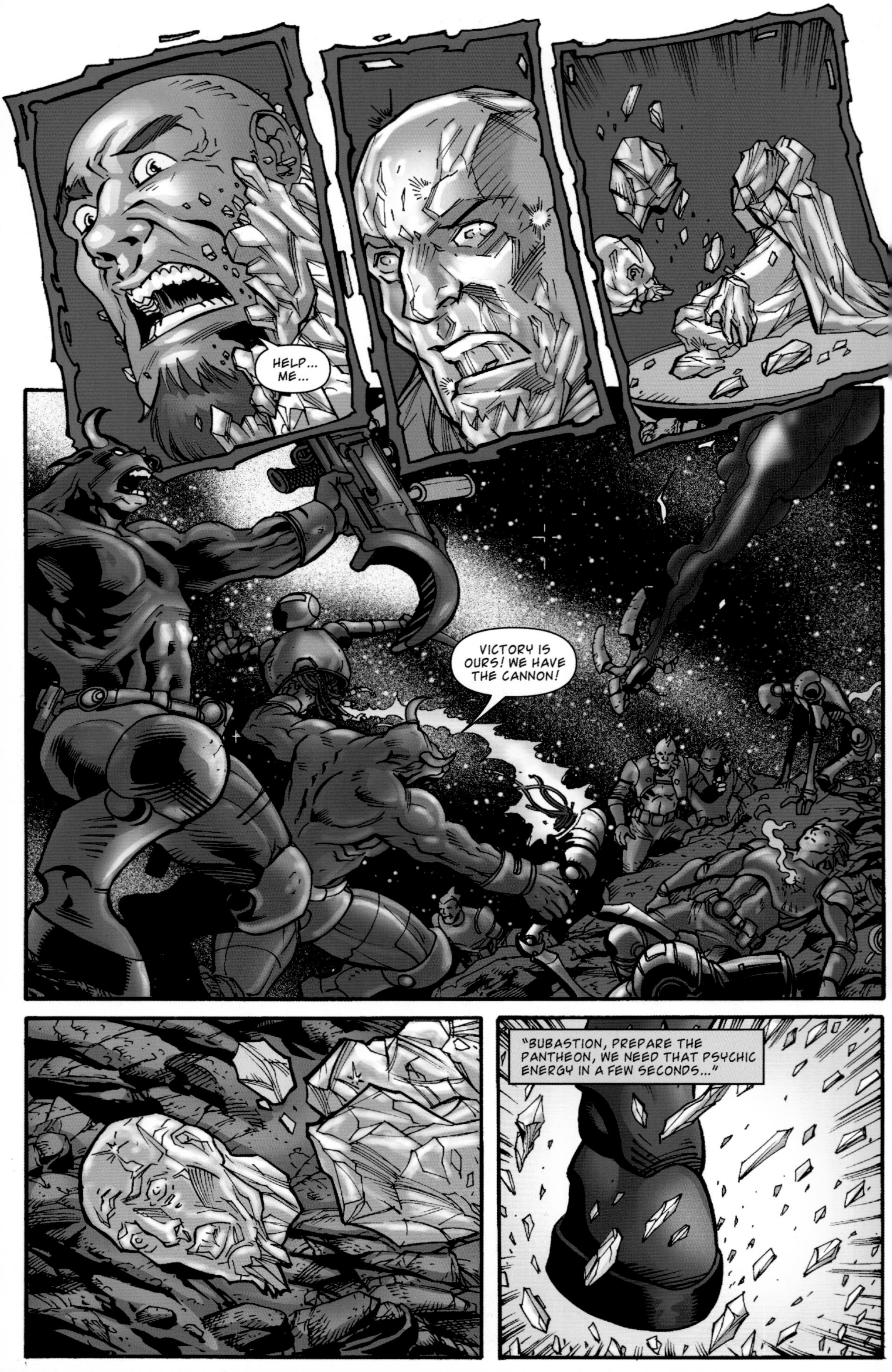
HELP... ME...
VICTORY IS OURS! WE HAVE THE CANNON!
"BUBASTION, PREPARE THE PANTHEON, WE NEED THAT PSYCHIC ENERGY IN A FEW SECONDS..."

"THEY ARE READY DOCTOR!"

THIS BETTER WORK, BUBASTION, OR IT'S THE SHORTEST, MOST PYRRHIC VICTORY IN HISTORY...

OH YES!

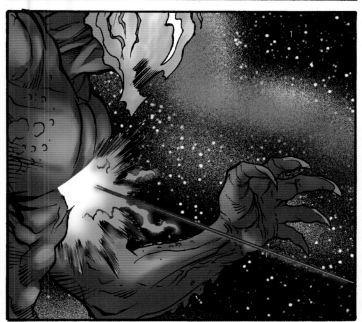

NOW, BUBASTION, WE NEED THE THOUGHTS OF A BILLION SOULS. NOW!

GOD, I HOPE THIS WORKS...

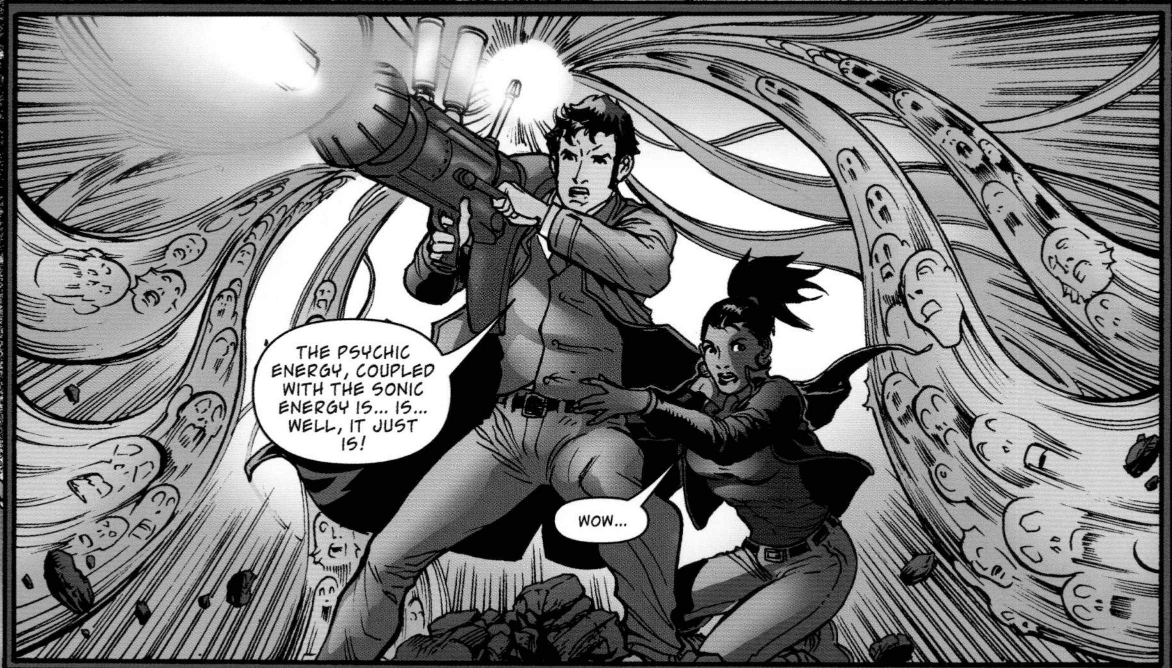
THE PSYCHIC ENERGY, COUPLED WITH THE SONIC ENERGY IS... IS... WELL, IT JUST IS!
WOW...

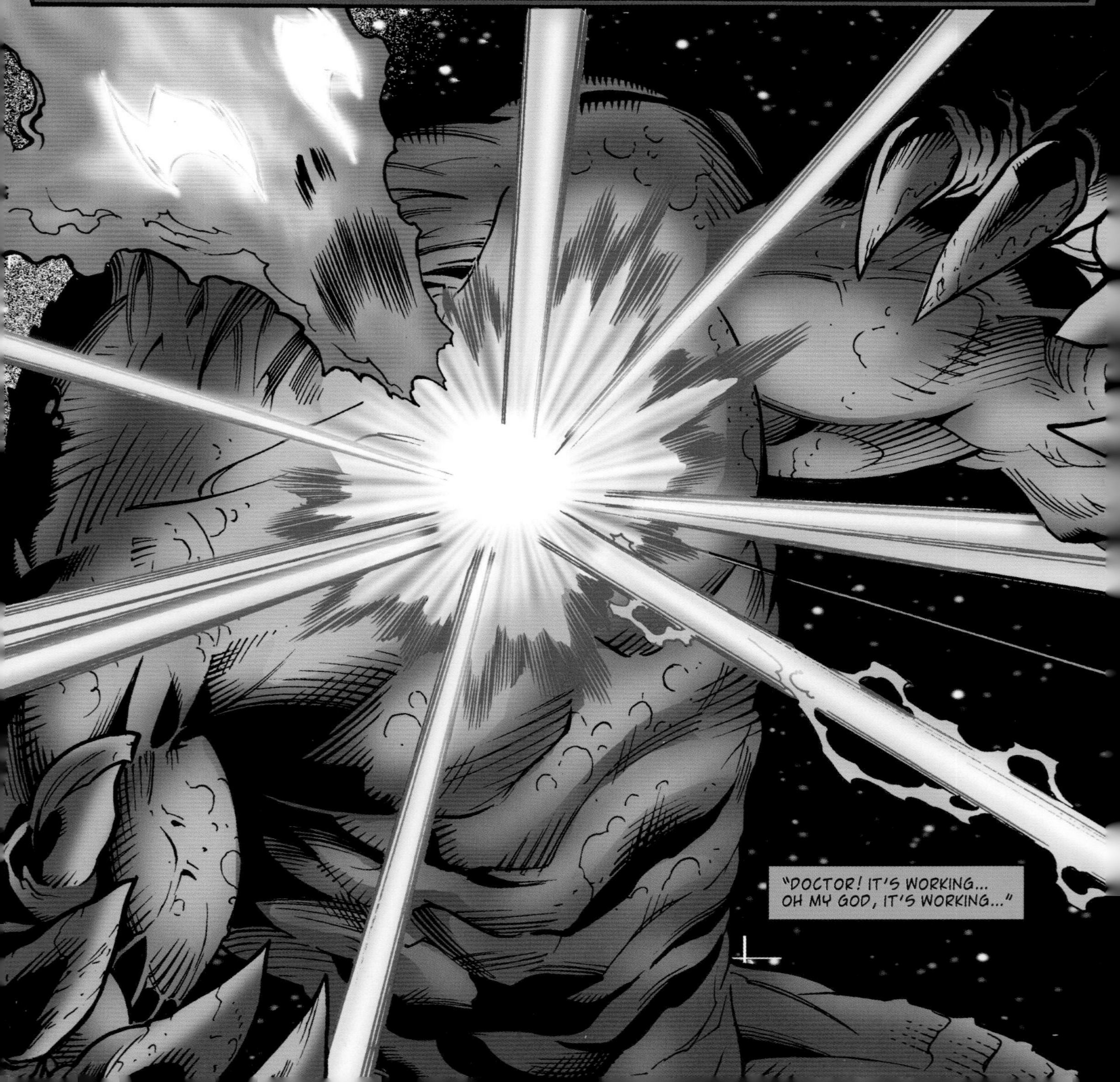
"DOCTOR! IT'S WORKING... OH MY GOD, IT'S WORKING..."

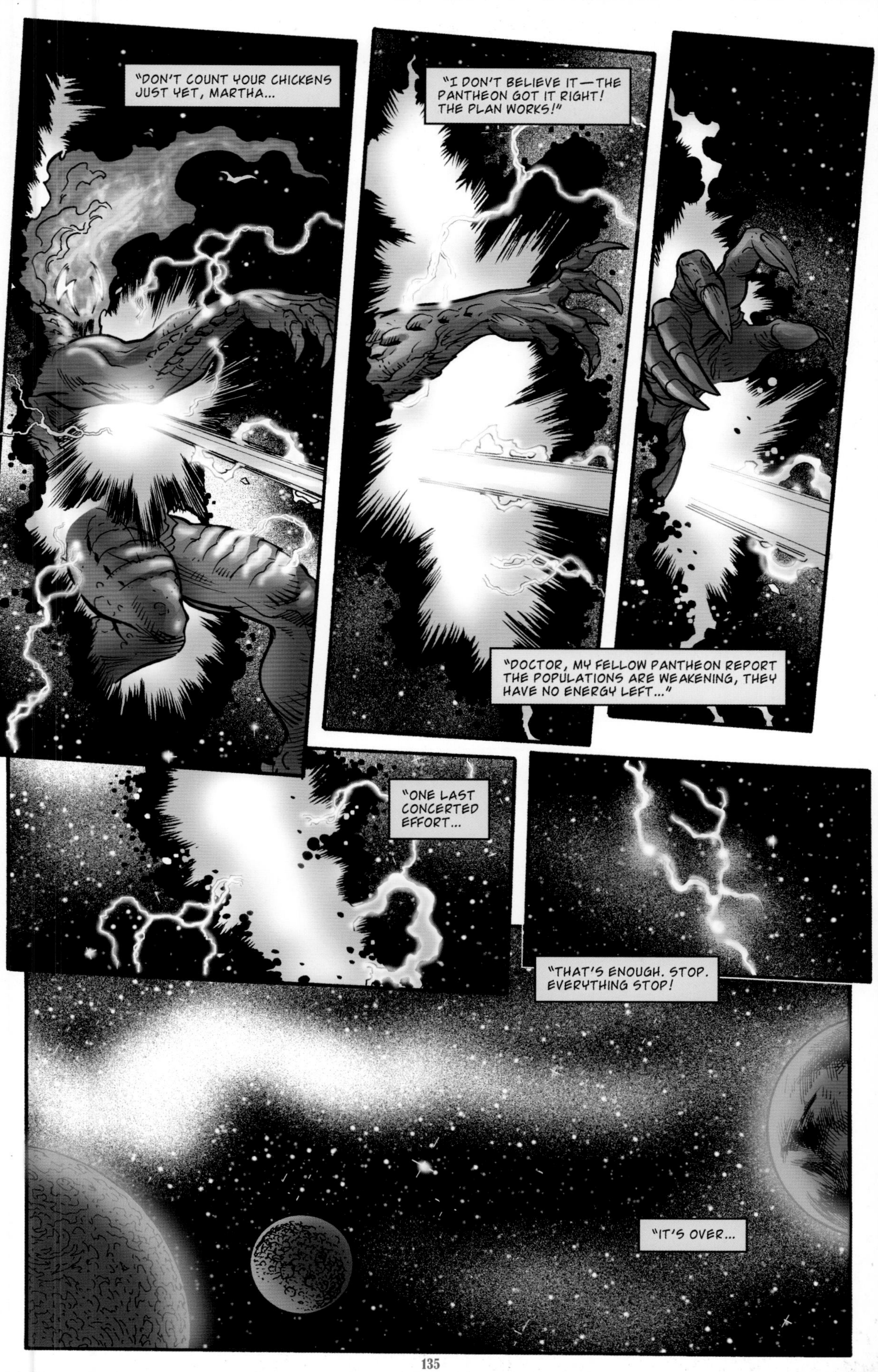
"DON'T COUNT YOUR CHICKENS JUST YET, MARTHA...
"I DON'T BELIEVE IT—THE PANTHEON GOT IT RIGHT! THE PLAN WORKS!"
"DOCTOR, MY FELLOW PANTHEON REPORT THE POPULATIONS ARE WEAKENING, THEY HAVE NO ENERGY LEFT..."
"ONE LAST CONCERTED EFFORT...
"THAT'S ENOUGH. STOP. EVERYTHING STOP!
"IT'S OVER...

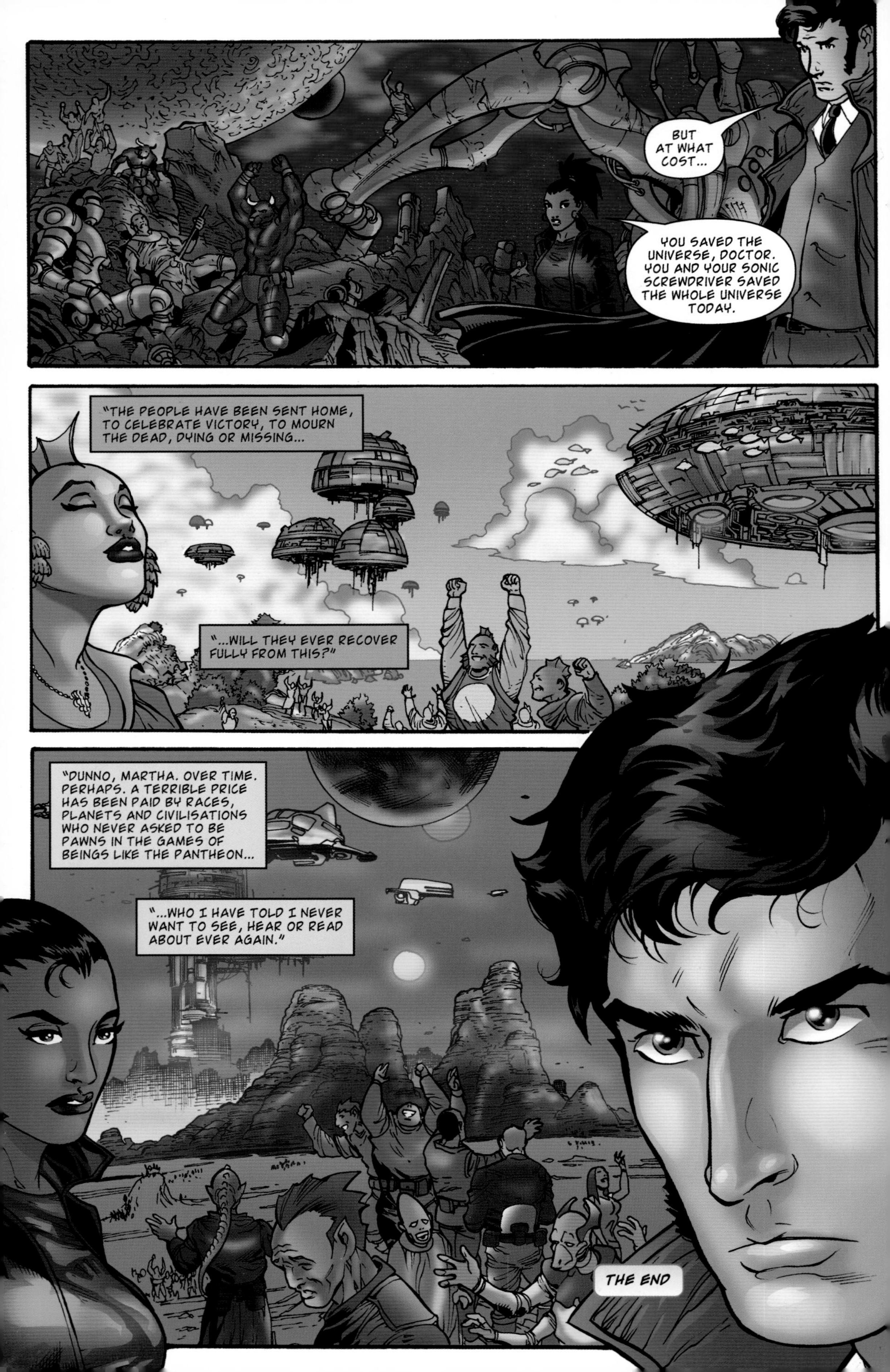
BUT AT WHAT COST...
YOU SAVED THE UNIVERSE, DOCTOR. YOU AND YOUR SONIC SCREWDRIVER SAVED THE WHOLE UNIVERSE TODAY.
"THE PEOPLE HAVE BEEN SENT HOME, TO CELEBRATE VICTORY, TO MOURN THE DEAD, DYING OR MISSING...
"...WILL THEY EVER RECOVER FULLY FROM THIS?"
"DUNNO, MARTHA. OVER TIME. PERHAPS. A TERRIBLE PRICE HAS BEEN PAID BY RACES, PLANETS AND CIVILISATIONS WHO NEVER ASKED TO BE PAWNS IN THE GAMES OF BEINGS LIKE THE PANTHEON...
"...WHO I HAVE TOLD I NEVER WANT TO SEE, HEAR OR READ ABOUT EVER AGAIN."
THE END

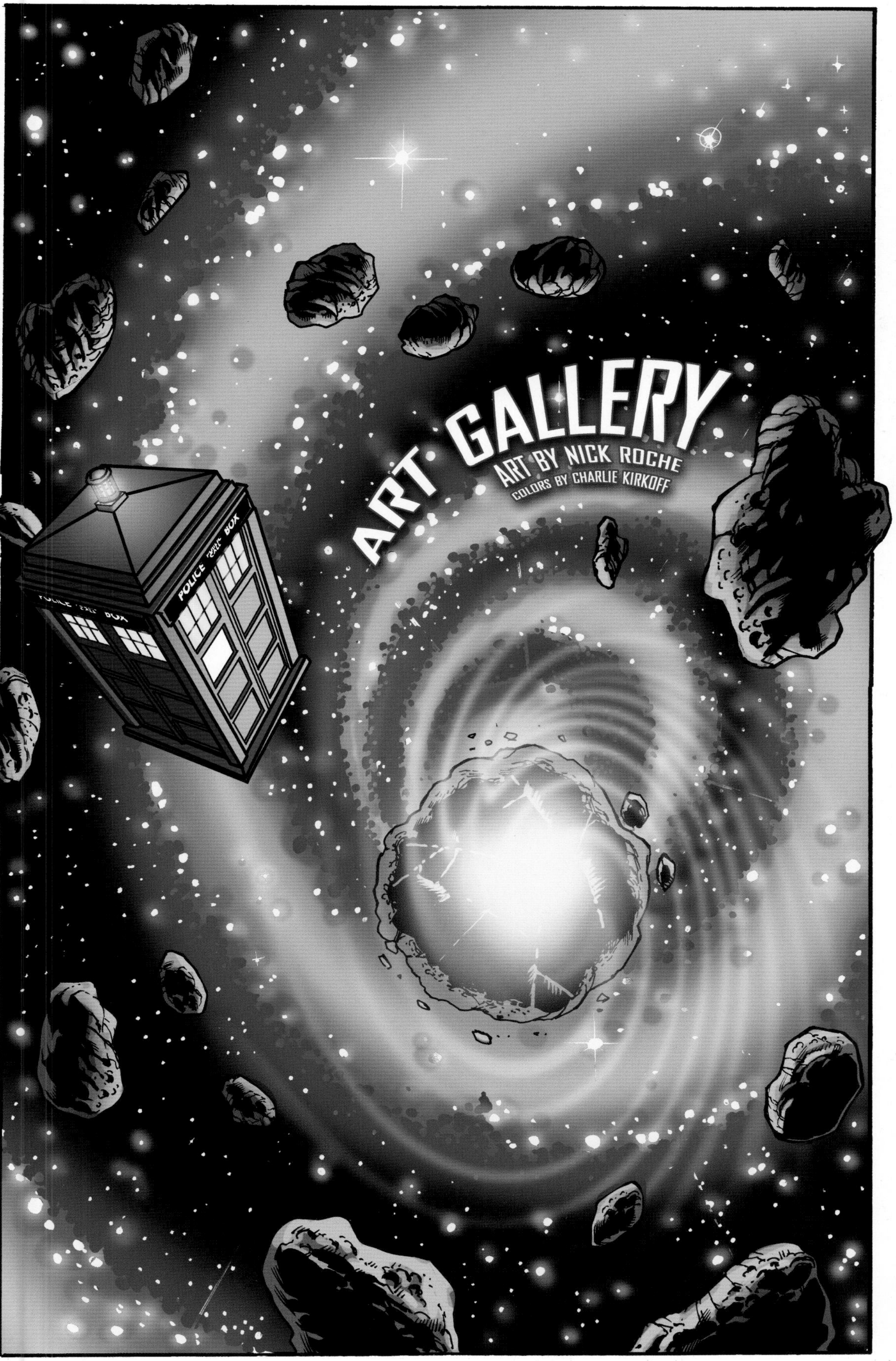
ART GALLERY
ART BY NICK ROCHE
COLORS BY CHARLIE KIRKOFF
POLICE PUBLIC CALL BOX

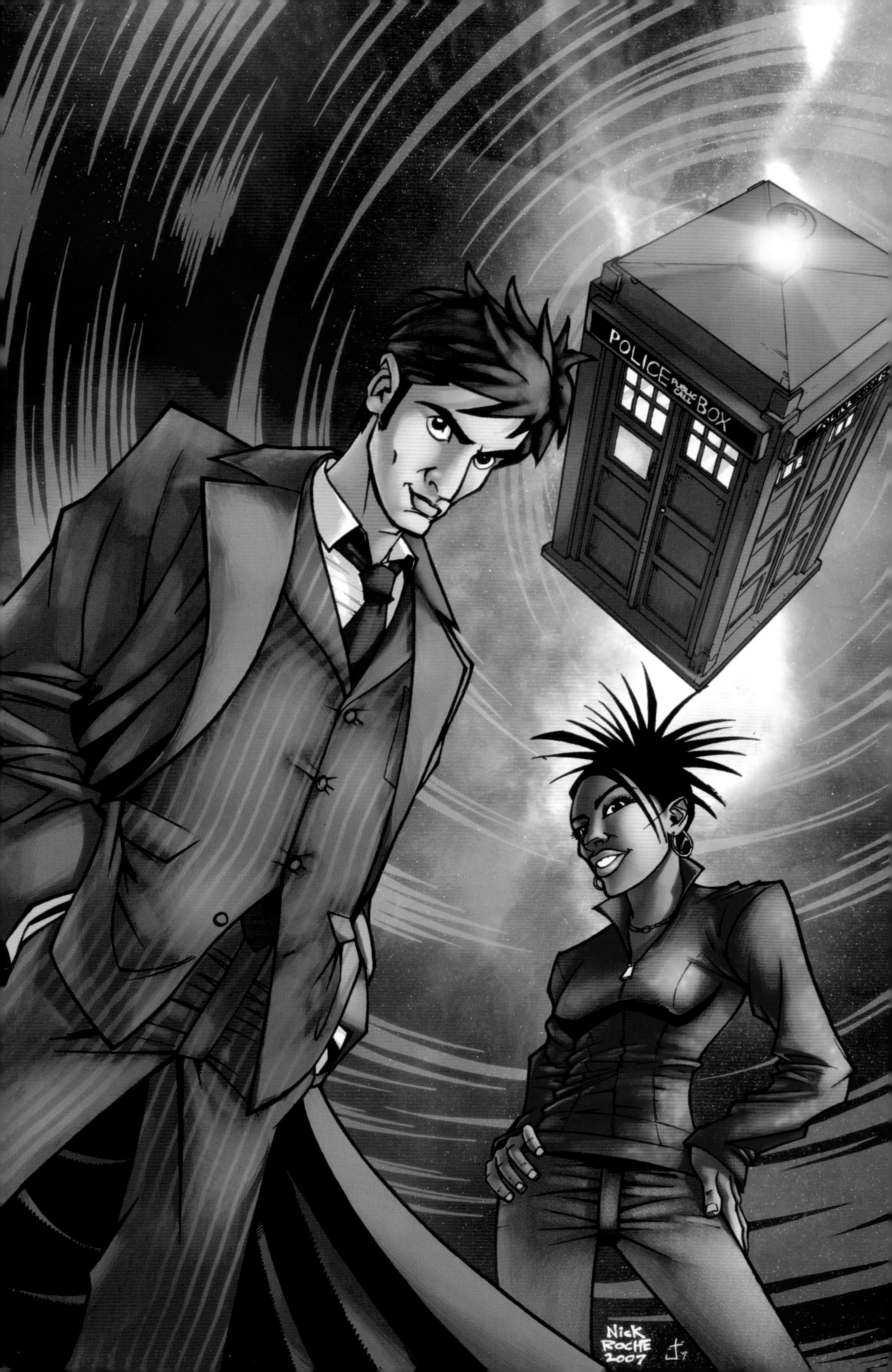
POLICE PUBLIC CALL BOX
NICK ROCHE 2007

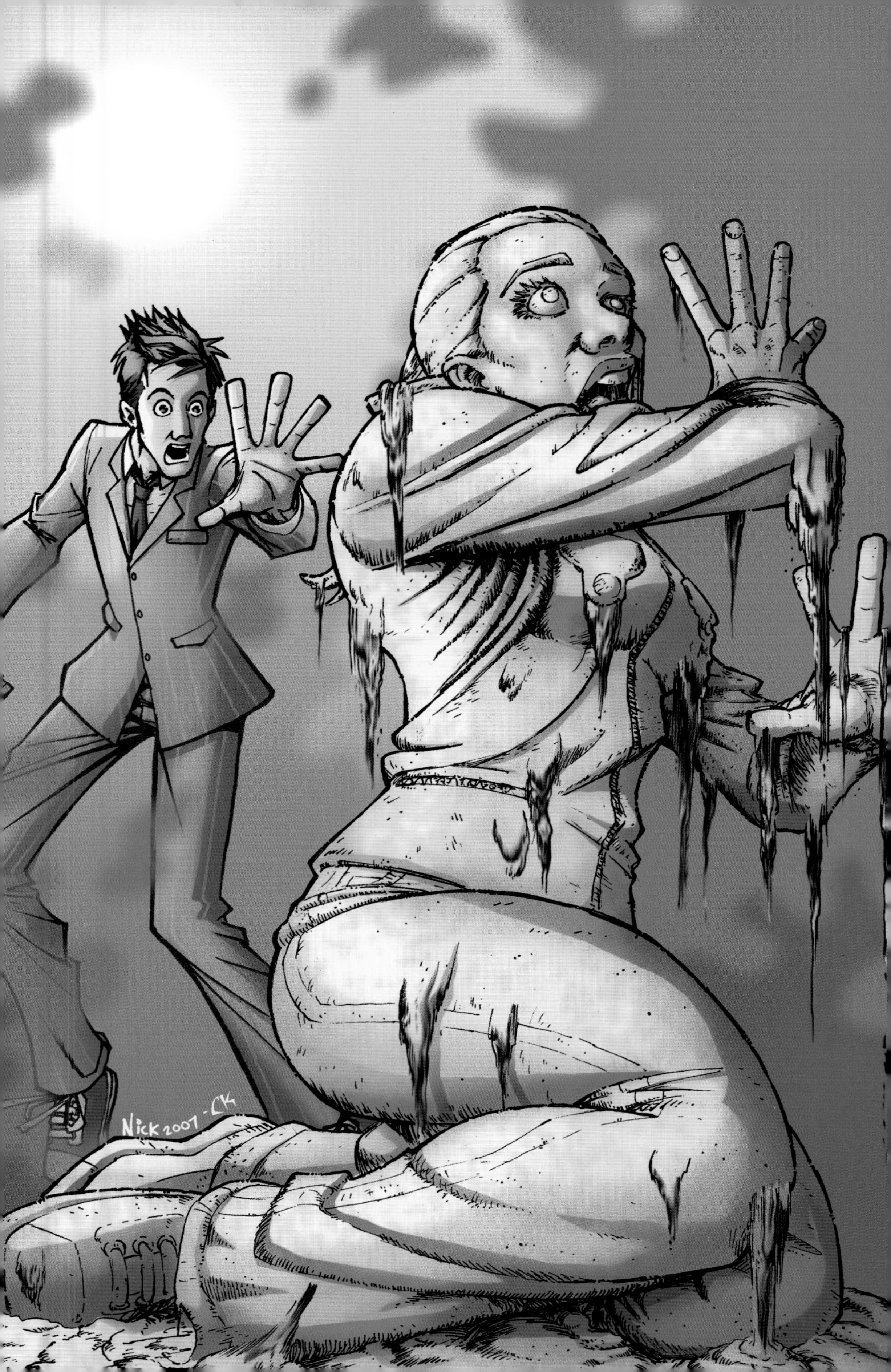
Nick 2007 - CK

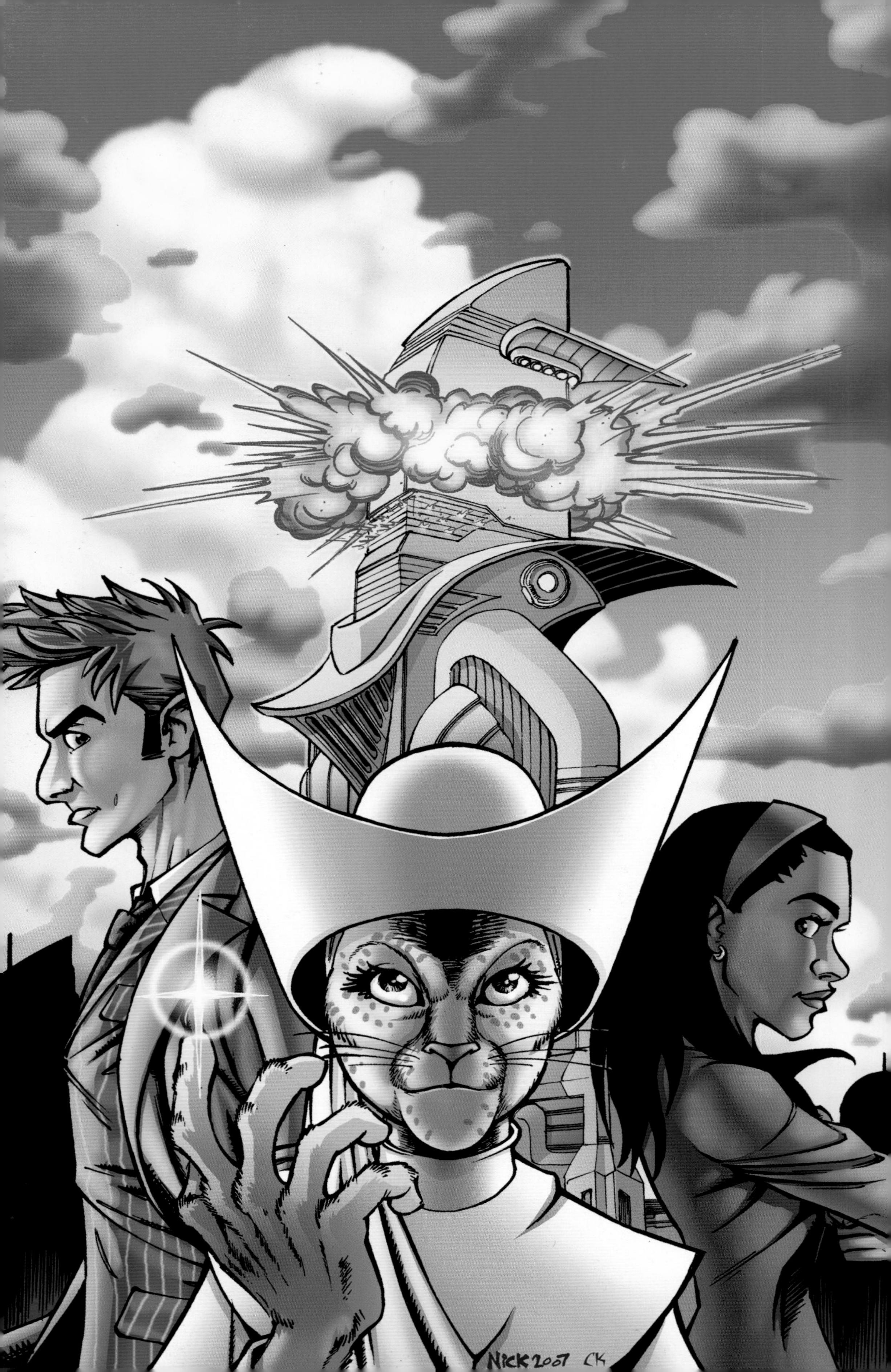
NICK 2007 CK

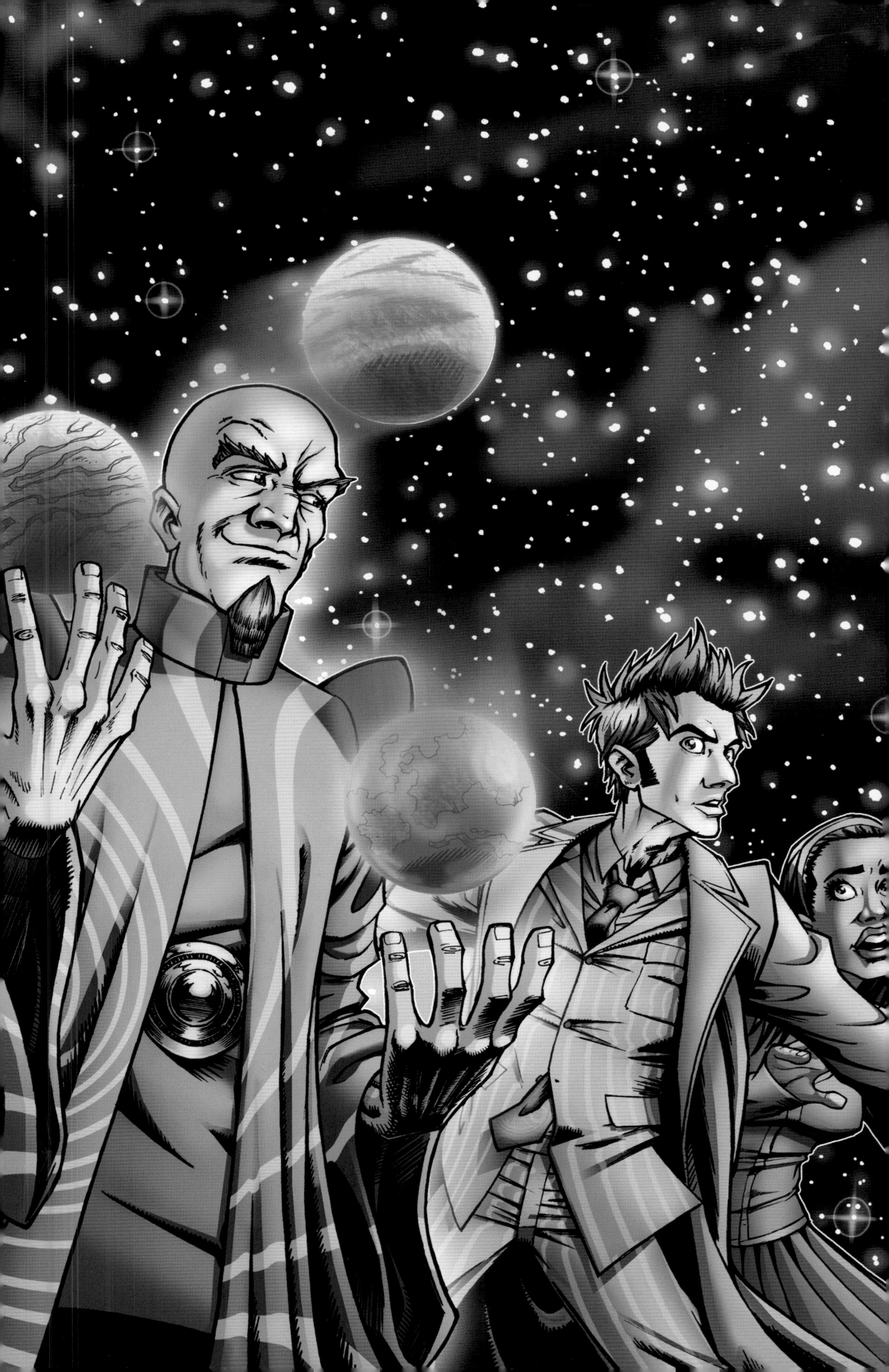

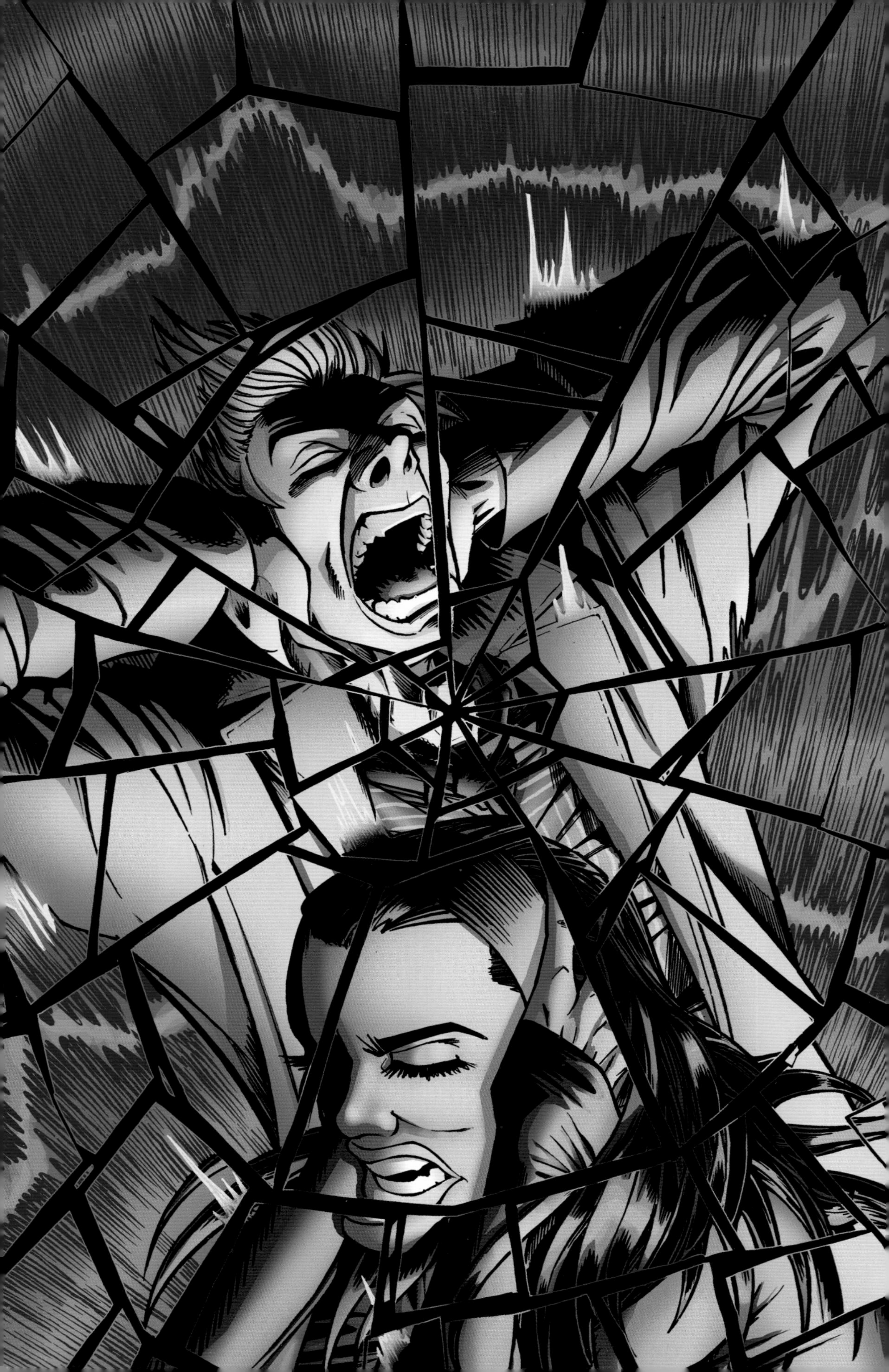

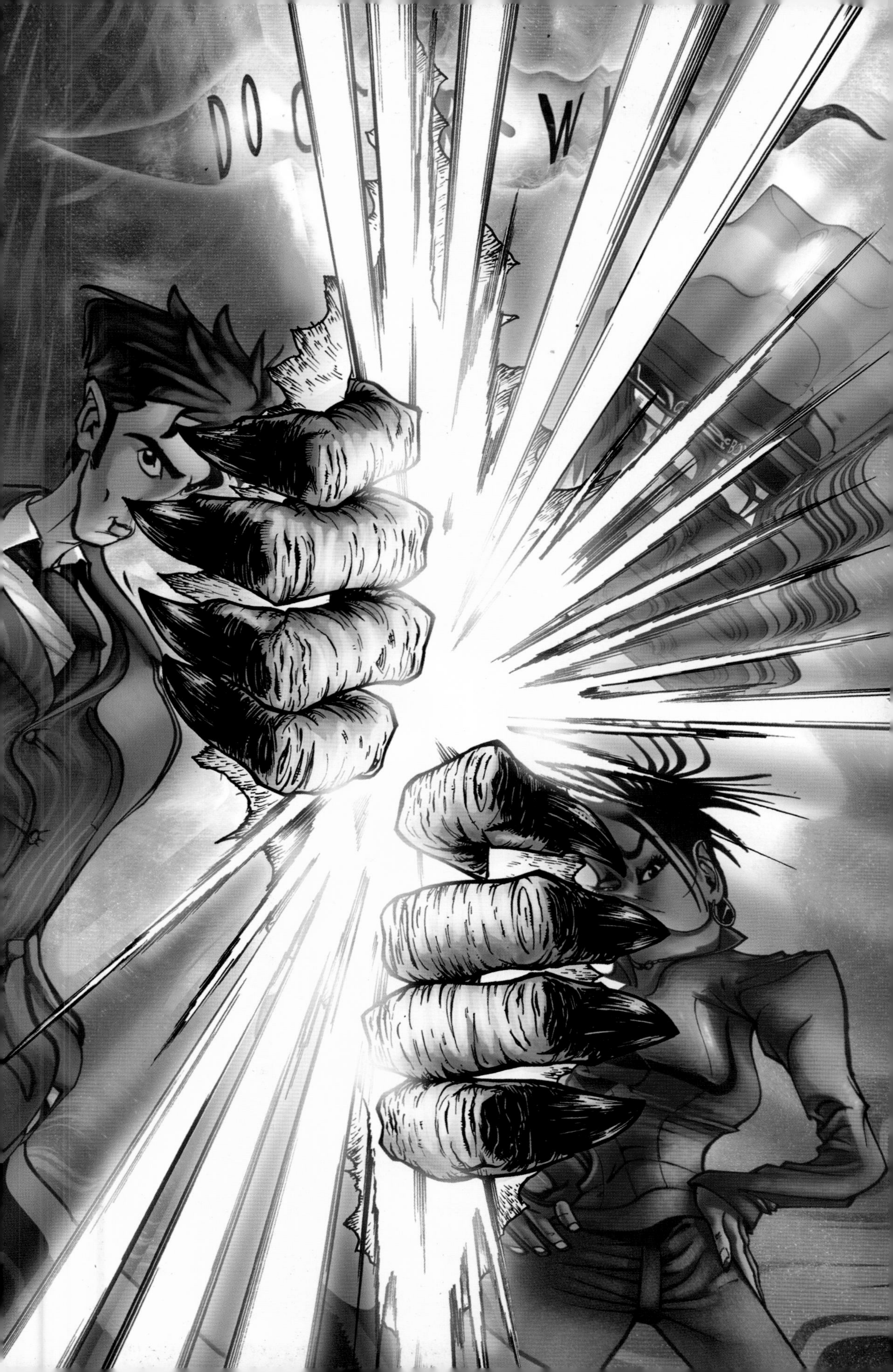

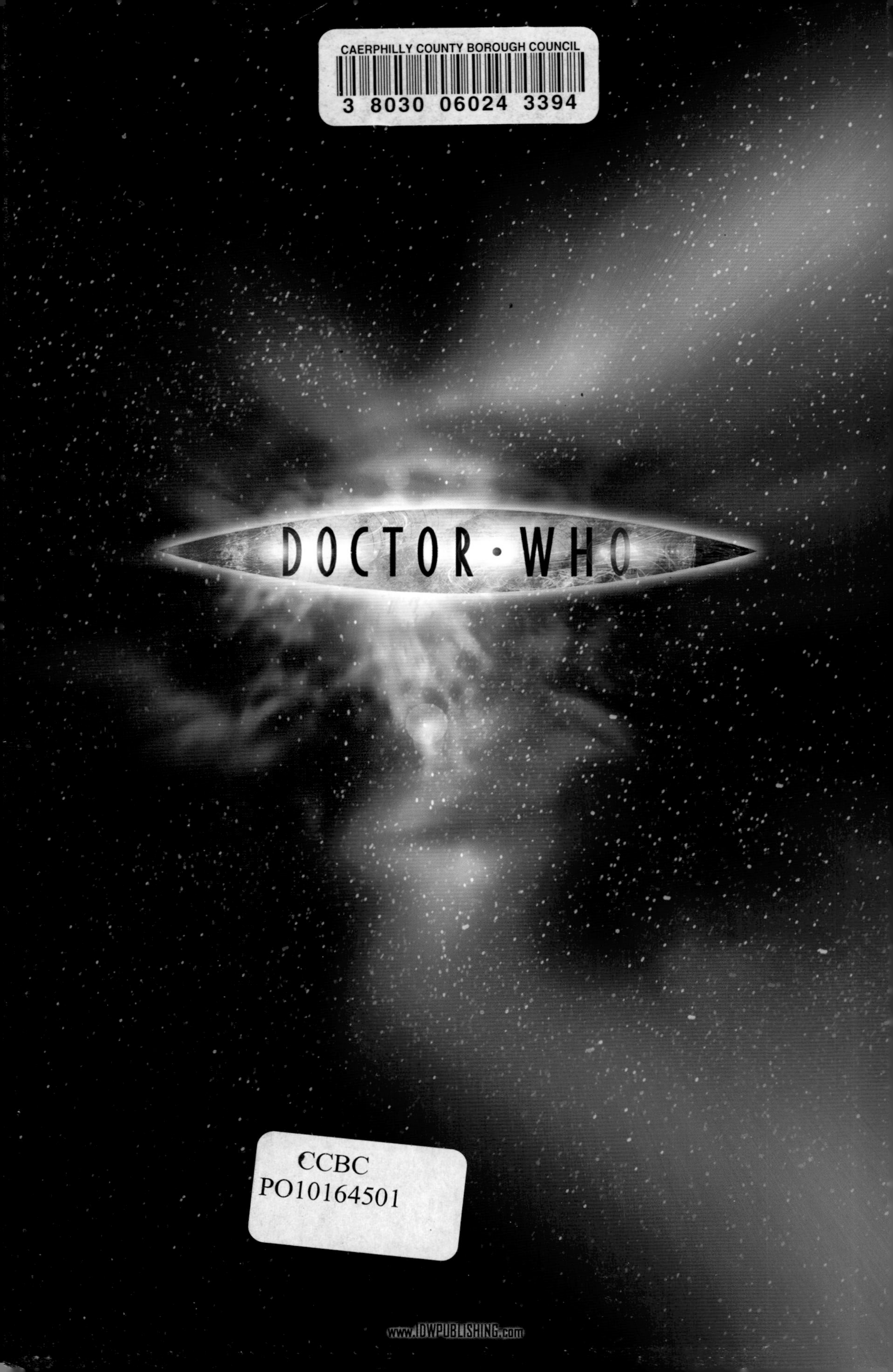
DOCTOR · WHO

www.IDWPUBLISHING.com